The Language of Canadian Politics
A Guide to Important Terms and Concepts

The Language of Canadian Politics
A Guide to Important Terms and Concepts
3rd edition

John McMenemy

Wilfrid Laurier University Press

We acknowledge the financial support of the Government of Canada through the Book Publishing Industry Development Program for our publishing activities.

National Library of Canada Cataloguing in Publication Data

McMenemy, John, 1940-
    The language of Canadian politics : a guide to important
terms and concepts

3rd ed.
ISBN 0-88920-372-5

1. Canada – Politics and government – Dictionaries. I. Title.

JA61.M33 2001   320.971'03   C2001-930466-8

© 2001 Wilfrid Laurier University Press
Waterloo, Ontario, Canada   N2L 3C5

Third impression 2003

Cover design by Leslie Macredie

∞

Printed in Canada

Contents

D

E

F

G

H

I

J

K

L

M

N

O

P

Q

R

S

T

U

V

W

Notes to Readers

This is the third revision of *The Language of Canadian Politics*, and while the contents have changed significantly since the first publication in 1980, the purpose and design of the book remain the same. People interested in Canadian government and politics—whether students, professionals, or the general public in Canada or elsewhere—have been well served by members of the Canadian political science community who have produced a number of comprehensive introductory and specialized books on Canadian politics. What distinguishes *The Language of Canadian Politics* from other books is its format: brief essays on more than five hundred subjects, written directly and concisely, and presented alphabetically, that provide the reader with essential information about the subject, with cross references to related topics. A perusal of the Table of Contents that precedes this note will indicate the variety of topics addressed: institutions, ideas, concepts, programs, processes, laws, events, and so forth, both historical and contemporary, that inform political discussion, debate and conflict in Canadian politics.

Canadian politics and the language of political discourse is sufficiently distinctive that *The Language of Canadian Politics* can help orient a student or a member of the public generally to various subjects. Some subjects are rather arcane: established program financing has been replaced by the Canada Health and Social Transfer; the Supreme Court has read missing words into the Canadian Charter of Rights and Freedoms; provinces can dissent from constitutional amendments; the Crown retains certain prerogative powers. Other elements of Canadian political discourse are familiar, but perhaps not entirely clear: patriation of the constitution; federal spending power; sovereignty association; Triple-E Senate; parachuted candidates; the Charter's notwithstanding clause; responsible government.

As mentioned above, the essays here deal with historical as well as contemporary subjects. For example, question period, the Prime Minister's Office, the press gallery, the federal political parties and the electoral process, the Secession reference and Clarity bill are discussed here. But readers will also find succinct essays on topics on the distant and recent past that continue to frame and inform contemporary discourse: for example, constitutional measures reaching back to the Royal Proclamation of 1763, the *Quebec Act* of 1774, and other constitutional arrangements up to the *Constitution Act* of 1867 and the significant amendments of 1982 to which, importantly, Quebec has not assented. Early events in the twentieth century such as Conscription, the Union government of the 'teens and the Progressive party of the 1920s, and later events such as the October Crisis of 1970 and the National Energy Program of the 1970s are included here because of their continued relevance to political attitudes and behaviour in Canada.

In addition, the cross-references permit readers to "exploit" the book for their own particular purpose. One reader might want to follow a route through the book that explains the nature of the party system and the electoral process, while others follow routes that explain developments in Canadian federalism, or the role of the courts, French-English relations, the legislative process, and so forth. *The Language of Canadian Politics*, then, is not so much a creation of the author as it is a tool of the reader.

However valuable this book as such a tool, for those who wish detailed information about some matter of Canadian government and politics, there are many useful books and Internet sites, some of which are listed below.

Select Bibliography:

The following books are examples of comprehensive works that approach the subject of Canadian government and politics in different ways. The most recent editions of these books can be consulted for detailed information on many of the entries. There are other comprehensive texts available, as well as collections of readings and works on particular elements of the Canadian political system.

Archer, Keith, Roger Gibbins, Rainer Knopff and Leslie A. Pal. *Parameters of Power: Canada's Political Institutions.* Toronto: Nelson.

Bickerton, James. and Alain-G. Gagnon. *Canadian Politics.* Peterborough: Broadview Press.

Brooks, Stephen. *Canadian Democracy: An Introduction.* Toronto: Oxford University Press.

Dyck, Rand. *Canadian Politics: Critical Approaches.* Toronto: Nelson.

Guy, James John. *People, Politics, Government: Political Science: A Canadian Perspective.* Toronto: Prentice-Hall.

Gibbins, Roger. *Conflict and Unity: An Introduction to Canadian Political Life.* Toronto: Nelson.

Jackson, Robert J. and Doreen Jackson. *Politics in Canada: Culture, Institutions, Behaviour and Public Policy.* Toronto: Prentice-Hall.

Select Internet Sites:

There are many Internet sites that can be used for research purposes. From the few listed here, there are links to many others. For example, the Government of Canada website contains links to provincial and territorial government websites and federal agencies, and the Canadian Political Science Association website contains links to other electronic research sites.

Government of Canada:	www.canada.gc.ca
Parliament of Canada:	www.parl.gc.ca
Privy Council Office:	www.pco-bcp.gc.ca
Supreme Court of Canada:	www.scc-csc.gc.ca
Elections Canada:	www.elections.ca
Canada Information Office:	www.infocan.gc.ca
Canadian Broadcasting Corporation:	www.cbc.ca
Globe and Mail:	www.globeandmail.com
National Post:	www.nationalpost.com
Bloc Québécois:	www.blocquebecois.org
Canadian Alliance party:	www.canadianalliance.ca
Liberal party of Canada:	www.liberal.ca
New Democratic party:	www.ndp.ca
Progressive Conservative party:	www.pcparty.ca
Canadian Politics on the Web (Nelson Canada [publisher]):	www.polisci.nelson.com/canpol.html
Canadian Political Science Association:	www.uottawa.ca/associations/cpsa-acsp

Acknowledgements

I thank those who have commented on the first and second editions and encouraged me to produce this third revision. Many of these readers were students as well as anonymous reviewers who, as instructors, had used the earlier editions in their courses. Because of them each revision has been an improvement on the previous one, and I look forward to comments on this edition as well. Thanks are due the staff of Wilfrid Laurier University Press, with whom I have worked closely over the years on this and other projects.

John McMenemy
Waterloo, Ontario
2001

The Language of Canadian Politics

A

Aboriginal rights. See **Land claims and settlements (Native; Aboriginal); Native (First Nations) self-government.**

Access to Information Act **(Canada).** See **Freedom of information.**

Accountability. The requirement that an individual or group explain and accept responsibility before another individual or group for actions taken by them and by those under their supervision.

In the Canadian parliamentary system, the constitutional convention of responsible government requires the political executive (that is, the prime minister or provincial premier and cabinet) to respond to criticism in the legislature and to retain the "confidence" of the House of Commons or provincial legislature, in order to remain in office. Executive accountability is both collective and individual. Not only is the cabinet collectively responsible to the legislature, but each minister is personally accountable for administrative behaviour in the area of designated responsibility.

While accountability is a central feature of responsible government in the Canadian constitution, legislatures seldom defeat governments or precipitate the resignation of ministers. The disciplined party system and the secrecy which has traditionally enveloped the cabinet and public administration usually enable governments and ministers to survive opposition criticism. Nonetheless, the principle of accountability is sufficiently strong to allow the opposition to make a public case which the electorate will eventually decide. See **Collective (cabinet/ministerial) responsibility**; *Ministerial responsibility*; **Responsible government; Secrecy.**

Act (statute). A bill that has passed three readings in the legislature and received royal assent.

When royal assent is given, bills become acts; they are given chapter numbers, with the name of the sovereign and the year, and are published. Acts become effective statutory law when proclaimed, but in some cases not until invoked by the governor-in-council (that is, the cabinet) through an order-in-council which is also published—in the case of the federal government in the *Canada Gazette*. Some acts delegate authority to particular government bodies to make regulations which have the force of law. These regulations, or statutory instruments, are also published. Periodically statutes are published, bringing legislation amended since their original passage up to date. For example, federal legislation is periodically updated as the *Revised Statutes of Canada (R.S.C.)*.

Activists (party). People who, in terms of political participation, are involved with party activity beyond simply voting for a party, but few of whom actually make important decisions in party councils that pertain to election campaigns or parliamentary conduct between elections.

Specifically, an activist is a person who engages in "gladiatorial" rather than simply "spectator" roles: for example, holding membership in a party, contributing money to a party, serving as an officer of a party, attending local party meetings or party conventions, working for a candidate during an election campaign or being a party's candidate. It is debatable whether some backbench legislators are best described as activists or elites; they might best be described collectively as "leading activists."

Activists of all parties tend to be of higher social rank than the passive supporters of their respective parties in terms of education, occupation and income. Lawyers and business managers are numerous among the ranks of party activists. Trade union officials are much more numerous among New Democrats than among activists in other parties. Activists tend to be proportionately more numerous in regions where their respective party currently receives substantial electoral support. Thus, for example, Liberal activists have been predominantly from central Canada while Reform party/Canadian Alliance activists have been predominantly from western Canada.

Administration (public). The instruments and processes by which government policies are formulated, implemented and reviewed.

Study of the administration of state policy traditionally focussed on organization, human resources, finance and accountability within the public bureaucracy. Early studies of public administration in Canada frequently commented on the coherence and collegiality of the "bureaucratic elite." However, given the expansion of state activity in society and the economy in the twentieth century, and more recent administrative restructuring, including downsizing, there is increasing internal competitiveness. Scholars now also study the policy-making role inherent in public administration as part of a larger "subgovernment" linked to a wider and distinct set of "policy communities." See **Policy (-making; analysis; communities; instruments; public...)**; **Public service (administration)**.

Administrative (executive) federalism. A term frequently used to describe Canada's federal system in which federal-provincial relations are characterized by a high level of interdependence, emphasizing multilateral and bilateral ministerial and administrative consultation, negotiation and administration of public policy. The term is also used pejoratively, in criticism of a secretive and exclusive, as opposed to a public and inclusive, policy-making process. See **Federalism**.

Administrative law. A branch of legal studies dealing with the establishment of public agencies—particularly regulatory agencies and crown corporations—their procedures and decisions, the rights of persons affected, and oversight by the relevant legislature, executive and the judiciary. The expansion of state activities in the twentieth century led to government regulation of virtually every aspect of social and economic behaviour. Consequently, people's lives became increasingly affected by the specific rules and regulations (subordinate legislation) of administrators acting under enabling legislation passed in legislatures. See **Regulatory agencies (regulations)**.

Administrator (of Canada). The designation for the chief justice of the Supreme Court of Canada when exercising the powers and authority of the governor general in the event of the governor general's death, incapacity, removal or absence from Canada. Should the chief justice likewise be unavailable, the designation of "Our [that is, the Crown's] Administrator" is granted to the senior judge of the Supreme Court present and able to exercise vice-regal powers. This executive succession in Canada is outlined in the Letters Patent Constituting the Office of Governor General of Canada (1947). See **Governor General; Letters Patent (1947)**.

Aeronautics Case (1932). See **Treaty power**.

Affirmative (Positive) action. Programs initiated by government to improve the position of people belonging to groups considered subject to systemic discrimination in society and the economy.

An example from the 1960s is the indirect recruitment and promotion of French Canadians within the federal public service through language requirements. However, the phrase usually refers to recruitment, promotion and compensation programs designed later for women, Native Peoples, members of other ethnic minorities and people with disabilities. Critics of affirmative action refer to such programs as reverse discrimination. Affirmative action programs respecting "race, national or ethnic origin, colour, religion, sex, age, or mental or physical disability" are constitutionally sanctioned in the equality rights section of the Canadian Charter of Rights and Freedoms (s.15:2). See **Canadian Charter of Rights and Freedoms (1982)**.

Agenda (of meeting; public/private). An enumeration of items to be discussed at a meeting; otherwise, a person or group's publicly acknowledged or privately held objectives or purposes in the short or long term, as in "the government's agenda."

Ambassador. A diplomat accredited to represent the federal government to other national governments or international organizations such as the United Nations.

Historically, official relations between governments have been maintained through ambassadorial representation. However, since the advent of secure, instantaneous world-wide communication and high-speed air travel, the scope of ambassadorial activity has been reduced while the direct involvement in foreign policy of the prime minister, the minister of foreign affairs and their senior aides in Ottawa has increased. The governor-in-council, effectively the prime minister, appoints ambassadors. Postings to some capitals, such as Washington, London and Paris are often made for political partisan purposes, and public service associations are quick to criticize these and other appointments which they consider intrusions into their professional domain.

Amendment (legislative; constitutional). The alteration of the wording of a bill or motion before a legislature; frequently the alteration of a statute in a subsequent bill.

The principle of the supremacy of parliament implies that any legislature can amend its own statutes; thus amendments to ordinary legislation carry by a majority (at least 50 per cent plus 1 of those voting). Because of the constitutional convention of responsible government, the adoption of an opposition-sponsored amendment to government bills or motions may be interpreted as want-of-confidence in the government, possibly leading to the formation of a new government or dissolution of the legislature for a general election.

Constitutional statutes usually include a more complex amendment procedure. Canada's *Constitution Act, 1982*, for example, contains several amending formulae (Part V), in most cases involving provincial legislatures as well as Parliament. Its provisions are thus said to be "entrenched." See **Constitution Act, 1867, and subsequently amended; Entrenchment.**

Appointment power. The power of the political executive (the prime minister and provincial premiers), under the authority of the Crown, to fill certain public offices. While this includes cabinet membership, the power usually refers to senior appointments in the public service, including boards and commissions, and the judiciary. Discussions of constitutional reform have included proposals to circumscribe this power at the federal level by establishing a limited role for the Senate and possibly provincial governments in certain appointments. See **Senate; Supreme Court.**

Aspect Doctrine (constitution). A ruling by the Judicial Committee of the Privy Council that "subjects which in one aspect and for one purpose" come within provincial jurisdiction under a section of the *British North America Act, 1867* (since 1982, the *Constitution Act*) "may in another aspect and for another purpose" come within federal jurisdiction under another section.

In *Hodge v. The Queen* (1883), the appellant argued that a conviction under an Ontario statute which regulated liquor trade in the province was invalid, despite clear enumeration of tavern licences in section 92. The appeal was based on *Russell v. The Queen* (1882) in which the Judicial Committee of the Privy Council upheld a federal statute that provided for local prohibition under the "Peace, Order, and good Government" clause of section 91, as the question of prohibition was not specifically enumerated under provincial jurisdiction in section 92. The two statutes dealt with different aspects of the same thing—the liquor trade—and the use of the "Peace, Order, and good Government" clause in the Russell case was not allowed to deny a province's jurisdictional competence clearly stated in section 92. See **Judicial Committee of the Privy Council (JCPC)**; *Russell v. The Queen* (1882).

Associate/Assistant deputy minister. Senior ranks of permanent executive officials in the public service. A department may be administered by several associate and assistant deputy ministers responsible to a deputy minister who in turn is responsible for overall management of the department, and for providing advice and support to the minister. See **Deputy minister**.

Asymmetrical federalism. A federal political system which, in addition to the differences in jurisdictional competence (hence political autonomy) between national and subnational legislatures that is the essence of federalism, also admits differences in competence among the subnational legislatures relative to each other.

Asymmetrical federalism would exist *de jure* in Canada if one province had entrenched constitutional powers not held by the others. Supporters of the Social Union Framework Agreement of 1999, that established rules for joint federal-provincial relations on social policy, argue that it represents *de facto* asymmetrical federalism, preferably styled "collaborative" federalism. Critics argue that separate bilateral or selectively multilateral federal-provincial agreements in major social policy fields could lead to "checkerboard" federalism.

The debate over Quebec's constitutional status in Confederation, as well as federal spending power, centres on the nature of Canadian federalism. Variation in jurisdictional competence among provinces *de jure* would raise numerous questions, for example, about the proper role of senators and members of parliament in debating and voting on matters which fell within the legislative competence of Parliament for parts of Canada other than the province and constituency they represented. See **Distinct society clause; Federal-provincial tax-sharing agreements (fiscal federalism); Federalism; Social Union Framework Agreement (1999); Spending power; Sovereignty association.**

Auditor General. The federal officer who audits public accounts and investigates the financial affairs of most agencies of the federal government, including accounting practices, financial management and reporting, and the verification of expenditures for authorized purposes.

The governor-in-council (effectively the prime minister) appoints the auditor general with the rank of deputy minister for a 10-year renewable term (until the age of 65), who is removable within-term only by a resolution of both houses of Parliament. In accordance with the *Auditor General Act*, the auditor general has considerable independence in reporting annually on the public accounts of the federal government, many crown corporations, agencies and funds, to determine value for money spent. The auditor general can also make special reports. In examining and reporting on government accounts and expenditures, the auditor general's staff are to have access to all records relating to the accounts of the government and are to receive any information and explanations from public officials which the auditor general deems necessary. However, the cabinet may deny access to material it deems confidential, thus creating the possibility of a court challenge from the auditor general and political controversy in Parliament. The staff is appointed under the *Public Service Employment Act*, but the auditor general is responsible for personnel management within the office and may also contract for professional services from outside the civil service.

The auditor general's report is transmitted to the House of Commons and its Public Accounts Committee, chaired by an opposition member of parliament. The Senate's Committee on National Finance may also examine the report, but it is the report itself and its examination by the House committee that attracts the most public attention. The auditor general's staff assist the committee during its examination of the report. Because of this, and because the Office of the Auditor General is itself audited by a committee of cabinet, the Treasury Board, political tension is inherent in the relationship between the government and the Office of Auditor General. See **Budget and budgetary process; Comptroller General; Treasury Board; Treasury Board Secretariat.**

B

Backbencher. A member of a legislature who is neither a member of the cabinet nor, on the opposition's side, a party leader or designated party critic.

The public role of backbenchers in the House is basically to engage in parliamentary activity that complements their party's policy and political strategy. The main public outlets for parliamentary activity by backbenchers are the committee system and private members' legislation. However, the strictures of party discipline invoked by the party whip still apply in committee. Backbenchers themselves frequently cite the in-camera sessions of the party caucus as their major forum of independent activity. Proposals for parliamentary reform usually include the loosening of party discipline, to allow for a more visibly independent role for backbenchers. See **Caucus; Members of parliament (MPs).**

Balance of power (legislative). Influence, if not power, held by a "third" party in a legislature in which no party has a majority of seats. In order to remain in office, then, the government party must obtain sufficient support of opposition parties (or opposition members voting)—usually from a party other than the official opposition—to win a vote in the House. In Canada such support is usually based on informal understandings.

Ballot. A specially prepared paper which electors use to designate their choice in secret for candidates in an election or for an option in a referendum.

The ballots are carefully guarded before, during and, for a period of time, after an election. In provincial and federal elections, unofficial counts are tabulated on election night and official counts declared later. As an act of protest, electors may refuse a ballot presented to them at a polling station and have the ballot officially recorded as "rejected." Otherwise, ballots cast are tabulated as valid, or declared "spoiled" if the elector's preference is unclear or the ballot is not marked in a way designated as acceptable. Elections have been increasingly organized and portrayed in the mass media as a "horse race" among party leaders. However, in Canada's parliamentary system, voters choose one among several local candidates nominated to represent their particular constituency. In each constituency, then, the ballot contains the names of the candidates for that constituency, listed alphabetically, along with the name of the political party to which each candidate belongs. Parties may designate a scrutineer in each polling station in a constituency to oversee the count which is conducted by the deputy returning officer, the person in charge of the polling station. See **Electoral system; Returning Officer (RO) and Deputy Returning Officers [DROs]**).

Bandwagon effect. The assumed tendency of some people to subscribe to a cause or vote for a party only because it is expected to prevail. Some argue that this behaviour is encouraged during election campaigns by the publication of public opinion polls. Others argue that, in the absence of convincing evidence, one can assert the existence of a countervailing effect, as voters support an "underdog" in order to decrease the expected margin of victory of the prevailing candidate or party.

Bank of Canada (central bank). A crown corporation established by Parliament in 1934, responsible for monetary policy and for protecting the external value of the currency, and in general "the economic and financial well-being of Canada".

The Bank of Canada can achieve these objectives because it is the final source of payment in the Canadian economy through its issuance of authentic bank notes, and the amount of money in circulation. The Bank also achieves a particular monetary policy by altering the bank rate, that is, the top end of a band of overnight lending rates at which it, or other financial institutions, will make loans or advances to major financial institutions. The credit policies (interest rates and terms of borrowing) of financial institutions exert great influence on saving and spending decisions in the economy. Thus the bank rate of the central bank leads to changes in the "prime rate" at which financial institutions will lend money to borrowers and the interest they will pay on various forms of deposit. The Bank of Canada can also influence interest rates by buying (to lower interest rates) or selling (to raise interest rates) government securities. The central bank does not engage in commercial banking. If the Bank perceives an economy growing faster than desired, the Bank will dampen inflationary trends by fostering a rise in interest rates. Otherwise, the Bank will seek lower interest rates when it feels that spending should be encouraged to avoid economic recession. The Bank also serves the Canadian government as banker and advisor on fiscal matters and the management of the public debt.

On the international level, the central bank protects the value of the currency by entering into transactions, for example, to buy and sell foreign exchange. It opens accounts in, and accepts deposits from, other central banks and international monetary agencies. Thus, when there is a "run on the dollar," the Bank may "prop up" the dollar's value on foreign exchange markets through purchases of Canadian dollars with foreign, notably United States, exchange, and by raising the bank rate. The Bank advises the government on international financial issues and participates in international meetings such as those sponsored by the International Monetary Fund, the Organization for Economic Co-operation and Development, and the Group of Seven Industrial Countries.

The bank is managed and its monetary policy determined by a governing council comprising the governor, senior deputy and deputy governors. A board of directors, chaired by the governor, and including the senior deputy governor, twelve outside directors and the (non-voting) minister of finance, reviews the Bank's policies other than its monetary policy. The minister of finance recommends to cabinet the appointment of the outside directors to three-year terms. The federal government also appoints the governor and senior deputy governor, but for seven-year terms.

Until 1967, there was some uncertainty over the relationship on monetary policy between the minister of finance and the governor of the Bank, its chief executive officer. The central bank began as a privately owned corporation in 1935, but since 1938, as a crown corporation, the federal minister of finance has held all share capital issued by the Bank. Since its decennial review by Parliament in 1967, *the Bank of Canada Act* grants the Bank responsibility for formulating monetary policy, but in the event of a disagreement between the government and the Bank, the minister of finance may give the governor a specific, written directive on monetary policy to be made public, "and the Bank shall comply with such directive" (s.14). However, governments are reluctant to engage in public debate with the Bank, let alone issue a directive that would likely result in the governor's resignation and a crisis of confidence in the government's management of the economy. Since the 1990s, the Bank and the government jointly declare the objectives of monetary policy.

Nonetheless public debate occurs occasionally over the general objectives of monetary policy and the appropriateness of that policy at a given time. For example, on general objectives, from 1984 to 1993 the Conservative government of Brian Mulroney and the governor were agreed that, between the two objectives of maintaining price stability to control inflation and achieving full employment, the former was the pre-eminent goal of monetary policy. Critics argued at the time that such monetary policy exacerbated recessionary effects such as unemployment. Also, some critics suggest that indivisible "national" monetary policy is designed to deal with the problems of the dominant central-Canadian segment of the economy which may be different from those of other regional economies in the country. See **Monetary policy**.

Bar (of the House). A barrier at the entrance to a legislative chamber, beyond which no "stranger," or non-member, is normally admitted. At the formal opening of a session of Parliament, members of the House of Commons are summoned to the bar of the Senate to hear the Speech from the Throne that outlines the government's legislative intentions for the session. Also, persons may be "summoned to appear before the bar of the House" to answer charges that they have slighted the dignity of the legislature or violated the privileges of members.

Bellwether riding. A constituency that, in general elections, has repeatedly elected a candidate whose party subsequently formed the government. Some people therefore cite results in those constituencies as possible indicators of the eventual election outcome. The phrase itself is an allusion to the practice of attaching a bell to a sheep to lead the flock. A more reliable designation of bellwether ridings would involve applying the most current regional public opinion data on voter intention to the last election results, with some allowance for possible candidate and other local effects.

Bicameral. An adjective denoting two chambers in the legislature as opposed to only one chamber (unicameral). The federal Parliament of Canada is bicameral by virtue of having a lower house—the House of Commons—and an upper house—the Senate, while all provincial and territorial legislatures in Canada are unicameral.

Bicultural cleavage. A deep-seated social division in Canada based on ethnic, religious and linguistic factors, reflected in constitutional statutes, political conventions and ongoing constitutional and policy debates.

The bicultural cleavage is usually expressed in terms of the minority French-speaking and Roman Catholic community on one side and the majority English-speaking and Protestant community on the other side. Over time the religious factor has diminished in importance and the linguistic factor and the question of the jurisdictional competence of Quebec—the only autonomous, majority French-speaking political jurisdiction in North America—have become the dominant issues between the communities.

The bicultural cleavage is generally considered the most powerful of cleavages in federal politics because of the cohesive political force of francophones, especially in Quebec. Certainly it is an historic cleavage, originating in the final conquest of New France by the British in 1759-60 and being expressed in the subsequent, at times uneasy, cohabitation of the two communities. Following disturbances in 1837 in Lower Canada (designated Canada East in 1840 and Quebec since 1867), the Governor of British North America, Lord Durham, recommended to the British government a policy of assimilation. However, the political cohesion of French Canadians and the achievement of responsible government in the Province of Canada in the 1840s resulted in a pattern of bicultural accommodation, which became the model for post-Confederation Canada.

Since Confederation in 1867, each cultural community—notably francophones throughout the country and minority-group anglophones and, more recently other ethnic communities (called "allophones") in Quebec—has been sensitive to changes that might put it at a disadvantage in relation to the other group, and many issues have arisen to create anxiety and to heighten tension on the bicultural cleavage. The earliest of such issues in post-Confederation Canada were the hanging of Louis Riel in 1885 and the passage of the *Jesuit Estates Act* in Quebec in 1888, and later the conscription crises during the First and Second World Wars. More recent issues include the provisions following from the federal *Official Languages Act* (Canada, 1969), and the language and constitutional policies of successive federal and Quebec governments, notably those of the sovereignist Parti Québécois, since the 1960s.

At the federal level, the formula of political accommodation developed in the nineteenth century still holds. A party will generally possess the support of the French-speaking community if its leadership in Quebec is integrated in the mainstream of that society and its leadership in English-speaking Canada is sympathetic to the cultural aspirations of French Canadians. Judging by the success of the Conservative party in the late nineteenth century and of the Liberal party in the twentieth century, electoral success with respect to this cleavage tends to be reinforced in subsequent elections. The party of French-Canadian favour is usually in office and able therefore to reward that favour in concrete terms. Other parties that do not have the support of French Canadians may, by contrast, harbour or appear to harbour unfavourable attitudes toward French Canada. The leadership of the successful party naturally magnifies and exaggerates these perceptions in order to maintain the electoral allegiance of French Canadians and thus style itself "the party of national unity." When none of the established parties seems to satisfy French Quebeckers, support may develop for a "third party," such as the Nationalistes in the early 1900s, the Ralliement des créditistes in the 1960s, and the Bloc Québécois that rose to prominence in the early 1990s. **See various entries on subjects mentioned above**.

Big M Drug Mart Case (1985). A decision by the Supreme Court of Canada that declared the federal *Lord's Day Act* to be a violation of section 2 ("Fundamental Freedoms") of the Canadian Charter of Rights and Freedoms.

This early Charter decision, among others, illustrated the Court's broad purposive interpretation of the Charter to ensure the "full benefit" of its protection to Canadians—in this case, freedom of conscience and religion—as traditions evolve. The purpose of the legislation was to enforce a common day of pause from commercial activity, but was related to the Christian Sabbath and thus discriminated against other religions. That Big M Drug Mart could successfully raise the issue of religious freedom on behalf of "others," while having no religious conscience or point of view itself, is an example of the broad non-interpretive approach to judicial review adopted by the Court. Legislation in Ontario with a similar purpose, but without a religious connotation (*Retail Business Holidays Act*), was sustained in a Supreme Court challenge (*R. v. Edwards Books and Art Ltd.*, [1986]). See **Canadian Charter of Rights and Freedoms (1982); Judicial review (interpretive; non-interpretive); Supreme Court**.

Bilingualism and biculturalism. A phrase describing the federal French-English language policies based on provisions of the *Official Languages Act, 1969*. The Act declared French and English to be the official languages of Canada, with equal "status...rights and privileges as to their use in all the institutions of Parliament and the Government of Canada."

To achieve equal status for both languages, the Act required that federal departments and agencies provide service in both languages in designated bilingual districts. The Act also provided for a commissioner of official languages to oversee the enforcement of the Act. The most obvious impact of the Act was probably the extension of French-language radio and television service across Canada in the 1970s and regulations respecting the use of both languages in commerce.

A contentious aspect of the Act involved recruitment to, and promotion within, the federal public service to create a functionally bilingual service. The modification of the merit system—by the introduction of language requirements and the creation of single-language units within the civil service—was also designed to increase French-Canadian representation in middle- and upper-level positions where, historically, French Canadians had been underrepresented.

Opposition to "official bilingualism" includes criticism of successive federal governments thought to be too solicitous of francophone support. Supporters view constitutionally entrenched "B and B" as part of a citizen-rights, or "personality" approach to Canadian nationality as distinct from a territorial-rights approach that would likely lead to variations in language rights across provinces and territories. See **Commissioner of Official Languages**; *Official Languages Act* (**Canada, 1969**).

Bill. See **Act (statute)**.

Bill 63; 22; 101; 178; 86 (Quebec). Various statutes in Quebec enacted since the 1960s, dealing with the use of the French language in government, the courts, education and commerce in Quebec. See **Charter of the French Language (Quebec)**.

Bill of Rights (*Recognition and Protection of Human Rights and Fundamental Freedoms Act* (**Canada, 1960**). A federal statute, introduced by the Conservative government of John Diefenbaker, that enumerated the "human rights and fundamental freedoms" of Canadians.

As an act of Parliament, the Bill of Rights, which was superseded by the Canadian Charter of Rights and Freedoms in 1982, applied to federal jurisdiction only. Unlike the 1982 Charter, the Bill was not entrenched in the constitution. Thus, as an "ordinary" parliamentary statute, it could be amended, made inoperative with respect to some legislation, or repealed by a parliamentary majority. Its application and judicial enforcement was inconsistent, but nonetheless it focused attention in subsequent constitutional discussions and negotiations that resulted in the constitutional entrenchment of the Charter. See **Canadian Charter of Rights and Freedoms (1982)**; **Civil liberties; Supreme Court**.

Bloc Québécois. A federal party, formed in 1990, and dedicated to the sovereignty of Quebec.

With the second-largest number of seats in the House of Commons, it formed the official opposition from 1993 to 1997. Since then, it has become a "third party" in federal politics while the provincial Parti Québécois remained the primary political force promoting sovereignty for the province.

The Bloc originated with five members of parliament elected earlier as Conservatives, three as Liberals and one MP elected in a by-election under the party label. It was the most popular party in Quebec in the 1993 election, winning 49 per cent of the provincial vote and 54 seats. The party's leader, Lucien Bouchard, had been recruited to federal politics and the Conservative party by his personal friend, Conservative leader Brian Mulroney. When Bouchard was elected in 1988 as a Conservative MP, Prime Minister Mulroney made him the leading francophone member of the cabinet. Bouchard resigned from the cabinet in 1990, following the defeat of the Meech Lake Accord which he felt was, in any event, an inadequate response to Quebec's needs. The Bloc Québécois also opposed the Charlottetown Accord of 1992 as "less than Meech." Soon after its formation, the Bloc represented a clear threat to the Conservative government. Indeed, the Bloc's success in 1993 occurred at the expense of the Conservative government. In addition to losing its Quebec base, the government party also lost support in western Canada and was reduced to unofficial standing in the House of Commons with only two MPs, while the Liberal party formed the government.

Following Bouchard's departure from the Bloc to lead the Parti Québécois and to become the premier of Quebec, the federal Bloc's role in the sovereignist movement declined. In subsequent federal elections, it continued to receive considerable support from francophone Quebeckers, but was reduced to "third-party" status in legislative strength with the Liberals maintaining dominance. In the election of 2000, the Liberals won the largest share of the popular vote in Quebec over the BQ for the first time (44% and 40%, respectively), gaining seats at the BQ's expense, although the voter turnout was only 62 per cent. Comparisons could be made with the origins and the impact on Liberal and Conservative fortunes of Henri Bourassa's Nationalistes early in the twentieth century and of Réal Caouette's Créditistes in the 1960s. See **Fragment splinter parties; Nationalistes, the; Parti Québécois (PQ); Ralliement des créditistes**.

Block payments. Unconditional federal transfer payments to the provinces for social programs, introduced in the late 1970s, in contrast to earlier conditional transfers on a federal-dollar-for-provincial-dollar expenditure basis.

From the federal government's perspective, periodically negotiated block payments were preferable to the blank cheque of "fifty-cent dollars" by which it had earlier supported provincial expenditures in approved social programs. From the viewpoint of some provinces, block payments "disentangled" the federal government from provincial policy-determination in allocating funds for certain programs, though federal standards would still have to be met. Critics objected to the unconditional aspect of the block transfers which would not prevent provincial governments from "underfunding" such programs as post-secondary education and medical health insurance, and thus detract from the quality of programs and accessibility.

In 1996, the federal Liberal government combined transfers of funds and the shifting of tax points for post-secondary education, health insurance, through Established Program Funding, and for social assistance and welfare services under the Canada Assistance Plan (CAP) into one block grant designated the Canada Health and Social Transfer. In addition to the criticism of block funding noted above, this change was also criticized for not continuing federal conditions for social assistance under CAP except for prohibiting minimum residence requirement for recipients, and also because tax points would generate different levels of provincial revenue across provinces. See **Canada Assistance Plan (CAP, 1966-1995); Canada Health and Social Transfer (CHST); Established Programs Financing (EPF); Federal-provincial tax-sharing agreements (fiscal federalism)**.

Borrowing power. The ability of federal and provincial governments and some crown corporations to incur indebtedness to finance expenditures, subject to approval by the legislature. The borrowing power of municipal governments is restricted by provincial governments. Borrowing by the senior governments is constrained by interest rates which in turn are affected by a government's or crown corporation's credit rating, and by the public's sensitivity to the extent of current indebtedness and the cost of servicing the debt.

British connection. A reference to the political and sentimental ties between Canada and the United Kingdom, epitomized by the continued role of the British monarch as Canada's monarch and head of state, and by Canada's membership in the Commonwealth of Nations, which includes most of Britain's former colonies.

Increasingly, the British connection meant less in Canadian politics and sentiment throughout the twentieth century. In the late-nineteenth and early-twentieth centuries, Britain was the dominant foreign model of domestic behaviour, and development of Canada's economy was dependent on British capital. But as the glory of Empire receded and the United States replaced Britain as the main external source of capital and political influence, the US became the predominant source of models of cultural and social values, and the British connection was relegated to largely symbolic importance. Britain's membership in the European Union and the increasingly heterogeneous nature of the Canadian population also contributed to the decline of British influence in Canada. The last occasion on which the British connection led to domestic partisan conflict was during the Suez Canal crisis of 1956. The Liberal government then refused to support Anglo-French and Israeli military intervention in Egypt. The Conservatives objected particularly to Prime Minister Louis St. Laurent's reference to the "supermen of Europe" no longer being able to dominate the world. However, when the Conservatives were in power from 1956 to 1963, relations between Canada and Britain worsened, especially when Canada actively opposed the British Conservative government's intention to enter the European Economic Community (Common Market). Canadian initiatives in the Commonwealth with respect to the apartheid regime in South Africa, for example, did not always receive British support. The Conservative sponsored Canada-United States Free Trade Agreement of 1989, followed soon after by the North American Free Trade Agreement including Mexico, should have dispelled any remaining thoughts that the British connection had much continuing practical significance either in domestic party politics or in foreign and international trade policies.

British North America Act. See **Constitution Act, 1867, and subsequently amended**.

Brokerage politics. Political behaviour based on practical actions best suited to achieving and maintaining power.

Brokerage politics is justified as the proper management of social tensions in a heterogeneous society through pragmatic decision making to maintain social harmony. Critics of the concept ask who benefits most from brokerage politics, suggesting that in framing and managing the political discourse, brokerage politicians deliberately magnify the importance of traditional social cleavages involving ethnicity, religion, language and geography, and thus discourage the public from developing a class perspective on society and demanding redistributive public policies. Such a development presumably would not favour the wealthy and powerful interests in society that have historically financed the two most "practical" brokerage parties, the Liberals and Conservatives.

Budget and budgetary process. The establishment of the government's priorities for spending among existing and proposed programs by the public administration and the cabinet and its committees, with parliamentary scrutiny and approval—an expenditure management system.

The process is complicated, and varies in detail among jurisdictions. Constitutionally, the prerogative of introducing money or supply bills (appropriation acts) belongs to the cabinet alone. The legislature's role is to examine and vote on departmental estimates and the government's budget. Although there is a wider pre-budget consultative process than in the past, the final decisions in the budgetary process still take place in a highly competitive environment within the largely private confines of the administration and cabinet.

The focus of financial administration and control in the federal government is a statutory cabinet committee on the expenditure budget—the Treasury Board, and its Secretariat—the Department of Finance and the cabinet secretariat, the Privy Council Office. However, the process begins in the complex pattern of demands made on the government from groups in society as well as the public administration itself. These demands are accommodated in cabinet committees that receive and evaluate policy priorities from the departments and government agencies. The Department of Finance submits to the cabinet its proposals for fiscal, or taxation, policy for the budgetary year based on the Department's evaluation of likely revenues and expenditures. This evaluation occurs well before the relevant fiscal year. Within this fiscal framework, the Treasury Board develops an annual expenditure plan and co-ordinates the estimates process.

In calendar terms, federal government departments submit their plans to the Treasury Board Secretariat each spring, indicating proposed spending for authorized programs. Departmental reviews are also examined by cabinet committees and standing committees of the House of Commons. In the autumn, the government releases budget consultation papers that are then examined by the Commons' standing committee on finance. The cabinet, Finance, the Treasury Board Secretariat and the Privy Council Office then review the government's budget strategy and, in January-February, the cabinet—but notably the prime minister and the minister of finance—decide upon the budget.

The minister of finance presents the government's annual budget in an address to the House of Commons usually in February, after the main estimates have been introduced. The budget address reviews the state of the economy from the government's point of view, the operation of the government in the previous fiscal year, and the forecast for the next year—the economic "outlook." The minister will also announce revenue measures, changes in the existing tax rates, rules and tariffs (announcements of resolutions to change commodity taxes are effective immediately and legislative approval is retroactive). The budget speech is delivered within the context of a motion approving the government's budgetary policy, which then leads to a wide-ranging "budget debate" in the House touching on the government's overall performance. When the motion is passed, budget resolutions and tax bills are introduced.

The final stage of the budgetary process is parliamentary scrutiny and approval. Main estimates and supplementary estimates are referred to committees of the House of Commons. Standing orders of the House deal with the timing of consideration of both main and supplementary estimates with respect to the current and the upcoming fiscal years. There are three supply periods in which the government's supply motions, or appropriation acts, are debated. On allotted days, motions made by the opposition take precedence and motions of non-confidence are debated. On the last allotted day in each supply period, the Speaker interrupts debate and asks for a vote on all supply business then before the House. Following parliamentary approval of expenditures, provisions of the *Financial Administration Act* regulate the expenditure process and an annual report by the auditor general on the government's financial statements is tabled in the Parliament for examination and debate.

The governor general's warrant is an important exception to parliamentary examination of government expenditures prior to actual disbursement of money. On the report of the Treasury Board that there is no appropriation for an expenditure which, according to a report by the relevant minister, is urgently required, the governor-in-council (that is, the cabinet) may order a warrant authorizing the expenditure. Warrants must be reported in the *Canada Gazette* and reported to Parliament, when debate can then take place. See **Auditor General**; **Estimates**; **Treasury Board**; **Treasury Board Secretariat**.

Bureaucracy. For social scientists, an administrative system associated with large social organizations characterized by hierarchy and status, specialized training, clear lines of supervision and accountability, objective judgmental criteria for recruitment, career advancement and the maintenance of records. In popular usage, bureaucracy is a pejorative word, usually with reference to the public sector and signifying excessive size, formality and inflexibility, jurisdictional interests, specialized vocabulary or jargon and a tendency to self-perpetuation—traits described collectively as involving "empire building" and "red tape." See **Public service (administration)**.

By-election. An election held to fill a legislative seat which has become vacant since the last general election.

The timing of federal by-elections is left to the prime minister, who, within six months of formal notification to the Speaker that a vacancy has occurred, may name any date. Thus, a by-election may occur within a short time of the notification of the vacancy or may be postponed so that it is not held, due to an eventual issuance of writs for a general election. A by-election may be called quickly if, for example, the prime minister or provincial premier has engineered the vacancy for political purposes or otherwise sees advantage in a by-election. By-elections may be important if the government party holds only a slim majority of seats in the legislature. Otherwise, by-elections are exercises that test in a limited way the government's popularity without threatening its existence.

C

Cabinet. The political executive—the government-of-the-day—which formulates government priorities and policies and is responsible for the introduction and passage of public legislation embodying those policies, the execution and administration of the policies, and the finances of government.

The federal cabinet is the active part of the Queen's Privy Council for Canada. Provincial cabinets are known formally as Executive Councils. The following describes the federal cabinet, a model which is followed in the provinces except in the specific examples of power of appointment.

The cabinet comprises the prime minister and ministers who have a relationship on one side with the governor general and on another with the House of Commons. A person becomes prime minister after an invitation from the governor general to form a ministry or government. The prime minister dominates the cabinet, selecting people for the cabinet and "advising" the governor general on their appointment, later their re-assignment to different portfolios or removal altogether from cabinet. In this "advisory" role to the governor general, the prime minister also effectively determines the date of the dissolution of Parliament and the issuance of writs for the next general election. The government remains in office as long as it has the support or "confidence" of the House of Commons. When Parliament is dissolved for an election, the cabinet remains in place throughout the election campaign and may remain in office afterwards to seek the confidence of the new House. Only when the prime minister—and not any individual or group of ministers—resigns, does the government cease to exist. The organization and operation of the cabinet, or political executive, is also largely the prerogative of the prime minister, assisted by the cabinet secretariat, the Privy Council Office.

As mentioned above, the principle of responsible government requires that the government retain the support of the House in order to stay in power. The House, however, is organized on the basis of a disciplined party system. Thus, the member of parliament whom the governor general invites to be prime minister is the party-selected leader of the party which holds a majority of seats in the House or, lacking a majority, is able to win the support of a majority of members of parliament on important policy votes. Custom, usage and convention restrict a prime minister's choice of ministers. Federal cabinet ministers must have seats in the House of Commons or, less desirably, in the Senate. The MPs selected by the prime minister to be cabinet colleagues are always from the same party, unless with only minority representation in the legislature the prime minister forms a coalition government with another party. The prime minister will also attempt to have a cabinet that is recognizably representative of important regional, ethnic, religious, occupational and social interests.

Collective responsibility and secrecy are important conventions of cabinet government in Canada. Not having any legal status other than as part of the Queen's Privy Council for Canada, the federal cabinet acts formally as the advisory Privy Council. Thus, the governor-in-council is the governor general acting on the advice of the cabinet through an order, or minute, of council which has the force of law. Not only does the government then speak with one voice, but members are bound for life by the Privy Council oath of secrecy. A former member of a cabinet still remains a member of the Privy Council. Thus, opinions that a current minister expresses publicly are those of the cabinet. A minister may disagree publicly with the cabinet's view only after first resigning from it, and even then may not disclose details of cabinet discussions or documents.

The disciplined party system in the House, along with the custom of collective ministerial responsibility based on a formal relationship to the Crown, gives the government-of-the-day an outward appearance of strength, efficiency and single-mindedness with which to fend off the opposition. Political patronage associated with government (for example, the prospects for judicial, administrative, diplomatic and senatorial appointments, as well as the possibility of a private post-political career assisted by government patronage) also ensures the cohesion of the cabinet. Perhaps the most notorious potential use of the historic, but largely formal, relationship between cabinet and Crown to protect the government is the potential use of the *Official Secrets Act.* This Act enjoins all Canadians from possessing, distributing and publicizing information deemed to be injurious to the state. This pressure could be applied against those (usually public officials and journalists) whose actions might embarrass the government, but hardly threaten the state.

The cabinet is also protected by parliamentary custom. For example, ministers need not answer questions about activities in portfolios no longer held by them. Thus, opposition MPs may be questioning a current cabinet minister on the behaviour of a predecessor while the alleged miscreant sits mutely as a minister holding another portfolio.

Basically, then, the government and individual ministers remain in office as long as they have the support of the majority of MPs, or as long as public opinion fails to rally behind the opposition's criticism. Prime ministers in Canada are well known for defending their ministers; rarely does a ministerial resignation result from opposition party criticism. As for the prime minister, other than in the case of defeat in the House on a vote of confidence, the governor general is not likely to ask for a prime minister's (that is, a government's) resignation except in a clear case of malfeasance and when there is another MP available who would have the support of the House or when public opinion—as expressed in the next election—would likely support the forced resignation. See **Cabinet organization; Governor General; Inner cabinet;** *Official Secrets Act;* **Prime minister**.

Cabinet organization. The organization of cabinet is the prime minister's and provincial premiers' prerogative in heading the political executive of their respective jurisdictions, and frequently reflects their government's political agenda and their personal leadership style.

The following describes the federal cabinet, but the same general principles apply to provincial cabinets. Until the 1960s, the federal cabinet was a small body operating informally with little assistance required from its secretariat, the Privy Council Office (PCO). However, the contemporary federal cabinet, with two dozen or more members, has an elaborate committee system and secretariat. Prime ministers organize cabinets—the committees, their membership and terms of reference—to suit their purposes, and the rules of cabinet secrecy and collective responsibility apply to all aspects of cabinet business.

The Treasury Board, however, is an important exception to the foregoing comment on prime ministerial prerogative in the organization of the political executive. The Treasury Board is a statutory committee of cabinet— that is, it exists by an Act of Parliament and is formally a committee of the Queen's Privy Council for Canada. The Treasury Board is chaired by a cabinet minister named the president, and includes the minister of finance and four other ministers. With its own Secretariat, and including the Office of the Comptroller General, it is responsible for examining and making recommendations on proposed government expenditures, for reviewing expenditures and financial controls, and for personnel management in the public service.

Federal cabinets contain several committees and levels of committees, from senior-level co-ordinating committees to lower-level policy committees. Since 1968, cabinets have grown in size and their role has become largely to ratify most recommendations from "below" and to debate only the most pressing political issues as defined by the prime minister. Consequently, most federal cabinets have included a committee, frequently called the committee on priorities and planning, an influential "inner cabinet."

The cabinet secretariat, or Privy Council Office, the Prime Minister's Office (PMO), and interdepartmental committees of senior civil servants are major influences in cabinet policy making. In 1940, an order-in-council designated the clerk of the Privy Council as secretary to the cabinet. Since then, however, the clerk has been designated the prime minister's deputy minister, the PCO thus becoming clearly the "administrative arm" of the prime minister as well as providing staff support and records for all cabinet business. The PMO is the prime minister's personal staff, the "political arm" headed by the chief of staff (sometimes called "principal secretary"). The PMO advises and supports the prime minister, and, under the "authority" of the prime minister, also counsels cabinet ministers. Interdepartmental committees may be established informally or by order-in-council to co-ordinate advice from the administration to relevant cabinet committees. Consisting of deputy ministers or associate and assistant deputies, these committees are often the site of interdepartmental rivalries and bargaining over competing interests within the public bureaucracy. See **Budget and budgetary process; Cabinet; Inner cabinet; Prime minister; Ministers (of the Crown); Prime Minister's Office; Privy Council Office; Regulatory agencies (regulations); Secretaries of state; Treasury Board; Treasury Board Secretariat.**

Cadre parties. Parties, such as the federal Liberal and Conservative parties, whose origins were in the legislative environment in the nineteenth century. They are managed by a small elite, centred around and possessing the confidence of the leader, that includes senior parliamentarians, selected extra-parliamentary officials, policy specialists, fund raisers, media consultants, market survey analysts and organizers.

While such parties developed an extra-parliamentary organization among the public in the twentieth century, they remain traditionally elite-dominated in terms of policy making and campaign decision making. The decision making in parliamentary, or cadre parties can be characterized as pragmatic and flexible, as these parties are focused on the achievement and retention of elective office and political power. The policy positions of parliamentary or cadre parties are difficult to predict except that the leadership usually seeks to maximize popularity by brokering support from as many interests as possible. Their extra-parliamentary organizations do not determine policy, but only offer advice to the leader who determines policy in the context of electoral requirements. Party policy is therefore subject to unexpected reversal.

By contrast, movement parties, such as the Co-operative Commonwealth Federation and Social Credit parties, and later the New Democratic and the

Reform/Canadian Alliance parties, originated in the twentieth century, outside the established political elite. As grassroots movements, they possessed a membership-based, extra-parliamentary organization whose behaviour and policy positions had to be respected by the leader and the parliamentary caucus of the party. See **Brokerage politics; Conservative (Progressive Conservative) party; Liberal party; Movement parties.**

Calgary Declaration (Framework; 1997). Following the second referendum in Quebec on sovereignty association in 1995 in which the Yes option was only narrowly defeated, a statement on Canadian unity forged by nine of ten provincial premiers (excluding Quebec's sovereignist Premier Lucien Bouchard) and the territorial leaders of Yukon and Northwest Territories.

Both the constitutional Meech Lake and Charlottetown accords of 1987 and 1992 failed to be adopted in large part because of their declaration of Quebec as a "distinct society," that, in the critics' view, would have given Quebec legislative powers not held by the other provinces. In view, however, of the narrow defeat of the referendum and an imminent election in Quebec, the provincial premiers attempted, in a meeting in Calgary, Alberta, to compose a statement that might satisfy Quebeckers, yet maintain the principle of the equality of provinces.

The seven-point statement spoke of the rights of individual Canadians, diversity, tolerance and compassion, Native peoples, the French and English languages, multiculturalism and mutual respect among their governments. On the key points, however, "All provinces, while diverse in their characteristics, have equality of status" (2), and "unique character of Quebec society" was substituted for "distinct society": "In Canada's federal system, where respect for diversity and equality underlies unity, the unique character of Quebec society, including its French speaking majority, its culture and its tradition of civil law, is fundamental to the well being of Canada. Consequently, the legislature and Government of Quebec have a role to protect and develop the unique character of Quebec society within Canada" (5).

It appeared, however, that francophone Quebeckers were largely unimpressed, if at all aware, of the premiers' statement. In 1998, the sovereignist Parti Québécois government was re-elected with a majority, though with a slightly smaller share of the popular vote than the Liberal party. Premier Bouchard promised a third referendum when, in his view, a victory was likely. For its part, the federal Liberal government developed a two-pronged post-referendum strategy: on the one hand having Parliament move to recognize Quebec as a distinct society and devolving the federal veto in the general amending formula of the constitution to several regions, Quebec constituting a region; on the other hand, having Parliament enact the so-called Clarity bill on future referendums on secession following a ruling by the Supreme Court on a federal reference on the legality of a unilateral declaration of independence. See **Charlottetown Accord (1992); Clarity bill; Meech Lake Accord (1987); Parti Québécois; Secession Reference; Sovereignty association.**

Campaign (election). An organized and competitive effort under law by political parties and individual candidates in local constituencies to mobilize public support to win legislative office and thereby gain executive political power.

Federal and provincial election campaigns begin formally when Parliament or the provincial legislature is dissolved and writs are issued for a general election on a given day. However, government parties often stage "pre-writ campaigns," especially as expenditures incurred then for political market research and advertising may not count as campaign expenditures and may in fact be borne by the public as a government, rather than a party, expense. Electoral success for a candidate involves winning more votes than any other candidate in a constituency, while success for a party is having its official candidates win the most seats—preferably a majority—in the next House of Commons or provincial legislature. In liberal democratic theory, competitive elections are an opportunity for citizens to review the past performance of the government party, assess the alternatives and influence the composition and policy direction of the government.

Organization and finance are crucial aspects of federal and provincial campaigns which have focussed increasingly on television for party advertising, coverage of the leaders' tours, and leadership debates. Mass marketing techniques used in business, such as omnibus and targeted public opinion surveys as well as focus groups, have been adopted by parties to test and improve "messages" designed to bond emotionally an increasingly unpredictable electorate to their party leader. These messages are then transmitted by television or by the use of computer-assisted telephone communication, direct mail and the Internet, often to specific segments of the electorate thought to be strategically important to the parties' electoral fortunes. The use of sophisticated marketing instruments and skills has caused some commentators to describe election campaigns as essentially opportunities for parties to manipulate rather than inform public opinion.

Election campaigns are centrally directed party campaigns. Little attention is given to the local candidates except in marginal seats where a local-candidate effect might be crucial to the outcome. The candidate selection process is subject largely to party regulation which, though formally centralized, is usually very localized. Occasionally party leaders "parachute" candidates into a riding if there is no organization "on the ground," or when they want to find a "safe" seat for a high-profile candidate who has no connection with the constituency. After the fact, a leader of virtually every party has had occasion to exercise a veto over some candidate's successful nomination when embarrassing information about the candidate later became known.

Various laws on campaign donations to, and expenditures by, officially registered parties and candidates, as well as tax credits to contributors, have existed since the 1960s, in order to counteract the inequities of party finance and to introduce greater probity in party politics generally. So-called "third party" advertising on behalf of parties and local candidates by interest groups and private individuals remains a contentious matter in Canadian elections. Third-party activity is prohibited in Quebec provincial elections, while several legislative attempts to restrict third-party advertising in federal elections have been successfully challenged in the courts as violations of the Canadian Charter of Rights and Freedoms. During the federal election of 2000, however, "pending complete constitutional review" the Supreme Court of Canada lifted an injunction granted in Alberta against recent amendments to the *Canada Elections Act* that limited third-party advertising (*A.G. of Canada v. Stephen Joseph Harper*). The amendments had been made in the expectation that the Supreme Court of Canada would ultimately uphold the law as a reasonable limitation of rights, as allowed under section 1 of the Charter. Otherwise, the lack of any control on third parties makes the stringent controls on political parties and candidates incongruous, and perhaps irrelevant. See **Electoral law (controls; subsidies); Leaders' debates**.

Canada Act, 1982 **(U.K.)**. An Act of the British Parliament "to Give Effect to a Request by the Senate and House of Commons of Canada," effectively patriating the Canadian constitution.

Until 1982, amendments to Canada's basic constitutional document, Britain's *British North America Act*, required a joint address from the Canadian Parliament to the British Parliament. The joint address by the Canadian Parliament on patriating the constitution was supported by all provinces except Quebec, the only predominantly francophone jurisdiction in Canada. The opposition of all parties in Quebec—federalist and sovereignist—led to years of ultimately abortive constitutional negotiations, against the backdrop of Quebec's possible secession from Confederation.

Britain's *Canada Act* enacted Canada's *Constitution Act, 1982* and declared that no British Act would subsequently extend to Canada as part of its law. The *Constitution Act* included several amending procedures that involved only Canada's federal and provincial legislatures (Part V), as well as the entrenched Canadian Charter of Rights and Freedoms (Part I) that included provisions respecting minority-language education rights and federal official languages policy, statements respecting Aboriginal rights (Part II) and equalization and regional disparities (Part III). The *British North America Act* was renamed the *Constitution Act*, 1867 and also amended to include a section on federal and provincial powers respecting non-renewable natural resources, forestry and electrical energy (s.92A). See **Canadian Charter of Rights and Freedoms (1982); Charlottetown Accord (1992); Constitution Act, 1867 and subsequently amended; Meech Lake Accord (1987); Natural resources; Patriation of the constitution; Sovereignty association**.

Canada Assistance Plan (CAP, 1966–1995). A comprehensive, shared-cost program between the federal and provincial governments to provide social assistance. In 1996, CAP was replaced by the Canada Health and Social Transfer, a block grant that also comprised federal assistance for such provincial services as post-secondary education and health insurance. Under CHST, federal funding was actually reduced and the only condition with respect to social assistance programs was that there be no minimum residence requirement. See **Canada Health and Social Transfer (CHST)**.

Canada Clause (Preamble, Charlottetown Accord, 1992). A preamble to the *Constitution Act* proposed in the failed Charlottetown Accord of 1992 which "would [have] guide[d] the courts in their future interpretation of the constitution, including the Charter of Rights and Freedoms."

The clause defined Canada's "fundamental characteristics," including parliamentary democracy, federalism and the rule of law; Aboriginal governments as "one of three orders of government in Canada"; a definition of Quebec as a distinct society; the "vitality and development" of French- and English-language minority communities; racial and ethnic diversity and equality; individual and collective rights; gender equality; and equality of the provinces. The clause would also have affirmed the role of the government and legislature of Quebec "to preserve and promote the distinct society of Quebec," while declaring that nothing in the clause derogated from the powers of Parliament, the provincial legislatures, or Aboriginal governments.

Critics of the Canada Clause in the Charlottetown Accord included opponents of the distinct society clause as it related to the role of the Quebec legislature and government. Some opponents also argued that the Canada Clause created a hierarchy of rights under the Charter and excluded those mentioned in the Charter but not specifically mentioned in the Canada Clause, such as the physically disabled. Some objected to the wording by which "Canadians and their governments" were committed to some characteristics while only "Canadians" were committed to others.

Canada Council. A federal agency created in 1957 to fund the arts in Canada— the projects of Canadian artists and the activities of Canadian art organizations, including orchestras, dance, theatre and opera companies, art galleries, publishers, and film and video organizations.

The creation of the Council was a major recommendation of the (Vincent Massey) Royal Commission on National Development of the Arts, Letters and Sciences. The Council administers funding programs, but the grants are awarded competitively on the advice of advisory committees of artists and arts professionals. From time to time, funded activities result in public controversies, but the Canada Council remains one of several well-established federal institutions which fosters a distinctive cultural identity among Canadians. Most provinces have similar arts councils.

Canada Gazette. A federal government publication which contains all proclamations issued under the authority of the governor-in-council and government notices such as orders-in-council, regulations, advertisements, or parliamentary matters requiring publication.

The *Gazette* comprises three parts. Part One, published weekly, contains information required by federal statute or regulation to be published, other than material designated for Parts Two or Three. This includes proposed government regulations, certain orders-in-council, and notices of hearings and decisions. Part Two, published biweekly, includes regulations and classes of statutory instruments and documents of government departments and agencies as defined by the *Statutory Instruments Act.* Part Three contains acts of Parliament and their proclamations, published as soon as possible after Royal Assent. Similar publications exist in the provinces.

Canada Health and Social Transfer (CHST). A block payment since 1996 in the form of cash transfers and the transfer of tax points by the federal government to the provinces to fund post-secondary education, health insurance and social assistance programs in the provinces.

The CHST replaced Established Programs Funding for education and health insurance, and the Canada Assistance Plan (CAP) for social assistance. It was instituted by the Liberal government in the face of continued opposition of some provincial governments over federal "entanglement" in areas of provincial jurisdiction; it was also part of the federal government's "off-loading" of costs of public services to the provincial governments in order to eliminate its budget deficits and reduce the federal debt. The federal government also preferred direct personal transfer programs over indirect transfers through the provinces, expecting that the more publicly visible direct transfers to individuals would confer greater electoral benefits.

The inclusion of tax points in the program had consequences especially for those provinces whose economies did not include a strong tax base. Moreover, some critics were concerned that some provinces might not spend even the smaller dollar amount on social services. Although it was funding provincial social services to a lesser degree, the federal government insisted that it would still enforce the conditions of the *Canada Health Act*. It did, however, eliminate all conditions under the CAP for social assistance except for prohibiting a minimum provincial residency requirement. See **Block payments**; **Federal-provincial tax-sharing agreements (fiscal federalism)**; **Medicare**.

Canada Labour Code. A federal law that regulates employment practices and standards in the federal public service and private-sector industries under federal jurisdiction, such as the transportation industry.

Because labour legislation involves conditions applied to the rights of employers and employees, and therefore to local works and property and civil rights, the courts have affirmed that otherwise labour legislation comes under the authority of provincial legislatures (*Constitution Act, 1867*, s.92:10, :13). The Canada Labour Code also applies to works which Parliament declares to be for "the general Advantage of Canada or…Two or more of the Provinces" (s.92:10[c]).

The Code is administered, in different sections, by the Public Service Staff Relations Board and by the Canada Labour Relations Board. See **Labour Conventions Reference (1937)**.

Canada Mortgage and Housing Corporation (CMHC). A federal crown corporation established in 1946 to administer the *National Housing Act* (NHA): that is, to facilitate the flow of capital into mortgages at favourable interest rates for new and existing owner-occupied, rented, or co-operative-owned housing. However, the CMHC, and its regional offices in particular, are involved through federal-provincial agreements in a variety of endeavours which have had a dramatic impact on urban Canada.

The CMHC is essentially a financial institution servicing new communities by aiding public land assembly and the expansion of municipal sewerage and water supply systems, assisting in the construction and financing of new housing, and in improving established urban neighbourhoods through planning and residential rehabilitation. The Corporation is also involved in the construction and administration of housing in areas of special need, for example, in the construction of housing for senior citizens and housing projects for Natives. CMHC also supports and conducts research and sets construction standards for the private sector. Its policy and research section advises CMHC on its policies, analyzes the housing market, and evaluates relations among the three levels of government (federal, provincial and municipal) on housing and related policies.

The scope of activity by this federal corporation has extended considerably beyond its original role of facilitating the flow of mortgage money in the economy. CMHC policy was largely responsible for the sprawling, low-density suburbs of single-family dwellings and the "bulldozer" urban renewal projects in city centres during the 1950s and 1960s, which replaced low-income housing and old central retail business districts with high-income housing, national chain stores, and new public buildings such as city halls, art galleries, and concert halls. Since the 1970s, CMHC policy has focussed on inner-city renovation and rehabilitation.

CMHC has been a target of provincial criticism because of federal involvement in an area of provincial jurisdiction (*Constitution Act, 1867*, s.92:8: Municipal Institutions in the Province), although the legal instrument is usually a federal-provincial umbrella agreement allowing for federal policy and cost-sharing roles. The federal government's involvement in the growth and development of many of Canada's cities is also facilitated by its land ownership and constitutional responsibilities in matters such as harbours, railway and air transportation.

Canada (Quebec) Pension Plan (CPP, QPP, 1966). A compulsory, earnings-related employee and employer contributory pension plan which covers most of the Canadian work force.

The federal government introduced the income insurance plan at a time when the provinces were increasingly critical of the centralization of fiscal and social policy. Considerable opposition from Quebec resulted in the separate, but basically similar, Quebec Pension Plan. Pension credits accumulated under the CPP or the QPP may be transferred to the other. Concerned that the CPP would provide insufficient income for prospective pensioners, the federal government introduced the Registered Retirement Savings Program that allows Canadians to defer taxation on income invested for retirement years.

Canada-United States Free Trade Agreement (1989). A comprehensive agreement between Canada and the United States to facilitate trade between the two countries, notably by reducing protectionist barriers and creating a dispute settlement mechanism.

The Agreement (FTA), negotiated by the Conservative government in 1988, was largely unnoticed by the US public, but subjected to considerable debate in Canada, including opposition by both the Liberal and New Democratic parties in the House of Commons and obstruction by Liberals in the Senate. Parliament was dissolved and the Agreement featured prominently in the subsequent general election in which the Conservative government was re-elected and passage of the FTA thus ensured.

Organized forces for and against the FTA agreed only that it was of profound importance to the future of Canada. Those supporting the FTA argued that, in an era of increased economic globalization and the formation of large trade blocs, Canada's future would be assured in a close relationship with the United States in competition with the blocs based on the European Union and Japanese economies. Supporters argued that the dispute settlement mechanism could be used to defend Canadian interests against US protectionism, while opponents held that the US was not really committed to the principles of the FTA when its interests were adversely affected. Opponents argued that further integration of the small Canadian economy with the large US economy would result in a rationalization that would eliminate jobs, companies and even whole industries—including cultural industries—and threaten distinctive government social policies such as medicare and regional development programs. Nonetheless, the Conservative government held firm and in the 1990s joined with the US and Mexico in talks to achieve a North American Free Trade Agreement, if only to protect Canadian interests under the Canada-US FTA. See **Dispute settlement mechanism (Canada-US Free Trade Agreement, 1989); North American Free Trade Agreement (NAFTA) (1992); Reciprocity.**

Canadian Alliance party. The populist, social conservative successor to the western-based Reform party, established in 2000.

Although he lost the Alliance leadership contest to Stockwell Day, a former Conservative cabinet minister in Alberta, Reform leader Preston Manning engineered the transformation of Reform to the Alliance, in his attempt to "unite the right." Although Reform formed the official opposition in the House of Commons following the election of 1997, it failed in its basic objective to create a solid base of electoral support in Ontario and Atlantic Canada. Thus began Manning's ultimately unsuccessful attempt to create a merger with the Conservative party whose western electoral base Reform had captured in 1993 and retained in 1997, but which remained an electoral force in the East. When the Conservative leadership rejected Manning's overtures, Alliance strategy shifted to undercutting the Conservative leadership by winning over the party's members and supporters. In the general election of 2000, the Alliance surpassed Reform's popular vote in 1997 by only 6 per cent, winning 26 per cent of the vote, but maintained its status as official opposition with an increase of six seats and failed again to achieve a significant electoral breakthrough east of Manitoba, while the Conservatives lost eight seats, winning thirteen and managing barely to retain official party status in the House of Commons.

Traditionally, the Conservative party has been a voice of the moderate political right, including a view that public policy, including social policy, entails a role for the federal government in the interest of social cohesion and order. Though desiring to displace the Conservatives as the voice of the political right, the Alliance program remained radically right wing and "decentralist": a single rate of taxation; the rate of government growth linked to inflation and population growth; stricter prosecution, sentencing and parole provisions in the criminal justice system; potential two-tier, private and public, provincial health care systems with no national standards for federal funding; elimination of funding for multiculturalism and various other federal programs including those for regional development; federal government withdrawal from a variety of policy fields, while retaining responsibility essentially for foreign affairs and an enhanced defence establishment, monetary policy, banking, trade and criminal law. Alliance also retained the traditional populist element of western-Canadian politics: party discipline would be relaxed as members of parliament would be obliged to vote according to a consensus of their constituents and citizens would be able to launch initiatives, including referendums whose outcomes would be binding on the federal government. Thus, short of an Alliance government amending the Criminal Code itself, social conservatives might use public initiatives, for example, to reinstate capital punishment and impose legal restrictions on access to therapeutic abortions.

In the election of 2000, the Alliance won only two seats east of Manitoba, in rural areas of the key province of Ontario, while the governing Liberal party increased its majority over 1997. The Conservative party, the moderate social democratic New Democratic party and the nationalist Bloc Québécois all lost seats to the Liberals. Among explanations for the election results was the limited appeal of the social conservatism of the Canadian Alliance, as well as the inexperience of its leader and his aides in federal politics. See **Conservative (Progressive Conservative) party**; **Populism**; **Reform party**.

Canadian Broadcasting Corporation (Radio-Canada; CBC). A federal crown corporation created in 1936 that provides country-wide radio and television services in English and in French, in some Native languages in selective parts of the country, notably in its Northern Service, and in various languages in its International Service.

The CBC's parliamentary mandate requires a "balanced service" of information, entertainment and enlightenment to encourage the expression of a Canadian identity and to enhance national unity. Parliament funds the CBC through annual appropriations and the CBC generates advertising revenue in its television services and commercial revenue through sales of program-related products. The CBC's centre for English services is in Toronto, for French services in Montreal, and for administration in Ottawa. The governor-in-council, that is, the federal government, appoints the CBC president and the board of directors, and the Corporation is subject to the regulatory powers of the Canadian Radio-television and Telecommunications Commission (CRTC).

Because of its public funding and its "nationalizing" political mandate, the CBC is subject to considerable parliamentary, governmental and public scrutiny and criticism. Apart from occasional charges of broadcasting immoral dramatic performances and biased public affairs programs, the Corporation has been subject to complaints that its French-language news and public affairs programming was consistently framed within a Quebec *nationaliste* perspective. There has also been dissatisfaction in the western and eastern areas of the country with central Canadian-based news and information programming, the lack of region-based programming, and cutbacks in local news and public affairs programming. The CBC's English- and French-language all-news television services, "Newsworld" and "Réseau de l'Information" (RDI), available only on cable, cover many political events "live" and emphasize programming from different regions of the country. See **Canadian Radio-television and Telecommunications Commission (CRTC)**; **Mass media of Communication**; **Press Gallery**.

Canadian Charter of Rights and Freedoms (1982). Part I of the *Constitution Act, 1982*, that guarantees Canadians protection of individual and certain collective rights against all levels and institutions of government, subject to interpretation by the courts, the invoking of a legislative override clause, or amendment through the general procedure for amending the constitution.

The Charter guarantees freedoms already enjoyed by Canadians and formulates new rights. For example, the Charter contains the traditional liberal freedoms of conscience and religion, thought and speech, and common law protection with respect to search and seizure, arrest or detention and fair judicial procedures. Section 24.2 on enforcement permits the admissibility of illegally obtained evidence if, in a judge's consideration, not doing so "would bring the administration of justice into disrepute." The Charter also includes established democratic rights respecting the franchise and the requirement for periodic elections and regular sittings of legislatures. The Charter reaffirms English and French as the official languages of Canada (the Parliament, government and the courts) and confirms New Brunswick as an officially bilingual province.

The Charter broke new constitutional ground respecting mobility rights, equality rights, minority-language educational rights, gender equality and multiculturalism. The sections on mobility (s.6) and equality (s.15) rights declare individual rights subject to affirmative action programs to combat social and economic disadvantage as well as disadvantage arising from racial, national, or ethnic origin, colour, religion, sex, age, or mental or physical disability. The Charter guarantees public education rights to English or French linguistic provincial minorities where numbers warrant (s.23). Section 28 guarantees the Charter's rights and freedoms "equally to male and female persons" and section 27 requires the courts to interpret the Charter "in a manner consistent with the preservation and enhancement of the multicultural heritage of Canadians." Section 24.1 grants the courts power to enforce remedies to the denial or infringement of Charter rights and freedoms "as the court considers appropriate and just in the circumstances."

The Charter may be amended only by a resolution of the House of Commons and Senate, and of two-thirds of the legislatures in provinces having together at least 50 per cent of the population of all the provinces. Otherwise the guarantees in the Charter may be limited in two ways: a Charter violation may be "saved" by section 1, which subjects the guarantees "only to such reasonable limits prescribed by law as can be demonstrably justified in a free and democratic society." Also, section 33, the *non obstante* or notwithstanding clause, permits legislatures to enact laws which violate sections dealing with fundamental freedoms (s.2), legal rights (ss.7-14), and equality rights (s.15), for five-year renewable periods.

In 1986, the Supreme Court established a test by which legislation or administrative regulation or procedure could violate guaranteed rights and freedoms, and thus be "saved" by section 1. Known as the Oakes Test, the successful application of section 1 requires demonstration that the objective of the law or rule is "pressing and substantial," that the means involve a minimal violation or restriction and are "rationally connected to the objective," and that the benefit will outweigh the cost of the limitation. Thus lawyers for a government will frequently argue that a disputed matter before a court is not a violation of the Charter, but, if deemed to be a violation, is nonetheless saved by section 1, demonstrating its consistency with the Oakes test.

The inclusion of the controversial section 33, known as the "legislative override," was a concession to supporters of the principle of parliamentary supremacy within the context of federal-provincial division of powers. The section has been little used, and when used has generated controversy. From 1982 to 1984, the

Parti Québécois government invoked section 33 in each new bill as standard prac-tice, reflecting its opposition to the constitutional changes in 1982. In 1984, the successor Liberal government in Quebec discontinued the practice, but invoked section 33 in five instances, the fifth being very controversial. In 1984, the Court ruled that Quebec's language law, the Charter of the French Language (Bill 101, 1977), violated the federal Charter with respect to minority-language education (s.23—outside the scope of s.33, the notwithstanding clause) (A.-G. *Quebec v. Quebec Association of Protestant School Boards*). Four years later, the Court dealt another blow to the language law, declaring its prohibition of commercial signs in languages other than French a violation of freedom of expression (s.2) (*Quebec v. Ford*). The Liberal government countered by amending the law (Bill 178), invok-ing section 33 of the Charter, to allow revised restrictions on commercial signage to operate notwithstanding the Charter. However, the Court having ruled the objective of preserving a "French visage" in Quebec was acceptable, the Liberal government further amended the law in 1993, without reference to section 33, to allow for bilingual outdoor signs as long as French was predominant. The only other use of section 33 occurred in Saskatchewan in 1986, when, fearing a success-ful challenge under section 1 ("freedom of association"), the Conservative government employed the override in legislation compelling striking public employees to return to work. The Conservative government in Alberta considered invoking section 33 with respect to its human rights legislation, to counter a Supreme Court decision (*Vriend v. Alberta, 1998*) that effectively read "sexual orientation" into the provincial legislation as a prohibited basis of discrimination. However, it decided not to circumvent the court's ruling. Successive federal Liberal and Conservative governments have indicated their unwillingness to use section 33. Thus, it increasingly appears that section 33 may become, like some other provisions of the constitution, a power not exercised.

Since 1982, courts at all levels have dealt with literally thousands of Charter cases. In their broad exercise of judicial review, the courts have been concerned not to usurp the legislative function of Parliament and the provincial legislatures, especially regarding remedial decree litigation under section 24.1. Inevitably, however, the courts have become perceived at least as quasi-political institutions, partly because of their decisions, but also because some governments have preferred to have controversial issues resolved by judicial decision rather than their legislative action. Other consequences of the entrenchment of Charter rights include more public attention to the judicial appointment process and reviews by academics and journalists of decisions by individual justices, especially those on the Supreme Court; the proliferation of so-called Charter interests and groups— frequently referred to as the Court Party—whose political strategies focus on achieving favourable court decisions compelling governments to alter legislation or regulations; concomitantly less attention to the legislative process and politicians as policy makers (on the one hand less incentive to achieve political accommodation but on the other a heightened regard for potentially adverse judicial rulings).

A number of Supreme Court judgments have defined a broad non-inter-pretive or purposive approach to judicial review under the Charter. For example, on judicial review, the Court ruled that, contrary to the intent of the framers of the Charter, "the principles of fundamental justice" (s.7) would involve where necessary the review of legislation on substantive grounds (*Motor Vehicle Reference*, 1985); that both the purpose and effect of legislation would be examined to provide Canadians with the "full benefit" of the Charter's protection (*R. v. Big M Drug Mart Ltd.*, 1985); that protection would extend to organizations such as business as well as to individuals (*Hunter v. Southam, Inc.*, 1984), involving section 8, "unreasonable search and seizure" in anti-combines investigations); that the concept of "fundamental justice" and "security of the person" (s.7) would involve Court-defined standards of procedures rather than administrative procedures established under enabling legislation. Specifically, administrative convenience (efficiency and cost) was rejected as reason sufficient to limit a Charter right (*Re Singh and Minister of Employment and Immigration*, 1985). The Court also established that executive decisions (cabinet orders-in-council) in matters such as foreign affairs and defence would be subject to review under the Charter (*Operation Dismantle v. The Queen*, 1985).

Some early Charter decisions had considerable impact on public policy debate. Thus it could be said that the Court has performed an indirect legislative function. In the past, the Court would decide cases on the basis of "legal facts." However, the Court as a whole must now entertain "social facts" in order to establish whether there has been a violation of the Charter and then to decide on the application of section 1. Some justices appear to be more open to consideration of substantive issues of rights under the Charter (a non-interpretive approach to judicial review), while others, less willing to engage in "judicial policy making," focus on legal analysis and precedent (an interpretive approach to judicial review). For example, in *Operation Dismantle*, the Court decided that it would hear the case against the federal government's agreement to allow the United States to test unarmed cruise missiles over Canadian territory as a contributory factor to the deprivation of "the right to life, liberty and security of the person." In his ruling for the majority against the claim that missile-testing would enhance the likelihood of nuclear war with Canada as a target, the chief justice said that with the best evidence available it could only speculate about the likely outcome of the cabinet's agreement. In *Morgentaler, Smoling and Scott v. The Queen* (1988), the Court was presented with "social facts" that were relevant in determining that conditions set out in the Criminal Code to procure abortions were a violation of women's security of the person (ss.7, 28). In this case, data from Statistics Canada and a government-sponsored report which found access to abortion across the country to be uneven and delayed, and which associated the current law with increased health risks to women, constituted relevant evidence and were used variously by the justices to come to their respective decisions. Although all but one justice sustained Parliament's right to legislate in the matter of abortion, Parliament was subsequently unable to agree upon substitute legislation (given a tie vote in the Senate). Following *Morgentaler*, the Court also ruled on "right to life and security of the person" against foetal rights (*Borowski*), paternal rights in the matter of abortion (*Daigle*), and against voluntary assisted suicide (*Rodriguez*).

The Supreme Court has used section 24.1 on enforcement to "read missing words" into legislation as an alternative to nullifying unconstitutional legislation and thus denying others the benefit of the legislation (*Schacter v. Canada [Employment and Immigration Commission]*, 1992). In this case involving differential parental leave benefits conferred under the federal *Unemployment Insurance*

Act, the Supreme Court was dealing with an appeal of the Federal Court's finding that the legislation constituted a denial of rights and of its extension of the benefit by reading the exempt group into the legislation (*Schacter v. Canada*, 1990). In 1995, the Supreme Court read "sexual orientation" into section 15 on equality rights as a prohibited basis for discrimination, although it "saved" the disputed federal legislation on old-age spousal benefits for a same-sex couple under section 1. However, in 1998, section 1 could not save Alberta's *Individual Rights Protection Act* as noted above in the *Vriend* case. In 1999, the Court found Ontario's *Family Law Act* similarly wanting in discriminating on the basis of sexual orientation (*M. v. H.*). Remedial decree litigation has also been pursued with respect to minority-language education rights. For example, in *Mahé v. Alberta* (1990), the Supreme Court compelled the Alberta government to create a minority-language school board in Edmonton to allow francophones administrative control over buildings and instruction.

Parliament has amended legislation to deal with Charter decisions of the Court. Sexual assault cases, for example, have come before the Court involving presumption of innocence and the admission of evidence of a complainant's previous sexual activity (*R. v. Daviault*, 1994; *R. v. Seaboyer*, 1991; *R. v. Ewanchuk*, 1999). Parliament has amended the Criminal Code to overcome some aspects of Supreme Court rulings, notably with respect to the admission of medical records in sexual assault cases, and the Court has partially reversed itself with respect to the admission of confidential counselling records of complainants in such cases. Parliament has also amended legislation to counter the Court's decisions in other matters such as "unreasonable search and seizure" (s.8): to make it easier to obtain a warrant to enter a building in order to pursue a suspect in flight (*Feeney*, 1997) and to obtain samples for DNA analysis (*Stillman*, 1997).

Unintended consequences can result from the Court's decisions, as in its attempt in 1990 to define "a reasonable time" for a person charged with an offence to be tried (s.11). Having accepted evidence respecting delays in various courts in several provinces, the Court ruled that delays of six to eight months "might be...the outside limit of what is reasonable" (*R. v. Askov*, 1990). Subsequently, hundreds of charges, including serious criminal charges, were dismissed, withdrawn, or stayed in Ontario courts. One justice attempted an unprecedented off-the-bench clarification of its policy making in *Askov*, and the Court reversed itself later, leaving "reasonable time" to be determined by provincial Courts of Appeal and placing the onus on an accused to demonstrate harm from the delay (*R. v. Morin*, 1992).

The Charter has been cited in cases involving common law freedoms impugned by statute, and to clarify precedence when elements of common law are in conflict. Legislation restricting commercial activities on particular religious grounds has been declared unconstitutional (*R. v. Big M Drug Mart Ltd.*, 1985), but valid if based on non-religious grounds (*R. v. Edwards Books and Art Ltd.*, 1986). Film censorship is acceptable under section 1 when the criteria are "prescribed by law" (*Re Ontario Film and Video Appreciation Society and Ontario Board of Censors*, 1984). The Criminal Code's prohibition on the dissemination of hate literature, and provisions respecting obscenity laws, have also been upheld as "reasonable limits" on the freedom of expression (*R. v. Keegstra*, 1990; *R. v. Butler*, 1992). However, the dissemination of injurious views that are deliberate falsehoods does not violate the Charter (*R. v. Zundel,* 1992). Quebec legislation restricting television advertising directed at children was ruled constitutional (*Irwin Toy Ltd. v. Quebec [Attorney-General],* 1989). Federal legislation prohibiting public servants from working for a political party or candidate was deemed unconstitutional (*Osborne v. Canada [Treasury Board],* 1991). Freedom of association was interpreted as an individual rather than a collective right. Thus, the right of organized labour to strike is defined by ordinary legislation rather than being a right guaranteed under section 2 of the Charter (*Re Public Service Employees Relations Act [Alberta],* 1987). However, the Supreme Court upheld the Rand Formula whereby unions collect dues from both members and non-members and represent all workers in a bargaining unit, and sanctioned unions' use of non-members' dues for political purposes not related to negotiating and implementing a contract (*Lavigne v. Ontario Public Service Employees Union,* 1991). In the absence of a statute respecting secondary picketing in British Columbia, a union unsuccessfully appealed its conviction based on common law as a violation of Charter rights (s.2). The Supreme Court rested its decision not on section 1 ("reasonable limit"), but on the absence of any statute impugning Charter rights, thus making the case one of private litigation to which the Charter did not apply (*Retail, Wholesale & Department Store Union, Local 580 et al. v. Dolphin Delivery Ltd.,* 1986).

Courts in Canada have generally allowed the common law freedom of an accused person to presumed innocence in a fair trial (s.11) to take precedence over freedom of the press (s.2). Ruling in 1994 on an appeal of a publication ban imposed on a television program that dealt with matters that were subject to criminal proceedings (*The Boys of St. Vincent*), the Supreme Court held that Charter rights are in principle equal. Publication bans can be imposed only "to prevent a real and substantial risk to the fairness of the trial [and when] the salutary effects of the publication ban outweigh the deleterious effects to the free expression of those affected by the ban."

There have been important lower-court decisions involving the Charter. In 1984 and 1993, courts in Alberta held that provisions of the *Canada Elections Act* that restricted so-called "third-party" advertising in federal elections were a violation of fundamental freedoms (s.2) that could not be reasonably "justified in a free and democratic society" (s.1) (*National Citizens' Coalition Inc. v. A.-G. Canada,* 1984). Remedial decrees were issued by courts in several provinces respecting minority-language educational rights of francophones. The Ontario government referred its *Education Act* to the provincial Supreme Court, certain that it would be declared unconstitutional, thus obtaining a judicial imprimatur for extending French-language education services in the province (*Reference Re Education Act of Ontario and Minority Language Education Rights,* 1984). The Ontario courts declared the powers of the province's Board of Censors violated the Charter, and the Ontario Supreme Court read "sexual orientation" into the Canadian Human Rights Code as a prohibited basis for discrimination. Although this applied to federally regulated workplaces only in Ontario, the Canadian Human Rights Commission said it would apply the ruling in federal areas of jurisdiction throughout Canada.

Academics and journalists have also focussed attention on the consequences for the larger political system of the sharing of legislative and executive/administrative policy making with the courts. Some have noted the enhanced positioning on the public agenda of those interests designated in the Charter, especially in section 15, and the more prominent role for the leadership of social movement organizations promoting those interests. Some commentators have suggested that the Charter has contributed to the rise and prominence of single-issue interest groups and social movements that are less deferential to political elites and ill-disposed to the traditional processes of political bargaining, accommodation, and to a diminution of public identification with political parties and leaders, the traditional brokers of interests and conflict managers in the Canadian political system.

Canadian Human Rights Commission (Act; Chief Commissioner). A federal commission established in 1977 under the *Human Rights Act* and headed by the chief commissioner to investigate and report on cases of alleged discrimination on the grounds of race, national or ethnic origin, colour, age, religion, sex, marital status, family status, physical disability, or pardoned criminal offence in areas under federal jurisdiction. The Commission also enforces the principle of equal pay for work of equal value by men and women. See **Canadian Charter of Rights and Freedoms (1982)**.

Canadian International Development Agency (CIDA). The federal agency responsible for administering Canada's bilateral and multilateral official development assistance (foreign aid) program, including assistance to voluntary nongovernmental organizations and incentives to the private sector for investment in developing countries. The CIDA program encourages environmentally sound, sustainable economic and social development, health and nutrition, basic education, human rights, child protection and prevention of HIV/AIDS.

Originally held by a branch of the Department of Trade and Commerce, it was transferred to External Affairs (now styled Foreign Affairs and International Trade) in 1960. Originally the External Aid Office, it was renamed CIDA in 1968. Funds devoted to Canada's international aid program, as a percentage of gross domestic product, is among the lowest among industrialized countries.

Canadian Judicial Council. A body established by Parliament in 1971 which is chaired by the chief justice of the Supreme Court of Canada and includes all chief justices, associate chief justices, chief judges and associate chief judges of courts appointed by the federal government.

The Council is a formal site for the exchange of views on the education of judges and on court administration in general. However, the most sensitive aspect of the Council's mandate is the investigation of complaints about judges' behaviour. Thus the Council reinforces the important constitutional principle of the independence of the judiciary, as previously such complaints were investigated by the minister of justice. The senior administrator of the Council is the commissioner for federal judicial affairs who also administers the process of judicial appointment and salaries on behalf of the Department of Justice.

Canadian Parliamentary Guide. A publication of the federal government that includes "thumbnail" biographies of current federal member of parliament and senators, names of officials of Parliament, the membership of the cabinet, and the electoral history of federal constituencies. The Guide also contains selective provincial electoral data.

Canadian Press/Broadcast News. A private-sector, French- and English-language news-gathering and disseminating co-operative whose members include newspapers and radio and television stations across Canada. Each member submits stories from their location to CP/BN, which rewrites, translates and distributes them to other members. CP/BN also has employee-reporters who file stories for distribution to all members. As local mass media outlets have been subsumed within a few corporate chains, especially since the 1960s, they also have access to their chain's news services. At the same time, the large media corporations can influence the operation of CP/BN. CP also has an exchange program with other agencies outside Canada, notably its counterpart in the United States, the Associated Press (AP).

Canadian Radio-television and Telecommunications Commission (CRTC). A federal agency that regulates broadcasting in Canada and certain telecommunication carriers, for example, on ownership, content, competition and rates.

The Canadian Broadcasting Corporation, itself a major part of the national broadcasting system, regulated broadcasting until the Board of Broadcast Governors assumed the role in 1958 and was in turn succeeded by the CRTC. Authorized to regulate all aspects of the Canadian broadcasting system, the Commission sets standards of broadcast behaviour and considers requests for new licences or renewal of licences in the context of the Commission's policies. The Commission's powers extend, with opposition from some provinces, to the cable systems which intercept radio and television signals over the air and deliver them by landline (sometimes involving microwave relay transmitters) to subscribers. The cable industry also operates the Cable Public Affairs Channel (CPAC) that broadcasts debates of the House of Commons, proceedings of some parliamentary committees and events that have significance for public policy. The CRTC also hears requests for new cable operators' licences or renewal of licences, and sets performance standards for these companies. For broadcasters, the most publicly contentious regulations of the Commission pertain to Canadian ownership and corporate mergers, and to requirements for Canadian content in programming. For cable companies, in addition to policy on ownership, contentious regulations involve priority ranking of broadcast stations and community programming on allocated channels. In recent years, attention has focussed on the issue of direct satellite-to-home transmission, the development of Canadian speciality channels, pay-per-view channels and services in the far North.

Since its inception, the CRTC has been an important forum for public debate on the "nationalizing" role of Canadian broadcasting in all aspects of the CRTC's supervision of the broadcasting system. It widely advertises its hearings on matters of significance to encourage public participation. It requires regulated companies similarly to advertise their particular applications to the CRTC, for example, for licence renewal, rate increases, or change in service. The same public process used to regulate broadcasting is replicated in its supervision of the federally regulated telecommunications industry. The federal government's ability to regulate telecommunications effectively is challenged by increased convergence of print and broadcasting media, cable and telecommunication companies in larger and fewer corporate conglomerates. See **Delegated power; Regulatory agencies (regulations)**.

Canadian Security Intelligence Service (CSIS). A federal intelligence-gathering service dealing with espionage and terrorism. CSIS is responsible for security checks on immigrants and refugees and on applications for certain federal civil service positions and security-related private-sector employment.

In collecting information, CSIS may enter private premises covertly, eavesdrop electronically, intercept and read mail, and gain access to otherwise confidential data on persons and groups held by federal agencies and, through agreements, to information held by provincial agencies (for example, on employment, income tax, health, marital and other personal information). Approval for the more intrusive activities must be obtained from the solicitor general and a warrant (valid for one year and renewable) from a judge of the Federal Court. The reasons for a warrant, the name of the judge granting it, and the length of its existence remain confidential. Unlike rules affecting the Royal Canadian Mounted Police, persons under surveillance or investigation by CSIS need not be informed after the fact.

CSIS was formed in 1984 following the exposure of a variety of illegal and politically embarrassing activities involving the RCMP Security Services in the 1970s. Long-standing recommendations for a civilian "spy agency" to replace the paramilitary police force were revived in the report of a royal commission investigating RCMP activities. In order to reinforce "civilian control," a Security Intelligence Review Committee (SIRC), appointed by the federal government, was also created to review CSIS activities. SIRC hears appeals on denial of security clearances, investigates alleged abuses, makes recommendations and issues an annual report. The House of Commons has only limited access to information about CSIS, notably through the annual appearance of SIRC before the standing committee on justice.

As an intelligence service, CSIS reports to the federal government: the solicitor general (the minister responsible), the Privy Council Office, that is, the cabinet secretariat that has a section for security and intelligence matters, a cabinet committee on security and intelligence, and government departments that require intelligence information, such as Foreign Affairs and Immigration.

CSIS has been seriously criticized on several broad policy- and operations-related counts as well as specific operational matters. Examples of the former include its excessive reliance in its early years on RCMP personnel, failure to recruit and operate in French, failure to distinguish between subversive activity and political dissent, adoption of United States' perspectives on foreign policy even when they conflicted with Canadian foreign policy, and failure to recruit personnel from minority ethnic groups. On operations, it has been charged that, while focusing on trade unions, peace activists, international church organizations and largely discredited sectarian dissident groups, CSIS failed to apprehend genuine terrorist threats in Canada, such as those, for example, involved in Turkish, South Asian and Chinese domestic politics. Although SIRC reported that CSIS had warned the government about the danger of violence among Natives before the armed insurrection among Mohawk activists at Oka, Quebec, in 1990, CSIS has otherwise been reproached for insensitivity in dealing with "Native extremism," for example, Innu opposition to low-level NATO jet training flights over Labrador. It has also been criticized for inattention to international industrial espionage and for continuing disputes with the RCMP that allegedly compromise investigations. In 1994, it appeared that CSIS had mismanaged the use of human sources, that is, informants, regarding its surveillance of neo-Nazi, white-supremacist organizations and individuals. Finally, CSIS has received poor marks regarding government security clearance and for the failure of individual officers to protect highly sensitive files in their possession.

Like other national security organizations, the failures of CSIS are broadcast more widely than its successes. Nonetheless, there have been repeated calls for more effective scrutiny of CSIS by a parliamentary committee whose oversight might extend to the RCMP, the Department of Defence and the Communications Security Establishment. See **Communications Security Establishment (CSE); Royal Canadian Mounted Police (RCMP); Security Intelligence Review Committee**.

Candidate. Usually a reference to someone who may be, or has been, formally nominated for elective office. The term is also used to refer to someone who may be under consideration for an appointive position. With reference to elective public office, see **Campaign (election)**.

Canvass. Systematic personal contact of electors by party workers during an election campaign.

Using telephone or door-to-door contacts, the purpose of the canvass is to identify personal or household voting preferences, to encourage favourable respondents to participate in the campaign and to provide party workers on election day with lists of likely party supporters to ensure that they have voted. The canvassing of electors has been especially important for parties with large numbers of committed activists and insufficient money to reach voters through indirect, mass marketing techniques. Changes in election financing and increased use of sophisticated marketing techniques by all parties, however, have made the traditional canvass by party workers a less prominent feature of the campaign. But the canvass may still be an important technique in highly competitive constituencies or in constituencies where important local effects or conditions are operating irrespective of the national party campaigns.

Capital crime and punishment. Planned and deliberate murder, or murder in the course of violent acts, punishable by life imprisonment with eligibility for consideration for parole. Parliament eliminated the death penalty for murder in 1976. In recent years, supporters of capital punishment generally have shifted their focus from reinstatement of capital punishment to the elimination of consideration for parole.

Career public (civil) service. A public administration in which recruitment and promotion is based on the merit principle (prescribed requirements of the position and qualifications for applicants) and disciplinary action is based on demonstrated cause and proper procedure, to ensure a state administration of professionally qualified personnel. By contrast, patronage appointments made for partisan purposes or as part of the spoils of victory will not last longer than the government leader who made them. See **Public service (administration)**.

Carter v. Saskatchewan (A.-G.) (1991). A Supreme Court ruling on the constitutionality under the Canadian Charter of Rights and Freedoms of electoral boundaries legislation requiring consideration of nonpopulation factors as opposed to the principle of representation by population, or voter equality.

The principle of representation by population requires that electoral constituencies have approximately the same number of voters. However, nonpopulation factors, or distinct community interests—for example, overrepresentation of rural voters—have long been tolerated in redistribution of electoral constituencies. Nonetheless, for some people the Charter required voter equality (s.3), thus making even generally accepted forms of malapportionment unconstitutional. The *Carter* case involved an appeal of the Saskatchewan Supreme Court's rejection of provincial legislation that required consideration of nonpopulation factors, specifically the overrepresentation of rural voters and underrepresentation of urban voters. The Supreme Court of Canada ruled 6-3 to uphold Saskatchewan's legislation mandating the consideration of nonpopulation factors. No justice, including the dissenters, opposed the consideration of non-population factors. The dissenting justices, however, objected to the statutory requirement of malapportionment. For them, voter equality should have been mandated by law, allowing for a reasonable balancing of nonpopulation, or community, interests by the independent electoral boundary commission. See *Electoral Boundaries Readjustment Act* **(redistribution)**; **Redistribution (electoral)**.

Caucus. Legislators of a particular political party who meet privately and regularly to discuss policy and parliamentary strategy and tactics. The "women's caucus" on Parliament Hill, however, is a rare example of a cross-party caucus and is given some credit for sensitizing male colleagues in respective party caucuses on some policy issues as well as on parliamentary behaviour and services.

Traditionally, a party caucus does not vote on issues before it; instead, discussion proceeds until the party leader articulates a consensus. Theoretically at least, because legislators are bound by party discipline not to express dissenting views in public, *in camera* discussions may be frank. However, members of caucus might "leak" information afterward for their own purposes. When the House of Commons is sitting, party caucuses meet at least once a week. In addition, particularly in large party caucuses, there will be separate meetings of party members from particular regions and major urban areas of the country.

On the government's side, the concern of private (that is, non-ministerial) members about the role of caucus is particularly strong. Like opposition backbenchers, they lack the resources of a cabinet minister to contest the government's decisions. But unlike their opposition counterparts, they cannot publicly criticize the government in the legislature or in committees without risking political sanctions. Governments therefore usually "preview" their legislation in caucus before introducing it in the legislature. While this consultation does not often result in major changes to the proposed measures, backbench "revolts" may occasionally bring about changes and possibly delay a bill's introduction. In recent years, the federal government caucus has had influence over government legislation regarding gun control, bank mergers and regulation and even the budget. When government caucuses are large, a committee system based on region and policy areas might be established to provide backbench advice more routinely. Government backbenchers, sensitive to public opinion in their constituencies, are usually upset if the government appears to be paying more attention to advice from the public administration or non-elected ministerial political staff than to advice from caucus.

Because opposition parties do not have responsibility for introducing and defending legislative proposals, their caucuses are basically designed to devise effective parliamentary strategy and tactics to criticize the government. At least theoretically, decision making in opposition caucuses can be more collegial, and parliamentary responsibilities more equitably distributed. However, if the party has recently suffered electoral defeat, the caucus may be consumed by internal intrigue. Opposition party leaders in Canada manage their caucuses in part through the designation of "critics," thus giving these members a degree of responsibility in caucus, visibility in House debate, and the hope of cabinet appointment should the party win the next election.

Parliamentary government in Canada is based on the principle of disciplined parties. In minor cases of maverick behaviour, a party leader might deny miscreant members parliamentary party positions such as committee memberships. In extreme cases, party leaders might expel members from caucus, forcing them to sit as independents. Maverick behaviour usually involves voting against the party's position on a major issue, but can also involve embarrassing the party with impolitic remarks. On rare occasions, members may not only leave their party, but "cross the floor of the House" and be accepted into another party caucus. A standard ploy of parties in power is to lure important but disgruntled opposition members (and indirectly their supporters among the public) with the promise of a particular policy change or a position in government.

Censure. An expression of strong disapproval or condemnation. Frequently, an opposition move to censure a minister is part of normal partisan debate. In formal usage, though, a legislature may discipline anyone, including its own members, in order to maintain its integrity or independence.

In Canada, censure, when imposed, usually involves legislators' use of unparliamentary language or lack of decorum. Members "named" by the Speaker are required to apologize or leave the chamber for the remainder of the day. In extreme cases, MPs have been expelled from the House of Commons or refused admission when faced with, or found guilty on, criminal charges. Canadian parliamentary institutions have not suffered serious external threats, and an alleged threat to a legislature's independence is more likely to be dealt with in the courts as a potentially criminal act than before the legislature itself.

Census. Decennial (since 1871) and quinquennial (since 1956) inventories of Canada's human resources conducted by the federal government.

The fundamental reason for the decennial census is to redistribute seats in the House of Commons as required in the *Constitution Act, 1867* (s.8). However, the census, which compels Canadians by law to respond fully and honestly to the census questionnaire, provides information on numerous demographic variables for private and public purposes. The data are used as social indicators to measure socio-economic well-being and to detect needs such as improved education facilities, housing, or minority-language service in certain areas of the country. Comparing data across several censuses, observers can plot demographic changes such as urbanization, age and regional migration patterns that can result in the alteration of federal and provincial government programs or the development of new programs to meet projected needs.

Census data are also important to decision makers in the private sector of the economy and to scholarly researchers. Census data include detailed information, for example, on age, sex, marital status, language, tenure of shelter, level of education, labour force activity, income, migration, urban-rural location, ethnicity, religion and family size of the population. The census also provides data on household facilities, as well as manufacturing and agricultural statistics. The private sector can obviously use such information to develop products and services. Social scientists can use the data as standards by which to observe, describe and explain human behaviour.

Central agency. An informal designation of key executive/administrative organizations in government.

The phrase may specifically refer to important departmental and non-departmental agencies in government finance and administration (for example, at the federal level, Department of Finance, Privy Council Office, Treasury Board Secretariat, and the Public Service Commission); or it may refer more generally to any group whose terms of reference extend its influence horizontally across all policy areas. The latter definition would include, in addition to the above, the Prime Minister's Office. Such agencies are "central" because they establish policies that other administrative groups must follow, or they co-ordinate and supervise policy making across the administration. See entries on each of these agencies.

Central bank. The national agency responsible for the country's monetary policy: that is, the regulation of credit and currency. See **Bank of Canada (central bank)**.

Centralization (decentralization). Usually a reference in national politics to the increasing (or decreasing) power of the central or federal government vis-à-vis the provinces; also, a reference to the location of political power at the centre with attendant antagonism towards the centre from the alienated population of the periphery, or hinterland. In urban politics, the phrase often refers to the debate over metropolitan or regional forms of government which involve the creation of a superior tier of government and the elimination or weakening of long-established area municipalities within the defined region. On national politics, see **Division (distribution) of powers; Federalism**.

Centrist. An individual or group advocating moderate responses to political demands, or only incremental changes to public policy. The term is derived from the debate over redistributive social policy which distinguishes egalitarians—those left of centre—from those who would tolerate a more hierarchical social structure—those right of centre.

Charlottetown Accord (1992). An agreement on major constitutional changes reached by the federal, provincial and territorial governments, and Native groups two years after the defeat in 1990 of the Meech Lake Accord of 1987 and following extensive public consultations, but which was subsequently rejected in a country-wide referendum, 55 to 44 per cent.

Earlier, the Meech Lake Accord had issued from the so-called Quebec round of constitutional negotiations designed to accommodate Quebec to the *Constitution Act, 1982.* The negotiations leading to the wide-ranging Charlottetown Accord involved not only Quebec's five demands from the Meech negotiations, including distinct-society status, but the demands of several provinces for fundamental reform of the Senate, restrictions on federal spending power and review of the federal-provincial division of powers, territorial demands concerning the process to achieve provincial status, demands from Native Peoples for recognition of their inherent right of self-government, federal proposals regarding the economic union of Canada, the demands of private groups for a social charter, and revision of the constitution regarding regional disparities, equalization and regional development.

Unlike the Meech Lake Accord that resulted from exclusive and private federal-provincial government negotiations, the Charlottetown Accord was negotiated following extensive public consultations and was submitted to Canadians for approval in a referendum. The Accord received popular approval in Prince Edward Island (74%), Newfoundland (63%), New Brunswick (61%), and the territories (61%). Voters in Ontario were equally divided (49.8% "Yes"), but opposed elsewhere (in descending order of support, Nova Scotia, 49% "Yes"; Saskatchewan, 45%; Quebec, 42%; Alberta, 39%; Manitoba, 38%; British Columbia, 31%).

There were various explanations for the rejection of the Accord and its consequences. Notably, the Accord was a comprehensive package of compromise proposals, and critics in the referendum campaign were not obliged either to present inclusive criticism of the package or alternative proposals. For example, there was opposition among both sovereignist and federalist francophones in Quebec who felt that the proposals regarding the powers of Quebec were inadequate. Some supporters of an elected Senate reform opposed the entire Accord because the proposals in the Accord related to Senate reform would have allowed provincial legislatures to determine whether the senatorial elections in their province would be direct or indirect. Some observers interpreted the rejection of the Accord as a general repudiation of the political elite by a normally deferential public, heralding a fundamental change in Canada's political culture. Others noted that it would be harder in the future for political leaders to engage in accommodative bargaining on the constitution.

While federal and provincial governments subsequently focused their attention on economic and financial matters, agreements were negotiated on some elements of the Accord that did not require formal constitutional amendment, notably regarding Aboriginal interests and the exercise of federal spending power. See **Canada Clause (Preamble, Charlottetown Accord, 1992); Distinct society clause; Canada Health and Social Transfer (CHST); Division (distribution) of powers; Economic union of Canada;** *Indian Act*; **Meech Lake Accord (1987); Native (First Nations) self-government; Referendum; Senate; Social**

Union Framework Agreement; Spending power; Supreme Court; Territorial governments.

Charter groups; interests. Private organizations that support interests specifically recognized in the Canadian Charter of Rights and Freedoms or have interests that may be addressed implicitly in various sections of the Charter.

As a result of the entrenchment of the Charter in 1982, some organized interests in society have claimed to have constitutional "protection" and therefore preferred status with respect to public policy. Others have used sections of the Charter to advance their views on public policy. The leadership of organizations representing these mass-based interests—sometimes referred to as social movement organizations— reflect a new style of public participation in policy making in post-Charter Canadian politics. On the one hand, they demand a more consultative decision-making process (as distinct from the operation of executive/administrative federalism that focuses on collegiality, confidentiality and compromise for mutual benefit), but are prepared to be more confrontational than many traditional interests, to forgo a collegial relationship with government actors and seek remedy through litigation in the courts to achieve the "full benefit" of the Charter. Active Charter interests notably include women, the elderly, the mentally and physically disabled, various ethnic minorities, gays and lesbians, and environmentalists. Some commentators have described such groups and interests collectively as the Court Party. See **Canadian Charter of Rights and Freedoms (1982); Social movement organizations**.

Charter of the French Language (Quebec). Quebec legislation originally enacted in 1977 (Bill 101) that, embodying the language policy of the Parti Québécois government, made French the official language of government, courts, schools and the economy of Quebec.

The Charter was the culmination of debate in Quebec on language policy involving three party governments: earlier, Bill 63 of the Union Nationale government in 1969 (the *nationaliste* party displaced later by the Parti Québécois) and Bill 22 of the Liberal government in 1974. In 1979, the Supreme Court declared sections relating to the legislature (that is, government) and to the courts to be a violation of the *Constitution Act, 1867* (s.133). Following successful challenges to the language Charter after adoption of the Canadian Charter of Rights and Freedoms in 1982, Quebec's Liberal government amended the language legislation (Bill 178) and invoked s.33 of the Charter to eliminate its further application to the language Charter.

The provisions of Bill 101, declared unconstitutional in 1979, had provided that only French versions of legislature debates, government documents and court proceedings were to be official. In 1984, the Supreme Court struck down the provisions of the language Charter regarding education as violations of s.23 of the Canadian Charter of Rights and Freedoms (Minority Language Educational Rights) (*A.-G. Quebec v. Quebec Association of Protestant School Boards*). The language law had restricted primary and secondary school instruction in English to children who had siblings in English-language schools in the province when the Bill was enacted, or who had one parent who had studied in an English-language school in Quebec. Exceptions had been made for temporary residents of the province and Native Peoples.

In 1988, the Supreme Court declared unconstitutional certain provisions of the language Charter dealing with the "francization" of business (*Quebec v. Ford*). Since 1977, the language Charter had been an important element in the successful conversion to the French language of business hitherto conducted almost entirely in English. One part of the law required that commercial signs outdoors be in French only, to create a *visage linguistique*. The Supreme Court ruled that the outright banning of signs in languages other than French was a violation of a fundamental freedom (s.2), but not the objective of a "marked predominance" of one language over others. Following heated debate in Quebec, the Liberal government amended the language law, allowing a predominance of French over other languages on indoor commercial signs, but maintaining the monopoly of French outdoors, and invoking the notwithstanding clause of the Canadian Charter of Rights and Freedoms (s.33) to preclude further court challenges. In 1993, the Liberal government amended the law (Bill 86) without reference to section 33 of the Charter, to permit other languages on outdoor signs as long as French was included and was the predominant language.

For both linguistic communities the debate was politically potent because of its symbolism. For many francophones in Quebec, only that jurisdiction in all of North America can effectively secure a place for the French language, and the "external" application of a constitutional statute to which Quebec's National Assembly had not given consent—the *Constitution Act, 1982*—should not be allowed to restrict Quebec's attempts to ensure the survival of French. Others, notably anglophones in Quebec, felt that the government's persistence fuelled intolerance among Québécois nationalists for minority-language groups in the province, as the law, though designed to enhance the French language, discriminated against others. The provincial Liberal party is largely satisfied with its reformulation of the language legislation. However, many activists in the Parti Québécois continue to encourage their leadership to adopt more restrictive measures. See **Canadian Charter of Rights and Freedoms (1982)**.

Chief Electoral Officer (Elections Canada). The officer of Parliament and office responsible for the conduct of all federal general and by-elections under the *Canada Elections Act*. Each province has a similar office to supervise its elections.

The federal chief electoral officer is appointed by a resolution of the House of Commons. Traditionally, the office has been responsible for the administration of fair and impartial elections, including the training and appointment of returning officers, the national register of voters and the confirmation of registration, the preparation and distribution of ballots, and the actual conduct of the poll and post-election reporting. Elections Canada is also responsible for administering provisions of the Act regarding subsidies to candidates and the expenditures of both parties and candidates, and of "third parties," that is, interest groups and private individuals, and the investigation of alleged violations of the Act and the prosecution of offenders. The chief electoral officer also assists the electoral boundaries commissions in the periodic redrawing of the boundaries of federal constituencies.

Chief Justice. The designated leader of a provincial supreme court and of the Supreme Court of Canada.

While appointments to the superior courts are those of the governor-in-council, effectively the responsibility of the federal minister of justice and the prime minister, the designation and appointment of a chief justice rests with the prime minister. The chief justice of the nine-member Supreme Court of Canada is sworn into the Queen's Privy Council for Canada prior to taking the oath as chief justice. When present, the chief justice presides at sittings of the Court; otherwise the most senior puisne ("ranking after") justice on the panel presides. The chief justice allocates the Court's workload, establishing panels of justices to hear cases. The chief justice is expected to be exceptionally learned and intellectually influential with respect to the other justices. The decisions of all justices are published, but the reasoning of the chief justice may receive particular attention, especially if it is part of the majority, to sense the "direction" of the Court in the post-Charter era of judicial review. In the extended absence or incapacity of the governor general, or if the office is vacant, the chief justice exercises the functions of that office as the Administrator of Canada. As ex-officio chair of the Canadian Judicial Council, comprising all chief justices and associate chief justices of superior courts, the chief justice may conduct investigations into the conduct of federally appointed judges. See **Canadian Charter of Rights and Freedoms (1982)**; **Supreme Court**.

Chief of staff (principal secretary). The administrative head of the political support staff for an executive office such as that of prime minister, provincial premier, or minister, and usually thus a key political advisor.

At the federal level, the head of the Prime Minister's Office was designated principal secretary under Prime Minister Pierre Trudeau, but chief of staff under later prime ministers. Personally selected by the relevant political office-holder, the chief of staff is the principal source of daily political counsel who manages the office, at the pleasure of the office-holder, to satisfy personal partisan needs. The attributes of the chief of staff usually reflect the office-holder's assessment of those needs. In the case of a prime minister or provincial premier, this may reflect policy development shortly after an election and electoral strategy as time for an election approaches. Consequently, the chief of staff of a head of government is politically closer to the prime minister or premier than many cabinet ministers and speaks— usually only privately—with considerable authority. See **Prime Minister's Office**.

Chief of the Defence Staff (Vice-Chief; Deputy Chief). Senior military advisors to the minister of national defence, appointed by the governor-in-council, that is, the federal cabinet, effectively the prime minister.

Civilian advisors in the Department of National Defence also assist the minister of national defence who is responsible for the Canadian Forces, national defence policy and emergency preparedness. The chief of the defence staff has overall responsibility for administration of the Canadian Forces, the vice-chief is chief of staff of headquarters, and the deputy chief is responsible for operations. On the civilian side of National Defence, a deputy minister is the senior advisor responsible for ensuring that government policy is reflected in administration, plans and operations.

Citizen. A person who is a native-born or naturalized member of a nation-state, with rights and obligations in that state.

The concept of Canadian citizenship as distinct from being a British subject was established in law in 1947. The federal *Citizenship Act* establishes the conditions for those not born in Canada for acquisition of citizenship, and also deals with the loss or resumption of citizenship. The federal *Immigration Act* embodies the federal government's immigration policy, including refugee resettlement and the processing of claims by visitors for refugee status, and the granting of permanent residence which may lead to the acquisition of citizenship.

Civil law (Civil Code; *Code civil*). Private law practised in Quebec and rooted in the French Napoleonic Code and Roman law, as distinct from the uncodified English-based common law which is practised in the other provinces.

The legal system of the former French colony was reaffirmed following the Conquest, in the British Parliament's *Quebec Act, 1774*, and finally in the *Constitution Act, 1867*. The Civil Code which constitutes the civil law governs personal, family and property relations in Quebec. Recent revisions of the Code dealt with issues raised by new reproductive and medical technology and current social values (for example, rights respecting surrogate motherhood and paternity, adoptive children, guardianship, and access of teenagers to medical counsel and abortion). Three of the nine justices of the Supreme Court of Canada are from the Quebec bar or courts, and five justices constitute a quorum, thus ensuring that a panel of the Supreme Court includes justices legally trained and experienced in civil law when such cases come before the Court.

Civil liberties. The phrase traditionally refers to the freedom of individuals to act without legal restrictions, for example, freedom of assembly and of speech, of religion, of the right to petition, freedom from detention and from arbitrary arrest, and the right to a fair and public trial with legal representation. In recent years, discourse on civil liberties has included freedom from hunger, illness and illiteracy, and from discrimination for reasons of sex, age, religion, ethnicity, sexual orientation, national origin and physical or mental disability.

Until 1982, Canadian legislatures were supreme in their areas of jurisdictional competence and therefore able to modify the common law liberties of individuals by statute. This applied particularly at the provincial level, where responsibility rests for "Property and Civil Rights" (*Constitution Act, 1867*, s.92:13), although federal responsibility for Criminal Law (s.91:27) was often cited to deny validity to some restrictive provincial statutes. In 1982, the Canadian Charter of Rights and Freedoms was entrenched in the constitution and now represents Canada's basic law regarding civil liberties. Federal and provincial legislation regarding privacy, access to personal information held by government agencies and human rights legislation also deal with the civil liberties of Canadians. See **Canadian Charter of Rights and Freedoms (1982)**; **Canadian Human Rights Commission**; **Duff Doctrine**; *Privacy Act, 1983* **(Canada)**; **Supreme Court**.

Civil service. A collective reference to government employees who constitute the administration of government. See **Career public (civil) service**; **Public Service (administration)**; **Senior civil servants**.

Clarity bill (on secession from Confederation). Federal legislation enacted in 2000 that sets the conditions under which the House of Commons would respond to referenda in Quebec on secession from Confederation.

The legislation was introduced by the Liberal government following the narrow defeat in 1995 of the second referendum in Quebec on sovereignty association and in the context of the Supreme Court of Canada's ruling in 1998 on the government's constitutional reference on secession. The sovereignty association option was defeated in 1995 by less than 1 per cent of the vote. The Supreme Court ruled that on a "clear" question supported by a "clear" majority, the secessionist movement would have to be recognized.

Under the legislation, within 30 days of the tabling of a referendum question, the House of Commons (the Senate is pointedly excluded) would determine if the question were clear. In doing so, it would take into account the views of all political parties in Quebec's legislature as well as the views of representatives of Native peoples in Quebec and other views it considered appropriate. Then following the referendum, the House would consider whether there had been a "clear expression of a will by a clear majority of the population" on secession from Canada. Consideration would include the proportion of eligible voters who participated as well as the size of the majority supporting secession and any other relevant criteria. Otherwise, the federal government would not enter negotiations on the terms of secession.

The Clarity bill was introduced despite divisions within the federal cabinet and the opposition of the federalist Quebec Liberal party, as well as the governing sovereignist Parti Québécois. The measure split the federal Conservative party, whose leader, Joe Clark, described it as "a roadmap to secession," and it deprived the Reform party, now the Canadian Alliance, of a major criticism of the Liberal government. The New Democratic party supported the measure while the federal Bloc Québécois, like the PQ, opposed it as a denial of Quebeckers' right to self-determination. In Quebec, the PQ government responded with the enactment of Bill 99 ("An Act Respecting the Exercise of the Fundamental Rights and Prerogatives of the Quebec People and the Quebec State"), asserting the province's right of self-determination, to determine alone the legal status of Quebec. See **Secession Reference**; **Sovereignty association**.

Class cleavage. A social division delineating communities of interest based on the distribution of wealth.

Class may be defined in subjective terms (that is, self-perception of class) or according to such objective indices as level of education, income and occupation. Class issues involving the distribution of wealth include such matters as the tax system and business law, or generally the role of government in regulating activities in the private sector of the economy. Public policies that would redistribute wealth, infringe upon rights of capital or private-sector managers, or result in more public disclosure and regulation of company activities (for example, in labour relations or consumer protection) are said to be "left-wing" policies; policies to the contrary, which emphasize the operations of the market as the chief site of social decision making and would be more tolerant of a hierarchy of wealth and power, are described as "right-wing."

Unlike other Western industrial societies, the class cleavage in Canada does not appear to generate independently as much political debate as do traditional identities with culture and region. When left-wing class attitudes are expressed, they are often filtered through cultural, regional and other perspectives. Thus, a Québécois worker might inveigh against "English business," a hard-pressed westerner against "Eastern business," or a feminist against the attitudes of "businessmen."

The two historically important political parties, the Liberals and Conservatives, have focussed public attention on regional, cultural and other issues, hoping to project a public image of mild social reformism without alienating the business community and thereby retaining its "confidence." This strategy is usually referred to as brokerage politics (see **Brokerage politics**). The only major political party in Canada with a decided left-wing image, the social democratic New Democratic party, has not been a strong electoral force in federal politics, but it has made an impression in certain provinces, where class consciousness is possibly strengthened by other traditional communities of interest. The fact that labour law is, in large part, a matter of provincial jurisdiction, also helps to explain apparently stronger class voting in some provinces than in the country as a whole.

Nonetheless, redistributive questions have not been entirely ignored by federal governments, especially when the NDP or its predecessors in the Co-operative Commonwealth Federation and Independent Labour or Progressive members of parliament held the balance of power in the House of Commons. In the 1960s, for example, the minority Liberal government enacted important redistributive legislation, including federal medicare, social assistance and pension legislation. While the tax reform legislation of that decade did not result in the dramatic reforms recommended earlier by a royal commission on taxation, a partial capital gains tax was one redistributive measure introduced. In a similar context, the review of foreign capital investment and the National Energy Policy were enacted by a minority Liberal government in the 1970s.

In 1982, the constitution was amended to entrench federal equalization payments to qualified provinces and commit federal and provincial governments to reduce disparities in economic opportunities and to provide "essential public services of reasonable quality to all Canadians" (*Constitution Act, 1982*, s.36). This "social charter" was particularly relevant to Atlantic Canadians whose provinces are particularly reliant on equalization payments. (See **Equalization grants [unconditional transfer payments]**)During the debate in the 1980s and 1990s over the Canada-United States Free Trade Agreement and the North American Free Trade Agreement, major public concern focussed on protection for Canada's "social safety net" and current and future regional development programs. The Canada-United States Free Trade Agreement was successfully negotiated in part because the question of defining "subsidy" was set aside. Also, debate on constitutional reform in the 1990s included calls for a social charter to be entrenched, to protect social and regional development programs.

In recent years, scholars have focussed attention on possible changes to the class-based or left-wing agenda. Increasing public interest in issues touching on protection of the environment and social and personal identity issues often touching on questions of morality, such as the rights of women, gays and lesbians, opposition to nuclear power, and community development, has been defined as concerns about "quality of life." This "postmaterialist" agenda frequently conflicts with traditional materialist left-wing concerns such as economic development to achieve full employment and increased personal income. This materialist-left agenda is associated historically with industrial development in the West during the nineteenth and twentieth centuries. In the earlier preindustrial period, the left-right division in Western society signified anti-church versus pro-church and nationalist versus imperialist sentiments. Thus the political left may yet again be in the process of modifying its agenda, now to accommodate postmaterialist concerns (See **Postmaterialism**).

While the historical attitude of the Liberal and Conservative parties has been to play down class issues, neither wishes at the same time to be perceived solely as an upper-class or "big business" party. The electoral success of the federal Liberals in the twentieth century and the concomitant weakness of the federal Conservatives was partly based on the more flexible Liberal approach to class questions, and the more sharply defined image of the Conservatives as an upper-class or "big business" party. When in office from 1984 to 1993—especially in the later years during an economic recession—Conservative support for free trade, its introduction of the value-added Goods and Services Tax (GST) in 1991, its policy on interest rates, reducing the public debt and government services, and its policy to make Canadian business more "globally competitive" generally reinforced that party's right-wing image. In the 1993 election, the Conservatives under new leadership failed to distance themselves from those policies, while the Liberal leadership appealed to the public with generalized references to encouraging "hope" and "dignity" among hard-pressed citizens. Yet, when in office following the 1993 and 1997 elections, the Liberals essentially adopted a right-wing fiscal and economic agenda popularized by the Reform party that had electorally surpassed the Conservatives in those elections and formed the official opposition in 1997. But in advance of the election in 2000, and mindful that the social democratic NDP had made electoral inroads against the Liberals in Atlantic Canada in 1997, the Liberals shifted their policy leftward, sensing correctly that public opinion favoured increased public investment in social policy fields, and was generally unsupportive of the fiscal and social conservatism of Reform and its successor, the Canadian Alliance.

Historically, both the Conservative and Liberal parties have been dependent upon the private and legally unlimited largesse of relatively few Montreal- and Toronto-based businesses. The Canadian Alliance, successor to Reform and its conservative economic and social policies, hoped to increase support from the corporate sector. The NDP receives only modest financial support from corporations. Both the Conservatives and the Liberals have been involved in major fundraising scandals when in office and have always been subject to charges of business favouritism and patronage in public policy proposals, the awarding of government contracts and various public appointments. Changes to election and party finances since 1974 in Canada have made it easier for the parties to diversify their sources of support. However, the Liberal and Conservative support is still drawn largely from well-off social and business circles.

Clawback. Provisions in personal income tax regulations designed to target benefits on the basis of need. Historically, benefits such as child (family) allowances and old age pensions were universal programs, that is, the allowance was granted regardless of income. Universal benefits avoid the necessity of a qualifying means test that necessarily involves the invasion of privacy and considerable administrative costs. In the 1980s, the desire by governments generally to reduce expenditures resulted in the targeting of some social benefits indirectly through income tax "clawbacks": people with higher taxable incomes progressively lose the dollar value of the particular social benefit. See **Indexing/de-indexing**.

Clerk of the House of Commons (of the Senate). The permanent head of the House of Commons (Senate) staff, holding the rank of deputy minister. The clerk of the House of Commons is responsible for the records of the House and ensures that the Order Paper is prepared for each parliamentary day's business. The clerk is the recording officer of the House, maintaining minutes and recording divisions. Operating under the direction of the Speaker, the clerk supervises the staff of the House. The clerk of the Senate is likewise the chief administrative officer of that chamber and performs functions comparable to those of the clerk of the House. However, because the Senate is formally the superior body, its clerk is also the clerk of the Parliaments and is the custodian of the original acts of Parliament that have received royal assent. The seal of the clerk of the Parliaments is affixed to the copies of all Acts, including those to be produced in the courts.

Clerk of the Privy Council. The person designated as secretary to the federal cabinet, a position in existence since 1940 and established by statute in 1975.
    The clerk/secretary is the highest-ranking federal civil servant and thus the head of the federal civil service as well as the cabinet secretariat which is responsible for co-ordinating the activities of cabinet and cabinet committees. This official is also designated the prime minister's deputy minister and therefore has a special relationship with the prime minister and, though usually a professional public administrator, nonetheless holds the position at the prime minister's "pleasure." The clerk is in constant communication with the prime minister, offering information and advice on government policy, organization and personnel. Consequently, the clerk/secretary is more influential than many cabinet ministers. The designation within the cabinet of president of the Privy Council is an honorific title and does not imply influence over the operation of the Privy Council Office and the clerk. See **Privy Council Office**.

Closure. Procedure by which a government can curtail legislative debate on a measure and bring it to a vote.
    As the legislature's roles are the conflicting ones of criticizing and enacting government legislation, the government's strategic objective is to conduct business expeditiously, while the opposition seeks to diminish public confidence in the government. In order to prevent protracted and possibly politically harmful debate —commonly called filibustering—by the opposition, procedural rules of the House of Commons allow the government to impose closure, effectively terminating debate.

Because the imposition of closure in 1956 to end the so-called pipeline debate was partially credited with the Liberal government's electoral defeat in 1957, federal governments were subsequently reluctant to impose closure. In 1969, however, the government used closure to introduce changes in the standing orders (procedural rules) of the House of Commons to revise the rules on limiting debate. House rules provide for limitation of debate at each stage of a bill's passage through the House. When the government cannot obtain the agreement among the parties in setting time limits for debate, the government may propose an "allocation-of-time" motion on which there can be only limited debate. Since then, the imposition of closure on debate has become common practice by both Conservative and Liberal governments.

Coalition government. A government-of-the-day that includes members from more than one political party.

Formal or informal coalitions are required in a parliamentary system when the government party does not hold a majority of the seats in the legislature. While formal coalition governments have been common in provincial politics, there have only been two cases in federal politics: the coalition for Confederation in 1867 and the Union government from 1917 to 1920.

Conservative Prime Minister Robert Borden led the Union government, which included anglophone Liberals, to expedite conscription and conduct a wartime election. The Union government divided Canada deeply between English and French. Neither the Conservatives nor the Liberal-Unionists appeared to benefit from the coalition experience. By the time of Borden's retirement and the selection of Conservative Arthur Meighen to succeed him, some Liberal-Unionists had returned to their party while others joined the new Progressive party. The Conservatives lost the next election to the Liberals.

Since then, minority-government parties and smaller parties in the opposition have preferred to deal with each other on an informal basis, for example the minority Liberal government and the New Democratic party between 1972 and 1974. There are inherent difficulties for the junior partner in such informal alliances, as the senior partner actually in office will likely reap any subsequent electoral benefits, as the Liberals did in 1974.

Collective (cabinet/ministerial) responsibility. The principle by convention that the cabinet, though comprising many individuals with possibly as many minds, speaks as one and is responsible or accountable as a body to the legislature for all actions and policies of the government.

The concept of responsibility which is individual (that is, ministerial), as well as collective, is central to the accountability of the political executive to the legislature, and thus to parliamentary democracy in Canada. The government must retain the "confidence" of the legislature (the House of Commons in the bicameral Parliament) to remain in office. The convention of responsible government predates Confederation, having been established in various British North American colonies in the 1840s. See **Accountability**; **Cabinet**; **Ministerial responsibility**; **Responsible government**.

Collectivism. A value orientation that esteems group loyalty and individual commitment to a notion of the common good.

Some people argue that collectivism is a distinctive feature of Canadian political culture in the North American context; that Canadians place a higher value than Americans on authority, mutual assistance and social order than on the freedom of individuals to pursue personal goals as each sees fit. The origins of this collectivism may be found in the persistence of a minority French-speaking society through various forms of group accommodation with the majority English-speakers, the need for collective action to deal with significant regional economic disparities, and possibly even as a reaction to unpleasant events in United States domestic history and foreign policy.

Constitutional phrases are sometimes cited to illustrate this difference in national political cultures: American society is inspired by the phrase "Life, liberty and the pursuit of Happiness" (Declaration of Independence), while Canadians honour "Peace, Order, and good Government" (*Constitution Act, 1867*). For whatever historic reasons, collectivism is an important part of Canada's political culture because of the continued use of government policy or state intervention to ensure cultural, regional and personal well-being. In recent years, however, some scholars have detected a weakening of at least the deferential or elitist aspect of collectivism in Canada's political culture.

Combines (anti-combines legislation; competition policy). Alliances or close associations of private companies that may restrict trade, facilitate price-fixing, or otherwise misuse their dominant position in the economy.

Anti-combines legislation prohibits business practices that "unduly" lessen competition at all stages of production, distribution and retailing in trade and commerce. The federal Department of Industry administers the *Competition Act* while the Competition Tribunal, established under its own Act, adjudicates on possible violations of competition policy such as corporate mergers or marketing agreements.

Prosecutions, especially successful ones, are rare. Some critics charge that the competition policy and its enforcement are designed to give the appearance of government supervision without excessively disturbing large scale business. Because prosecutions are judicial rather than administrative in nature, judicial rules of evidence apply, involving costly gathering of admissible evidence and court proceedings with the usual provisions for appeals. Furthermore, action with respect to the enforcement of competition policy must conform to the Canadian Charter of Rights and Freedoms. In *Hunter v. Southam* (1984), the Supreme Court ruled that protection afforded by the Charter from "unreasonable search or seizure" (s.8) extended to the fact-finding activity of government investigators regarding suspected business violations of competition policy: the search and seizure of documents required prior authorization from an impartial person— normally a judge—who had to be convinced on reasonable and probable grounds that an offence had been committed and that evidence was located in the place to be searched.

Although the *Hunter* decision made it more difficult for the government to enforce the *Competition Act*, in 1992 there were three Supreme Court decisions that upheld federal competition policy and the powers of the Bureau of Competition Policy. In one case, the Court ruled that the government does not have to prove intent to lessen competition, but only establish that a "reasonable business person" would know that a particular arrangement would do so (*Nova Scotia Pharmaceutical Society et al.*). In other cases, the Court affirmed the power of the Bureau to determine whether a company has eliminated competitors and to punish a company that refused to comply with its orders.

Commission (board, agency, tribunal). A government-appointed group established by statute or statutory instrument to administer public policy, often possessing regulatory, investigative and adjudicative powers.

The so-called administrative state comprises many such bodies to which the legislature delegates quasi-legislative and quasi-judicial power through enabling legislation to devise and enforce regulations—subordinate legislation—"as may be deemed necessary for giving full effect" to the particular Act. The governor-in-council, effectively the cabinet and notably the prime minister (or provincial premier), appoints directors who oversee a commission's staff. The commissions, agencies and tribunals have semi-independent status that allows them to make and enforce regulations without partisan consideration, though they may be guided by general government policy. They report to the legislature through designated ministers. Prominent examples at the federal level include the Canadian Human Rights Commission, Canadian Radio-television and Telecommunications Commission, Canadian Transportation Agency, Competition Tribunal, Immigration and Refugee Board, National Parole Board, National Energy Board, Tax Court of Canada and Tariff Board.

Some federal administrative activity is personalized in a commissioner, such as the Commissioner of Official Languages, Information Commissioner, Privacy Commissioner (the first ensuring the administration follows federal language law; the last two ensuring some protection against the excesses of the administrative state), and the Superintendent of Financial Institutions. Lesser-known federal agencies deal with copyright, federal jurisdiction in labour relations, pensions, patents, unemployment insurance and other matters, all reflecting the wide range of government activities. Commissions are also important at the provincial level where the constitution grants jurisdiction, for example, in environmental protection, labour relations, municipal government, and assessment of property tax. In addition to ordinary statutes requiring such bodies to adopt specific procedures to ensure openness, fairness and public accountability, the Canadian Charter of Rights and Freedoms has been successfully invoked in the courts to provide protection against arbitrary administrative power. See *Hunter v. Southam* (**1984**), and **Singh Case** (*Re Singh and Minister of Employment and Immigration* [**1985**]).

Commission for Environmental Cooperation (NAFTA). A trilateral agency established under the North American Free Trade Agreement, with headquarters in Montreal, to prevent conflicts between trade and the environment, and to investigate and seek enforcement of environmental protection laws by the three NAFTA signatories, Canada, Mexico and the United States. The Commission comprises a council with cabinet-level representation from each country, assisted by a secretariat. The Commission also has a public advisory committee

Under the NAFTA Agreement on Environmental Cooperation, nongovernmental organizations or individuals can submit complaints to the Commission's secretariat alleging noncompliance by any of the countries to its own environmental law. If, given the response of the relevant government, the secretariat deems the complaint worthy, it can recommend to the ministerial council that a "factual record" regarding the complaint be prepared, with its publication on a two-thirds vote of the council. See **Environmentalism**; **North American Free Trade Agreement (NAFTA) (1992)**.

Commissioner of Official Languages (language ombudsman). The federal officer responsible for ensuring the recognition of equal status for French and English languages in the operations of the government of Canada.

The commissioner advises the public of the requirements of the *Official Languages Act*, receives complaints and conducts investigations of alleged violations. Most complaints deal with the inadequacy of federal service in French. Appointed for a seven-year term, the commissioner reports annually to Parliament, but may make special reports dealing with matters that the office considers particularly pressing. See **Bilingualism and biculturalism**; *Official Languages Act* **(1969)**.

Committee of the Whole (Supply; Ways and Means). All members of a legislature meeting as a committee chaired by the deputy speaker.

Until 1969, the House of Commons met as committee of the whole to examine bills clause by clause after second reading. Most bills are now examined by relevant standing committees and legislative committees; supply, through designated Supply Days in the House; and estimates, in standing committees. In addition to appropriation (expenditure; supply) bills following the examination of estimates in standing committees, the committee of the whole considers emergency measures (such as back-to-work legislation in the case of industrial action affecting the public welfare) and non-controversial measures whose passage can thus be expedited.

The purpose of the change from the committee of the whole to legislative and policy area designated standing committees was to involve more members of parliament in the legislative process and to allow for specialization. The change has not been a complete success, especially for members of the opposition, whose criticism of the government is now diffused in committees that do not receive as much attention from the mass media as do sittings of the House. However, with respect to public policy, there have been examples of the diminution of partisanship in many cases of committee deliberation, increased use of committees by private interests seeking to influence policy debate as well as specific legislation, and acceptance by the government of amendments to its bills. See **Standing (select, special, joint) committees (of the House and Senate)**.

Common law. Law based on legal precedents, or case law, as opposed to statutory or codified law.

Private law in all parts of Canada except Quebec is based on common law derived from England, while criminal law, which is codified and uniform throughout the country, is rooted in British criminal jurisprudence. The common law has been very important in the development of the Canadian constitution. For example, the discretionary or prerogative powers of the Crown and government derive in part from common law, restricted from time to time by statute. Civil liberties in Canada are also rooted in the common law and until 1982 were subject to the principle of parliamentary supremacy and judicial decisions respecting federal-provincial jurisdiction.

In 1982, the adoption of the Canadian Charter of Rights and Freedoms codified civil rights, profoundly modified the principle of parliamentary (or legislative) supremacy, and enlarged the scope and impact of judicial review. A case before the Supreme Court in 1994 dealt with conflicting elements of common law now enshrined in the Charter—an accused person's right to presumed innocence and a fair trial (s.11), and freedom of the press (s.2) (in an appeal of a court-ordered ban on televising *The Boys of St. Vincent*). Past judicial practice had established a hierarchy of common law rights, with the former taking precedence over the latter, for example, in the form of prohibitions on the publication of information touching on actual or prospective trials. The Supreme Court ruled that Charter-based rights are in principle equal and that a "hierarchical approach to rights, which places some over others, must be avoided, both when interpreting the Charter and when developing the common law. When the protected rights of two individuals come into conflict, as can occur in the case of publication bans, Charter principles require a balance to be achieved that fully respects the importance of both sets of rights." Such cases have subsequently been decided by the judiciary in, for example, restricting media coverage of the murder trial of a defendant before a co-defendant's trial on similar charges and evidence. See **Canadian Charter of Rights and Freedoms (1982); Civil law (Civil Code); Civil liberties**.

Commonwealth (The British...of Nations). An association of approximately 49 independent nations and some associated states, including Canada, which were former colonies or trusts of the United Kingdom.

The Commonwealth has a secretariat in London responsible for conferences pertaining to both governmental and nongovernmental programs relating, for example, to trade, technical co-operation, youth, science and athletics. The Commonwealth originated in imperial conferences held in the early decades of the twentieth century, but it constitutionally dates from the Statute of Westminster, 1931. The British monarch, who is also the monarch and head of state of Canada and of several other Commonwealth countries, serves as head of the Commonwealth. The main body of the association consists of the heads of government who hold an informal meeting every two years. More recently, the Commonwealth's secretariat has been used in attempts to mediate serious disputes within and between Commonwealth states. Countries have occasionally been expelled (and reinstated in the case of South Africa) or had their membership suspended pending the return to civilian from military rule (as in the case of Nigeria in the 1990s). Such action, however, is not consistently followed (as in the case of Pakistan at the same time), nor is mediation by the Commonwealth necessarily welcomed (as in the case of Fiji in 2000). See **British connection; Statute of Westminster (U.K., 1931).**

Communications Security Establishment (CSE). A highly secret organization under the Department of National Defence that has the capacity to monitor electronic communications and electro-magnetic "transmissions." It is linked internationally with similar allied national monitoring organizations and resources, most importantly the United States National Security Agency. Unlike the example of the Canadian Security Intelligence Service and its oversight body, the Security Intelligence Review Committee (SIRC), there is no independent oversight body for, and no parliamentary scrutiny of, the CSE. In 1996, however, the federal government appointed a CSE commissioner to oversee the monitoring of communications by the CSE, especially where they might involve the privacy of Canadians. In annual reports to the minister of defence who tables them in Parliament, the commissioner has essentially asserted the lawfulness of CSE activities. See **Canadian Security Intelligence Service (CSIS)**; **Security Intelligence Review Committee (SIRC)**.

Community (the Francophone; la Francophonie). An association, founded in the early 1960s, of approximately 37 French-speaking or partly French-speaking states and associated states.

The term *la Francophonie* also refers more generally to relations among French-speaking states and nongovernmental organizations. The French government was initially ill-disposed to the idea when a spirit of independence took hold in most French colonies in Africa in the early 1960s, but later came to appreciate the positive foreign policy implications for France of such an association. For its part, the Canadian government has sought to demonstrate abroad the bilingual and bicultural aspect of Canadian society by associating itself with *la Francophonie*. As a member of the Community, Canada is involved in multilateral and bilateral trade, as well as technical, youth, education and athletic endeavours through the Agency for Cultural and Technical Co-operation and in various conferences of ministers (for example, education and youth). The Canadian government has approved the participation of Quebec most notably, but has also engaged Manitoba, New Brunswick and Ontario in some Agency and conference activities. Quebec and New Brunswick have the status of "participating governments" in the Agency.

Compact theory of Confederation. An interpretation of Confederation in 1867 as the outcome of a treaty, or compact, among colonial participants.

In one version, the provinces were understood to be the successors of the colonial elites, heirs to a negotiating role in Confederation, whose consent was required for amendments to the constitution. Another version views Confederation as a compact between the political leadership of francophone and anglophone British North America. This version would grant a constitutional veto to the government of Quebec. The theory, however, had no legal foundation, though it provided a handy excuse for government procrastination. Prime Minister William Lyon Mackenzie King managed to take different positions on compact theory within a three-year period. The "unemployment insurance" amendment of 1940 was postponed until the approval of all provinces was received. King told the Commons: "We have avoided a very critical constitutional question... whether...in amending the British North America Act it is absolutely necessary to secure the consent of all provinces..." (Canada, House of Commons, *Debates*, June 21, 1949, 1117-118). However, in the postponement of the redistribution of seats in the Commons in 1943, King did not consult the provinces and refused to relay the Quebec premier's request that the British Parliament reject the federal amendment. It was King's opinion then that "the [compact] theory...does not appear to be supported either in history or in law" (Montreal *Gazette*, July 16, 1943).

In 1982, the *British North America Act* was amended through an address of Canadian Parliament to the British Parliament, with the support of all provinces except Quebec. The *Constitution Act, 1982* patriated the constitution by establishing a general amending procedure (among others) that required neither unanimous provincial consent nor the necessary consent of Quebec.

Competition policy. See **Combines (anti-combines legislation)**.

Comptroller General of Canada. Appointed by the federal government at deputy minister rank, the comptroller general is an administrative officer of the Treasury Board responsible for standards of financial controls, reporting systems and program evaluation of federal departments and agencies. The government appointed the first comptroller general in 1978 in response to criticism in 1976 by the auditor general that the government had in effect lost control of the treasury. In 1993, the Treasury Board Secretariat absorbed the functions of the Office of Comptroller General and the secretary of the Treasury Board was designated the comptroller general. See **Auditor General; Treasury Board Secretariat**.

Concurrent majority. See **Double majority**.

Concurrent powers. Jurisdictional competence held jointly by the national and subnational levels of government in a federal system. In Canada, the *Constitution Act, 1867* designates agriculture and immigration as areas of jurisdictional competence held by both Parliament and the provincial legislatures (s.95). The Act was amended in 1951 (s.94A) to add old age pensions as an area of concurrent power (and further amended in 1964). In the case of conflicting legislation, the Act provides for federal paramountcy in agriculture and immigration, but no federal legislation on pensions can "affect the operation" of any provincial legislation on that subject. In 1982, s.92A and "The Sixth Schedule" were added to clarify federal and provincial jurisdiction in non-renewable natural resources, forestry resources and electrical energy.

Conditional grants (special-purpose transfer payments). Also referred to as grants-in-aid, federal monies transferred to provincial treasuries for agreed-upon, shared-cost programs.

At the close of the First World War, conditional grants were experimental and involved programs with fixed terms. By the end of the century, the federal government was systematically reducing its level of financial commitment to expensive shared-cost programs that it had developed since the Second World War in such provincial policy fields as social assistance, hospital and medical care, and postsecondary education. Through the exercise of federal spending power in such joint federal-provincial efforts, minimum national standards of public service were established despite provincial opposition to federal "entanglement" in their jurisdictional prerogatives.

The initial federal response to provincial criticism and rising costs came in 1965. Under the *Established Programs (Interim Arrangements) Act, 1965*, the provinces were given the option of contracting or opting out of shared-cost programs. Only Quebec took up the offer to assume all administrative and financial responsibilities for programs in return for a specified percentage of the individual income tax on the income of the province's residents (tax abatement) and, in certain programs, an associated equalization and operating cost adjustment grant. After 1965, the federal government established limits on federal payments in shared-cost programs. Under the *Fiscal Arrangements and Established Programs Financing Act, 1977*, the federal government replaced conditional grants for medical and hospital insurance and for postsecondary education with unconditional grants known as block funding and abatement of tax points.

Successive federal governments in the 1980s and 1990s sought to control expenditures partly through reducing the size of their grants. For their part, provinces responded to the decrease in federal assistance and rising costs by increasing their revenue, shifting funds from one program to another, but increasingly by reducing levels of service and accessibility. In 1996, Established Program Funding was replaced by a negotiated block payment and transfer of tax points to the provinces under the Canada Health and Social Transfer.

Beyond concern over continued deficit financing and a growing public debt, the federal government was also concerned that its financial assistance to programs delivered by the provincial governments did not result in sufficient public visibility and credit for the federal government. Thus, a combination of provincial concern over federal spending power in areas of provincial jurisdiction, the governments' mutual concerns about public indebtedness and the federal government's concern for greater public visibility in delivering public services contributed to a lowering of federal funding with fewer conditions attached to federal assistance for provincial programs. See **Canada Health and Social Transfer (CHST); Federal-provincial tax-sharing agreements (fiscal federalism); Social Union Framework Agreement; Spending power.**

Confederation. The formation of Canada as a federal union of the British colonies of the Province of Canada, New Brunswick and Nova Scotia with a constitution otherwise similar to that of the United Kingdom, through provisions of the *British North America Act* (UK), on July 1, 1867.

Confederation was a response of several colonial elites to their domestic selfinterest, expansionist sentiment in the United States and the changing focus of British imperial interests. The internal impetus came from the United Province of Canada, where political and French/English conflict had immobilized the political forces of Canada East (formerly Lower Canada, later Quebec) and Canada West (formerly Upper Canada, later Ontario). Initially well-disposed to Maritime union because of the smallness and isolation of their colonies, politicians from New Brunswick, Nova Scotia and Prince Edward Island met in Charlottetown in 1864 to discuss their future. Canadian politicians, who had by then formed a grand coalition to pursue the project of a larger union, attended the Maritime conference to advance their proposition. The conference in Charlottetown was followed by one in Quebec City to consider formally a federal union. The Quebec conference adopted 72 resolutions, including one to seek "the sanction of the Imperial and Local Parliaments...for the union...."

Only the Province of Canada, however, had much enthusiasm for the union. Newfoundland and Prince Edward Island refused to participate. The government of New Brunswick was defeated in an election on the issue, and the Nova Scotia government simply reaffirmed its support for a Maritime union. The Canadian government then lobbied the British government, which pressured the eastern colonies. In a conference in London held late in 1866, representatives from Canada, Nova Scotia and New Brunswick agreed to 69 resolutions that became the basis of the *British North America Act*. Since 1982, the Act and its later amendments are cited as the "*Constitution Act, 1867* and subsequently amended."

Under the original Act, Canada was created as a federation with a strong central government and a "Constitution similar in Principle to that of the United Kingdom" (preamble). French and English were made the official languages of Parliament, the federal courts, and the legislature and courts of Quebec. Established minority Catholic and Protestant rights in education were guaranteed in all provinces, which now included Ontario and Quebec as well as New Brunswick and Nova Scotia. The bicameral Parliament comprised a lower house—the House of Commons— elected on a limited franchise and an upper house—the Senate—appointed on the basis of regional representation. Recognizing the weak financial basis of the provinces, the principle of federal statutory subsidies was established. The western British North American territories known as Rupert's Land and the Northwest Territory were later annexed to Canada and administered by the Canadian government. In 1870, Manitoba was created as a province on the same bilingual basis as Quebec. British Columbia "entered" Confederation in 1871, followed by Prince Edward Island two years later. In 1905, Alberta and Saskatchewan were created out of the western territory by federal statute. In 1949, Newfoundland "joined" Confederation.

The legislative responsibilities of the Parliament and provincial legislatures were outlined in several sections of the Act, notably ss.91-95. The preamble to s.91, which described Parliament's general responsibility for the "Peace, Order, and good Government of Canada" in matters not exclusively assigned to the provinces, illustrates the compromise of the framers of Confederation to have a federal state with a dominant centre rather than a unitary state. The importance of the federal government was also evident in the specific responsibilities assigned to Parliament, including declaratory power over provincial works and the federal nature of the office of provincial lieutenant-governor, including the powers of reservation and disallowance. Until 1982, judicial review of the Act in Canada and the UK (by the Judicial Committee of the Privy Council until 1949) pertained largely to establishing jurisdictional competence between the two levels of government.

In 1982, the constitutional basis of Confederation was profoundly altered through an address to the British Parliament from the Canadian Parliament supported by all provincial legislatures except the National Assembly of Quebec. The *British North America Act* was patriated as the *Constitution Act* including the Canadian Charter of Rights and Freedoms against which legislation (and, in time, executive and administrative orders and procedures) could be tested in the courts. The Act includes a declaration recognizing (though not defining) "existing aboriginal and treaty rights" of Indian, Inuit and Métis. It also contains a commitment to the promotion of equal opportunities for Canadians and to the principle of federal equalization payments to the provinces to achieve comparable levels of public services across the country. The Act was patriated with the entrenchment of several amending formulae involving, variously, the Canadian Parliament and provincial legislatures. See **Constitution Act, 1867 and subsequently amended** and other entries on subjects mentioned here.

Confederation of Regions party (CoR). A provincial political party that existed briefly in New Brunswick from the late 1980s until its decline in the 1990s, to oppose official bilingualism in the province that Conservative and Liberal governments had supported since 1969 (*Official Language Act* [New Brunswick]).

In 1982, New Brunswick was constitutionally declared bilingual with respect to its legislature, courts and communications with government offices. The province is the centre of Atlantic Canada's historic minority French-speaking Acadian population. CoR's support peaked in 1991, electing several members to the provincial legislature, drawing support from English-speakers in the south and particularly in the area of the capital, Fredericton. The Liberals won the election, in part as CoR drew support of voters who had previously voted Conservative and for whom the Liberals were not an acceptable alternative. CoR's limited electoral success was counter-productive: in 1993, the province's official bilingualism was further entrenched in the constitution with respect to cultural and educational institutions. See **Bicultural cleavage**; **Third parties (political)**; **Two-party system**.

Conference of First Ministers. Meetings of the heads of the provincial and federal governments, usually held annually.

Styled earlier as dominion-provincial and federal-provincial conferences, these meetings have been held more regularly since the 1960s. The conferences are usually convened in Ottawa and chaired by the prime minister, to establish agreement on policies of federal and provincial concern. The "summits" receive extensive coverage by the mass media, and the formal sessions are usually broadcast. The public meetings largely involve formal statements of government views by the heads or relevant ministers, as well as occasional exchanges among the politicians conscious of their "viewing audience back home." Effective negotiations therefore usually take place in private meetings. The Conference of First Ministers is the most visible and formalized aspect of federal-provincial relations.

The Conference epitomizes the federal-provincial style known as executive or administrative federalism, whereby the political future of the country is guided by agreements negotiated privately by officials of the 11 political executives, some to be ratified later by usually compliant legislatures. Following the failure of the constitutional Meech Lake Accord in 1990, negotiated in the style of executive federalism, constitutional discussions were enlarged to include consultative forums involving diverse public groups. Afterward, ministerial meetings on the constitution were enlarged to include the territorial governments and representatives of selected Native groups. The Charlottetown Accord of 1992, which was rejected in a national referendum, had included a constitutional requirement for an annual meeting of first ministers, including territorial government leaders, but without entrenching an agenda as had the ill-fated Meech Lake Accord of 1987. Aboriginal representatives were to be invited when items being discussed directly affected Aboriginal peoples.

The prime minister and premiers can no longer afford to be seen as an elite determining the future of the country behind closed doors. However, the highly integrated nature of government policies and relations in Canadian federalism still requires on-going and high level federal-provincial consultation and agreement. See **Canadian Charter of Rights and Freedoms (1982); Dominion-provincial conferences; Executive (administrative) federalism; Intergovernmental committees.**

Conference of Ministers (of Education, Finance, etc.). Councils of ministers that meet regularly to discuss and co-ordinate various federal-provincial policies and programs relevant to their portfolios. See **Intergovernmental committees.**

Conference of Provincial First Ministers. A meeting of provincial premiers held on an annual basis since the 1960s. The first interprovincial heads-of-government meeting took place in 1887, but did not become a permanent feature of Canadian federalism at that time. The meetings gradually acquired political significance through the 1970s and 1980s as regular federal-provincial consultation or executive federalism became the framework within which political conflicts, especially on constitutional change, were to be resolved. See **Intergovernmental committees**.

Confidence (of the House; Chamber of...). Support on a money bill or other major legislation by a majority of members of a legislature required for a government to remain in office, thus maintaining the constitutional principle of responsible government. Given the disciplined party system in Canadian legislatures, confidence should be problematic only in the case of minority governments. In the case of the bicameral Parliament, the elected House of Commons is a confidence chamber, but not the appointed Senate.

As a constitutional convention, legislators define confidence by the observance or modification of precedents. In 1968, the minority Liberal government was defeated on third reading of a money bill in the House of Commons. However, the Liberals argued that the outcome of the vote on third reading—usually a formality—resulted from a tactical error by the government whip and that a winter election would not be in the country's interest. Moreover, and more to the point, the Liberal party was in the midst of a leadership campaign to replace the retiring Lester Pearson. Prime Minister Pearson marshalled forces inside and outside government to persuade the Conservative leader of the opposition, Robert Stanfield, to allow the House to meet, promising that a confidence motion would then be introduced, debated and put to a vote. Stanfield acceded and the government was sustained in the vote.

Conflict of interest. A personal pecuniary interest, direct or indirect, sufficient either to influence or to appear to influence the exercise of a legislator's or public official's duties.

A real conflict exists when one knows of a personal interest that is sufficient to influence one's public duty. A potential conflict arises when the known existence of a personal interest could influence a person's duties, provided that the duties have not been exercised. The notion of impartiality implied in the rule of law and the principle of equality, both enshrined in the Canadian Charter of Rights and Freedoms (preamble and s.15), are the constitutional bases for defining and prohibiting conflict of interest.

At the federal level, statutory provisions dealing with conflict of interest among parliamentarians and public service employees, notably in the Criminal Code, are acknowledged to be antiquated or ineffective, largely because they deal with breech of the public trust after the fact and do not apprehend potential conflicts of interest. Following a series of scandals and allegations in the 1970s and 1980s, a Liberal-appointed federal task force proposed a statutory code of behaviour for federal officials. Though elected in 1984 in a campaign that included criticism of Liberal patronage appointments, Conservative Prime Minister Brian Mulroney only implemented another set of prime ministerial guidelines for ministers and public officials. Consequently, like guidelines of earlier governments, these seemed to be an exercise in public relations rather than a delineation of constitutionally required behaviour. The Mulroney government was later beset by a series of scandals involving violations of the guidelines, which led to a judicial inquiry regarding one minister and criminal charges in other cases. In 1988, the government introduced legislation which would have applied to all MPs and senators. While it was stronger than the ministerial guidelines, it was weaker than the proposals of the task force, especially regarding party patronage. The measure died on the Order Paper later that year, was reintroduced in 1989 and studied by a joint parliamentary committee. This legislation also died on the Order Paper when Parliament was dissolved for the 1993 election. The subsequent Liberal government established an ethics counsellor, but responsible to the prime minister rather than to Parliament, to investigate alleged violations of the government's ministerial conflict of interest guidelines. Various investigations of ministers by the ethics counsellor since then, including even of Prime Minister Jean Chrétien's business affairs, have concluded that no conflicts existed.

Likewise, there are only guidelines cautioning federal civil servants against questionable behaviour or the appearance of it when in the employ of the government and, upon retirement from the public service, establishing a timeframe to discourage consulting and lobbying on behalf of interests previously overseen when in public employment. The lobby industry in Ottawa is replete with former members of parliament, including former ministers, former ministerial aides and former senior civil servants. See **Lobby (-ist; -ing).**

Conscription. The term commonly used in Canada for compulsory military service. The issue has always been a divisive one in Canada, particularly during the two world wars, dividing the francophone and anglophone communities. In 1917, there was considerable civil strife in Quebec when the Union government headed by Conservative Sir Robert Borden introduced conscription, manipulated the franchise and won a general election. This was one of the few instances in Canadian history when French Canadians were not represented on the government side of the House. The issue was raised again in 1940-44. Liberal Prime Minister William Lyon Mackenzie King, who had pledged opposition to conscription in the wartime election of 1940, conducted a referendum in 1942 to release the government from its pledge. Late in 1944, King sent home-service conscripts overseas. King's ambivalent position on conscription is remembered in his phrase "conscription if necessary, but not necessarily conscription."

Consensus. Agreement among members of a group that approaches, if not achieves, unanimity, without a vote. The designated head of the group defines the consensus. This approach to conflict resolution may be used in the event that unanimity is not likely, but a resolution is desired with as many members of the group as possible in agreement, thus maintaining collegiality and collective responsibility. Cabinet decisions in Canada are based on consensus. However, as prime ministers and premiers can profoundly influence the political careers of their ministerial colleagues, their personalities and views are crucial determinants in the development of the consensus.

Conservatism. Historically, a term used in Canada with reference to British Toryism or to European conservative political thought generally.

Since the 1960s, the use of the term has been confused with its contemporary meaning in the United States. In American usage, conservatism is a manifestation of early liberalism in which individualism, self-reliance and antipathy to the state are stressed, and in which progress or the improvement of the human condition is viewed as the inevitable outcome of unrestricted interaction among rational, self-interested individuals. By contrast, conservatism in the European and British tradition values order, rank and security above individual freedom, and obliges the state in the name of the community to restrain personal freedom for the common good.

In the 1990s and later, the phrase "social conservatism" became a slogan of the populist right, encompassing an ambivalent attitude toward the state: on the one hand against government interference and regulation, for example, in the economy, on equality rights for cultural minorities and gun control laws, but intense government involvement over other personal matters such as a woman's access to therapeutic abortions and the reinstatement of capital punishment.

Conservative (Progressive Conservative) party. A political party dominant in federal politics until 1896, more frequently than not the official opposition to Liberal governments during the twentieth century, and with only minor representation in the House of Commons since the election of 1993.

Begun in the 1850s as a Liberal-Conservative coalition in the United Province of Canada, the Conservative party took form as the "Confederation party" in the 1860s. At that time, ministerialism, or attachment to the patronage-dispensing government rather than to a party organization, determined the loyalty of legislators. Under the leadership of John A. Macdonald, the party was dominant until the 1890s. Since 1896, it seldom has held power federally, but is competitive in various provincial party systems. In 1988, the federal party formed a second consecutive majority government for only the first time since 1892, excepting the Union government's wartime victory in 1917. Its victory in 1984, then, was only the party's fourth majority win in the twentieth century (earlier 1911, 1930, 1958). Its defeat in 1993, when it gained 16 per cent of the vote, won only two seats and lost official-party standing in the House of Commons, was its most serious defeat. In the 1997 election, it regained official-party status winning twenty seats, but ranked after the Reform, Bloc Québécois and New Democratic parties. It rebuffed the Reform party's "unite the right" strategy when Reform transformed itself to the Canadian Alliance party in 2000, and barely managed to retain official-party status winning the minimum required twelve seats in the 2000 election with 12 per cent of the popular vote.

The Conservative party's lack of success nationally may be understood with reference to its nineteenth-century success and to the Liberal party's success in the twentieth century. The party then comprised an English-Canadian elite generally sympathetic to French-Canadian concerns, and a Quebec leadership that had the confidence of the French-Canadian population in that province. The Conservatives at that time also had a business orientation tempered by a progressive image of "the working man's party." At the level of political symbolism, the party was readily identified with Canadian nationalism. By contrast, the Liberal party lacked those characteristics in the nineteenth century, but possessed them in the twentieth.

Since the 1960s, the federal Conservative leadership—perhaps hesitatingly first under John Diefenbaker, but more assertively under Robert Stanfield and later Joe Clark—sought to integrate itself more effectively in Quebec. The party had never had a French-Canadian leader, and in the 1970s had fewer than five francophone members of parliament. In 1979, the party formed a minority government under Clark with only two MPs from Quebec elected as Conservatives, and only one of them a francophone. In the election defeat of 1980, the party elected only one MP from Quebec and gained 13 per cent of the provincial popular vote.

In 1983, the party selected Brian Mulroney, a fluently bilingual anglo-Irish Quebecker and corporate lawyer, as its leader. One year later, the party formed a majority government with sizeable representation from all regions, including Quebec (58 MPs to 17 Liberal MPs). As the Liberals and the nineteenth-century Conservatives had done earlier, Mulroney sought to reinforce Conservative power on the basis of a *Québec solide*. The prime minister appointed French Quebeckers to prominent positions in the cabinet and ensured that an appropriate level of public goods and services was allocated to that province. With constitutional reform a leading item in its agenda, the government worked sympathetically with the Liberal government in Quebec to obtain agreement among all provinces that would lead to Quebec's accommodation to the *Constitution Act*. In 1988, the government was re-elected with a reduced majority, but an increase in Quebec representation (63 to 12 Liberal MPs). In its second term, the government's Quebec strategy was doomed by the defeat of the constitutional Meech Lake Accord, the defection of Lucien Bouchard, the most prominent francophone cabinet minister and a putative successor to Mulroney, to become leader of the sovereignist Bloc Québécois, and the rejection in a country-wide referendum of the constitutional Charlottetown Accord. The party's disastrous election defeat in 1993 under Mulroney's successor Kim Campbell led to the leadership of Jean Charest, a minister in the Mulroney and Campbell cabinets, a Quebecker and the first francophone to lead the Conservative party. Party fortunes appeared to revive under Charest, given his performance in the Quebec referendum debate on sovereignty in 1995 and in the federal election campaign of 1997, but he was later wooed by the Quebec Liberal party to lead it against the sovereignist Parti Québécois now led by his former cabinet colleague, Bouchard. Joe Clark, who had earlier served as leader and briefly in 1979-80 as prime minister, returned to lead the party that was subject to a hostile merger proposal by the Reform party—

later the Canadian Alliance party—to "unite the right." In the 2000 election, the party barely managed to retain official party status, winning twelve seats including Clark's.

The Conservative party failed to alter its historic class and central Canadian image. The party retained a right-wing, upper-class, business image largely untempered by its earlier nineteenth-century image of mild progressivism. From the 1960s to the 1980s, when its leaders were successively the populist John Diefenbaker from Saskatchewan, the patrician Robert Stanfield from Nova Scotia, and the young Joe Clark from Alberta, the leadership had balanced its pro-business faction with the influence of so-called Red Tories. However, the rhetoric and action of Prime Minister Mulroney's Conservative government in economic and social policy after 1984 was dominated by policy to facilitate the restructuring of the economy in a North American context to ensure "global competitiveness." This was accompanied by government downsizing, a lessening of government regulation in the economy, a reduction in social expenditures, notably in transfer payments to the provinces for health, education and social assistance and introduction of an unpopular consumption (Goods and Services) tax. That these policies were enacted during the worst economic recession since the depression of the 1930s helped reduce the government's popularity to the lowest level of any government since opinion surveys were first conducted.

As Prime Minister Mulroney sought to establish the party's dominance through a Quebec strategy, he also hoped to establish a firm base of support in western Canada by elevating western Canadian members of parliament to prominent positions in his government and promoting western interests generally.

Neither the Conservative government's Quebec nor its western strategies succeeded. As the government fell in popularity, regional political parties rose that successfully challenged Conservative dominance in their respective regions of the country. In the 1993 election, called following the selection of Kim Campbell to succeed Mulroney, the nationalist Bloc Québécois, contesting only constituencies in Quebec, won 54 of the province's 74 seats with 13.5 per cent of the national vote, but 49 per cent of the votes in Quebec. The populist Reform party won 51 seats in western Canada and one in Ontario with 18.7 per cent of the national vote, but 43 per cent of the vote in Alberta and British Columbia together. With its 16 per cent of the total vote more evenly distributed throughout Canada, Conservative representation in the House of Commons was reduced to two MPs, including Jean Charest, who, as mentioned, succeeded Campbell as party leader.

In the 1997 election, Conservative fortunes revived somewhat, winning twenty seats, the Bloc Québécois lost some political steam with Bouchard's departure from its leadership, the Reform party failed to break out eastward from its western base, the New Democrats found new strength in Atlantic Canada and the Liberal party's majority in the House of Commons was reduced. Thus, when Joe Clark returned as party leader following Charest's departure to lead the Quebec Liberal party, he faced strategic problems familiar to Conservative leaders in the twentieth century: Quebec was still Liberal and Bloc territory, and the Reform party, later the Canadian Alliance, remained a dominant force in western Canada continuing aggressively to break through in Ontario. Although the Canadian Alliance failed to achieve significant electoral success east of Manitoba in the 2000 election, the Conservative party still faced the same problems, with the party barely gaining official-party status in the Commons. See various entries on subjects mentioned here.

Consociational democracy. A concept originating with Arend Lijphart, who sought to explain why some countries that possessed fragmented political cultures were nonetheless stable democracies. At the core of a consociational democracy is a set of leaders of important but separated groups, or subelites who choose to govern in mutually supportive ways rather than through basically competitive and stressful relationships. See his "Cultural Diversity and Theories of Political Integration," *Canadian Journal of Political Science* 4 (1971), pp1-14.

In *Democracy in Plural Societies: A Comparative Exploration* (New Haven: Yale University Press, 1977), Lijphart described Canada as a semi-consociational democracy. In Canada, the fragmentation of the political culture on ethnic grounds between English- and French-speaking Canadians is institutionalized in the federal system of government. Federal-provincial and interprovincial relations, rather than electoral and legislature-based conflicts among political parties each defined by ethnicity, constituted major consociational activity among the elite. Lijphart concluded that the Canadian political system would move either "in the direction of greater consociationalism—or in the direction of a more centrifugal regime with a partition of the country as its more likely outcome" (129).

While the concept has been used to explain tension management on the bicultural cleavage in Canada, the concept is more evident in a purer form in negotiations in the late-twentieth century regarding Native rights and constitutional reform, including the recognition of Native self-government. In this case, the leadership of prominent Native groups have negotiated, on behalf of a virtually separated Native population, with the political leadership of the non-Native population—the federal and various provincial governments.

Consolidated Revenue Fund. Money accumulated by the government of Canada which the cabinet allocates to departments and to certain public corporations with parliamentary approval. See **Budget and budgetary process.**

Constituency (riding). A geographic area defined for legislative representation. In the appointed Senate, representation is based on regional divisions defined in the *Constitution Act* (s.22). In the popularly elected House of Commons, the number and the boundaries of constituencies are determined when redistribution takes place following each decennial census (*Constitution Act*, ss.8, 51, 51A, 52). At the beginning of the twenty-first century, there were 301 constituencies, from each of which one member of parliament was elected. Provincial and territorial representation in the House was: Ontario 103, Quebec 75, British Columbia 34, Alberta 26, Manitoba 14, Saskatchewan 14, Nova Scotia 11, New Brunswick 10, Newfoundland 7, Prince Edward Island 4, Northwest Territories 1, Nunavut 1 and Yukon 1.

Constituency (riding) association. Local party organization in the constituencies of elected legislatures.

The purpose of a party's constituency association is to nominate a candidate and conduct an election campaign. Laws pertaining to campaign contributions and expenditures—for example, in federal politics the *Canada Elections Act*—require candidates of recognized parties and their designated agents to observe and maintain specific procedures and records. Otherwise, constituency organizations operate under party rules when selecting executives, nominating candidates for office, running their campaigns and conducting any other business. Party rules also designate procedures whereby constituencies may nominate delegates to party leadership and policy conventions. Particularly in large metropolitan areas, executives of several constituency associations of a party may attempt to maintain social and political activities between elections.

Not all parties have constituency associations in all ridings and some associations may exist only on paper. This might be the case where a party is virtually without popular support. But it might also be the case where a party is overwhelmingly dominant. In such cases, senior party officials advise the leader on the designation of a candidate. See **Campaign (election)**.

Constituent assembly. A group of people with the power to establish or amend a constitution or at least recommend changes to authoritative bodies.

In the aftermath of the failed attempts to amend the Canadian constitution through the Meech Lake Accord of 1987 and the Charlottetown Accord of 1992, some people argued for the establishment of a constituent assembly. The Canadian constitution can be amended only by legislatures (*Constitution Act, 1982*, Part V) and the Meech Lake Accord failed for want of approval of two provincial legislatures among the federal and ten provincial legislatures. There was popular opposition not only to the substance of the agreement, but to the process of behind-the-scenes, federal-provincial government negotiations leading to the agreement which was not to be altered by the legislatures. Consequently, the federal-provincial negotiation of the Charlottetown Accord was preceded by extensive public consultations and followed by a country-wide referendum in which it was rejected. Consequently, neither the process of executive negotiations alone nor negotiations following consultations and leading to a referendum seem workable as a means of amending the constitution. Thus, some people argued for a constituent assembly to be created by the legislatures to negotiate constitutional change with subsequent approval by the legislatures as required by the *Constitution Act*. However, the precedent of the referendum on the Charlottetown Accord suggested to others that a popular country-wide referendum on constitutional change could not be avoided.

Constitution. The basic law of a political community that defines rights and obligations of individual members of that community, establishes and describes the functions and relationships among executive, legislative and judicial institutions of that community, and a procedure for its amendment. Constitutions may be "written" documents, and may also include "unwritten" rules based on generally accepted cumulative patterns of behaviour, customs or conventions.

The Canadian constitution is drawn from several sources: the British *Constitution Act, 1867*, and subsequently amended, notably the amendment of 1982 which included the Canadian Charter of Rights and Freedoms and "domestic" amending formulae, and certain other British statutes (for example, from the Royal Proclamation of 1763 to the Statute of Westminster, 1931); certain

Canadian and provincial statutes that may be said to constitute the country's "organic law" (for example, acts dealing with the Supreme Court, citizenship, the establishment of provinces, the conduct of elections, and national emergencies); certain orders-in-council (for example, invoking legislation and enacting regulations under enabling legislation); certain fundamental values and informal practices based on custom, usage and convention (for example, the rule of law, the independence of the judiciary and responsible government); and judicial interpretation of written and common law aspects of the constitution. See various entries on subjects that are mentioned here.

***Constitution Act, 1867,* and subsequently amended**. An Act of the British Parliament that established Canada as a federal union with originally four and later ten provinces.

Titled the *British North America Act* until renamed in 1982, it describes the components of the federal, or central, government and distributes power between the two levels (federal and provincial) of government. Although it is the major written element of the Canadian constitution, it does not completely and accurately describe the constitution. Unwritten constitutional conventions supplement the Act and, in some cases, more accurately describe the constitution. Thus, a literal reading of the Act gives an inaccurate view of the country's political regime.

The succinct phrase in the preamble declaring Canada to have "a Constitution similar in Principle to that of the United Kingdom" is a better indication of constitutional behaviour than some of what follows in the Act, especially with reference to the executive and its relation to the legislature. Until 1982, with some exceptions, important sections of the Act could only be amended by the British Parliament on an address by the Canadian Parliament. In 1982, the British Parliament amended the Act on an address by the Canadian Parliament with the support of all provinces except Quebec. The 1982 amendment included several amending formulae involving only Canadian legislatures, thus patriating the Act. The amendment also included the Canadian Charter of Rights and Freedoms, against which all government action, including legislation, orders, regulations and administrative procedures can be tested in the courts, a statement on the rights of Aboriginal peoples, and a constitutional commitment to the principle of federal equalization payments to ensure sufficient revenues to the provinces to provide reasonably comparable levels of public services.

An appreciation of the constitution of Canada includes the written *Constitution Act* supplemented by unwritten convention and judicial review. For example, according to the Act, the governor general exercises supreme executive authority in Canada on behalf of the sovereign, advised by a Privy Council, members of which the governor general selects, summons and removes. The sovereign is the commander-in-chief of the military. The governor general appoints the Speaker of the Senate, all senators (who hold office until 75 years of age), and almost all judges. The governor general summons and dissolves the House of Commons and issues writs for general elections. Bills involving the expenditure of money can be introduced in Parliament only on the governor general's recommendation. The governor general may refuse assent to bills passed by Parliament and may disallow a provincial act. Generally, the same powers possessed by the governor general are also possessed at the provincial level by lieu-tenant-governors, whom the governor general appoints.

Unwritten constitutional conventions, however, describe the constitution more accurately than the *Constitution Act*. In fact, the governor general rarely acts according to personal judgment, but instead on the advice of a small component of the Privy Council—the cabinet, which is not mentioned by name in the Act and which, in turn, is selected by the prime minister, who is also not mentioned in the Act. The prime minister and other cabinet members, the government-of-the-day, must retain the support, or confidence, of the House of Commons to remain in office and must themselves have seats in the House of Commons (although some ministers may be in the Senate in addition to the government leader there). Should an election result in another party winning a majority or a significant plurality of constituencies, the prime minister would in all likelihood resign. The governor general would then ask the party-determined leader of the new leading party to form the next government.

While constitutional conventions can be altered by establishing new forms of practice or by statute, the amendment of the *Constitution Act* is complicated. Provisions for amendment, which existed prior to 1982 and involved the British Parliament, were superseded when the Act was patriated that year, with the inclu-sion of several "domestic" amending formulae outlined in Part V of the 1982 Act. The general amending formula requires a resolution of the Canadian Parliament (with majority support in each of the House of Commons and the Senate—although inaction or dissent by the Senate can be overridden by the House) and the legislatures of two-thirds of the provinces that combined have at least 50 per cent of the population of all the provinces (*Constitution Act, 1982*, ss.38, 47). A provincial legislature could avoid the effect of an amendment which derogated from its powers, rights, or privileges through an expression of dissent; and if the amendment involved the transfer of education or cultural matters from the provinces to the federal Parliament, a province could opt out with compensation (s.40).

Consent by majority vote of Parliament and all provincial legislatures is required to amend the *Constitution Act* respecting executive power (the Queen, the governor general and lieutenant-governors), minimum representation by province in the House of Commons, the use of French and English notably as official languages of Canada, the composition of the Supreme Court and, crucially, amendments to this part of the Act on amending procedures (s.41). The consent of Parliament and the legislatures of affected provinces only is required to alter boundaries between provinces and amend legislation pertaining to the use of English and French within a province (s.43). Parliament may, subject to sections 41 and 42, amend unilaterally certain sections of the constitution respecting the executive of Canada, the House of Commons and the Senate (s.44). A provincial legislature may, subject to section 41, amend its constitution unilaterally (s.45). The principle of proportionate representation of provinces in the Commons, as prescribed by the Constitution, Senate reform, the establishment of new provinces, or the extension of provincial boundaries into the territories and aspects of the Supreme Court other than its composition may be achieved through the general amending formula.

Following the referendum in Quebec in 1995 on sovereignty association, that was only narrowly defeated, the federal Liberal government of Prime Minister

Jean Chrétien, unable to pursue successfully an amendment that would accommodate Quebec to the constitution, promised that no amendment that required Parliament's approval would be introduced that lacked support of the legislatures of designated regions, including Quebec. The other "regions" were Ontario, British Columbia, the prairie West and Atlantic Canada. In the case of the last two, two thirds of the legislatures representing at least 50 per cent of population in the respective region would constitute approval (thus effectively granting the legislature of Alberta a veto in that region).

Finally, as mentioned above, the Senate has only a suspensive veto over amendments that require its support (ss.34, 41, 42, 43), including amendments affecting the method of selecting senators, provincial representation, the residence qualifications and powers of the Senate (s.42). If the Senate fails to adopt a resolution within 180 days of the House of Commons doing so, an amendment can proceed if the House adopts the resolution again after that period (s.47).

The *Constitution Act* has always been subject to judicial review. However, judicial review was considerably broadened with the 1982 amendment that included the Canadian Charter of Rights and Freedoms. Until 1949, the *Constitution Act* was subject to judicial interpretation by the Judicial Committee of the Privy Council in the United Kingdom. Since then the Supreme Court of Canada has been the final court of appeal. Until 1982, judicial review focussed almost exclusively on the jurisdictional competence of Parliament and provincial legislatures described in the Act; that is, challenges to legislation, including challenges based on common law rights and civil liberties, were tested largely against the distribution of legislative powers between the two levels of government.

Judicial interpretation defined the limits of the federal government's paramountcy, especially on the question of residual power. Generally, judicial rulings from London reduced federal power asserted in the "Peace, Order, and good Government" clause of section 91 (preamble) in favour of provincial power asserted in the "Property and Civil Rights" clause in section 92:13, while the Supreme Court later tended to reaffirm federal paramountcy either through the "Peace, Order and good Government" clause or through federal Trade and Commerce power (s.91:2).

Since 1982, however, the role of judicial review has been expanded. While each level of government remains, strictly speaking, supreme within its area of legislative competence, all government action, including executive agreements and administrative procedures and regulations of federal, provincial, territorial and municipal governments, may be tested against the provisions of the Canadian Charter of Rights and Freedoms. See various entries on subjects that are mentioned here.

Constitutional Act, 1791 (**U.K.**). The Act that superseded the *Quebec Act, 1774*, and by which Quebec was divided into Upper and Lower Canada, each colony having a British-appointed governor, advised by an appointed Executive Council, with an elected Legislative Assembly (lower house) and an appointed Legislative Council (upper house).

Several factors were involved in dividing Quebec and introducing representative government. One was the influx of Loyalists following the American Revolution who demanded political and legal rights such as they had enjoyed in the American colonies, including representative government, English common law, habeas corpus and trial by jury. The *Constitutional Act* enhanced the prospects for the survival of French culture through the establishment of Lower Canada where French-speakers would continue to comprise the majority of the population. One of the earliest acts of Upper Canada was the replacement of French civil law imposed by the *Quebec Act* (subject to local modification) with English common law, while French civil law was maintained in Lower Canada. The *Constitutional Act* was replaced in 1840 with the Union Act that established the United Province of Canada. See **Quebec Act, 1774; Union Act, 1840.**

Constitutional amendments. See **Amendment (legislative; constitutional);** *Constitution Act, 1867,* **and subsequently amended**.

"Consultative mechanisms" (forums and reports on constitutional reform). Various means used by governments in Canada in the early 1990s to obtain views from the public on constitutional reform.

   The eleven first ministers and their senior officials privately negotiated the Meech Lake Accord in 1987 to obtain Quebec's support for the *Constitution Act, 1982,* but failed to achieve unanimous provincial ratification through similar, last-minute, high-pressure negotiations in 1990. This abortive exercise in constitutional reform brought to a head public opposition to the style of federal-provincial relations known as executive or administrative federalism, which argued pejoratively that Canada's future should not be determined "behind closed doors by eleven middle-aged white men in suits." Various groups, but notably those representing the interests of Natives, women, the disabled, labour, environmentalists and the poor, argued that constitutional change should involve broadly based public consultation and approval, possibly including a referendum. Those who had voiced opposition to the Meech Lake Accord had objected to the requirement of legislatures to vote the proposal up or down without amendment. Some legislatures held no committee hearings on the Accord, while others held perfunctory hearings.

   After 1990, the federal government and several provinces organized various forums on constitutional change in which representatives of public interests were invited to participate. At the federal level, the Citizens' Forum on Canada's Future (Spicer Committee) organized hundreds of small group meetings and regional and national forums to discuss constitutional reform before presenting its *Report to the People and Government of Canada.* The federal government also established a joint parliamentary committee to study the constitutional amending formula (Beaudoin-Edwards). The government published proposals for discussion in 1991 (*Shaping Canada's Future Together*) which were examined in public hearings by another joint parliamentary committee (Beaudoin-Dobbie). The government also organized five nationally televised regional forums, including public interest group representatives, to discuss the proposals. These forums or consultative assemblies were far removed from the style of executive-dominated politics that is deeply rooted in pre- and post-Confederation Canada.

   These federal government-sponsored activities had counterparts in several provinces, notably Quebec, which set the pace for the federal response described above. With the defeat of the Quebec round of constitutional negotiations in the rejection of the Meech Lake Accord, nationalist sentiment in Quebec was revived.

The provincial Liberal government responded first with the party's Allaire report, which recommended a very decentralized federation with the federal government solely responsible only for currency, customs and excise, debt management and defence, with other responsibilities either shared or solely provincial concerns. The government established a broadly based commission, including the two major provincial parties, Liberal and Parti Québécois, and sectional interests (Bélanger-Campeau). In addition to enlarged provincial authority for Quebec, the commission recommended separation from Canada unless the "rest of Canada" proposed a satisfactory new constitutional regime, and set a deadline for a referendum in Quebec on sovereignty.

Following these public consultations, the first ministers resumed negotiations which led to the Charlottetown Accord which was rejected in a country-wide referendum in 1992. Constitutional negotiations still require federal-provincial diplomacy and constitutional amendment formally requires only the approval of Parliament and provincial legislatures. However, while executive federalism without public consultation appears now to lack legitimacy, the process of ratification by referendum also has its drawbacks. Supporters of the Charlottetown Accord, notably the first ministers, were obliged to defend a comprehensive set of compromise proposals while opponents could criticize particular components without an obligation to present a comprehensive alternative. As well, the referendum defeat makes problematic the success of future intergovernmental constitutional negotiations. In the aftermath of the rejection of the Charlottetown Accord, some people argued for constitutional negotiations through a constituent assembly as a compromise between the processes of executive federalism which led to the defeat of Meech and of direct democracy which led to the defeat of Charlottetown. See **Charlottetown Accord (1992); Meech Lake Accord (1987)**.

Consumer Price Index (CPI). A measure of change in the retail prices of goods and services bought by a representative cross-section of the population.

The CPI is published monthly by Statistics Canada. A CPI is also reported for regions and metropolitan areas. The CPI is based on seasonally adjusted spending patterns on a weighted fixed list of several hundred items which is changed from time to time better to reflect consumer behaviour. The index is reported using "a particular year = 100" reference base. Thus, the CPI is a measure of changes in the cost of living and the purchasing power of the Canadian dollar.

The CPI has considerable significance beyond that of an economic monitor. Some social benefits such as the old age pension supplement and private pension benefits are indexed to the CPI; that is, the benefit increases as the CPI rises in a given period. Also, many labour contracts include cost-of-living adjustments (COLA), which allow for wage and salary increases based on the CPI.

Continentalism. A term used pejoratively by Canadian nationalists to describe Canada-United States relations in terms of a continental region, the result of which, particularly since 1945, is for Canada to lose the capacity for independent policy making and its distinctive identity.

While the impact of continentalism could be observed in cultural terms (in the publishing, popular music, film and television industries), the debate over Canada-US relations has more often focussed on the economy and the large amount of US-based equity (ownership) capital invested in Canada. The debate on continentalism in the late 1960s and 1970s gave rise to the left-nationalist "Waffle" movement within the New Democratic party, to the centrist Committee for an Independent Canada, and to debate within the federal Liberal government and the eventual establishment of policy to review foreign investment. The alliance of economic nationalists faded until renewed in the late 1980s and 1990s in opposition to the Canada-US Free Trade Agreement and later the North American Free Trade Agreement with the United States and Mexico that sought to "harmonize" the three national economies. With the transformation of the General Agreement of Tariffs and Trade to the World Trade Organization, of which Canada is a member, Canadian nationalists are as likely to denounce economic and social "globalization" under the WTO as continentalism in North America under NAFTA. See **Canada-United States Free Trade Agreement (1989)**; **North American Free Trade Agreement (NAFTA)**; **World Trade Organization (WTO)**.

Contracting (opting) out. A provision whereby a province may remove itself from the effect of a federal-provincial agreement, usually with compensation. One example involves dissenting from a constitutional amendment; another, from shared-cost federal-provincial programs.

Under the *Constitution Act, 1982*, an amendment "that derogates from the legislative powers, the proprietary rights or any other rights or privileges of the legislature or government of a province" may be adopted without unanimous provincial consent. However, the amendment will not have effect in a province whose legislature has "expressed its dissent" (ss.38, 39). In cases where the amendment transfers provincial powers to Parliament "relating to education or other cultural matters," the federal government "shall provide reasonable compensation" to any dissenting province (s.40).

Under the *Established Programs (Interim Arrangements) Act, 1965*, provinces could withdraw from and receive financial compensation for several major federal-provincial shared-cost programs: hospital insurance, old-age assistance, allowances for blind and disabled persons, the welfare portion of unemployment assistance, technical and vocational training for young people, and the health grant program. The Act also allowed for withdrawal from several smaller and temporary programs, and was later amended to include the Canada Assistance Plan. The formula was proposed in response to objections by Quebec and other provinces to federal conditional grants in areas of provincial jurisdiction. Only Quebec exercised the option.

Controverted election. A constituency election challenged, or "petitioned," because of alleged irregularities or corrupt and illegal practices. Electoral petitions alleging corruption or irregularities that would disqualify an elected member of the House of Commons are investigated and tried without jury by two superior court justices for the province in which the disputed election took place. The judicial determination that may declare the challenged election void is, subject to appeal to the Supreme Court of Canada, final and reported to the Speaker of the House of Commons. The report to the Speaker may include an additional report which the judges feel ought to be presented to the House of Commons. If the judges differ in their determination, the member is deemed elected. Persons may subsequently be tried for corrupt or illegal practices.

Convention (constitutional). See **Custom, convention and usage**.

Convention (party). Meetings of party activists to discuss policy and select a leader or executive officers. Conventions of the Conservative and Liberal parties have been held more regularly since the early twentieth century, while the New Democratic party has a constitutional requirement for biennial conventions. In the 1990s, the populist Reform party—now the Canadian Alliance—styled its regular meetings as assemblies.

As parties of nineteenth-century origin, the Conservative and Liberal extra-parliamentary organizations developed in the twentieth century in response to requirements as defined by the parliamentary leadership. Leaders are selected for an unspecified time, but since the 1970s have been subjected to various kinds of review procedures. Resolutions adopted at Liberal and Conservative policy conventions constitute advice only to the leader. Contests at conventions for executive positions in the extra-parliamentary organization may be surrogate challenges to the leader's control of the party apparatus.

The New Democratic party succeeded the Co-operative Commonwealth Federation, a mass movement party which was established in the 1930s. The NDP constitution requires a biennial convention, styled "the supreme governing body" of the party. The convention selects a leader for a two-year, renewable term, determines policy and selects a Federal Council to act on its behalf until the next convention. The Reform party, which was founded in 1987, likewise held its assemblies approximately every 18 months. As a new conservative populist party, its very existence, policy and electoral fortunes were directly related to the personal influence of its founder-leader, Preston Manning, whose "unite the right" proposal led to the transformation of the Reform party to the Canadian Alliance party in 2000, whose initial policies and organization were similar to those of Reform.

The Liberal and Conservative experience with extra-parliamentary organization, and with conventions in particular, developed in the twentieth century generally in concert with the requisites for electoral success, given the gradual increase in population, the ongoing expansion of the franchise, and hence an increase in the number of constituencies to be organized and voters to be wooed. The development of electronic mass media of communication, especially television, and changes in election finance laws, also encouraged the expansion of membership and the holding of conventions to capitalize on attendant publicity. While the CCF-NDP experience with conventions is based in its grassroots origins outside the established political elite, that party's leadership also expected electoral benefits to flow from the appearance on television of the party in convention as dynamic and public-spirited.

Rules among all parties respecting delegate selection usually ensure outcomes that will benefit the party. The Liberals and Conservatives employ the device of the leadership appointment of numerous ex-officio delegates while the delegates from affiliated trade unions at NDP conventions usually provide a stabilizing influence over constituency and youth delegates.

Conventions to select party leaders as distinct from those to discuss policy are an awkward transplant to Canada's parliamentary party system of the presidential nomination process among parties in the United States. Ostensibly democratic compared to earlier selection of party leaders by the parliamentary caucus, the leadership convention was prone to various criticisms. In 1999 and 2000, the federal Bloc Québécois and the Canadian Alliance, respectively, selected their leaders on a one member-one vote basis rather than through a convention of representative delegates, following the mixed experience of some provincial parties that had earlier used member and mixed member/convention procedures. See **Leadership conventions (selection)**.

Co-operative Commonwealth Federation (CCF). A grassroots socialist party, founded in 1932 and reconstituted as the New Democratic party in 1961.

The CCF program was based on the Regina Manifesto, which called for "genuine democratic self-government, based on economic equality" through public ownership of major industries and government planning. In contrast to the Conservative and Liberal parties, the CCF stressed membership participation in policy making and in party finance. The party achieved its greatest success in the mid-1940s. In September 1943, a Gallup poll showed a slight lead for the CCF over the Liberals and Conservatives in national popularity. The party formed the official opposition in Ontario in the same year and won an election in Saskatchewan in 1944. However, the victory in Saskatchewan, which was repeated several times until 1964, was the only electoral breakthrough for the party. The CCF fell to third place in Ontario through the 1940s and 1950s, although it formed the official opposition in British Columbia throughout the 1950s.

Important factors in the loss of public support for the CCF included an extensive, well-organized, "Red scare" propaganda campaign. The Canadian government also conformed to the post-Second World War "Cold War" foreign policy of the United States against the ideologically left-wing Soviet Union and, later, China. Also, during the Korean War and the heyday of McCarthyism in the United States in the 1950s, the opponents of the CCF denounced the social democratic party as though it were a totalitarian left-wing organization. Finally, the 1950s were a period of improvement in the living standards of many Canadians and the CCF's criticism of capitalism seemed incongruous under such circumstances.

Consistent with changes that took place in socialist movements throughout western Europe, the CCF modified its outlook in the Winnipeg Declaration of 1956. Economic and social planning and regulation now took priority over public ownership as a means to achieve social justice. From 1958 to 1961, the CCF leadership transformed the party structure to allow for greater participation of trade unions, and generally to create an image which would be more appealing to a youthful, urban, self-perceived socially mobile, and central Canadian population. The party emerged from this process as the mildly reformist New Democratic party. See **League for Social Reconstruction; Movement parties; New Democratic party (NDP); Regina Manifesto; Socialism**.

Co-operative federalism. A political slogan associated with the federal Liberal government under Lester Pearson's leadership in the 1960s. It described a trend under Pearson to settle federal-provincial jurisdictional disputes through accommodative intergovernmental bargaining rather than through court decisions. Phrases such as "administrative" or "executive" federalism have also been used to describe federal-provincial diplomacy since then. Critics viewed the outcome of co-operative federalism as further legitimizing federal spending power in areas of provincial responsibility and thus altering the federal nature of the Canadian political system. See **Federalism**.

Council of Maritime Premiers. A body comprising the heads of government of New Brunswick, Nova Scotia and Prince Edward Island. Created in 1971, the Council possesses legal status granted by each of the Maritime legislatures to act as an agent in specific administrative matters. With its own secretariat, the Council is a permanent structure for interprovincial negotiations on joint policy proposals. The Council is an instrument to protect the respective interests of member governments as well as to organize regional programs based on shared views. See **Intergovernmental committees**.

Count (election), official and unofficial. The tabulation of votes cast in general and by-elections.

In federal elections, the deputy returning officer in each polling station conducts the unofficial count on election night, immediately after the closing of the polls. All candidates are permitted to have a representative (scrutineer) at polling stations throughout the day and during the unofficial count. After the unofficial count, the ballots in each station are returned to the ballot boxes, which are sealed and delivered to the returning officer of the constituency. The returning officer is responsible for safeguarding the boxes and ballots until conducting the official count later, at which time ballots cast by military personnel and other non-resident electors are included. In the event of a narrow victory or alleged irregularities, a judge conducts a recount. Finally, the returning officer certifies to the chief electoral officer the name of the winning candidate, the total number of votes cast for each candidate and the number of rejected or spoiled ballots.

Courts. See **Judicial system**.

Criminal Code of Canada. Law pertaining to crimes against society, rooted in large part in English criminal jurisprudence, and applied uniformly across Canada in contrast to private or civil law, which is based on the Civil Code in Quebec and on common law elsewhere.

Under the *Constitution Act*, Parliament is responsible for criminal law (s.92:14) which must conform to the Canadian Charter of Rights and Freedoms. Latter-day changes to the Criminal Code have included amendments relating to sexual orientation, abortion, bail reform, the jury system, eavesdropping on or recording of private conversations and rules regarding evidence in cases of alleged sexual assault. A notable testing of the Criminal Code against the Charter involved the voiding of provisions dealing with the procurement of therapeutic abortions (*Morgentaler, Smoling and Scott v. The Queen* [1988]). Subsequent attempts by the federal government to enact amendments to the Code on abortion failed. See **Canadian Charter of Rights and Freedoms (1982)**.

Crossing the floor. An act by which a legislator, elected as a party candidate, leaves that party voluntarily and sits "across the floor" from former colleagues as a member of another party or an Independent member.

This action results from an irreconcilable difference between the member and the party leadership, and is usually preceded by obvious signs of disaffection. It is a rare event for a member to change parties because, though defectors may be welcomed to another party, they might not be re-elected as a candidate of the new party in the same constituency. It is also a rare event for a member to become an Independent voluntarily, because elections and House procedure—including recognition by the Speaker to address the House—are based on party affiliation. Even more rare is the victory of an Independent candidate against party-affiliated candidates in a general election. In the federal election of 1997, however, an Independent candidate who had been ejected from the governing Liberal caucus in the previous Parliament did win re-election as an Independent, but was defeated in 2000.

Crown. The supreme executive authority in Canada which derives from the monarchy of the United Kingdom and therefore bears constitutional likeness to it. In fact, the Canadian monarch, sovereign, or head of state is the same person as the British monarch and is represented in Canada by the governor general.

The *Constitution Act, 1867* declares the "Executive Government and Authority of and over Canada…to continue and be vested in the Queen [Victoria]" and, by implication, her successors (s.9). British constitutional development involved the wresting of prerogative powers from the monarch by Parliament. This occurred, not through the seizure of the power of the state, but by the Crown's acceptance of advice from the prime minister and the maintenance of royal legitimacy. Today, the monarch, or the governor general as the monarch's representative (s.10), does virtually nothing except on the "advice" of constitutional advisors styled "the Queen's Privy Council for Canada" (s.11). The effective part of the Privy Council is the cabinet, the government-of-the-day, formed largely from, and with the continued confidence of, the House of Commons. See **Crown prerogatives; Governor General.**

Executive power is held by the Crown, but as Canada has a federal system of government, the Crown is represented in each province as well as in the federal level of government. In the provinces, the lieutenant-governors act virtually always on the advice of their respective Executive Councils or provincial cabinets. An important exception is that, as the office of lieutenant-governor is a federal office, the governor-in-council, or federal cabinet and effectively the prime minister, may direct a lieutenant-governor to reserve or disallow provincial legislation. See **Disallowance; Reservation**.

In the monarch and the leader of the cabinet, the prime minister (or premier in a province), Canada and the provinces have a dual executive. The Canadian monarch "reigns, but does not rule" while the political executive or cabinet rules, but formally has no authority in its own right—only as advisors to the Crown. Supporters of the monarchy and parliamentary democracy make much of this distinction, as several prerogatives remaining to the Crown, notably regarding the dissolution of a legislature and the holding of an election, and the appointment of a government, are seen as a constitutional protection against the abuse of power by a government-of-the-day. See **Crown prerogatives**.

Crown corporation. An organization that may be organized similarly to a private-sector enterprise, but which is established by specific acts or pursuant to enabling legislation of a federal or provincial legislature, and is owned by the Crown (or government).

Government appointments to boards of directors frequently have patronage overtones, while the administration of crown corporations tend to be based on professional merit. Although crown corporations report to the legislature through a designated minister, there is a so-called "arm's length" relationship with the government. Without being involved in the day-to-day operation of a crown corporation, a government can influence it through policy directives, budgetary allocations and, if necessary, legislative amendment to its statute. The legislature reviews the financial affairs of crown corporations, and officers of crown corporations may appear before legislative committees. Thus a degree of public accountability co-exists with independent corporate initiative in the achievement of public policy goals.

At the federal level, the *Financial Administration Act* establishes classes of crown corporations, each involving different degrees of independence from the government, and usually involving corporations that exist for qualitatively different purposes. Some crown corporations exist for monetary reasons (the Bank of Canada and the Canadian Mint); others to promote business generally (e.g., the Business Development Bank) or specific industries (e.g., the Canada Mortgage and Housing Corporation, Canada Wheat Board, Atomic Energy of Canada Limited); still others for cultural purposes (e.g., the Canadian Broadcasting Corporation, National Film Board, Canada Museums Corporation); for regional development (e.g., Atlantic Canada Opportunities Agency) and for purposes of national integration that cannot be achieved solely or at all through the private sector (e.g., VIA Rail and Canada Post).

As public-sector organizations, crown corporations exist to achieve public policy goals and therefore provide service ahead of, or instead of, profit. However, Canada, like many other countries, experienced a recent trend to government downsizing and the privatization of crown corporations. Prominent examples of federal government privatization include Air Canada, an international air carrier, and Petro-Canada, a major player in the "oil patch." Nonetheless, the federal government remained an active regulator of the transportation and energy industries. Thus, Canada's economy still contains a strong element of "public enterprise" and public management.

Crown prerogatives. Unrestricted by statute, a residue of discretionary authority possessed by the Crown and which is delegated to the governor general through Letters Patent, the Instrument and the Commission of Appointment. Otherwise, with the exception of the powers of reservation and disallowance of provincial lieutenant-governors, the Crown and its representatives act entirely on the advice of their Councils (cabinets), which are themselves accountable to their respective legislatures, and eventually to the electorate.

The discretionary powers, or crown prerogatives, are historically shrinking. The most important of the prerogatives remaining in Canada pertain to the Crown's role in dissolving Parliament and provincial legislatures before the expiry of the five-year term and appointing a prime minister or premier. In the twentieth century, there was only one instance of the governor general exercising such discretionary power. In 1926, the governor general, Lord Byng, refused to grant dissolution on the "advice" of Prime Minister William Lyon Mackenzie King, whose Liberal party had won only the second largest number of seats in a three-party House of Commons in an election eight months earlier. As prime minister, King had exercised the right to remain in office unless defeated in the newly elected House. Now, however, the House was debating an opposition motion of censure that King's minority government was likely to lose. Byng rejected King's request for dissolution of Parliament and another election as there appeared to Byng to be the possibility of the Conservative leader, Arthur Meighen, forming a workable alternative government even though the Conservatives, while holding more seats than the Liberals, did not have a majority either (see **King-Byng Dispute**).

A strict constitutionalist will argue that, upon their resignation—either voluntary or as a result of an election defeat— prime ministers (provincial premiers) do not have the right even to advise the governor general (lieutenant-governor) unless asked. Usually, though, an electoral outcome resulting in a prime minister's resignation also carries with it an obvious candidate as successor. A resignation in office as party leader will result in a leadership contest that will, again, present the governor general with an obvious successor as prime minister. Were, however, the prime minister to die in office and the government party not present the governor general with a clear indication of support for a successor, then an exercise of well-informed, astute, discretionary action would be necessary.

The basic constitutional obligation of the Crown is to ensure that there is a government in office that has the on-going support of the legislature. For some, crown prerogatives imply an emergency power to dismiss a government whose behaviour violates the constitution. Especially in view of the King-Byng Crisis, it appears that for a governor general or lieutenant-governor to exercise such discretionary power, the present situation would have to involve clearly a violation of a fundamental constitutional principle, and there would have to be no reasonable doubt among the public about the appropriateness of such independent action. Wise counsel to a governor general or lieutenant-governor might also be to allow time for party politicians and public opinion to resolve the matter. See **Crown**; **Governor General**; **Letters Patent**; **Lieutenant-governor**.

Cultural duality. The division of Canadian society into anglophone and francophone communities, which has been fundamental to Canadian history and constitutional development since the Conquest of 1759-60.

Britain's *Quebec Act, 1774*, which allowed Roman Catholics freedom of worship and the right to hold public office, and retained civil law in the colony, represented the earliest legislative recognition of cultural duality. The *Constitutional Act, 1791* divided Quebec into Upper and Lower Canada and granted representative government to each colony. The Civil Code was retained in Lower Canada where the population was predominantly francophone. By 1840, when the British enacted the assimilative *Union Act*, bringing the two colonies together again, French society was firmly entrenched in British North America. The outcome of the union was not assimilation, but the creation of a number of political devices acknowledging the cultural duality of the Province of Canada.

The new federal state in 1867 recognized the duality of the country through various constitutional provisions. For example, the *Constitution Act, 1867* allocated matters of cultural significance such as education, property and civil rights, and matters of a local or private nature to the provinces, which now included Quebec with its predominantly francophone population. The Act established rights for the French and English languages in Parliament, in the Quebec legislature, and in the federal and Quebec courts; and it protected minority Catholic and Protestant education rights.

Quebec's political leadership generally accepted the Confederation agreement of 1867 until the 1960s and the "Quiet Revolution" in Quebec. Since then, the leadership of that province has argued for a recognition of Quebec as a distinct society with particular needs as the only jurisdiction in Canada (indeed on the North American continent) with a predominantly French-speaking population. Demands by French-speaking Quebeckers to become "maîtres chez nous" ("masters in our own house"), have ranged from various forms of formal recognition of special status for Quebec within the federal union to a new constitution based on an independent and sovereign Quebec associated economically with the rest of Canada.

Successive Liberal and Conservative federal governments, most with significant numbers of francophone MPs from Quebec in their ranks and all with important cabinet members from Quebec, have responded to this assertive nationalism—the Liberals notably with a policy of official bilingualism through the *Official Languages Act, 1969* and a patriated citizens-rights-based constitution in 1982 that entrenched a Charter of Rights and Freedoms containing, among other things, the federal language policy and minority-language education rights.

Neither the Quebec Liberal party nor the Parti Québécois supported the provisions of the *Constitution Act, 1982*, especially the section on minority-language education and the general amending formula that denied Quebec a veto over constitutional change. Through two rounds of constitutional negotiations in the 1980s and 1990s, a Conservative government failed in its efforts to accommodate Quebec to the constitution. Failure derived not only as a result of Quebec's position, but also those of some other provincial governments and public opinion opposed to any semblance of "distinct society" status for Quebec that would grant powers to the Quebec legislature and government not held in common by the other provinces. See **Bilingualism and biculturalism; Charlottetown Accord (1992); Distinct society clause; Meech Lake Accord (1987); Patriation of the constitution.**

Custom, convention and usage. Informal rules of constitutional behaviour that do not have explicit statutory sanction, but are based on long-established observance or precedents.

Conventions are treated as obligatory practices while custom and usage denote long-established but non-obligatory practices. In Canada, many such unwritten rules of the constitution actually modify or contradict obligations based in law. For example, British constitutional conventions respecting responsible government that were adopted in most North American colonies prior to Confederation were imported into the Canadian constitution in the preamble of the *Constitution Act, 1867* ("...a Constitution similar in Principle to that of the

United Kingdom"). Those conventions define executive power better than the specific provisions of the Act: by convention, the governor general chooses as prime minister the party-designated leader of the party which commands majority support in the House of Commons and the prime minister determines the composition of the cabinet, the effective executive. Constitutional conventions also determine the relations between the executive and the legislature. For example, cabinet members must have seats in the House of Commons (with some allowances granted for members from the Senate) and a minister without a seat must be actively seeking one; the cabinet remains in office only as long as it has the support of the House; that support is based on strict party discipline and is almost always assured in majority governments; following a reasonable length of time from the previous election and the first session of the Parliament, within the statutory five-year life of a Parliament the prime minister determines when it will be dissolved and therefore the date of the next election.

Statutory constitutional power may atrophy or be altered by constitutional conventions. The federal powers of reservation and disallowance of provincial legislation are permitted under the *Constitution Act*; but they have fallen into disuse (s.90 with reference to ss.55-57, 60-61). Similarly, the statutory declaratory power of the federal government to nationalize "Local Works and Undertakings" (s.92:10[c]) has not been exercised since the Second World War. That various federal governments have been prepared formally to abandon these powers in constitutional negotiations since the 1970s illustrates that, while these powers exist in law, they are not likely to be exercised in practice—although section 26, that effectively allows the prime minister to appoint additional senators, was effected for the first time more than 125 years after the constitution's enactment. Federal spending power is an example of the formal statutory provisions of Canada's federal constitution being altered by informal behaviour. The federal government's constitutionally unrestricted taxation power compared to the limited power of provincial governments under the statutory provisions of the constitution (ss.91:3; 92:2) has allowed the federal government to involve itself in areas of provincial jurisdiction. By offering federal funding for provincial programs that meet federal standards (and later modifying that support), the federal government thus affects provincial government priorities and establishes performance standards for provincial programs.

When there is a clash between law and convention or between conventions themselves, the matter is normally resolved through the exercise of political will. There can also be resort to the judiciary. During the constitutional negotiations preceding the adoption of the *Constitution Act, 1982*, the federal government referred to the Supreme Court the constitutionality of an address to the Parliament of the United Kingdom from the Canadian Parliament that would fundamentally change the constitution, but with the support of only two of ten provinces. The Court ruled that, though the federal action was legal, it violated constitutional convention because it lacked the "substantive agreement" of the provinces (*Reference re Amendment of the Constitution of Canada*, 1981). The Court did not define the term "substantive agreement," but the UK Parliament eventually acceded to the request of the Canadian Parliament when it obtained the support of all provinces except Quebec.

Constitutional conventions may be categorized according to the degree to which they sustain a constitutional principle. For example, an important convention would be one which, if unobserved, would significantly alter the relationship of political institutions or the relationship between government and citizens. At the other end of the scale, custom and usage can refer to behaviour which, if unobserved, would simply be inadvisable. An example of important conventions would be those related most directly, for example, to the principles of responsible government and the independence of the judiciary. That a government should resign following defeat of its budget in the House would be a clear case of a fundamental, non-statutory constitutional requirement, while the appointment of only Canadians as governors general since the 1960s would make the appointment of a non-Canadian inadvisable rather than unconstitutional. Individual ministerial responsibility is an area of some controversy where the importance of a constitutional principle is relevant. A minister who communicates privately with a judge on a case for whatever reason compromises the independence of the judiciary. However, ministers have not been compelled to resign for every administrative wrongdoing. Dispute on rules of behaviour with respect to ministerial responsibility and accountability in such cases will be settled by political will, and arguments to sway public opinion will probably focus on precedents as well as principle. See entries on various subjects mentioned here.

D

Declaratory power. The authority of Parliament to take control of "Local Works and Undertakings" which are otherwise provincial responsibilities, by declaring them to be "for the general Advantage of Canada or for the Advantage of Two or more of the Provinces" (*Constitution Act, 1867*, s.92:10[c]; see also s.91:29).

Such federal control could be assumed before or after the work or undertaking was completed. The courts have interpreted "Works" broadly, to include "integrated activities" as well as "things" or "facility." The imposition of federal control over the uranium industry during and after the Second World War is a case of the broad use of declaratory power. This constitutional provision illustrates the intention of the framers of Confederation to create a centralized federation.

In constitutional negotiations since the 1970s, successive federal governments have been prepared to modify the power in section 92:10(c). Although it has not been invoked since the 1940s, provincial governments have expressed concern about federal declaratory power. For example, Alberta has voiced apprehension about the potential use of declaratory power with respect to the petroleum industry. See **Economic union of Canada**.

Delegate theory of representation. A view that legislators should represent faithfully the views or the general will of their constituents, a populist notion that would keep elected members in a distant capital more than mindful of local grassroots opinion.

The theory found support in western Canada in the early part of the twentieth century as part of a deliberate attempt to undermine the established disciplined party system in which a legislator's vote was really determined by the party leadership. Western populists contended, not without reason, that the two major federal parties, the Liberals and Conservatives, were dominated by central Canadian financial and commercial interests. Around 1920, the United Farmers parties required their candidates to commit themselves to this theory prior to their nomination. Indeed, Alberta had a provincial *Recall Act* under the populist Social Credit government until 1937 when an attempt was made to unseat the premier. In the 1990s, the Alberta-based Reform party (since 2000, the Canadian Alliance) implicitly revived the delegate theory of representation, especially with its demands for the institution of referenda, and the New Democratic party government in British Columbia actually enacted a recall measure that involves, however, a strict time limit for submitting a petition that must include signatures only of qualified electors in the relevant constituency at the time of the previous election.

The delegate theory is in contrast to the traditional representative theory of parliament, according to which legislators are elected as parliamentarians to reflect on and articulate policy in the national interest, based on their own sound judgment. However, as mentioned above, the disciplined party system usually determines the votes of most members of parliament and provincial legislatures.

Delegated power. Legislative, administrative and quasi-judicial power delegated under enabling legislation to various government bodies, such as the governor-in-council (or provincial lieutenant-governor-in-council), that is, to the cabinet or to government bodies within the jurisdiction of the legislature.

Delegated legislative power is power to enact subordinate legislation by order-in-council or regulation. Delegated quasi-judicial powers are powers held by regulatory tribunals with possibly only limited appeal to the cabinet, or appeal to the courts. The Canadian constitution does not permit the interdelegation of power, that is, the delegation of the jurisdictional competence held by a legislature of one level of government to a legislature of the level lacking jurisdictional competence. However, the Supreme Court has permitted a government of the level that possesses jurisdictional authority to delegate policy administration to an administrative body of government of the other level that lacks jurisdictional authority (Nova Scotia Interdelegation Case, 1951). Delegated power can be revoked by subsequent legislation and federal-provincial agreements that establish delegated administrative power may also be revised or terminated.

In Canada, the delegation of power within its jurisdictional competence by a legislature is the basis of the modern administrative or regulatory state and is therefore widespread. There are many examples of the interdelegation of administrative power. For example, the federal government collects personal and corporate income tax on behalf of most provinces and federal inspectors assist in the enforcement of provincial food standards. See **Interdelegation Reference**.

Delegated legislative power is so common today that the law within a particular policy area is effectively formed by these executive and administrative bodies, rather than by the legislature. The legislature's role is to pass the so-called enabling legislation authorizing a certain agency to devise, promulgate and supervise regulations "as may be deemed necessary for giving full effect" to the particular Act. The most extreme example of delegated legislative power is the

Emergencies Act, Canada's "emergency legislation." The Act gives the governor-in-council (the federal cabinet) extraordinary regulatory power during declared emergencies. The Act thus transfers from Parliament to the cabinet the emergency powers which were granted Parliament under the "Peace, Order, and good Government" clause in the *Constitution Act, 1867* (preamble, s.91).

Legislatures also delegate quasi-judicial powers. A quasi-judicial tribunal makes regulations and orders, and establishes procedures that are a mixture of law and policy, and may easily revise its regulations, orders and procedures when considered appropriate. While statutory limitations on judicial review or appeals to the cabinet in the administrative process are based on a desire for efficiency, there is considerable scope for abuse of power by ministers, civil servants and members of administrative or regulatory bodies. To deal with potential abuse, the procedures of such tribunals should be accessible to all concerned, with efficient and wide distribution of information prior to and following public hearings. In several Charter decisions, the Supreme Court has ruled that procedures and decisions of both cabinets and administrative bodies at all levels of government, including municipal government, are subject to review under the Canadian Charter of Rights and Freedoms. See **Canadian Charter of Rights and Freedoms (1982)**.

Having "enabled" the growth of the administrative state, Parliament has been slow to supervise it. Only in 1971 did Parliament pass the *Statutory Instruments Act* and establish a joint Senate and House of Commons committee on the scrutiny of regulations to examine subordinate legislation. However, such legislation is so extensive that Parliament can do little other than conduct random checks and investigate only some apparent abuses. Finally, the creation of the office of ombudsman in several Canadian jurisdictions since the 1970s was, in part, recognition by legislators that they were incapable of dealing effectively with alleged abuses by administrative tribunals exercising delegated power under enabling legislation. See **Ombudsman; Regulatory agencies (regulations)**.

Department (of government). An administrative unit, sometimes called a ministry, that exists under an Act of the legislature and is headed by a cabinet minister and staffed by civil servants. In this unit, government policy in a particular area is formulated and implemented.

The minister is the political head of the department, its representative and defender in the cabinet and the legislature. The deputy minister is the administrative head and, although holding that position at the pleasure of the government, is usually a career civil servant. Because they possess management skills as much or more so than policy expertise, the government may shift deputy ministers across departments and agencies. The deputies, associate and assistant deputies, and directors of various departmental sections or branches constitute the senior departmental civil service. In the federal government, there is a close working relationship between the senior officials and their minister, but also between the officials and the Privy Council Office whose clerk is the head of the civil service and deputy to the prime minister.

Departmental organization is usually in a state of flux. A few federal departments have remained distinct over the years, while a number have operated under different names or been amalgamated with others. Customs and Internal Revenue, for example, operated as separate departments in the early decades of

Confederation, became National Revenue early in the twentieth century, and Canada Customs and Revenue Agency at the end of the century. Justice and Finance are two of the oldest and most senior of departments, indicating a long-term interest of the federal government. Foreign Affairs, established in 1909 as External Affairs, has also had high status in the civil service. The large Health portfolio illustrates epochal change in the scope of government policy interests. Public Works and Government Services assists other government departments. In the 1990s, both Conservative and Liberal governments downsized the public administration, eliminating some departments and merging others.

Deputy minister. The appointed administrative head of a department of government. A person may have deputy minister status as a chief executive officer of an operation of government other than a department, but which also reports to Parliament through a minister. Deputy ministers of departments hold office at the pleasure of the government, but are usually career civil servants who have developed managerial expertise, rather than partisan patronage appointments.

The functions of a deputy minister are both managerial and advisory. A deputy minister is a manager, directing administrative affairs but also recommending new policy and serving as an important advisor to the minister, the political head of the department. The deputy is particularly influential in relation to the minister because, unlike the minister who has several political roles and for whom the portfolio is probably a short-term responsibility, the deputy is a full-time official and a potentially longer-term department head. The deputy minister deals with other departments in related policy and program areas and, perhaps more critically, with senior officials of the cabinet secretariat, the Privy Council Office, who co-ordinate government business at the centre and whose head, the clerk, is the most senior public administrator and deputy minister to the prime minister. Given the integrated nature of the Canadian federal system, deputy ministers are also involved with counterparts in other jurisdictions. Committees of deputy ministers comprise one of the most important strata of governmental and intergovernmental committees. The results of their consultations frequently determine the pace and outcome of respective ministerial meetings.

Thus, while the role of deputy minister may appear largely administrative and managerial, a deputy minister's political role is also important. Administrative and managerial tasks may be delegated to the ranks of permanent assistant deputy ministers and directors as the deputy pays greater attention to the political role of that office both within the administration and in relation to other jurisdictions. Clearly, however, the minister is politically accountable, and an effective minister-deputy minister relationship involves an understanding and agreement as to their respective roles and mutual trust in each other's conduct in carrying out an agreed-upon agenda for the department.

Since the 1960s, the rank of federal deputy minister has been diminished somewhat in status, although it nonetheless remains high. This diminution of influence has occurred given an increase in the number of deputy ministers and the subsequent diminution of collegiality and an increasing bureaucratic competitiveness among them; the growth of ministerial political staffs, notably the increase in influence of the Prime Minister's Office; a greater role for other central agencies, such as the Privy Council Office and the Treasury Board Secretariat and the need to respond to various parliamentary commissioners respecting auditing, official-language policy, access to information and privacy legislation. Also the public generally has less confidence in government and is therefore less charitable towards both politicians and officials. It is a more common practice than in the past for deputy ministers to appear before parliamentary committees to answer for perceived administrative and policy shortcomings, though their political ministers are still responsible for defending government policy. Increasingly, there is a tendency for governments to rotate deputy ministers and sometimes to establish periodic exchanges with counterparts in the private sector. Especially when a new party takes office, it may suspect that its senior advisors in the administration were too closely involved with the outgoing government and its policies, and therefore shuffle some senior personnel in the administration and rely more heavily at least initially on its partisan political staff. While a dynamic equilibrium will eventually be established as a government party remains in office, the relationship among senior officials and political staff and among officials themselves will always be complex and sensitive.

Deregulation. The reduction or elimination of government control and supervision of private-sector economic activity.

Deregulation was a significant item on the agenda of the federal Conservative government of the 1980s and 1990s, and various provincial governments as well, which also included the privatization of selected crown corporations, reduction in government transfers to individuals and provincial governments, and reductions in levels of personal and corporate income tax. Notable areas of federal deregulation included the air transportation, energy and finance industries. Supporters of deregulation contended that "excessive" government regulation added to costs and protected companies from the "rigours" of competition, to the disadvantage of consumers. Also, deregulation was intended to make Canadian firms more innovative and competitive internationally. Critics argued equally adamantly that becoming competitive within an unregulated global economy would impair national sovereignty, the environment, social security benefits and public well-being. In the early years of the following decade, however, there were indications among the Canadian public of increasing concern about the reduction in "social investment" by federal and provincial governments, notably in health care and education.

Direct (indirect) taxation. Under the *Constitution Act, 1867*, direct taxation is the source of provincial revenue (s.92:2), including such taxes as personal and corporate income tax, and property and sales taxes. Defined by the Judicial Committee of the Privy Council in the manner of John Stuart Mill, a direct tax is a tax "demanded from the very persons who it is intended or desired should pay it" (*Bank of Toronto v. Lambe*, 1887).

This power, however, is not held exclusively by the provinces. Interpreting section 91:3 of the *Constitution Act* ("The Raising of Money by any Mode or System of Taxation"), the courts have agreed that the federal government has the power to levy both direct and indirect taxes. Thus, the provincial governments have access only to direct taxation, while the federal government has access to both direct and indirect taxation. Section 121 of the Act prohibits provincial tariff barriers and section 125 exempts public land or property belonging to "Canada or any Province" from taxation.

The revenue needs of the provinces increased significantly during the twentieth century to meet public policy needs within their jurisdictional competence in fields such as health, education and social assistance. But their independent access to revenue fields did not. Since the Second World War, the federal government has made significant transfer payments to the provinces in the form of conditional and unconditional grants, exercising a so-called spending power. Prior to the war, the provinces, though responsible for such areas as education, roads and unemployment relief, were clearly incapable of funding the necessary programs. The federal government appointed the (Rowell-Sirois) Royal Commission on Dominion-Provincial Relations in 1937. In 1940, the Commission recommended a shift of government functions and powers of taxation to the federal government and the introduction of a program of unconditional equalization payments. The report was not received enthusiastically by the provinces. However, it represented a departure point from the years of the fiscal straitjacket of the *Constitution Act* that, in the nineteenth century, gave the level of government with the least access to revenue some of the most costly legislative obligations of the twentieth century, and began the era of administrative, or executive federalism. See **Federal-provincial tax-sharing agreements (fiscal federalism); Rowell-Sirois Royal Commission on Dominion-Provincial Relations (1937-40); Spending power**.

Disallowance. The voiding of provincial legislation by the governor-in-council, that is the federal cabinet and more specifically the prime minister, on the recommendation of the minister of justice within one year of the receipt of the provincial Act. The power of disallowance is based in the federal government's appointment and control of the office of lieutenant-governor in the provinces. It mirrors a function of the imperial government in 1867 regarding the Canadian government (*Constitution Act, 1867*, ss.56, 58, 60, 61) and illustrates the intention of the framers of Confederation that Canada be a centralized, federal state.

Although frequently used in the early years of Confederation, federal disallowance power fell into disuse in the early twentieth century. In the late 1930s, however, the federal government disallowed many statutes dealing with federal matters which had been enacted under the Social Credit government in Alberta. Asked by the federal government for a reference on such powers, the Supreme Court declared the powers of disallowance and reservation to be unimpaired (Disallowance and Reservation Case, 1938).

The notion of the federal government as a paternalistic watchdog of the provinces is now out of fashion. The power of disallowance has not been exercised since 1943. By the 1970s, the federal Liberal government was willing to abandon both disallowance and reservation in a new constitution. In 1977, the government rejected suggestions that it disallow Quebec's *Official Language Act* (Bill 101), preferring to leave the matter to the courts and to the provincial electorate. See **Reservation**.

Discretionary power. Power to act on the basis of one's own judgment. Institutional discretionary power is found in the Canadian political system in the office of governor general in the form of crown prerogatives (the residue of authority unrestricted by statute) and in the quasi-judicial powers granted ministers and administrative tribunals under enabling legislation. The exercise of such power, both substantive outcome and procedure, may be tested in the courts against the provisions of the Canadian Charter of Rights and Freedoms. See **Canadian Charter of Rights and Freedoms (1982)**; **Crown prerogatives**; **Delegated power**; **Regulatory agencies (regulations)**.

Dispute settlement mechanism. Procedures under provisions of the Canada-United States Free Trade Agreement (1989) and later of the North American Free Trade Agreement (1992), but also under the World Trade Organization (successor to the General Agreement on Tariffs and Trade—the GATT), to administer the settlement of international trade disputes.

Challenges arise respecting anti-dumping and countervailing duties, internal subsidies and other domestic policies applied in one country against imports from another, or which grant preferences to imports from some countries over the same product from others, or that allegedly protect or enhance unfairly domestic industries with respect to foreign counterparts. Canada has been on both ends of such disputes, winning some cases and losing others. Dispute settlement mechanisms are heralded by supporters of "freer" international trade as a major factor in improving international relations generally; critics, however, view "free trade" as part of the "globalization" movement that strengthens the competitive advantage of large, multinational corporations centred in the developed regions over smaller businesses and national governments, especially those in less developed regions. See **Canada-United States Free Trade Agreement (1989)**; **North American Free Trade Agreement (1992)**; **World Trade Organization (WTO)**.

Dissolution of Parliament (the Legislature). The termination of a current Parliament, or of a provincial or territorial Legislature, with the issuance of writs for a general election to the lower house of Parliament, the House of Commons, or to a provincial or territorial legislature. (The upper house of the bicameral Canadian Parliament, the Senate, is an appointed body; all provincial and territorial Legislatures are unicameral.) Dissolution occurs automatically five years from the date of the return of the writs for the previous general election, or sooner on action by the governor general (lieutenant-governor), normally on the advice of the prime minister (premier). Only once in this century has the governor general refused a request from a prime minister to dissolve Parliament and instead appointed another government from the same House of Commons. A Parliament (provincial legislature) may be extended "in time of real or apprehended war, invasion or insurrection," if so voted by at least two thirds of the members of the House of Commons (Legislative Assembly) (*Constituion Act, 1982*, s.4). See **Crown prerogatives**; **King-Byng Dispute**.

Distinct society clause. A provision found first in the failed Meech Lake Accord of 1987 (later in the Canada Clause of the Charlottetown Accord of 1992 which was defeated in a country-wide referendum) that the Constitution be "interpreted in a manner consistent with...the recognition that Quebec constitutes within Canada a distinct society" and that affirmed "the role of the Legislature and

Government of Quebec to preserve and promote the distinct identity of Quebec....." The Meech Lake Accord, which resulted from a so-called "Quebec round" of federal-provincial constitutional negotiations, also affirmed the role of Parliament and all provincial Legislatures "to preserve" French-speaking minorities in provinces outside Quebec and the English-speaking minority in Quebec as "a fundamental characteristic of Canada."

Supporters of the Accord argued that the interpretive distinct society clause gave the National Assembly of Quebec no additional powers and none not possessed by other provinces, though it might be of some significance in future debate over the distribution of legislative powers between the federal and provincial governments. Opponents of the Accord felt otherwise.

The recognition of Quebec as a distinct society was one of five requirements established by the Quebec Liberal government in 1985 to obtain its consent to the *Constitution Act, 1982*. While the defeat of the Accord involved other criticisms, opposition to the distinct society clause was the focus of criticism, especially after the Quebec government invoked the notwithstanding clause of the Canadian Charter of Rights and Freedoms to protect its official-language law following a successful court challenge in 1988.

The Charlottetown Accord reached by the federal, provincial and territorial governments, and Native groups in 1992, in a subsequent so-called "Canada round" of negotiations, included a Canada Clause which required that the Constitution, including the Canadian Charter of Rights and Freedoms, be interpreted "in a manner consistent with" specified "fundamental characteristics." They included a definition of the "distinct society" of Quebec "which includes a French-speaking majority, a unique culture and a civil law tradition." The Clause then affirmed the Quebec government and legislature's role "to preserve and promote the distinct society of Quebec." Nothing in the Clause was to derogate from the powers of Parliament or the provincial legislatures. The Charlottetown Accord was defeated in a country-wide referendum, notably in six provinces, among them Quebec where nationalist francophones argued that the Accord represented "less than Meech." See **Charlottetown Accord (1992); Charter of the French Language (Quebec); Meech Lake Accord (1987).**

Division (distribution) of powers. The legislative competence of the federal and provincial levels of government, respectively, as outlined in the *Constitution Act* and interpreted by the Judicial Committee of the Privy Council (JCPC) until 1949, and the Supreme Court of Canada.

The division of legislative powers, which is fundamental to any federal system, is the source of much political dispute and controversy. Canada's *Constitution Act* grants broad residual power to the central or federal government to make laws for "the Peace, Order, and good Government of Canada in relation to all Matters not coming within the Claims of Subjects by this Act assigned exclusively to the Legislatures of the Provinces" (s.91, preamble). The Act then enumerates matters of federal competence—"but not so as to restrict the Generality of the foregoing"—including such significant fields as the regulation of trade and commerce (91:2), the raising of money by any mode or system of taxation (:3), currency (:14), banking (:15), defence (:7) and the criminal law (:27). See **Residual power**.

The enumerated legislative powers of the provinces (s.92) are not preceded by such a comprehensive phrase as the "Peace, Order, and good Government" clause mentioned above. The powers of the provinces include: direct taxation within the province for provincial purposes (92:2), the amendment of provincial constitutions, except the office of lieutenant-governor (:1), property and civil rights (:13), the administration of justice (:14), municipal government (:8), and most hospitals (:7). In section 93, the Act refers to provincial rights and obligations in education. While section 109 placed natural resources in the provinces under provincial jurisdiction, the federal "trade and commerce" power permitted federal involvement given the cross-border marketing of those resources. Section 92A on non-renewable resources and electrical energy, adopted in 1982, granted additional revenue-raising and resource-management powers to the provinces, without compromising established federal authority.

Section 95 establishes agriculture and immigration as powers to be held concurrently by both levels of government. An amendment in 1951 added old age pensions to concurrent powers. In disputed cases, the federal legislation takes precedence in agriculture and immigration while the provincial legislation takes precedence in the matter of pensions. Section 132 refers to the treaty-making powers of the federal government, which have been modified by the Court in consideration of the enumerated powers in sections 91 and 92. See **Treaty power**.

The Act also grants the federal government extraordinary powers over the provinces. Section 56 allows the governor-in-council (federal cabinet) to disallow provincial legislation, and sections 58-61 create the "federal" office of lieutenant-governor in each province. The lieutenant-governor has the power to reserve any provincial bill for consideration by the governor-in-council. Section 92:10[c] permits Parliament to nationalize any "local work or undertaking" in a province simply by declaring it "to be for the general Advantage of Canada or for the Advantage of Two or more of the Provinces." These federal powers, however, have fallen into disuse and successive federal Conservative and Liberal governments have offered in constitutional negotiations to abandon them. See **Declaratory power; Disallowance; Reservation**.

Until 1982, the history of Canadian federalism was basically an account of disputes over the division of powers. Generally, from the 1880s to the 1930s, federal powers waned due to judicial decisions weakening the "Peace, Order, and good Government" clause and strengthening the "Property and Civil Rights" clause, and defining the scope of the criminal law and treaty-making powers of the federal government. Indeed, some argue that the JCPC effectively rewrote the *Constitution Act*, interpreting it literally and ignoring the centralist intentions of its framers. Others maintain that the JCPC protected the federal nature of the union. More sensitive to the contemporary needs of Canadian society than the JCPC, the Supreme Court, which has been the final constitutional arbiter since 1949, has sought to reconcile the federal constitution to those needs. For example, in 1951 the Supreme Court declared that neither Parliament nor any provincial Legislature could directly delegate its power to the other level (*Nova Scotia Delegation Reference* [1951]), although indirect delegation was allowed from a legislature of jurisdictional competence at one level to an administrative agency at the other level that lacked jurisdictional competence (*PEI Potato Marketing Board v. H.B. Willis Inc. and A.G. of Canada*, 1952). See **Judicial Committee of the Privy**

Council; Supreme Court of Canada. Canadian federalism since 1982 still involves jurisdictional disputes, but circumscribed by the Supreme Court's additional role of testing government action at all levels against the Canadian Charter of Rights and Freedoms. See **Canadian Charter of Rights and Freedoms (1982)**.

In the latter part of the twentieth century, the federal and provincial governments devised ways other than legal confrontation to finance costly programs in policy fields of provincial jurisdiction that many provinces could not afford, given their limited power of taxation and weak tax base compared to the federal government's greater power of taxation and access to revenue. Policy fields such as health, education and social assistance which were considered by the framers of the federal constitution in the nineteenth century to be either minor or of primarily regional concern became matters of major concern for the twentieth-century public. Variously styled co-operative, administrative, or executive federalism, federal-provincial diplomacy since the 1960s has occasionally included references to the court for jurisdictional rulings (for example, on offshore mineral rights) to facilitate federal-provincial negotiations and agreements. See **Federal-provincial tax-sharing agreements (fiscal federalism); Spending power**.

Nonetheless, the provinces remain jealous of their jurisdictional powers. All provinces are attentive to additional incursions by the federal government and some are particularly sensitive to maintaining the principle of jurisdictional equality among provinces, especially in view of Quebec's demand for constitutional recognition of its distinctiveness within the federation. Constitutional negotiations following constitutional patriation in 1982 focussed on the division of powers, including the federal disallowance, reservation, declaratory, spending and residual powers; federal withdrawal from certain policy areas such as labour training, housing, forestry and mining; the possibility of federal and provincial constitutional agreements in the fields of immigration and culture; permission for interdelegation of powers; and a provincial role in nominations to the Supreme Court and important federal agencies such as the central bank, the Bank of Canada. Because the constitution was effectively patriated—without Quebec's assent—through the adoption of a domestic amending formula involving various combinations of the federal and provincial legislatures, revision of the formula has also been a prominent item on the constitutional agenda. In the 1990s, the federal and provincial governments negotiated federal withdrawal from some lesser policy fields without constitutional amendments.

Division of the House. The recording of votes in a legislature. In the House of Commons, the Speaker first puts a question to a voice vote and announces a decision. If at least five members rise to request a recorded vote, the Speaker orders "Call in the members," and division bells ring to summon members to the chamber. Divisions are carried by the majority of the members present. Until electronic voting is introduced, members must stand for identification when their votes are recorded and then resume their seats.

In the case of majority governments, the disciplined party system and the ever-watchful eye of the government party's whip ensures that the results of divisions are normally won by the government. Therefore an opposition party usually forces recorded votes on questions of confidence and second reading of bills or amendments to legislation which are important to the party. In the case of minority governments which do not control the majority of members, the mutual agreement of each party's house leader to house business, including votes, and the careful assurance of attendance or absence of members by each party's whip, are important for the government's survival on divisions of the House. At least for a short period following a general election that results in a "house of minorities," parties are likely to co-operate to avoid the censure of public opinion.

Members who expect to be absent during a vote may, with the approval of the party whips, "pair" with a member of parliament on the other side of the House. In such a case, neither MP votes; thus, the government's and opposition's relative strength remains unaffected. "Pairing" is obviously more important when a minority government is in office and members must be absent from the House on public or private business.

Dominion (of Canada; government; status; Day). A now seldom-used term with reference to Canada as "One Dominion under the Crown of the United Kingdom" comprising several provinces (*Constitution Act, 1867*, preamble and s.3 [before 1982, the *British North America Act*]) or to the national, federal, or central government, or Parliament of the Dominion.

Created as a Dominion within the British Empire, Canada's "dominion status" refers to the autonomy possessed by Canadian authorities with respect to the imperial government or Parliament of the United Kingdom at a given time (see **Statute of Westminster [U.K., 1931]**). In 1879, the Canadian, or Dominion, Parliament established July 1, the day the BNA Act came into effect in 1867, as Dominion Day. The term was largely abandoned in the late-twentieth century because of the pejorative overtone of "domination" and of its French equivalent, "Puissance," both externally with respect to the United Kingdom and internally with respect to federal-provincial relations. The country is simply known as Canada. The dominion or central government is commonly referred to as the federal government, and dominion-provincial conferences as federal-provincial conferences or as conferences of first ministers. Since the patriation of the constitution in 1982, Confederation has been celebrated on July 1 as Canada Day.

Dominion-provincial conferences. Referred to later as federal-provincial conferences and still later as conferences of first ministers, meetings involving the prime minister and provincial premiers or their representatives, held in 1927, 1935, 1945-46, 1957 and 1960-61. The term federal-provincial conference now also refers to innumerable meetings involving not only the heads of government but also ministers with particular portfolios, or senior officials of particular departments or with particular policy responsibilities.

Most of the conferences which were styled dominion-provincial concerned the division of legislative powers and the search for agreement on a "domestic" amending formula for the *Constitution Act, 1867*. For example, the Dominion-Provincial Conference on Reconstruction of 1945-46 concerned the report of the (Rowell-Sirois) Royal Commission on Dominion-Provincial Relations, which was established by the dominion (federal) government in 1937 and which recommended in 1940 wider policy responsibility and powers of taxation for the dominion (federal) government. See **Intergovernmental committees**.

Double majority. A procedure requiring approval within a political unit of a majority of members of each designated sub-unit. For example, the "double majority" convention existed in the nineteenth century in the United Province of Canada which had two sections equally represented in the legislature—the predominantly francophone Canada East (Quebec after Confederation in 1867) and the predominantly anglophone Canada West (later Ontario).

Following the adoption of responsible government in 1848, a convention developed whereby the government was required to have the support of the majority of members of both sections of the colony's legislature and not just a majority of the legislature as a whole. The device was a contributing factor to political deadlock which led to negotiations between Canada and the Maritime colonies in the 1860s, culminating in Confederation in 1867.

Duff Doctrine (constitution). A judicial opinion in 1938 that the preamble of the *British North America Act, 1867* (since 1982, the *Constitution Act*), which asserts that Canada is to have a constitution similar in principle to that of the United Kingdom, precludes provincial legislatures from restricting "free public discussion of public affairs, notwithstanding its incidental mischiefs…" and other rights essential to the operation of parliamentary government, while Parliament "possesses authority to legislate for the protection of this right…" (*Reference re Alberta Statutes* [1939]).

The so-called Duff Doctrine is associated with Chief Justice Duff, who wrote the decision in the Reference concerning the Alberta *Accurate News and Information Act, 1937*, which would have subjected newspapers to government censure and required "corrections" of stories. The doctrine was written as an *obiter dictum*, that is, as an opinion which was not central to the decision on the case and therefore represented only a guide for subsequent judicial interpretations. Because Duff based federal competence in the "powers requisite for the protection of the constitution itself," he felt that Parliament could only protect and not itself restrict the right of free public discussion of public affairs. Duff's view was reasserted subsequently in several decisions by other justices of the Supreme Court regarding provincial legislation. However, until 1982, legislation affecting civil liberties in Canada was tested in the courts largely against the federal-provincial division of powers in the *British North America Act, 1867*. In 1982, the Canadian Charter of Rights and Freedoms was constitutionally entrenched in the *Constitution Act, 1982*, and all government legislation as well as executive and administrative orders, regulations and procedures can now be tested against the provisions of the Charter.

E

Economic nationalism. A phrase associated with the opinion, especially widespread during the 1960s and 1970s, that the federal and provincial governments should act to slow the rate of increase and reduce the amount of non-resident equity (ownership) capital in the Canadian economy, thereby reversing the "continentalist" policies of federal governments since 1945.

Since the 1980s, economic nationalists have generally opposed continental trade agreements, as well as the "globalization" of international trade agreements such as those of the World Trade Organization, whose binding decisions restrict the options available to federal and provincial governments in responding to domestic socio-economic needs.

The roots of late-twentieth century economic nationalism may be found in the report of the federal (Walter Gordon) Royal Commission on Canada's Economic Prospects in the 1950s and in Gordon's later career in the federal Liberal government of the 1960s. Important in the latter were his abortive "foreign take-over" tax when he was minister of finance in 1963, and a Gordon-commissioned study on foreign ownership by economist Mel Watkins (1968). A House of Commons committee (Wahn) report in 1970 and a government review (Gray) the following year added fuel to the fires of controversy. Kari Levitt's *Silent Surrender: The Multinational Corporation in Canada* (Toronto: Macmillan Co. of Canada Ltd., 1970) was an important academic work on the subject at the time.

The greatest pressure from outside the Liberal government came from the political left and was organized originally as a faction within the New Democratic party. Its founders, Watkins and historian James Laxer among them, styled the group "the Waffle" because they initially hesitated at its founding in the late 1960s to argue for extensive public ownership as a solution to foreign control of the economy. In 1969, the Waffle attempted unsuccessfully to have the federal NDP adopt its manifesto. In 1971, Laxer unsuccessfully challenged veteran New Democrat David Lewis for the federal party leadership. In 1972, the Ontario NDP denounced the Waffle as an unacceptable "party within a party" and forced the group from the party.

The Committee for an Independent Canada, which was also established at this time, comprised mostly Liberals and Conservatives. Walter Gordon and Conservative organizer and fundraiser Eddie Goodman were prominent in the CIC's ranks at its founding. Publisher Mel Hurtig and economist Abraham Rotstein were also prominently associated with the organization.

The federal government and some provincial governments did respond to the issues raised by the economic nationalists. The most notable federal responses were the introduction of the Canada Development Corporation, designed to develop Canadian-owned and managed private corporations and investment opportunities for Canadians, and the Foreign Investment Review Agency, to assess the benefit to Canada of proposed foreign purchases of established Canadian companies or new businesses.

Economic nationalism waned in the late 1970s and 1980s, especially during the period of Conservative government from 1984-1993, but continues in views expressed notably by the Council of Canadians. The Conservatives concentrated on reducing government's role in the economy generally, defeated the opponents of its Canada-United States free trade agreement in its re-election in 1988, and negotiated the North American Free Trade Agreement with the US and Mexico in the 1990s. Upon their return to office in 1993 and following their re-election in 1997, the Liberals essentially continued Conservative economic policy, focussing on the elimination of the budget deficit, encouraging other free-trade agreements and generally encouraging free trade through such organizations as the World Trade Organization. See **Continentalism; Globalization**.

Economic union of Canada. One of the major objectives of Confederation in 1867, the creation of an integrated economy and common market in British North America. The *Constitution Act, 1867* prohibits provinces from establishing tariff barriers against each other's products (s.121) and grants jurisdiction to the federal Parliament in matters crucial to establishing and maintaining an economic union, notably trade and commerce, banking and currency, patents, interprovincial transportation, and immigration (s.91). By the late-twentieth century, however, provincial governments had established a variety of barriers to the mobility of labour, capital, goods and services.

During constitutional negotiations in the early 1990s, the federal Conservative government failed to obtain provincial support to revise section 121, which would have granted new federal power "to make laws for the efficient functioning of the economic union." Under the proposal, federal legislation on management of the economy would have required the support of "at least seven provinces representing 50 percent of the population," with a restrictive opting-out procedure. The proposal was designed "in the face of recent and ongoing continental and global economic change" ("Shaping Canada's Future Together: Proposals," Supply and Services Canada, 1991). Large-business organizations supported the federal proposal, but various interest groups representing, for example, women, labour, the poor and environmentalists, joined provincial governments in opposing it. In 1993, the newly elected Liberal government continued Conservative efforts to eliminate internal trade barriers but without resorting to constitutional amendments. Although a federal-provincial framework agreement was reached to prevent discrimination against the mobility of goods, services, labour and investment capital across provincial borders, conflicts still arose between provinces concerning various discriminatory practices.

Electoral Boundaries Readjustment Act **(redistribution).** Provisions for the drawing of boundaries of constituencies in the House of Commons, following the redistribution of seats based on population distribution according to the decennial census. An important object of the Act is to remove the task from the government to independent commissions, one for each province and the territories. Otherwise, the business of drawing electoral boundaries would have been left in the hands of politicians in office who would be tempted to establish constituency boundaries to maximize electoral support for their party (to gerrymander the boundaries).

Each of the federal boundary commissions, which are established after each census, comprises three members: a judge, appointed by the provincial chief justice, who takes the chair, and two others appointed by the Speaker of the House of Commons—usually an academic, the provincial chief electoral officer, or another nonpartisan official. The chief electoral officer calculates the number of constituencies to be assigned to each province and territory (redistribution) following rules in the *Constitution Act, 1867* as amended by the *Representation Act*, and prepares maps showing the distribution of population in each province. Each commission exercises impartial judgment in drawing boundaries of the allocated constituencies according to the *Electoral Boundaries Readjustment Act.*

Malapportionment, in which some constituencies are overpopulated relative to others, is generally tolerated for geographic reasons, particularly between densely and sparsely populated parts of a province, with consideration for accessibility and rate of population growth, but also for socio-political reasons, recognizing community or diversity of interests of the inhabitants of a particular area. Federal legislation permits a deviation in constituency size normally not greater than plus or minus 25 per cent of the determined national electoral quotient, or average number of voters per constituency in the country. However, in 1991 the Supreme Court upheld Saskatchewan's legislative mandating of consideration of nonpopulation factors (in that case, allowing the overrepresentation of rural voters) as distinct from the principle of voter equality under the Canadian Charter of Rights and Freedoms.

Preliminary recommendations of the commissions are subject to public comment. Following the hearings, the chief electoral officer transmits the final reports to the Speaker of the House for tabling. Members then have approximately thirty sitting days to object to the proposed changes. Naturally, members of parliament and the political parties are soon familiar with changes proposed for their seats, applying the previous election results to the proposed constituencies. If unsuccessful at the preliminary stage, objections supported by 10 MPs can be filed with the Speaker, debated, and a copy of the debate sent to the relevant commission for review. Finally, each report is adopted by order-in-council.

The process of federal boundary readjustment or redistribution is lengthy. Redistribution based on the 1961 census was completed for the 1968 election, redistribution based on the 1971 census was used first in the 1984 election and data from the 1981 census were first used in the 1988 election. The election in 1997 was the first based on the 1991 census, a Conservative majority in the Senate having defeated legislation passed by the Liberal majority in the House of Commons to delay implementation.

Given the length of time between the census and redistribution, and the process of urbanization in Canada, the tolerated malapportionment between urban and rural areas tends to be accentuated, with urban populations being considerably underrepresented, notably in British Columbia, Alberta and Ontario. In 1992 the (Pierre Lortie) Royal Commission on Electoral Reform and Party Financing recommended greater adherence to the principle of proportionate representation while respecting the constitutional protection of provinces with smaller populations. See ***Carter v. Saskatchewan (A.-G.) (1991); Gerrymander; Malapportionment; Redistribution (electoral).***

Electoral law (controls; subsidies). Provincial and federal election laws that variously provide tax credits for contributions to parties and candidates, control expenditures, provide for public disclosure of names of financial supporters, allow access to the mass media and limited compensation for designated election expenses from the public treasury, control "third party" advertising and set rules regarding the disclosure of results of public opinion surveys .

There continues to be debate over the effectiveness of legislation in different jurisdictions. For example, because the expenditure ceilings are usually in effect only following the issuance of writs for an election, there is considerable uncontrolled pre-campaign activity. The federal *Canaada Elections Act,* for example, exempts expenditures on research from the limits on campaign expenditures, including omnibus surveys, focus-group tests and daily tracking of public opinion. The publicly supported mailing and constituency office privileges of sitting members, and a government party's access to the treasury for government advertising campaigns, represent pre-writ advantages over challengers.

Legislative limitations in federal elections on participation by "third parties," that is, individuals and groups other than registered political parties, their candidates, constituency associations, and their agents, have been successfully challenged in the courts as violations of fundamental freedoms protected in the Canadian Charter of Rights and Freedoms. In 1984, the Alberta Supreme Court ruled that federal legislation permitting only registered parties and their candidates to spend money in federal elections violated fundamental freedoms protected in the Canadian Charter of Rights and Freedoms (*National Citizens' Coalition v. A.-G. of Canada*). The ruling was not appealed and, though the ruling applied only to federal elections in Alberta, the prohibition was not enforced elsewhere, and federal campaigns prior to the campaign of 2000 were conducted with third-party or direct interest group participation. The 1988 campaign was noteworthy for the controversial participation of organizations other than registered political parties either in support of or opposition to the Canada-United States Free Trade Agreement (FTA). Thus, while there were financial and advertising controls on parties, including a twenty-four-hour moratorium before election day, there were no controls on other organizations. Because only the Conservative party was defending the FTA while the Liberal and New Democratic parties were opposing it, it is generally thought that the Conservatives were advantaged by the third-party campaigning in support of the FTA, either reinforcing the intentions of Conservative supporters or causing pro-FTA Liberals to vote Conservative.

Following the 1988 election, the federal Conservative government established the (Pierre Lortie) Royal Commission on Electoral Reform and Party Financing. In 1992, the Commission made wide-ranging proposals on the conducting of federal elections, including party and candidate financing, and restrictions on third-party participation that it felt would survive a court challenge. It also proposed controls regarding the selection of party leaders and election candidates.

Scholarly studies of the effects of third-party advertising in Canada have generated mixed results. Some studies have concluded, for example, that the Conservatives might have been helped by third-party campaigning in 1988, or that the effects of the pro- and anti-advertising cancelled each other, thus no cumulative effects. Studies on effects in specific constituencies targeted by third parties concluded that the problem was over-estimated, especially as election campaigns in Canada tend to be broadly focused, and in the multi-party system a campaign directed against a particular party candidate would not necessarily result in a vote for a group's preferred party candidate.

Despite the recommendations of the Royal Commission and subsequent amendments to federal legislation, courts at the provincial level continued to rule that, while fairness in election campaigning is an appropriate objective of legislation, there is no firm evidence that third-party activity is harmful. Nonetheless, the federal government renewed attempts to limit third-party expenditures in federal elections and to prevent collusion between third parties and political parties, in further amendments to the *Canada Elections Act* in 1999. The amendments imposed strict registration, expenditure and reporting requirements on third parties. A third party that spends more than $500 must register, and can spend up to $3,000 in a constituency, but no more than $150,000 in total. Contributions received for election advertising six months prior to the election must be reported, with names and addresses disclosed of those who contribute more than $200. The government might have been influenced by a decision of the Supreme Court of Canada that sustained the principle of limitations on third-party campaigning in Quebec's referendum law. In *Libman v. Quebec (Attorney general)*, the Court ruled in 1997 that the limits on "independent spending" in Quebec's referendum law, though a violation of section 2 of the Canadian Charter of Rights and Freedoms, was "saved" by section 1 that allows "reasonable limits," in this case to promote fairness. Moreover, "the limit on independent spending must also be stricter than that granted to the national committees [established to advance the Yes and No options], since it cannot be assumed that independent spending will be divided equally to support the various options." However, once again the restrictions on third-party advertising in federal election campaigns were subject to a court challenge. During the federal election of 2000, in an 8-1 decision the Supreme Court of Canada lifted an injunction that had been ordered by an Alberta court against the amendments, without however judging their constitutionality, the majority citing the "rule against granting the equivalent of final relief in interlocutory challenges to electoral statutes, even in the course of elections governed by those statutes." The Court also noted the principle that "at this stage of the proceeding," other than "in clear cases," it is assumed that the challenged, but "duly enacted law" will "produce a public good"; the onus is on the applicant who asserts otherwise to establish that suspension of the law would be in the public interest (*A.G. of Canada v. Stephen Joseph Harper*).

The amendments in 1999 also reinforced a ban on both advertising and the publication of new public opinion surveys results on election day. Further requirements were introduced concerning the reporting of results of public opinion survey. They involved, for example, disclosure in the first instance of sponsors, the firm that undertook the survey, when and how the sample was drawn, how many people participated and the margin of error regarding the results. Newspapers and Internet sites were required to publish the wording of the questions and how a copy of the questionnaire might be obtained. These amendments followed an earlier Supreme Court ruling against more restrictive federal legislation.

Electoral system. The means by which votes cast for party candidates are translated into legislative seats held by the parties, the basis upon which governments are formed.

Elections to the provincial legislatures and to the House of Commons are based on the single-member constituency system with plurality win, or the first-past-the-post system. That is, the winner is the candidate who receives more votes than any other candidate irrespective of the percentage of the total number of votes cast. Thus a candidate may win with a plurality, but not a majority of the votes cast.

There are other types of electoral systems. For example, in federal elections in the United States, there are different electoral systems for election to the presidency, the Senate and the House of Representatives. In the Federal Republic of Germany, half of the Bundestag's deputies are elected by the single-member constituency system with plurality win, while the other half are elected on a system of proportional representation using the party list system. In Israel, the Knesset is elected by proportional representation applied to party lists of candidates. Other specific rules and procedures pertaining to elections concerning, for example, candidate selection, voter eligibility, and campaign procedures and financing are usually referred to as election laws.

No electoral system is neutral. Each has inherent biases. The system used in Canada's multi-party elections results, in effect, in two levels of electoral reality: "voter reality," the percentage of overall public support for each party, and "legislative reality," the number of constituencies each party has won. Governments, however, are appointed on the basis of seats held in the Commons (or the provincial legislature), regardless of any discrepancy between the percentage of seats and the percentage of votes for that party. Therefore, the reality that counts in the formation of a government is the number of seats won by each party; the percentage of popular support for each party is irrelevant.

The discrepancy between these two levels of electoral reality attracts considerable academic and some public attention, especially when there are extraordinary discrepancies in election results, but also when considering the long-term consequences of rational short-term considerations that party strategists employ to exploit the biases inherent in the system. For most of the twentieth century, for example, Conservative representation in the House of Commons from constituencies in Quebec rarely equalled or surpassed the party's share of popular vote in that predominantly French-speaking province. This helped to reinforce an image of the party as a largely anglophone group unsympathetic to francophone interests. Some commentators have also noted that interpretations of Canadian political history based on legislative majorities can misrepresent the past when viewed from the perspective of the overall proportion of party support in the period being studied. For example, the considerable Liberal majority of members of parliament elected in the Depression election of 1935—usually styled a "landslide" of support for the Liberals—was based on the same share of popular vote held by the party when it lost the previous election of 1930. Thus, the party's "landslide" was based on the split vote among the Conservatives and new parties more so than on an overwhelming increase in support for the Liberals compared to the 1930 results.

The elections of 1993 and 1997 resulted in extraordinary discrepancies between "voter reality" and "legislative reality" for some parties and also highlighted the tendency of the electoral system to reward parties with concentrated regional support (including a sovereignist Bloc Québécois) at the expense of parties with diffused country-wide support. In 1993, the Conservative party's 16 per cent share of the popular vote, nationally distributed, resulted in only two seats (0.7%), while the Reform and Bloc votes—18.7 and 13.5 per cent, respectively—were each sectionally concentrated, in the West and Quebec, resulting in 52 and 54 seats (18 per cent each), respectively—the sovereignist Bloc forming the official opposition. All Bloc votes were cast in Quebec ridings (49 per cent of the provincial vote total), while Reform's supporters comprised 52 per cent of voters in Alberta and 36 per cent in British Columbia. With its 6.9 per cent of the total vote concentrated in Saskatchewan (26.6%), the New Democrats won nine seats with the support of fewer than half the number of Conservative voters. In 1997, the election results, in order of popular vote, gave the Liberals 51.5 per cent of the seats with 38.5 per cent of the vote; Reform, 19.9 per cent of the seats (19.4% of the vote); Conservatives, 6.6 per cent of the seats (18.8% of the vote); New Democrats, 7 per cent of the seats (11% of the vote); Bloc Québécois, 14.6 per cent of the seats (10.7% of the vote). The results of the 2000 election also contained the usual anomalies: for example, the party with the largest share of the popular vote—in this case the Liberals with 41 per cent—usually receive a disproportionate share of seats—57 per cent; parties with a small, but with a widely distributed vote share fare worse than those with a small, but regionally concentrated vote share—in this case the Conservatives with 12 per cent of the vote spread across the country won 4 per cent of the seats while the Bloc Québécois with 11 per cent of the vote concentrated in Quebec won 13 per cent of the seats.

The drawing of constituency boundaries—or redistribution—occurs regularly following each census, in order to ensure reasonably equal voter power among Canadians. Procedures have been established to minimize gerrymandering, the drawing of boundaries to maximize the effect of the controlling party's popular support. However, malapportionment is permitted in recognition of the need for communities of interest, notably in sparsely populated areas, to be effectively represented. See **Electoral Boundaries Readjustment Act (redistribution)**; **Malapportionment**; **Redistribution (electoral)**.

Elites. Small groups of people who exercise considerable power in society. One may speak separately of economic, cultural, political and bureaucratic elites, and collectively of a national elite or ruling class, as well as regional elites.

In urbanized and industrialized societies generally, there tends to be a plurality of elites forming temporary coalitions of interests on different issues, rather than a well defined, permanent ruling class as in more traditional societies. However, in modern societies that retain remnants of an earlier feudal order, one may detect an "establishment" associated with inherited wealth, family status, certain schools and universities, and professions such as law, business and public administration.

There is much in the literature of political science and sociology on the role of elites in public policy and decision making. Studies of community power have led to "ruling elite" and "plural elite" models of community power. The methodology of the investigators may explain their different conclusions. If one follows a reputational method of study, one might arrive at the ruling class model; if one adopts a decisional approach, examining a variety of issues, the plural model might be confirmed. Nonetheless, in pluralist societies, some interests are better organized and financed than others and consequently have more influence on decision making in that society.

In the manner of John Porter in *The Vertical Mosaic: An Analysis of Social Class and Power in Canada* (Toronto: University of Toronto Press, 1965), some Canadian academics adopt an understanding of power as conflicts, not between those who are "in" and those who are "out," but rather among those who are "in":

holding decision-making roles in important sectors of society, the elites "compete to share in the making of decisions of major importance for the society, and they co-operate because together they keep the society working as a going concern" (27).

For Porter and for Robert Presthus (*Elite Accommodation in Canadian Politics* [Toronto: Macmillan of Canada Ltd., 1974]), the major forces dominating the political system are the political (elected) and bureaucratic (career public-sector) elites along with an elite based in the private sector of the economy, comprising representatives of large-scale business and financial interests. Moreover, these groups share a class background characterized by a high level of education that results in a secularism which values moderation, bargaining and accommodation. This secularism may be contrasted with the particularism of the lower strata of each group, which may occasionally complicate the bargaining process. In the 1960s, Arend Lijphart devised the term "consociational democracy" to describe countries that had fragmented political cultures but were stable democracies. In such countries, he argued, the elite make a conscious decision to accommodate their differences while defending the particular values and interests of their constituency, or subgroup. Lijphart later classified Canada as a semi-consociational democracy, in which the cultural fragmentation was institutionalized by the elite in intergovernmental relations (*Democracy in Plural Societies: A Comparative Exploration* [New Haven: Yale University Press, 1977]) (see **Consociational democracy**).

A characteristic of such a horizontally accommodative elite system is the movement of personalities back and forth across groups, in addition to recruitment to the top vertically from within the groups. This is particularly evident in federal politics in Canada, where the Liberal party has been pre-eminent since 1896. Especially from the 1930s to the 1950s, but also at other times, the Liberal party has been not so much a power structure in itself as a coalition for power that has included people "imported" into leading party positions from other elites. Though the weaker of the two parties of nineteenth-century origin, the social, educational and professional background of Conservative leadership throughout the twentieth century is also instructive on the matter of political elite recruitment in Canada.

Historically, the federal system in Canada enhanced the elite structure of Canadian society. However, a consequence of the entrenchment of the Canadian Charter of Rights and Freedoms in 1982 has been to alter the nature of political discourse in Canada. Alan C. Cairns has commented on both periods. In 1977, before the advent of the Charter and the rise of so-called Charter interests, he spoke of the two levels of government creating powerful support for their survival in their public employees and in the support of parties and interest groups in a complex network of mutually supportive relations ("The Government and Societies of Canadian Federalism," *Canadian Journal of Political Science* 10 [1977], pp695-725). In 1987, he spoke of a movement away from federal-provincial to citizen-state dialogue, at least in constitutional matters (*Charter versus Federalism: The Dilemmas of Constitutional Reform* [Montreal: McGill-Queen's University Press, 1992). More broadly, however, the Charter and judicial review of government action under the Charter have defined "citizen interests" and legitimized new "equality interests" in public debate among groups not heretofore granted status, such as Native Peoples, women, the mentally and physically disabled, and gays and lesbians. A consequence, then, of the Charter is an apparent broadening of the pluralist elite nature of Canada's political community (see **Canadian Charter of Rights and Freedoms [1982]**).

Emergencies Act (**Canada, 1988; emergency powers**). Federal emergency legislation under the "Peace, Order, and good Government" preamble of Section 91 of the *Constitution Act*, enabling the governor-in-council, that is the cabinet, to declare and respond to emergencies with the approval of Parliament.

The Act is successor to the *War Measures Act, 1914*, whose invocation in peacetime in 1970 was criticized, largely retrospectively, and whose unchecked application in wartime, especially to confiscate property and intern thousands of citizens, has also been retrospectively condemned. Also, since 1982 Canada has had an entrenched Charter of Rights and Freedoms to which all legislation, including emergency legislation, must conform.

The *Emergencies Act* is distinguished from its predecessor by the admission of several types of emergencies with appropriate powers, including time limits on the declaration of emergency, and by the degree of parliamentary oversight. The Act defines public welfare, public order, and international and war emergencies, and indicates specific requirements for the declaration and the executive orders and regulations that can pertain to the specific emergency. A motion to confirm a declaration of emergency must be presented to Parliament within seven days (if not sitting, Parliament must be called within seven days; if prorogued, "at the earliest opportunity"). A defeat of the motion in either the House of Commons or the Senate nullifies the declaration. A motion to revoke a declaration filed by at least twenty members of parliament or ten senators must be debated within three sitting days and the question put within ten hours. A motion passed in either House revokes the declaration. The Act specifies a length of time for each type of emergency, from thirty days for a Public Order emergency to 120 days for a War emergency. A motion to confirm an extension of an emergency must be tabled in Parliament within seven days of its proclamation, with a ministerial report giving reasons and naming the orders to remain in effect, and must receive the support of both houses. An all-party parliamentary review committee meets in private during the emergency to review all orders and regulations, including those exempt from publication in the *Canada Gazette* under the *Statutory Instruments Act*, and to report regularly to Parliament. Within sixty days following the expiry or revoking of a declaration, the government must hold an inquiry into the circumstances that led to the declaration, including the measures employed during the emergency, and table the report in Parliament within one year of the termination of the emergency. See **Emergency power**; *War Measures Act* (**Canada; emergency powers**).

Emergency power. Extraordinary power to be assumed by the federal Parliament in time of national peril, under the residual "Peace, Order, and good Government" clause of the *Constitution Act* (s.91, preamble), specifically under provisions of the *Emergencies Act, 1988*, successor to the *War Measures Act.*

The occasion on which to invoke the powers and their duration are fundamentally political questions, determined by the cabinet with Parliament's approval. During the First World War, Parliament passed the *War Measures Act*, which gave authority to the governor-in-council to make orders and regulations which "it may deem necessary or advisable for the security, defence, peace, order and welfare of Canada...." It was under the authority of the Act, for example, that the federal government passed orders-in-council during the Second World War, expropriating the property of Canadians of Japanese origin and forcibly detaining them in camps in the interior of British Columbia. When the Second World War ended in 1945, Parliament passed the *National Emergency Transitional Powers Act*, which declared that the state of emergency under the *War Measures Act* still existed. The powers, renewed during the Cold War and the Korean Conflict under the *Emergency Powers Act, 1951*, expired in 1954.

In 1970, the *War Measures Act* was invoked for the first time in peacetime, upon the government's assertion of an "apprehended insurrection" when the Front de Libération du Québec kidnapped a British trade official and a Quebec cabinet minister in separate incidents in Montreal (the cabinet minister was murdered shortly afterwards by his captors, and the trade official was released following negotiations). Serious doubts were expressed during and after the events of 1945-54 and 1970 about the emergency measures. The successor *Emergencies Act* distinguishes among emergencies with appropriate regulatory powers and provides for more immediate parliamentary debate, ongoing secret parliamentary review of regulations, and a report to Parliament following the emergency. The *Constitution Act, 1982* requires Parliament (and the provincial legislatures) to sit at least once a year (Canadian Charter of Rights and Freedoms, s.5) and allows no House of Commons or provincial legislature to continue for more than five years except "in time of real or apprehended war, invasion, or insurrection" and when "such continuation is not opposed by the votes of more than one-third of the members" of the relevant legislature (s.4). See **Emergencies Act (Canada, 1988; emergency powers); October (FLQ) Crisis (1970); War Measures Act (Canada; emergency powers)**.

Employment equity. See **Equity legislation**.

Employment Insurance (EI). Earlier styled as "unemployment insurance," a federal income-maintenance program established during the Second World War.

In 1937, the Judicial Committee of the Privy Council declared a federal scheme for unemployment insurance, part of Conservative Prime Minister R.B. Bennett's "New Deal" legislation, to be a violation of provincial jurisdiction. In 1940, the *British North America Act* (since 1982, the *Constitution Act*) was amended to give jurisdiction unequivocally to the federal government (s.91:2A). In 1941, a federal *Unemployment Insurance Act* allowed for benefits to those unemployed who had earlier contributed premiums when employed. Under the Act, the governor-in-council appoints commissioners to administer the Act through several regional offices. The Act also allows for appeals to independent referees by claimants.

Regulations pertaining to EI are subject to constant political debate and alteration: some people argue that the qualifications for employment insurance payments are too lax, while others argue that they are too strict. There have also been arguments over whether the EI program, which had become a costly general welfare program actually built into the operation of some regional economies, should be strictly an insurance program. Some have argued that a negative income tax, or minimum guaranteed income, would be preferable as an income-maintenance program.

Entrenchment, constitutional. Formal requirements of a constitutional statute, subject to judicial interpretation, and which can be amended only through a complex and difficult procedure. Such requirements regarding the exercise of legislative and administrative power are thus said to be entrenched in the constitution.

Until 1982, all legislatures in the Canadian federal union were supreme within the context of the federal-provincial division of powers as adjudicated by the courts. However, the *Constitution Act, 1982* fundamentally altered the nature of the constitution and Canadian federalism, notably with the entrenchment of a Charter of Rights and Freedoms, the constitutional recognition of Aboriginal rights and of the principle of federal equalization payments, and domestic amending formulae. All legislation as well as executive and administrative regulations and procedures at all levels of government are subject to challenges in the courts based on the provisions of the Charter that can be amended only by a resolution of Parliament and two-thirds of the provincial legislatures having at least 50 per cent of the population of Canada's provinces. In addition to the well-known liberal democratic rights, the Charter also entrenches mobility, equality, official-languages and minority-language educational rights, and the principle of maintaining multicultural heritage, with judicial interpretation giving meaning to these rights. See **Canadian Charter of Rights and Freedoms (1982).**

Enumeration (of powers). The delineation of the legislative competence of Parliament and of the provincial Legislatures in Canada, as outlined in the *Constitution Act, 1867*, and subsequently amended (see notably parts VI, VII, and s.132 in Part IX). See **Division (distribution) of powers.**

Enumeration (of voters). The registration of people as eligible voters prior to federal and provincial elections.

Until the 1990s, the voters' list for federal elections was created anew prior to each election on the basis of door-to-door visits by enumerators. Since 1996, however, a permanent register of voters has been established that is updated from various sources including income tax returns and provincial data bases. Registered voters receive a mailed card indicating their eligibility to vote and directions as to time and place. People not included on the list of eligible voters can appeal during the election campaign and on election day itself to be declared eligible to vote.

Environmentalism. A social movement with varying degrees of political influence since the 1960s, concerned about ecological damage from both private- and public-sector activity, in matters ranging from the use of nuclear power to individual behaviour affecting the ecosystem.

On the assumption that unrestrained economic growth and development is counter-productive in that it harms the ecosystem on which all life depends, the movement promotes laws and regulations to submit developments to environmental assessments, conserve non-renewable resources, protect endangered fauna and flora in environmentally sensitive areas and habitats, and secure the atmosphere from industrial and urban pollution, including acid rain and depletion of the ozone layer.

Environmentalism, broadly interpreted, may be seen as an aspect of postmaterialism. Some social scientists hold that a difference in values exists between an older generation raised in the context of scarcity and deprivation, and therefore focused on the pursuit of material well-being, and a younger generation raised in a period of relative economic security, and therefore focused more on non-material aspects related to the quality of life, including the protection of the environment from degradation associated with the economic growth agenda of the materialist generation. Canada's environmentalists are part of a larger, international "Green" movement.

While most governments include a department of the environment and have enacted legislation in response to the environmentalist agenda, the level of human and financial resources, and the regulatory power of such departments can vary considerably from jurisdiction to jurisdiction and from one government to another within a jurisdiction. Consequently, Canada's active and influential social movement network of environmental lobbyists has effectively used the courts to pursue their objectives. For example, through their efforts—and sometimes in legal consonance with organizations representing Native Peoples—the courts have given the federal government power to order environmental studies of provincial projects that touch on any aspect of federal jurisdiction and, in some cases, have ordered federal environmental reviews of whully provincial projects. Provincial governments have challenged federal environmental assessment as a intrusion into provincial jurisdiction, while at the same time, federal governments that place a high value on amicable federal-provincial relations have not welcomed such judicial involvement in those relations. Although Canada has experienced increasingly effective political lobbying and legal activism by the "Green" movement regarding environmental protection, unlike some European countries, there is no electorally significant Green political party.

Standards of environmental protection were a major concern for opponents of the North American Free Trade Agreement involving Canada, Mexico and the United States. While the courts have widened federal responsibility in environmental matters, the extent of Canada's effective compliance with the North American Commission for Environmental Cooperation established in Montreal under NAFTA depends on the commitment of federal and relevant provincial governments. See **North American Free Trade Agreement (NAFTA) (1992); Postmaterialism.**

Equality rights. See **Canadian Charter of Rights and Freedoms (1982); Equity legislation.**

Equalization grants (unconditional transfer payments). Unconditional financial payments made by the federal government to provinces, according to a specific formula, in order to achieve revenue equalization among provinces.

Following the expiry in 1946 of the federal-provincial Wartime Tax Agreements of 1941, the federal government, in bilateral agreements with all provinces but Ontario and Quebec (1947-52), continued to "rent" provincial personal income and corporation taxes, as well as succession duties, and paid individually negotiated provincial subsidies beyond a minimum level. In the 1952-57 period, only Quebec remained completely aloof from these arrangements. The 1950s arrangement included a guaranteed amount of "rent" regardless of the revenue yield of the tax fields vacated to the federal government—the earliest form of unconditional equalization payments to "have-not" provinces. In 1956, new federal-provincial arrangements for 1957-62 led to the determination of unconditional federal subsidies for provincial revenue equalization based on objective criteria. The formula for determining the grants was designed, at that time, to bring the provincial per capita yield of personal income and corporation tax and succession duties to the per capita yield of the same taxes in the two wealthiest provinces in each year. By then, all provinces participated to some extent, including Quebec, which received an equalization payment as well as a tax abatement in place of rental payments, equal to what the province would have received had it entered the agreement to vacate the three standard tax fields.

Since 1957, the principle of equalization of provincial revenue has been reaffirmed in five-year agreements and in 1982 was entrenched in the *Constitution Act, 1982* (Part III, s.36). All governments are constitutionally committed to promote "equal opportunities for the well-being of Canadians," encourage "economic development to reduce disparities in opportunities," and provide "essential public services of reasonable quality to all Canadians." The essential mechanism is "making equalization payments to ensure that provincial governments have sufficient revenues to provide reasonably comparable levels of public services at reasonably comparable levels of taxation," and the formula for calculating equalization payments remains subject to periodic federal-provincial negotiations. See **Federal-provincial tax-sharing agreements (fiscal federalism)**.

Equity legislation. Enactments by federal and provincial legislatures dealing originally with gender-based inequity in the workplace, with reference to hiring, promotion, benefits, compensation and policy dealing with sexual harassment. Later, equity requirements were extended to include ethnicity and physical ability.

The primary focus for advocates of workplace equity is the provincial legislatures, as labour legislation falls under provincial jurisdiction with the exception of employment by the federal government and in federally regulated industries. Apart from the justice of the demands for equity based on available statistics, legislation setting guidelines or mandating specific goals for both the public and private sectors is supported by the "equality rights" provisions of the Canadian Charter of Rights and Freedoms. Section 15 guarantees "equal protection and equal benefit of the law without discrimination and, in particular, without discrimination based on race, national or ethnic origin, colour, religion, sex, age, or mental or physical ability." It also sanctions laws or programs designed to improve the conditions of individuals disadvantaged on those specific grounds. Further, section 28 affirms that rights and freedoms in the Charter "are guaranteed equally to male and female persons." See **Canadian Charter of Rights and Freedoms (1982); Charter groups; interests**.

Established Programs Financing (EPF). From 1977 until 1996, federal-provincial cost-sharing arrangements for post-secondary education and hospital and medical care insurance involving tax abatements and periodically negotiated formulae for block funding, enacted in the federal *Federal-Provincial Fiscal Arrangements and Established Programs Financing Act*. In 1996, Established Programs Financing and the Canada Assistance Plan for social assistance were combined into a single federal block grant designated the Canada Health and Social Transfer. See **Canada Health and Social Transfer (CHST)**; **Federal-provincial tax-sharing agreements (fiscal federalism)**.

Estimates. A government's spending proposals for which it requires approval of the legislature.

The following describes recent procedures for dealing with estimates at the federal level. Detailed departmental and agency spending estimates for the forthcoming fiscal year, approved by the Treasury Board and cabinet with a concern for the government's priorities in spending as well as for economy, are usually tabled in the House of Commons in February as the main estimates, the "Mains," in several "Blue Books." The government's main estimates take the form of a supply bill, or appropriation Act, and are accompanied by the detailed spending proposals of departments and agencies. The estimates for specific departments and agencies are then sent to the relevant standing committee of the House of Commons for intensive scrutiny. The committee members—at least the opposition members—question the designated or responsible minister, who is accompanied by senior civil servants to provide information and advice in responding. In some jurisdictions, the legislature sits as the committee of the whole, or a committee of supply, to question the minister and department officials. Although the estimates have been fought over, defended, and won in the private executive confines of government departments, Treasury Board Secretariat and cabinet committees, this is the first time they have been exposed to public criticism and defence. When the committees report back to the House of Commons, the estimates are voted on and passed through Parliament as one bill. The opposition uses the committee meetings and supply periods in the House (twenty-five days in three periods, also known as "Opposition days," or allotted days) to criticize not only government spending but policy priorities generally. As estimates have been prepared and made public well before the fiscal year begins, and because parliamentary approval can be delayed, Parliament may vote "interim supply" before the study of the main estimates is concluded and may be asked to approve "supplementary estimates" during the fiscal year.

All departments and agencies must spend appropriated funds as outlined in the detailed estimates examined by Parliament. A government body may deviate somewhat with the approval of the Treasury Board. However, Parliament requires the auditor general to investigate and report on spending for purposes other than those for which funds were appropriated (see **Auditor General**).

When Parliament is not in session and the government faces a serious appropriation shortfall, it can spend money through Governor General's Warrants. The governor-in-council (that is, the cabinet) issues warrants when the president of the Treasury Board reports that there is no appropriation for an expenditure which the relevant minister deems urgently required. These special warrants must be published in the *Canada Gazette*, reported to Parliament, and be approved as supplementary estimates. See **Budget and budgetary process**; **Treasury Board**; **Treasury Board Secretariat**.

Ethics counsellor. A federal office established in 1994 to monitor, and investigate alleged violations of, the government's conflict-of-interest guidelines for ministers and public officials.

In 1992, a parliamentary committee recommended the establishment of a parliamentary office to hold private information regarding all parliamentarians in confidence, to make some information public, to advise parliamentarians on their obligations, to investigate alleged violations, conduct public hearings and report to Parliament. The Liberal government appointed a career public official as ethics counsellor, accountable however to the prime minister rather than to Parliament. Thus the matter of conflict of interest has remained an area of prime ministerial prerogative and responsibility. Since the appointment, the ethics counsellor has made public determinations on several cases of alleged conflict, even involving Prime Minister Jean Chrétien, frequently to dismiss the allegations. See **Conflict of interest**.

Executive, the. That part or branch of government which is responsible for the presentation of a program to the legislature for its approval, and for the implementation of laws by the administration. The executive also has certain subordinate legislative and quasi-judicial powers through delegated power under enabling legislation.

Canada has a dual executive. The formal executive—the Crown and its representatives, the governor general and the provincial lieutenant-governors— and the political executive—the cabinets, or governments-of-the-day. The *Constitution Act, 1867* invests the "Executive Government and Authority of and over Canada" in the Crown, its governor general, and the Privy Council for Canada (ss.9-11), and the lieutenant-governors advised by the Executive Council of each province (ss.58-67). The cabinets constitute the *de facto* or effective provincial and federal executives, appointed by the Crown's representative and retaining the support of their respective legislatures. However, they have *de jure* or statutory existence only as the effective part of the Privy Council for Canada and the provincial Executive Councils. See **Cabinet**; **Crown**; **Crown prerogatives**; **Delegated power**; **Governor General**; **Letters Patent**; **Lieutenant-governor**; **Public Service (administration)**; **Quasi-judicial decisions**; **Regulatory agencies (regulations)**.

Executive (administrative) federalism. A term which describes a federal system such as Canada's, in which intergovernmental relations are paramount in accommodative bargaining, and are characterized by a high level of interdependence, with emphasis on multilateral and bilateral consultation, negotiation and functional operations among the federal, provincial and territorial governments.

This type of federalism contrasts with a more classical federal system in which intergovernmental relations are determined by a strict delineation of jurisdictional competence between the levels of government. It is frequently referred to as " inter-state" federalism as distinct from "intra-state" federalism where accommodative bargaining takes place within the executive and legislative institutions of the central, or federal government.

Executive federalism is by nature elitist, with accommodative bargaining taking place in closed meetings of government ministers and officials. But the entrenchment of the Canadian Charter of Rights and Freedoms in 1982 and the defeat of the constitutional Meech Lake Accord in 1990 led to some modification of executive federalism in constitutional negotiations. The Charter elevated so-called Charter interests among the public whose lead organizations thereby claimed to have an interest in negotiations that would lead to constitutional change. The Accord's defeat was seen, in part, as a public rebuke of executive federalism, wherein the country's future was seen to have been the prerogative of eleven first ministers and their aides engaged in private negotiations. Subsequently, the Charlottetown Accord of 1992 was negotiated by federal, provincial, territorial and Aboriginal leaders following extensive public consultation. Nonetheless it, too, was defeated in a national referendum. Constitutional amendments and intergovernmental relations in Canadian federalism generally still require a high degree of intergovernmental co-operation and approval at executive/administrative levels, followed by legislative approval. See **Canadian Charter of Rights and Freedoms (1982); Charlottetown Accord (1992); Federalism; Meech Lake Accord (1987).**

Executive assistant, ministerial (chief of staff; exempt staff). The chief of staff of a cabinet minister, hired and retained at the minister's "pleasure" (that is, exempt from protection under the *Public Service Employment Act*) to head a minister's personal staff.

At its inception in the 1960s, this ministerial staff dealt with constituency business and appointments. Over time, however, ministerial staff have increased in numbers, positioned politically between the minister and departmental staff, offering advice and briefing ministers on various political matters. Usually such personnel at the federal level, who are maintained on public salaries, are hired with the approval of senior members of the Prime Minister's Office and the Privy Council Office (notably for security checks). The minister determines how to allocate departmental, cabinet, party, and constituency responsibilities among the executive staff.

From the minister's point of view, an executive assistant or chief of staff should bring to the minister's attention information and points of view from outside the cognizance of the departmental senior civil servants, and thereby improve political judgment on issues within the minister's responsibility. The influence of ministers' personal staff relative to their departmental officials rose during the Conservative government of 1984-1993. At the outset of his government in 1993, Liberal Prime Minister Jean Chrétien reduced not only the size of the cabinet, but also the size of the ministerial exempt staff. Frequently the target of lobbyists when attached to a ministerial office, many ministerial staff have careers in consultative work with private lobbying firms once they have left office.

Executive Council. The formal name for a provincial government-of-the-day, cabinet, or ministry.

Executive Councils are mentioned in the *Constitution Act, 1867* only with respect to the lieutenant-governor (ss.63-66). The principle of responsible government is observed in the provinces by constitutional convention; that is, the lieutenant-governor appoints the Executive Council, but selects as premier someone who has the support of the legislature—usually the acknowledged leader of the party with the most seats—and then accepts the premier's recommendations on appointment to the Executive Council, or cabinet. Formally, the cabinet acts as the lieutenant-governor-in-council. The lieutenant-governor virtually always accepts the government's advice, subject to the federal aspects of the office (including appointment, tenure, and powers of disallowance and of reservation). See **Disallowance; Lieutenant-governor; Lieutenant-governor-in-council; Reservation**.

Extraterritoriality. The extension and application of the laws of one country to another. The extraterritorial application of United States law is particularly serious in Canada because of the extensive ownership of Canadian companies by US-based firms. Thus, Canadian exports, which involve components and technical data from the United States, have been subjected to the US *Export Control Act* of 1949. Also, United States Foreign Asset Control Regulations and the Cuban Assets Control Regulations as well as the *Trading With the Enemy Act* apply to American-owned operations abroad, even when no United States components are involved. In 1992, the United States adopted the *Democracy in Cuba Act* which prohibits foreign subsidiaries of American firms from dealing with Cuba. Finally, United States anti-trust (anti-combine) laws are also applied when Canadian subsidiaries of United States firms are merged. Successive Canadian governments have publicly expressed opposition to the application of the *Trading With the Enemy Act*, for example, concerning countries in Asia, Europe, the Caribbean area and Central America. There have been a few cases when Canadian-based but American-owned companies have lost export business because of the extraterritorial application of United States law. However, the greatest impact of extraterritoriality may be in the inhibition it places on Canadian managers and boards of American-owned firms when developing export markets.

Historically, statutes of the Imperial Parliament were paramount over any conflicting Dominion statutes under Britain's *Colonial Laws Validity Act* until renounced at the Imperial conferences of 1926 and 1930, and by the British Parliament in the Statute of Westminster of 1931. See **Imperial conferences; Statute of Westminster (U.K., 1931)**.

F

Federal Court. Established in 1971, successor to the Exchequer Court, the Federal Court consists of a Trial Division (a court of original jurisdiction) and an Appeals Division, or Federal Court of Appeals. The Trial Division has: original jurisdiction in claims against or by the Crown and in federal-provincial and interprovincial disputes; concurrent jurisdiction in claims against or concerning officers or employees of the federal government; some jurisdiction with respect to relief sought against federal boards, commissions and other tribunals; jurisdiction in certain property matters; admiralty jurisdiction; jurisdiction in appeals from income and estate tax assessments and citizenship court decisions; and residual jurisdiction where no other court has jurisdiction for relief under a law of Canada which, though not a statute of Parliament, falls "within the legislative competence" of Parliament.

The jurisdiction to hear and determine applications to review and set aside orders of federal tribunals is found in the Trial Division—except where the Appeal Division has statutory jurisdiction or where there is a statutory appeal elsewhere. In the second case, appeals may be allowed by statute to the Supreme Court, the governor-in-council (that is, the federal cabinet), or the Treasury Board. Also, federal tribunals may themselves refer a question of law, jurisdiction, practices, and procedure to the Appeal Division.

The Court of Appeal consists of the chief justice of the Court and ten other judges. The trial division consists of the associate chief justice and thirteen other judges. The Federal Court has the authority to invite retired federally appointed judges to act as deputy judges of the Court. The Court may also invite federally appointed judges who are still on the bench, but only with the consent of the relevant chief justice or provincial attorney general. The Court has district offices throughout the country and the Court's divisions can sit anywhere in Canada, as a convenience to those whose cases are being heard.

The Court's work frequently concerns cases involving, for example, the federal Public Service Commission and Public Service Staff Relations Board, Immigration and Refugee Board, Parole Board, Canada Customs and Revenue Agency, appeals with respect to the *Access to Information* and *Privacy* acts, and requests from the Canadian Security Intelligence Service for warrants to engage in surreptitious activities.

Federal-provincial conferences. Earlier styled dominion-provincial, meetings of the prime minister and provincial premiers or their representatives. As a generic term, it connotes frequent meetings involving ministers with similar portfolios and senior government officials of similar departments or with similar policy responsibilities. Meetings involving ministers and officials are usually held behind closed doors; meetings involving first ministers might begin and conclude with public sessions. See **Intergovernmental committees**.

Federal-Provincial Fiscal Arrangements and Established Programs Financing Act. See **Federal-provincial tax-sharing agreements** (fiscal federalism).

Federal-provincial tax-sharing agreements (fiscal federalism). Periodically negotiated agreements whereby the provinces and the federal government share tax revenues and the federal government provides conditional grants in specific shared-cost programs and unconditional equalization grants, to reduce regional disparities in the provision of government services.

This fiscal regime began during the emergency conditions of the Second World War, when the provinces agreed not to levy personal income and corporation taxes. In return, the federal government made a tax rental payment to the provinces and assumed the costs of certain social services. The Wartime Tax Agreement lasted until 1946. Since then, five-year arrangements were negotiated and enacted in federal legislation, since 1977 called the *Federal-Provincial Fiscal Arrangements and Established Programs Financing Act* (EPF). In 1996, federal Established Program Financing for provincial post-secondary education and health insurance, and the Canada Assistance Plan to fund income-maintenance in the provinces, were replaced with a federal block grant and tax points under the Canada Health and Social Transfer. The principle of unconditional federal equalization payments to "have-not" provinces in order to raise their level of public revenue to a periodically negotiated national provincial average of public revenue was entrenched in the *Constitution Act* in 1982. Equalization payments were unaffected by the other changes in federal-provincial fiscal relations in 1996.

The aim of the tax agreements is to reduce provincial disparity in the provision of public services in costly social policy fields of provincial responsibility. Canada's regime of so-called fiscal federalism reflects the federal government's spending power arising from its unrestricted taxation powers under the constitution, relative to the provinces' limited powers and widely disparate tax base, yet with constitutional jurisdiction in costly social policy fields.

Since the 1960s, the federal government has been increasingly criticized by provincial governments for the conditions it attaches to the conditional programs, effectively involving itself in policy making in areas of provincial jurisdiction. In response, the federal government introduced block funding that allowed the provinces discretion as to which programs they funded. But the federal government has also reduced its level of funding, preferring to fund its own programs with direct transfers to individuals, thus receiving more visibility and presumably reaping more political credit. But at the same time, the federal government still attaches conditions to shared-cost programs, notably with respect to the provision of health care. In 1999, the federal government and nine provinces, with Quebec dissenting, signed the Social Union Framework Agreement that set rules for federal-provincial social programs. See **Equalization grants (unconditional transfer payments)**; **Social Union Framework Agreement (1999)**; **Spending power.**

Federalism. A political system in which legislative power is distributed between a national, central, or federal legislature and a level of state or provincial legislatures.

In a theoretically pure, or classical federal system, there is no superior-inferior relationship implied in the divided authority. The national legislature retains jurisdiction in matters crucial to the integrity of the nation, while the subnational legislatures have autonomy in matters of local concern. In practice, however, federal constitutions are usually biased in one direction. The push-pull of political competition leads to inevitable conflict between the levels of authority and the domination of one by the other in different areas of political activity. An indication of constitutional bias is the location of residual power: that is, which level of authority is given the powers not otherwise enumerated in the case of either level of government. Jurisdiction in matters related to trade and commerce, banking and finance, and taxation are indications of effective political power. In case of disputes, governments may negotiate or seek judicial interpretation of the constitution.

In Canada, domination by the central or federal government characterized the early years of the federal system. In a short time, however, the provinces acquired a consciousness that led to a competitiveness that is characteristic of federal-provincial relations. Since the Second World War, an underlying cause of tension in Canadian federalism has been the high level of jurisdictional responsibility on the part of the provinces in social policy fields in an era of positive government and the welfare state, countered by the considerably greater access of the federal government to tax revenue and a self-assumed responsibility to ensure national minimum standards in public services through its so-called spending power. Attendant also with the enhanced role of the federal government is the tendency of contemporary policy questions to cut across the jurisdictional divide established in the nineteenth century.

For approximately twenty years after the Second World War, the federal government was pre-eminent in setting policy priorities, establishing conditions for shared-cost programs in areas of provincial responsibility and determining the formula for unconditional equalization payments to "have-not" provinces. After 1960, the provinces—some more than others—began to assert themselves. Quebec's political elite, in particular, made demands commensurate with its proclaimed role as defender of French civilization in North America. Since the 1970s, a significant majority of public opinion in Quebec has supported a fundamental restructuring of the province's relationship with the rest of Canada, either in a renewed federal state or as an independent nation state itself. Assertiveness by some other provinces, notably Alberta, was based on wealth accruing from natural resource development and conflicts that arose as these resource commodities involved interprovincial and international marketing and pricing policies. Apart from a reduction in the federal government's role in setting policy conditions in shared-cost programs, the Alberta government has articulated a general desire among western Canadians to reform federal institutions, notably the Senate, to improve the representation of regional interests at the federal level. Such changes would lead to a balance between an inter-state federal system characterized by accommodative bargaining among federal-provincial elites and an intra-state federal system in which accommodative bargaining is conducted in central, or federal institutions.

Canada's federal system is characteristically an inter-elite system, with federal-provincial disputes following Confederation in 1867 frequently settled by the judiciary variously sustaining provincial power or federal power. After the 1960s, when both constitutional and policy differences came to the fore, accommodative bargaining in Canada's federal system was usually styled executive or administrative federalism: conflict is managed in closed-door, intergovernmental negotiations involving ministers and government officials, receiving subsequently, if necessary, only perfunctory legislative scrutiny and approval.

The patriation of the *Constitution Act* in 1982, with the entrenched Canadian Charter of Rights and Freedoms, appears to have established conditions for subsequent modification of executive federalism. The Charter legitimized a number of Charter or equity interests in the public, which successfully projected their concerns onto the public agendas of both federal and provincial governments. The defeat of the Meech Lake Accord in 1990, which would have satisfied Quebec's demands for acceptance of the constitutional arrangements of 1982, was interpreted in part as a defeat of political elite dominance by the eleven first ministers and their officials who had attempted to determine the country's constitutional future behind closed doors. Constitutional discussions after 1990 included federal government-sponsored national forums involving a variety of mass-based interest groups (notably, business, labour, Native Peoples, women, the disabled, multicultural and welfare groups). Nonetheless, the Charlottetown Accord of 1992, negotiated by federal, provincial, territorial and Aboriginal leaders, was defeated in a national referendum. However, the constitutional regime of Canadian federalism still requires close collaboration and co-operation of the eleven federal and provincial governments in both public policy and constitutional matters. See **Division (distribution) of powers; Executive (administrative) federalism; Federal-provincial tax-sharing agreements (fiscal federalism)**.

Filibuster. The deliberate use of legislative debate and procedural tactics by opposition parties to protract consideration, and delay adoption, of government bills.

Legislative rules, or Standing Orders, permit the government on the one hand to introduce its proposals and the opposition on the other to have sufficient opportunity to criticize them. The opposition, however, may occasionally engage in drawn-out speeches, points of order, points of privilege, and even music-hall antics, to draw public attention to some allegedly heinous government measure or ministerial blunder. The major procedural countermeasure to opposition filibustering is closure, by which the government may impose time limits on debate. In such legislative confrontations, the opposition does not want public opinion to perceive it as unnecessarily obstructionist, while the government does not want to appear autocratic and dismissive of the legislature. See **Closure**.

Finance, Department of. A key federal department established in 1867, that is responsible for advice to the cabinet on economic and financial policy. It is a central agency, the focus of whose activity is the review of government revenues and expenditures, and the preparation of the budget and relevant taxation legislation. The Department of Finance is involved in any policy proposal which has a significant implication for revenue or expenditures, and is likely to have a major impact on the economy. The Department is also concerned with monetary policy and the activity of the central bank, the Bank of Canada, and with international decisions that may affect the Canadian economy.

The Department deals with tax policy and legislation (but not collection which is the business of Canada Customs and Revenue Agency); economic development policy, dealing with all sectors of the economy, including the activity of federal crown corporations; economic analyses to monitor and forecast national and international developments; international trade and finance, focussing for example on the World Trade Organization and regional free-trade agreements that deal with tariffs, other forms of subsidies and protection and countervailing duties, and international aid and debt management; the regulation of financial institutions such as federally chartered banks and trust companies; the international finance market, regarding the currency exchange rate and the balance of payments; federal-provincial relations and social policy, focusing on expenditure management with respect to federal-provincial programs; and co-ordination of federal government consultations with the private sector. The Department also orchestrates Canada's involvement in other international discussions such as the Economic Summit of leading industrialized countries (the G7 [8] and other groups of nations), the International Monetary Fund, World Bank and the meeting of G-7 and G-20 finance ministers. The deputy minister is a member ex officio of the board of directors of the central bank, the Bank of Canada. The governor of the Bank meets regularly with the minister of finance to discuss general economic conditions and monetary policy. The minister also recommends to cabinet the appointment for three-year terms of "outside directors" to the central bank's board of directors who review the central bank's management by its governing council of governor, senior deputy and deputy governors.

Not unexpectedly, then, the minister of finance is a senior cabinet minister, viewed by the public as primarily responsible for government policy related generally to the health of the economy. A requisite for government success is frequently said to be "the confidence of the business community." Consequently, in their private careers before entering politics, federal ministers of finance have usually been well connected to, and respected among, if not actually part of, the economic elite. See **Bank of Canada (central bank)**; **Budget and budgetary process**.

Financial Administration Act **(Canada)**. A major federal statute that includes requirements pertaining to accounting for revenues and the expenditure of money by the government of Canada. The Act defines and classifies departmental and nondepartmental organizations such as crown corporations, and gives authority for planning, programming and administrative policy operations in the government to the central body of administrative and financial management, the Treasury Board Secretariat. See **Treasury Board Secretariat**.

First Ministers' Conference. See **Conference of First Ministers**.

First-past-the-post electoral system. A term often used to describe the process by which votes are tallied in federal and provincial elections, and candidates declared elected—the single-member constituency system with plurality win. Under "first past the post," the winner in each constituency is the candidate who receives more votes than any other candidate, but not necessarily more votes than all other candidates' votes combined, that is, usually a plurality rather than a majority of votes cast. See **Electoral system**.

Fiscal federalism. A reference to the division in a federal system of government of taxation powers and revenue sources (tax fields), and hence of revenues, between the central and subnational governments, and a regime that is established to manage significant or structural disparities in the revenue base among governments.

Although the contemporary fiscal regime in Canada dates largely from the Second World War, the *Constitution Act, 1867* established the basic framework in sections describing the economic union and the economic and revenue-raising powers of the two levels of government. The federal-provincial fiscal regime at a particular time in Canada involves debate over provincial access to revenue through restricted powers of taxation compared to unrestricted federal power of taxation and a tax base that varies among provinces, in the context of provincial responsibilities in various costly policy fields, and conditional and unconditional federal government transfers of money and tax points to provincial governments, as prescribed since 1996 in the Canada Health and Social Transfer (earlier in the federal *Federal-Provincial Fiscal Arrangements and Established Programs Financing Act*). See **Canada Health and Social Transfer (CHST)**; **Economic union of Canada**; **Federal-provincial tax-sharing agreements (fiscal federalism)**.

Fiscal policy. A government's taxation (revenue) and expenditure policies that underlie its budget. Fiscal policy involves regulating (along with monetary policy) the level of economic activity through the allocation of financial resources to government, private-sector business and to individuals. A classic debate in politics involves how to manage economic growth while ensuring an equitable distribution of wealth in society, and how this can be achieved in times of economic slowdown through taxation, deficit budgeting and debt management. See **Budget and budgetary process**; **Finance, Department of**; **Monetary policy**.

FLQ Crisis. See **October (FLQ) Crisis (1970)**.

Fragment (splinter) parties. Political parties whose founding leaders have usually abandoned a hitherto successful career in a governing party because of major policy differences with their leader. The fragment or splinter group receives considerable attention because of the founder's prominence and the popularity of the grievance. However, lacking any real grassroots involvement and being removed from traditional sources of financial support, fragment parties and their leaders' political careers are usually short-lived.

Henri Bourassa's (earlier a Liberal cabinet minister) Nationaliste party in the early decades of the twentieth century, T. A. Crerar's (earlier a Liberal minister) Manitoba wing of the federal Progressive party in the 1920s, H. H. Steven's (earlier a Conservative minister) Reconstruction party and W. D. Herridge's (confidant of a Conservative prime minister) New Democracy in the 1930s are examples of fragment parties in federal politics. Paul Hellyer's (earlier a Liberal minister) Action Canada in the 1960s was a fragment party which did not last to contest an election. Finally, the Bloc Québécois, a federal party initially comprising former Liberal and Conservative members of parliament committed to Quebec sovereignty, gained prominence when Lucien Bouchard, a senior Conservative minister and personal confidant of the prime minister, resigned from the cabinet and party in 1989 and accepted the Bloc leadership. Unlike other fragment parties, however, the Bloc is an arm of an established grassroots movement—the sovereignty movement in Quebec represented by the Parti Québécois—and it formed the official opposition in the House of Commons from 1993 to 1997. The party became a lesser institutional focus of the sovereignty movement in Quebec after Bouchard resigned from federal politics to assume the leadership of the Parti Québécois and became the premier of Quebec. In the 2000 election, the BQ lost seats to the Liberals and its first place in the popular vote in the province. In any event, Bloc supporters intend the party to be short-lived for its raison d'être would be eliminated with the achievement of its objective of

Quebec sovereignty. In the meantime it remains the chief opposition to the Liberal party in federal politics in Quebec.

Franchise. The right to vote in elections, now virtually universal in Canada.

From 1867 to 1884, the franchise in federal elections in Canada, based on provincial law, was inconsistent across the country. A distinct federal franchise was established in 1885, which included a property qualification and allowed for multiple voting for electors who held property in more than one constituency. As well, only men qualified for the franchise. There was a return to the several provincial franchises for federal elections from 1898 to 1917, a combined franchise from 1917 to 1920, and finally a separate federal franchise from 1920 to the present.

Although the federal franchise is now extended basically to any Canadian 18 years of age or older, it was not always so. The property and gender biases have already been mentioned. The most flagrant manipulation of the federal franchise occurred in 1917, during the First World War. Then, the Union government disenfranchised Canadians of central European origin, extended the franchise to women in the military and close female relatives of soldiers, and created a floating military vote (see **Wartime Elections Act and Military Voters Act [Canada, 1917]**). Since then, however, the history of the federal franchise is an account of its gradual extension. Following the war, women were enfranchised on the same basis as men, and the franchise was extended periodically to lower age levels from the high twenties in the 1920s to the 'teens in the 1970s. Inuit effectively could not vote in federal elections until constituencies were created in the North in the 1960s and Indians received the federal franchise in 1960. At the provincial level, women were excluded from the franchise in Quebec elections until 1940, and until 1945 Canadians of Asian descent were excluded from voting in provincial elections in British Columbia. This exclusion existed in federal elections in British Columbia until 1948, as federal law then denied the franchise to anyone disqualified on the basis of race under provincial electoral statutes. In the late 1980s and 1990s, the few remaining categories of disenfranchisement—judges and people in mental or correctional institutions—were successfully challenged in the courts, using the Canadian Charter of Rights and Freedoms that guarantees "every citizen" the right to vote in federal and provincial elections (s.3).

(La) Francophonie. A collective term to designate countries that are wholly or partly French-speaking. See **Community (the Francophone; La Francophonie)**.

Free trade. The unrestricted flow of capital, labour, goods and services across national and subnational borders.

Within Canada, despite the objective of Confederation in 1867 to achieve a common market, various provincial trade restrictions developed. Provincial governments cannot formally erect tariff barriers, but they developed restrictive practices through marketing boards, labour law, the licensing of trades and professions, regulating the issuance of securities, and preferential government purchasing policies. In the early 1990s, the federal Conservative government unsuccessfully proposed constitutional changes to eliminate interprovincial trade restrictions and establish a federal role in managing the economic union, and the successor Liberal government continued Conservative efforts to eliminate inter-provincial trade barriers. However, various protective practices persist.

There were limited reciprocal trade agreements between the United States and British North America in the nineteenth century, and shortly after Confederation in 1867 there was a movement to engage further in reciprocal trade agreements with the US. But until 1911, both Liberal and Conservative governments supported the system of Imperial trade preferences with Britain and protective tariffs otherwise. In 1911, the Liberals lost an election in which they supported a reciprocal free-trade agreement with the US. Over 75 years later, with Britain firmly part of the European Union and the Commonwealth preferential trade system dismantled, the Conservative government initialled a free-trade agreement with the US in 1988 and won re-election largely on that issue. The Canada-United States Free Trade Agreement, formally concluded in 1989, was followed by negotiations among Canada, Mexico and the United States to conclude the North American Free Trade Agreement in 1992. Since the Second World War, the international community has been committed to lowering trade barriers through periodically negotiated agreements under the World Trade Organization, earlier the General Agreement on Tariffs and Trade (the GATT). See **Canada-US Free Trade Agreement (1989)**; **Economic union of Canada**; **Globalization (globalism)**; **North American Free Trade Agreement (NAFTA) (1992)**; **World Trade Organization (WTO)**.

Free vote. A division in a legislature when members, normally bound by party discipline, are free to vote as they wish.

In a disciplined party system such as Canada's, divisions in the legislatures usually take place along party lines, with each party leadership using inducements or sanctions available to them to maintain discipline among party members. This cohesion ensures stability in a system of responsible parliamentary government in which the government must retain the confidence of the legislature in order to remain in office. Occasionally, however, a question will arise for which the leadership of normally the most tightly disciplined party—the government party—may conclude that it cannot or should not maintain the discipline of the whip. In such cases, the government will permit a free vote (perhaps the cabinet members excepted), asserting that this dignifies the legislature by making its debate and subsequent division a matter of each member's conscience rather than one of confidence in the government. The opposition parties may likewise declare their members free of discipline or else maintain party cohesion to contrast their unity on the matter with disunity in the government party. Some supporters of parliamentary reform argue that party discipline is too strictly observed in the House of Commons.

Freedom of information. Reference to legislation under which the government is obliged to make information public. In 1983, the federal Liberal government enacted the *Access to Information Act* which was similar to legislation introduced by the short-lived Conservative government in 1979.

This and similar legislation in most provinces runs counter to the traditional practice of Crown privilege and confidentiality, and the natural tendency of governments to protect themselves from the public disclosure of information that might prove embarrassing. Therefore the adoption of such legislation in Canada was not only slow, but the statutes contain many broad categories of exemption. The federal legislation, for example, requires the government to reply to access demands within thirty days, subject to extensions if the request is complex or if third parties must be notified. Requests for information may be denied if disclosure would be injurious to the conduct of federal-provincial relations, international affairs, national security, the safety of individuals, the national economic interest, third parties, or the investigation of criminal activities, or if they would facilitate an offence, constitute personal information as defined in the *Privacy Act*, or violate other statutory provisions (for example, in the *Income Tax Act*). Finally, cabinet documents are also protected under a broad category called "Operations of Government," which includes "advice or recommendations" or "an account of consultations or deliberations involving officers or employees of a government institution, a minister of the Crown or the [minister's] staff."

Dissatisfied applicants may appeal to the information commissioner, whose staff will investigate complaints related to denial, excessive costs, delay, or any other problems associated with the request for information. The commissioner may appeal to the Federal Court to seek government compliance with a request for information, but of course this further delays the process of disclosure. In annual reports to Parliament, the commissioner has repeatedly complained about such delays, the statutory exemptions from the *Access to Information Act*, as well as a bureaucratic culture that does not accept the principle of freedom of information implied in the Act.

Fulton-Favreau Formula (1964). A proposal in 1964 to revise and patriate the constitution—the *British North America Act, 1867*—by adopting a domestic amending formula, named after the two federal ministers of justice who chaired federal-provincial constitutional negotiations (E. Davie Fulton, a Conservative, succeeded by Guy Favreau, a Liberal). Rejected by Quebec, the proposal was, however, a basis for subsequent discussions and the formula that was eventually adopted in 1982.

The Fulton-Favreau procedure would have required unanimous consent of Parliament and the provincial legislatures for certain changes (for example, legislative powers allocated to the provinces, the use of English and French, denominational education rights, and the determination of representation by province in the House of Commons). Certain aspects of the constitution relating to the federal government would have been amended by Parliament with the concurrence of at least two-thirds of the provincial legislatures which together represented at least half of the country's population (for example, the role of the monarchy and the governor general, Senate representation by provinces and the five-year limit on the duration of a Parliament). Otherwise, Parliament would continue to have the right to amend the constitution with respect to the government of Canada. Finally, the delegation of legislative power between the two levels of government would have been allowed by mutual consent of Parliament and at least four provincial legislatures. All provinces would have had to be consulted on such delegation and Parliament would assert that the delegation was of concern to fewer than four provinces.

Federal-provincial conferences continued to be held on the constitution. In 1971, the so-called Victoria Charter was also rejected by Quebec. In 1982, the BNA Act was patriated with a Charter of Rights and Freedoms and amending formulae reminiscent of the Fulton-Favreau Formula, and renamed the *Constitution Act, 1867*. Quebec was the only dissenting government and constitutional negotiations continued into the 1990s to accommodate Quebec's demands, a difficult process highlighted by the defeat of the Meech Lake Accord in 1990 for want of legislative approval in Manitoba and Newfoundland, public consultations and negotiations leading to the Charlottetown Accord and a country-wide referendum, and its defeat in that referendum in 1992. See **Charlottetown Accord (1992)**; **Meech Lake Accord (1987)**; **Victoria Charter (1971)**.

G

G-7 countries, meeting of. Annual meeting of the heads of government or state of the seven leading industrialized nations, including Canada, France, Germany, Italy, Japan, the United Kingdom, and the United States.

The meetings were initiated in the 1970s as an umbrella for meetings of senior finance officials and central bankers of five countries (Canada and Italy were added later; since 1997, the USSR/Russia has attended, the meeting then designated as the G-8) to co-ordinate national policies with reference to particular economic problems. The summit meetings themselves are largely ceremonial "photo opportunities" with discussion frequently focused on immediate political issues rather than long-term solutions to economic problems. The institution of the G-7 summit nonetheless is an acknowledgement of international commitment to achieve agreed-upon common macro-economic policies among finance officials of the leading industrialized economies. In recent years, a ministerial meeting of G-20 countries, including industrialized countries additional to the G-7 as well as some developing countries, have also met for discussions focusing on third-world development. See **World Trade Organization (WTO)**.

Gay and lesbian rights. A movement since the 1970s to end all forms of discrimination on the basis of sexual orientation.

The movement for gay and lesbian rights in Canada received initial encouragement with the removal in 1969 of Criminal Code prohibitions regarding sexual relations among consenting adults. It has since been reinforced considerably largely through court decisions involving the equality rights section 15 of the Canadian Charter of Rights and Freedoms, enacted in 1982. While governments, especially at the provincial level with few exceptions, have been reluctant to legislate independently of court decisions to eliminate discrimination in law, none has used the "notwithstanding clause" of the Charter (s.33) to protect discriminatory legislation from judicial review. Instead, they have responded, however reluctantly, to conform with court decisions. Ontario's New Democratic government in 1994 was the first in Canada to propose granting same-sex couples rights (and obligations) granted others, notably regarding the adoption of children, contracts for property and inheritance rights, in addition to family-benefits packages. In free votes, the legislation passed first reading, but was defeated on second reading. A few years later, the Conservative government of Alberta, deciding not to invoke s.33 of the Charter, acceded to a Supreme Court ruling that effectively included "sexual orientation" as a prohibited basis of discrimination in the province's human rights legislation (*Vriend*, 1999). While judicial rather than legislative decisions have ended discrimination with reference to such family law matters as same-sex benefits (*M v. H*, 1999), and employment (*Vriend*), other matters such as the legal definition of marriage and adoption rights remained unaffected, though still subject to challenge. In brief, among public institutions, the judiciary has led the way by effectively writing "sexual orientation" into section 15 of the Charter as a prohibited basis of discrimination not to be saved by the "reasonable limits" exemption provided in section 1.

Gender politics (gap). Discussion focusing on differences between men and women in political involvement, participation, representation, partisan preference and public policy attitudes.

Scholarly studies of gender politics in Canada have focused on obstacles to participation and representation by women, and the nature of the gender gap among party activists and voters generally. Some feminists argue that differences between men and women in social attitudes and policy preferences are based on different fundamental values. Women, they argue, are more motivated than men for "expressive" reasons such as service, and less than men for "instrumental" reasons such as the personal acquisition of power.

The entrenchment of gender equality in the Canadian Charter of Rights and Freedoms in 1982 (ss.15, 28) enlarged the domain of gender politics by legitimizing women's issues in Canada's political discourse and providing an impetus for the women's movement to challenge legal and institutional structures that had marginalized women in Canadian society. These challenges have focussed on reproduction rights, workplace-equity in recruitment, promotion and compensation, division of labour within the family and recognition of non-market, that is, household labour, and improved statutory provisions regarding family violence, child support and child care. In addition to pursuing these issues, the organized women's movement, comprising a network of diverse but loosely linked organizations, with the National Action Committee on the Status of Women at its centre, participated actively in constitutional discussions in the early 1980s and 1990s.

General Agreement on Tariffs and Trade (the GATT). A periodically renegotiated international agreement established in 1948 in the aftermath of the Second World War to reduce tariffs and other restrictions on international trade, now the World Trade Organization. See **World Trade Organization (WTO).**

General amending formula (*Constitution Act, 1982*). The general procedure by which the *Constitution Act* is amended: by proclamation issued by the governor general upon authorization by resolutions of the Senate (that can exercise only a suspensive veto [s.47]) and House of Commons and resolutions of legislative assemblies of two thirds of the provinces that have combined, according to the latest general census, at least 50 per cent of the population of all the provinces (s.38:1). There are several other amending formulae in the *Constitution Act*, pertaining to matters involving Parliament, individual provinces or several, but not all provinces.

Until 1982, because the major Canadian constitutional statute—the *British North America Act*—was an act of the Imperial Parliament in London, it could be amended only by that Parliament, albeit on a resolution of the Canadian Parliament. The persistence of this anomaly, given Canada's status as an independent nation-state in the twentieth century, lay with the inability of Canadian federal and provincial governments to agree on a purely domestic amending formula. A consensus was achieved in the early 1980s for the constitution's "patriation," lacking however the support of Quebec, in part because the general amending formula precluded the necessary consent of the National Assembly of that sole jurisdiction whose population was predominantly French-speaking. Quebec was not mollified by further subsections in section 38 and section 40 that any amendment that affected "the legislative powers, the proprietary rights or any other rights or privileges of the legislature or government of a province" (s.38.2) would not have effect in a province whose legislature expressed its dissent (38.3,4), with compensation to the dissenting province by the federal government if the transfer involved "education or other cultural matters" (s.40).

Following the referendum in Quebec on sovereignty association in 1995, which was only narrowly defeated, the federal Liberal government of Prime Minister Jean Chrétien, unable to pursue successfully amendments that would accommodate Quebec to the constitution, promised that no constitutional amendment that required the approval of Parliament would be introduced without the approval of the legislatures of "regions" of the country, with Quebec designated as a region. See *Constitution Act, 1867 and subsequently amended*.

Geographic cleavage. A social division delineating areal or spatial communities of interest. The cleavage is usually expressed in terms of the core, or metropolis, on the one side and the periphery, or hinterland, on the other. The core/metropolis is that part of a political unit which is densely populated. It is where most of the manufacturing, industrial, research and financial activity takes place, and it contains major centres of advanced learning, the arts, the dominant communication media and government. The remainder of the political unit is the periphery/hinterland.

In Canada, the national core has historically been the lower St. Lawrence Valley and the lower Great Lakes area, including Montreal, Toronto and Ottawa, or central Canada generally, comprising the provinces of Ontario and Quebec. The periphery comprises several distinct areas: the Maritime provinces of New Brunswick, Prince Edward Island and Nova Scotia, or Atlantic Canada when including Newfoundland and Labrador; the West, comprising Manitoba, Saskatchewan, Alberta and British Columbia, or the first three provinces alone as the "prairie West"; finally, the North, comprising three territories: Northwest Territories, Nunavut and Yukon. These regions and provinces can each be subdivided between core and periphery. For example, the lower mainland including Vancouver and Victoria constitute British Columbia's core, and the "interior" its periphery. Also, changes can take place over time. Edmonton and Calgary, the core of the resource-industry-based prairie West, have displaced Winnipeg, the historically dominant core of an agriculture-based prairie West.

The political attitudes and behaviour manifested in Canada's regions often reflect those of adjacent regions of the United States. The models of behaviour for people in the core were traditionally those of the British core (London), but more recently those of the United States northeast core, including New York City. Likewise, political attitudes and behaviour in the Canadian West have been historically influenced by the populist ideas and political movements of the US midwest and northwest.

It is difficult to isolate issues that are purely spatial in meaning, but once apparent, the "inter-state" nature of Canadian federalism promotes and perpetuates such issues in federal-provincial government relations, rather than within political institutions at the centre. Policies that highlight regional interests in Canada include transportation, natural resource, trade, agricultural, and regional development policies. Western disaffection toward the "East" or central Canada is often expressed in terms which also have bicultural or class overtones. This is because the bulk of Canada's francophone population and a high concentration of wealth and economic decision makers are found in central Canada and are well represented in federal institutions, both political and administrative, in Canada's capital region of Ottawa-Hull.

Western disaffection with political institutions, processes and policies deemed "central Canadian" has been manifested in radical political behaviour on both the political left and the right. Historically, the prairie provinces were creations of the federal Parliament, and the largely European population was enticed there in the early decades of the twentieth century by the Canadian government's promise of a better life. Moreover, the population had already experienced or had knowledge of radical behaviour in trade unions, rural co-operatives, and socialist and populist political parties. As already mentioned, there was also considerable knowledge about similar concerns and debate in adjacent US states. Thus, when expectations were not met, the western population readily rejected the "received" party system and its two "eastern" parties, the Conservatives and the Liberals, establishing western-based parties.

In contrast to the West, the eastern periphery is a long-settled region where traditional elites were more firmly established and better integrated in the economic and political institutions of Canada. Also, Atlantic Canada's economy, less advantaged than the West's by structural changes in the twentieth century, is more reliant on federal equalization, shared-cost and regional development programs. Therefore, long after Confederation, Atlantic Canada remained the most solid regional support base, both federally and provincially, for the Conservative and Liberal parties of the Confederation period of the late 1800s.

Because of its sparse and widely distributed population, its territorial status and therefore still limited political autonomy, the North has only recently begun to establish a regional political personality, including the development of indigenous Native-based political institutions and practices. Territorial government leaders participated in constitutional negotiations with federal and provincial first ministers for the first time in 1992. It is noteworthy that the resulting Charlottetown Accord, negotiated by federal, provincial, territorial and Aboriginal leaders, and defeated in a country-wide referendum, had its greatest regional public acceptance in Atlantic Canada and the North, and its greatest regional rejection in the West. In 1999, the territory of Nunavut was established in the eastern Arctic, the first jurisdiction whose population, however small, was predominantly Aboriginal.

The West, then, has been the origin and site for much radical political behaviour in Canada. Despite the federal New Democratic party's attempts to make inroads in central and eastern Canada, the West remained an important base of support for the left-wing NDP as it was for its predecessor the Co-operative Commonwealth Federation, notably in British Columbia, Manitoba and Saskatchewan. The West was also the bastion of support for the Progressive party in the 1920s and for the right-wing populist Social Credit party from the 1930s to the 1970s. The ideological polarization of politics in British Columbia is a periphery political counterpoint to the traditional party loyalties in the eastern periphery. In BC's provincial politics from the 1950s to the 1990s, the Social Credit and the CCF-NDP were the two major parties.

In federal politics, the decline of the Social Credit party in the 1960s, the rise and fall of the Conservatives in the prairie West from the 1960s to the 1990s, and the rise of the Reform party in the 1990s—since 2000 the Canadian Alliance—reflected a shift in partisan preferences within the populist constituency. The popularity of the federal Conservatives in the West was based in large part on the leadership of that otherwise "eastern" party by westerner John Diefenbaker, from 1957 to 1967, and on later provincial representatives such as Alberta Conservative leaders and premiers, Peter Lougheed and Ralph Klein. While Diefenbaker's immediate predecessor as federal Conservative leader was a central Canadian, his two immediate successors were from the periphery—Robert Stanfield from Nova Scotia and Joe Clark from Alberta—though neither would be called populist. In the 1990s, western disaffection from the Conservative party of central Canadian Brian Mulroney resulted in increased support, especially in Alberta, for the Reform party led by Preston Manning, son of former Alberta Social Credit Premier Ernest Manning. In the 1993 election, the right-populist Reform party won 18.7 per cent of the popular vote, mostly in the West but notably in Alberta (52%) and BC (36.4%), and elected fifty-two members of parliament, all but one from western Canada. In 1997, the Reform party formed the official opposition with only western representation, and in 2000 was reorganized as the Canadian Alliance, in an attempt to increase support east of Manitoba. In a leadership contest, the Albertan Manning was defeated by Stockwell Day, an Alberta Conservative cabinet minister, under whose leadership in the election later that year the Alliance fared little better than Manning's Reformers previously. No federal Liberal leader has come from the periphery, although the successful leader of almost thirty years, William Lyon Mackenzie King, once held a seat in Saskatchewan and had prominent western representatives in his cabinets. John Turner, briefly leader in the 1980s, held a seat in Vancouver, but his earlier parliamentary and business careers were based in central Canada.

Gerrymander. A manipulation of constituency boundaries to minimize the effect of the opposition vote. A gerrymander is achieved by drawing boundaries so that the opposition vote is likely to be concentrated in a few constituencies while the vote for the party responsible for the gerrymander will be at least narrowly greater than the opposition vote in most constituencies.

The word "gerrymander" comes from such a manipulation in Massachusetts in 1812 by the party of Governor Elbridge Gerry, which resulted in constituencies whose configurations resembled those of a salamander. Gerrymandering can take place effectively only when one party has control over the drawing of constituency boundaries. The possibilities for gerrymandering have diminished considerably in Canada since the 1960s, as federal and provincial legislatures have delegated the responsibility for redesigning constituency boundaries to impartial boundary commissions. See *Electoral Boundaries Readjustment Act* (**redistribution**).

Globalization (globalism). A collection of cross- or supranational pressures, generated notably by corporate businesses encouraging the lowering of barriers to international trade, but thereby affecting national politics and culture. In addition to regional free trade agreements, the chief characteristic of globalization involves the subjection of national and regional trade policies generally to the regulations flowing from international agreements such as those of the World Trade Organization, the International Monetary Fund and the World Bank—the WTO and IMF being the organizations that principally affect Canada and other industrialized national economies; all three affecting developing countries.

The process of globalization encourages enhanced worldwide corporate competition with minimal government controls on cross-national corporate behaviour regarding, for example, the flow of capital investment, labour laws, environmental protection, large-scale mergers of transnational corporations and technological innovation. Enhanced cross-national corporate competition also involves the recasting, if not elimination, of various national policies and programs regarding such cultural industries as publishing, broadcasting, film, video and sound recording.

Globalization represents a fundamental challenge to individual nation-states whose economic, trade and cultural policies, while more or less liberal domestically, have historically been protectionist with respect to other countries. Globalization also challenges the fundamental organization of international relations and politics. As distinct from internationalism, globalization implies one integrated worldwide economic unit managed by organizations named above, in which national borders and national policies are incrementally eliminated.

Because foreign trade accounts for approximately 30 per cent of Canada's national income and provides jobs for millions of Canadians, Canada was among the initial signatories in 1947 of the General Agreement on Tariffs and Trade (the GATT), now the World Trade Organization, and the Organization for Economic Co-operation and Development (the OECD). Periodic agreements among member-states involve the reduction of national barriers to foreign competition, and Canada has had to revamp or eliminate many domestic practices and policies to conform to the regulations and binding decisions of the WTO. In the 1990s, the International Monetary Fund advised Canada on specific policies to reduce the national deficit. As a trading nation, following the demise of the imperial trade preferences with the United Kingdom and excluded from an associate relationship with the European Union, the Canadian government vigorously pursued free trade agreements, first with the United States in 1987, and shortly thereafter with the United States and Mexico. The Canadian government continues to pursue bilateral free trade agreements with other countries.

Because Canada's population and economy is significantly smaller than the United States, nationalists in organizations such as the Council of Canadians have opposed globalization. Their most significant success in this respect was their participation with other national groups in the late 1990s to defeat the Multilateral Agreement on Investment (MAI). "Globalists" in Canada argued that the MAI, sponsored by various industrialized nations within the OECD, would have ensured that Canadian firms investing abroad would be treated fairly. "Nationalists" were concerned that the MAI would restrict the Canadian government's ability to regulate foreign investment and corporate behaviour in Canada. See **Canada-United States Free Trade Agreement (1989)**; **Continentalism**; **Economic nationalism**; **North American Free Trade Agreement (NAFTA) (1992)**; **World Trade Organization (WTO)**.

Goods and Services (ad valorem, value-added) Tax (GST). A federal consumption, or value-added tax introduced by the Conservative government in 1991, applied to virtually all goods and services sold at all stages of production and distribution. The few exempt and zero-rated (0 per cent-taxed) goods and services include basic foodstuffs, most health and dental services, educational services, and residential rents.

The GST, which replaced the federal manufacturers' sales tax, is similar to retail sales tax in that it is paid by the consumer; however, as it applies to all stages of production and distribution, businesses can recover the GST they pay for commercial purposes. The government also introduced a GST credit for which low-income people can qualify through income tax returns.

The tax was introduced despite considerable opposition. Indeed its adoption by Parliament was ensured only after Prime Minister Brian Mulroney, using an obscure section of the *Constitution Act* (s.26), had eight additional senators appointed to overcome a Liberal majority in the upper house. Criticism from the political left focussed on the regressive nature of the tax, that is, its ultimate incidence on the individual consumer bears no direct relationship to one's ability to pay; critics on the political right condemned the GST as a "tax grab." Despite the government's assertion it was "revenue neutral," revenue from the GST has been significantly greater than expected. The unpopularity and defeat of the Conservative government in 1993 was due in some measure to the GST. The successor Liberal government, having promised to eliminate it, did not; instead, it negotiated a "harmonized" federal-provincial sales tax (HST) with some provinces.

Government bills. Public bills or legislation introduced by the government and to whose passage it is committed. Consideration of government bills dominates the legislative agenda. A government may be politically embarrassed if forced by opposition criticism and public opinion to withdraw or significantly alter a bill. Because public division among government party supporters is even more embarrassing, a government usually discusses its intentions in caucus before introducing controversial legislation in the house. In Canada, major government bills, especially supply bills, are questions of confidence on which, if defeated, the government is obliged by convention either to seek dissolution of the legislature for an election or resign. See **Legislation; Responsible government.**

Governor General. The person who exercises the functions of the Crown in Canada under Letters Patent made effective by the sovereign. The appointment of the governor general is formally a function of the sovereign, but informally of the federal cabinet, notably the prime minister. The appointment is usually for five years although this term may be modified.

The *Constitution Act, 1867* describes a role for the governor general, but Letters Patent from the sovereign also delineate the governor general's role. Until the Imperial Conference of 1926, governors general were not only representatives of the formal non-resident head of state, but also of the British government in Canada. Since 1947, governors general have exercised the power and authority of the Crown in Canada with the advice of the sovereign's Privy Council for Canada, effectively the federal cabinet. Important powers include appointment of federal ministers of the Crown, notably the prime minister, and provincial lieutenant-governors, judges and administrative officials. They also include the power to dismiss federal ministers, notably the prime minister, and the power to summon, prorogue and dissolve Parliament, the latter in order to hold a general election. The *Constitution Act* grants the governor general exclusive power to recommend legislation which involves public expenditures or revenue from taxation. Under the Act, the governor general may also appoint senators, refuse royal assent to legislation and disallow provincial legislation.

However, in these important matters, the governor general acts on the advice of the Privy Council for Canada, as the governor-in-council, the effective part of which is the federal cabinet, or government-of-the-day. But there remains a residue of discretionary authority, or crown prerogative, pertaining to the dissolution of Parliament and the appointment and dismissal of the prime minister. In this respect, the governor general's primary constitutional duty is to ensure that there is a government in office that has the confidence of the House of Commons. The last time a governor general rejected a prime minister's advice was in 1926 when Governor General Byng refused Liberal Prime Minister Mackenzie King's request for dissolution of Parliament and an election, eight months after the previous election and when King's government was on the verge of losing a vote of confidence. Instead, he accepted King's resignation and appointed Conservative leader Arthur Meighen as prime minister. Unfortunately for both Byng and Meighen, the Conservative minority government lasted only three sitting days. Byng then had no recourse but to dissolve Parliament, and in the subsequent election the Liberals won a majority. Though the Liberals made Byng's "intervention" in 1926 an election issue, the governor general retains this extraordinary discretionary power to dismiss a government. However, a prudent governor general would be one inclined to let the political parties and the electorate resolve questions of political misbehaviour, and exercise the prerogative only in the most dire circumstances to protect the constitution, satisfied that such discretionary action will be deemed justified.

Since 1947, the office of governor general has been continually "nationalized." In 1952, following a succession of Britons in the office, Vincent Massey was the first Canadian appointed governor general. Since then, custom suggests not only that Canadians hold the office, but that there be appointed alternately an anglophone and a francophone. Vice-regal appointments have been seen to acknowledge Acadians, women, Canadians born elsewhere, and Canadians of neither French nor British ethnic origin. Also, since the 1970s, the federal government has "advised" the governor general to engage in activity appropriate to a head of state rather than a representative of a non-resident head of state. Domestically, the occasional presence of the governor general in the Arctic, for example, represents a display of national sovereignty over the archipelago; internationally, the governor general has made official state visits to other countries. See **Crown**; **Crown prerogatives**; **Governor-in-council**; **King-Byng Dispute**.

Governor General's warrants. Authorization issued through an order-in-council for unforseen emergency expenditure of public money not approved by Parliament. According to provisions of the *Financial Administration Act*, the governor-in-council issues warrants when the Treasury Board reports, on the advice of the relevant minister, that such authorization is necessary. The government must report the issuance of warrants in the *Canada Gazette* within thirty days. The expenditures must be included as part of the next supplementary estimates. Only the government has the authority to put supply bills before Parliament, but Parliament must sanction all expenditures, normally before the actual disbursement of the funds. See **Budget and budgetary process**.

Governor-in-council. The formal constitutional body through which the federal cabinet exercises executive power.

Under the *Constitution Act, 1867* and Letters Patent (1947), the governor general advised by the Queen's Privy Council for Canada constitutes the executive power. The cabinet or government-of-the-day, which the governor general appoints, has no statutory status by itself. Rather, the cabinet is the effective part of the Council, whose advice the governor general virtually always accepts. Thus, the governor-in-council is the governor general acting on the advice of the cabinet; and the executive instrument of the governor-in-council is an order-in-council or minute of the Council. The governor general does not attend cabinet meetings, but signs orders or minutes delivered from cabinet through the Privy Council Office.

In the provinces, a similar relationship exists between the lieutenant-governors and their Executive Councils—effectively the provincial cabinets or governments-of-the-day. The lieutenant-governor, however, is a federal officer. Under the *Constitution Act*, the governor-in-council, effectively the prime minister, appoints lieutenant-governors, and Parliament establishes their salaries. Though now a power not likely to be exercised, the governor-in-council, that is, the federal cabinet, may instruct provincial lieutenant-governors to reserve provincial legislation for the federal government's consideration and possible disallowance. See **Disallowance**; **Reservation**.

Green (coloured) paper. A government document that contains legislative proposals for discussion. Governments are not committed to the proposals in papers traditionally described as green papers, but can use their publication to gauge public opinion. Governments also publish green papers on matters of public interest on which it does not wish to commit itself at present. When a green paper is tabled in a legislature, it is usually sent to a committee which will hold hearings and report to the legislature on the proposals. Subsequently, the government might introduce legislation on the question, or if it wishes to delay further might publish a white paper, containing specific government proposals, for still further discussion.

Grit (Clear Grit). A popular term to refer to Liberals and the Liberal party in Canada. The phrase "Clear Grit" was popularized by editor and political reformer George Brown in Canada West in 1849-50. It indicates the quality of character which Brown thought necessary for members of his wing of the Reform party in the Province of Canada. The term was applied in the post-Confederation period to the Liberal party, which represented the same rural interests in Ontario and which included Brown himself as a prominent member.

Gross Domestic Product (GDP). A statistical statement which the federal government (Statistics Canada) publishes concerning economic activity, based on the Canadian System of National Accounts. This system is closely related to an international standard of national accounts. By totalling all costs incurred in production and subtracting imports, the GDP measures the market value of all final goods and services produced in a specific period by Canadian factors of production. Demand for Canadian goods and services arises from private and public spending, business investment and export demand. The GDP is a measure of the cycle of domestic economic expansion and recession, and generally of how well the economy is performing.

H

Hansard. The informal name for the verbatim record of debates in the House of Commons, Senate and provincial legislatures, named after the family of Luke Hansard, original printers of debates of the British Parliament.

Edited, translated and printed in English and in French, the House of Commons Hansard is publicly available after each day's sitting. A revised, indexed and bound edition is published later. An electronic version is also available. The official parliamentary English titles are *House of Commons Debates: Official Report* and *Debates of the Senate: Official Report.* The daily record, with minor editorial emendations by members of parliament and senators to correct grammar and achieve clarity, is compiled from shorthand notes of "reporters," who work from the floor of the legislative chamber during the debate. The term Hansard is also used informally with reference to the published record of committee meetings.

Have (have-not) provinces. A popular term which designates provinces which do or do not receive unconditional equalization payments or other adjustment grants from the federal government under federal-provincial tax agreements.

Various formulae have been in effect since the 1950s to calculate payments intended to raise the per capita revenue of each "have-not" province to a defined national average of provincial per capita tax revenue. The commitment of the federal government to the principle of equalization payments was entrenched in the *Constitution Act, 1982* (Part III). See **Equalization grants; Federal-provincial tax-sharing agreements (fiscal federalism)**.

Head of state. The person who holds the political office that embodies the authority and power of the state—in Canada, a non-resident monarch represented by the governor general of Canada, and within their respective provincial jurisdictions, the lieutenant-governors. Both constitutional statutes and conventions limit the powers of the Canadian head of state and its representatives. See **Crown; Crown prerogatives; Custom, convention and usage; Governor General**.

High Commissioner (Commission). The representative of Canada in each Commonwealth country and that of each Commonwealth country in Canada.

The terms, used instead of "ambassador" and "embassy" to distinguish member-states of the Commonwealth from other countries, are of nineteenth-century origin, when Canadian agents had no international status except as associates of British diplomats. Canada's representative in London was designated a high commissioner rather than an ambassador and had consular rather than diplomatic rank. This model was followed in the cases of Australia, New Zealand and South Africa when they gained self-governing status in their internal affairs in the early twentieth century. In time, Canada and the other dominions acquired status in external relations in their own right. Since the transformation of the British Empire to the large Commonwealth of Nations following the Second World War, the terms "high commissioner" and "high commission" have continued to distinguish the particular relationship of the former colonies with Britain and to each other in the Commonwealth. See **British connection; Commonwealth (The British…of Nations)**.

Horizontal agencies. An informal term denoting administrative bodies in government that, in addition to being hierarchically organized in a single structure, have influence over other government bodies across the entire administration. At the federal level, for example, the president of the Treasury Board has authority over cabinet colleagues and across the government through the Treasury Board Secretariat, in consolidating and co-ordinating policy and procedures regarding budgetary process and accounting for expenditures. The Privy Council Office (or cabinet secretariat) responsible to the prime minister, the Department of Finance and the Public Service Commission are other examples of horizontal agencies in the federal administration. See entries on each of these agencies.

House leaders. Members of parliament, one designated from each party, to manage party conduct in the House of Commons, and collectively to seek agreement on scheduling business in the House. The government's house leader, a member of the cabinet, is responsible for obtaining agreement among the parties on the Commons' timetable. Acting in close touch with their respective party leaders, the house leaders have the authority to negotiate a timetable and hold their respective parties to the negotiated agreement. Recognizing that the government and opposition parties have different objectives in parliamentary proceedings, House leaders may not come to an agreement, in which case the government can introduce a motion to allocate specific time to consideration of a bill. See **Closure**; **Filibuster**.

House of Assembly. The official name for the elected legislatures of Ontario, Nova Scotia and Newfoundland. The legislature in Quebec is styled the National Assembly, and those of the other provinces the Legislative Assembly. The organization and procedures of the provincial legislatures are not too dissimilar from those of the House of Commons, especially in matters of constitutional convention. See **House of Commons**.

House of Commons. The elected lower house of the Parliament of Canada, some of whose members constitute the government, ministry, or cabinet; others, the opposition parties' leadership (shadow cabinet or critics); and most, backbench supporters of the parties. At a given time a few members may be sitting as Independents, unattached to any party in the House.

The composition of the House is based on the principle of representation by population in single-member constituencies allocated proportionately among the provinces, with minimal territorial representation and with a redistribution of seats following each decennial census (*Constitution Act, 1867*, ss.51-52), and a floor for provincial representation (*Constitution Act, 1982*, s.41[b]). At the beginning of the twenty-first century, there were 301 members of parliament, or MPs, representing a national population of approximately thirty million.

The behaviour of MPs is almost invariably dictated by the government or opposition status of their party, and enforced by MPs designated as party whips. The MPs are elected in constituency contests among candidates, most of whom represent established political parties. The contests take place on the same day, in a general election; otherwise some MPs are elected in by-elections to fill vacancies that occur between general elections. The successful candidates sit with other MPs elected from their party. The House is divided by an aisle, with government MPs sitting on one side to the right of the Speaker, and opposition MPs on the other side, the two groups facing each other. MPs of the leading, or official opposition party sit to the left of the Speaker, with the opposition party leader and critics facing the prime minister and the cabinet, with smaller opposition parties also on the left side of the chamber. As each MP is assigned a desk, in the case of large government majorities, some government MPs may actually be placed for convenience on the opposition side; in the case of a House of minorities, some opposition MPs may be seated on the government side. House rules, or Standing Orders, define the number of MPs required for a party to have official standing in the House for purposes of participating in House and committee deliberations.

The principle of responsible government requires that cabinet ministers have seats in the House (or, though less politically desirable, in the appointed Senate), and that the government retain the support of the House on major bills, especially money bills. The governor general appoints as prime minister someone who is likely to command majority support in the House. But given formal party rules selecting a leader and the convention of party discipline, the exercise of this prerogative and the "swearing-in" of a government is usually a formality. Subsequently, the House responds to the government's agenda—government MPs positively, and opposition MPs critically. Except in cases of war and insurrection, a Parliament lasts no longer than five years (*Constitution Act, 1982*, s.4[2]). Normally, the governor general dissolves Parliament on the advice of the prime minister and issues writs for another election for a new House sometime within the constitutional five-year term.

As suggested above, the House of Commons is the site for two conflicting parliamentary roles: the surveillance and legitimation of government activity. The cabinet, acting formally in the name of the Crown, is responsible for the initiation of government legislation and must obtain parliamentary endorsement of its proposals and expenditures. The opposition's role is to criticize those proposals and government policy generally, undermining public support for the government in the next election, if not defeating it in a division of the House and thus forcing an election (see **Legislation**). In Parliaments where the government party has a majority of MPs, the opposition will not likely bring down the government, but it can influence the government's policy through various tactics, and upset its legislative timetable. Normally, the government controls the legislative timetable, but the opposition can also prolong debate on a government measure, perhaps forcing the government to impose closure (see **Closure** and **Filibuster**). Also, the daily oral question period, so-called "Opposition days," and motions to adjourn the House to debate urgent matters, are opportunities available to the opposition to throw the government off balance and to call into question its competence. In these various manoeuvres, the role of the mass media in transmitting the parliamentary debate to the public and generating public opinion is crucial. Since 1977, debates of the House of Commons have been available for broadcast by radio and television.

During the question period, the principle of responsible government is personified in exchanges between ministers and opposition critics. Some questions may be written down and placed on the Order Paper, to receive a printed reply later. The oral question period, however, permits direct questioning of ministers. Any member, other than those in the cabinet, may ask a question of a minister, but usually the leading opposition speakers and selected backbenchers on the opposition side of the House dominate question period. Ministers may be asked questions about activities in currently held portfolios only. Dissatisfied questioners may give notice that they intend to pursue a matter prior to adjournment later in the day. In that brief debate, ministers' parliamentary secretaries usually defend the government against the opposition attack (see **Question period**). Up to 25 days are allotted to the opposition in three supply periods to determine the subject of debate. Supply periods are those occasions in which the government is seeking passage of various supply, or appropriation, bills in a session (see **Budget and budgetary process; Supply period**). The object here is to force the government to defend measures which the opposition feels are weak points in the government's armour. The opposition may also move adjournment of the House to discuss an important matter of great urgency that has risen unexpectedly and is not likely to be considered in normal business that day. If the Speaker, a neutral MP usually in past practice from the government's side, determines that the request is appropriate, the motion to adjourn will be held over until the evening, at which time an extensive debate will take place on the subject, perhaps lasting through the night. When satisfied that the debate has been concluded, the Speaker will declare the motion to adjourn carried and adjourn the House until the next sitting, perhaps only a few hours hence. Even if the Speaker does not accept the motion to adjourn, the opposition will have raised the issue to the government's potential embarrassment (see **Urgent business [emergency debate]**).

The debate on the Speech from the Throne—formally a debate on a government motion commending the governor general for the address opening the session—and the debate on the budget brought down by the minister of finance are occasions for general debate. In those cases, the opportunity for backbenchers to participate in House debate is greater than in the situations discussed above, which tend to be dominated on both sides by frontbenchers. However, there has been a tendency in recent years to devote less time to the general debates.

The role of the private member (that is, an MP who is not a cabinet minister) is severely constrained by party discipline. Within this stricture, however, MPs participate in *in-camera* sessions of the party caucus and caucus committees. They may participate actively in committees of the House, introduce private members' legislation, and act as a constituency ombudsman, redressing grievances of constituents (see **Caucus; House of Commons committees; Standing [select, special, joint] committees [of the House and Senate]; Members of Parliament; Private members' legislation**).

The chief officer of the House of Commons is the Speaker, whose election from among MPs is the prime constitutional order of business when the House first meets after an election (*Constitution Act, 1867*, s.44), and whose duties are outlined in Standing Orders, or rules, of the House. Until 1986, the selection of Speaker was largely the prerogative of the prime minister, nominated by the prime minister and elected by the House which usually comprised a majority of government MPs. Since then, the Speaker has been elected by majority vote of the House in secret balloting, the results of which are announced without numbers mentioned by the Clerk of the House. The Speaker is responsible to the House and not to the government, although the Speaker is usually a government party MP. The Speaker's main function is to preside over proceedings impartially, but also to maintain the rights and privileges of MPs, dealing with points of order and of privilege, and occasionally requiring members to withdraw from the chamber for unparliamentary behaviour (see **Parliamentary privileges [immunities]**). The Speaker also manages the administration of the House and the permanent employees who staff the House and the committees (see **Speaker**). Because impartiality prevents the Speaker from expressing opinions publicly even on concerns of constituents, the government will be solicitous towards concerns expressed privately.

Other officers of the House include: the deputy and acting speakers, nominated by the prime minister and elected by the House, and such permanent and appointed officers as the Clerk of the House, principal clerks, the sergeant-at-arms, and parliamentary counsel. The deputy speaker occupies the Speaker's chair when the Speaker is absent and otherwise chairs the committee of the whole House. Like the Speaker, the deputy and acting speakers are MPs chosen at the beginning of a Parliament and usually for its duration. The Clerk, who holds the rank of deputy minister, is the recording officer and is responsible for advising all members, but notably the Speaker and House committees, on procedural matters, and for the safekeeping of House documents. The principal clerks act as reading clerks when documents must be read in the House, and are also responsible for ensuring that relevant documents are available to MPs. Parliamentary counsel prepare memoranda and opinions on legal and constitutional matters and advise MPs on proposed amendments or private members' legislation. The sergeant-at-arms attends the Speaker with the Mace, the symbol of the authority of the House vested in the Speaker, and is responsible for House fittings; in addition, the office of the sergeant-at-arms engages messengers, pages and temporary constables and labourers when necessary. Finally, there is an administrative organization of the House— involving personnel, building services and legislative services—that is responsible to the Clerk of the House; and there is a financial and management administration in the Board of Internal Economy, chaired by the Speaker and including government and opposition MPs.

House of Commons committees. Meetings of all or some members of parliament in forums subsidiary to the House of Commons. In addition to committees of the whole House, which are chaired by the deputy or acting speakers who are chosen shortly after the opening of the first session of a Parliament, there are standing and special committees of the House as well as joint and special committees with the Senate.

House rules require the striking, or appointment, of standing committees in major areas of public policy, each with approximately fifteen to twenty members, to consider estimates, or expenditure proposals, from government departments and agencies, government legislation and other matters relevant to their policy field as authorized by the House. There is also provision for standing joint committees with the Senate, including a joint committee that scrutinizes regulations and other statutory instruments (see **Statutory instrument**). Finally, special and special joint committees have been used, for example, to examine constitutional proposals.

Party representation on committees approximates the proportion of party representation in the House, and membership is determined by party leaders. Permanent employees of the House of Commons serve as committee staff. Verbatim records of proceedings of public sessions are published. The chairs of standing committees are, given government majorities, usually government MPs (except in the case of the Committee on Public Accounts). To maintain a degree of continuity and expertise, only pre-designated alternates or "associate members" may substitute for an absent member. In addition to standing committees scrutinizing government estimates and conducting a post-audit function and examining specific bills, special committees may, with government compliance, hold public hearings on policy matters prior to the introduction of legislation.

The advantage of the standing and special committee system is that public officials, including ministers, representatives of interest groups, and policy experts may be heard and questioned. Thus, the legislature becomes a more effective site for public education and future changes in public policy and possibly even changes to legislation already proposed. The mass media have given increasing but necessarily still selective attention to committee hearings, and some are televised on the parliamentary television channel when proceedings of the House itself are not being broadcast. Within sixty sitting days of the House receiving a committee report, the government is obliged to table a reply. Although standing committees, in particular, have recently acquired greater autonomy in determining their own agenda, party discipline may be enforced through the party whips, especially on the government side, should any committee's activity diverge too much from the government's interests. See **Committee of the Whole**; **Standing (select, special, joint) committees (of the House and Senate)**.

Hunter v. Southam (**1984**). A decision of the Supreme Court pertaining to protection against unreasonable search and seizure in section 8 of the Canadian Charter of Rights and Freedoms. The Supreme Court denied broad powers of search to the federal government in investigations and prosecutions under anti-combine legislation.

This was an early Charter decision by which the Court adopted a "broad, purposive analysis, which interprets specific provisions of a constitutional document in light of its larger objects." The Court, in this and other decisions, has adopted a non-interpretive approach to Charter cases to review legislation on substantive grounds to achieve for Canadians the full benefit of Charter protection. In effect, judicial review is a continuous process of constitutional clarification whereby generally expressed rights in the Charter are interpreted in a contemporary context to circumscribe legislative, executive and administrative power.

This particular case involved an authorization by the director of the federal Combines Investigation Branch to search the files of *The Edmonton Journal*, a Southam newspaper. The Court ruled on the purpose of search- and-seizure limitations to determine when it was reasonable to conduct a search and seize property. Since the purpose of such limitations is to protect privacy, the reasonableness of a particular search must be considered beforehand.An authorization must be made by a neutral and impartial person determining that the interests of the state are superior to the individual's right to privacy; also, authorization requires "probable" rather than "possible" grounds that evidence pertaining to an investigation would be found in the search. See **Canadian Charter of Rights and Freedoms (1982)**; **Judicial review (interpretive; non-interpretive)**; **Supreme Court**.

I

Immigration and Refugee Board. A court of record established by Parliament in 1988 to deal with matters previously dealt with by the Immigration Appeal Board and the Refugee Status Advisory Committee.

The operation of both the law and the appeal procedure with reference to immigration and refugee status is always controversial. There is usually an extensive backlog of cases, especially concerning refugee claims, which involves many members of parliament in their constituency service roles. The government has occasionally had to deal with controversial government decisions suggesting political favouritism, and with complaints about incompetent members of appeal panels established to facilitate processing of claims. There are also complaints that some board members are too lenient. The most important case, with respect to the political process generally, involved a successful appeal to the Supreme Court under the Canadian Charter of Rights and Freedoms. To facilitate the hearing of refugee claims, refugee claimants were no longer to appear before a panel, but to be represented, in effect, through a transcript of an interview with an administrative official. In *Re Singh and Minister of Employment and Immigration* (1985), the Court ruled the procedure unconstitutional. Guarantees in the Charter respecting "principles of fundamental justice" did not countenance administrative burdens and costs in the process of fact-finding with respect to adversarial hearings as sufficient to restrict "everyone['s] ... right to life, liberty and security of the person..." (s.7). See **Singh Case** (*Re Singh and Minister of Employment and Immigration* [1985]).

Imperial conferences. Forums of prime ministers and ministerial colleagues from the self-governing colonies and dominions of the British Empire, held occasionally between 1887 and 1930 in London. The conference was neither an executive nor a legislative body, though it would express opinions in resolutions. Topics of the early conferences included imperial federation, defence and tariffs; and in later years, foreign policy, national autonomy and independence.

In 1914, the British government assumed the dominions, such as Canada, to be at war upon its declaration that a state of war existed. Canada did join the imperial war effort from 1914 to 1918, but was a separate signatory to the war's conclusion and joined the League of Nations. The imperial conference of 1926 issued a declaration of equality between Britain and the dominions—Australia, New Zealand and South Africa, in addition to Canada—in imperial and international affairs. This declaration was a turning point from subordination in the Empire to association in a Commonwealth of nations. The declaration read in part: "They [the dominions] are autonomous Communities within the British Empire, equal in status, in no way subordinate one to another in any aspect of their domestic or external affairs, though united by a common allegiance to the Crown, and freely associated as members of the British Commonwealth of Nations...." The imperial conference of 1930 (the last so styled) requested that the British Parliament pass certain resolutions of the conferences of 1926 and 1930, clarifying the new association. Thus, the British Statute of Westminster (1931) became a constitutional statute, removing most statutory impediments to national autonomy and independence of the dominions. See **Statute of Westminster (U.K., 1931).**

Income tax. A tax levied by federal and provincial governments on all forms of income, personal and corporate, according to various rates on that income less permitted deductions, or taxable income, and subject to special surtaxes.

Graduated rates imply a progressive system of income tax according to the taxpayers' ability to pay: that is, the higher the taxable income, the greater the percentage of that income is subject to taxation. An income tax system with only one level of taxation is referred to as a "flat tax."

Permissible deductions from gross income, as well as deductions from the calculated "taxable income" before final determination of the tax due, represent government encouragement in those tax-deductible activities. Thus a dollar earned is not necessarily a dollar taxed, as some people more than others can lower their levels of taxable income and final tax due. Surtaxes are measures by which the government, having granted a universal benefit with one hand, may retrieve it from people of high income with the other, or levy purportedly temporary taxes to deal with urgent needs for revenue.

Indexing (de-indexing). The periodic adjustment of private contractual compensation and government payment of social benefits on the basis of changes in the cost of living. Indexing wages or private pension benefits to the cost of living is referred to as the Cost of Living Adjustment, or COLA clause. Governments wishing to "de-index" a benefit have learned through public opposition that it is easier to "claw back" a universal benefit from high-income earners through provisions of the income tax system. See **Clawback**.

Indian Act. A federal statute adopted in 1876 that established in Confederation a continuation of British imperial policy toward certain Aboriginal peoples of British North America that began with the Royal Proclamation of 1763.

Historically, British policy was designed to maintain the allegiance of Native Peoples they encountered regarding exploration, defence, trade, and eventually the ceding of land and economic rights to facilitate European settlement, through treaties and agreements setting aside "reserves" and providing "presents." The *Constitution Act, 1867* (before 1982, the *British North America Act*) granted authority over "Indians, and lands reserved for Indians" to the federal government (s.91:24) and the *Indian Act* consolidated this power which had already been exercised in the form of treaties similar to those with the British, though there remained Aboriginal populations, notably in British Columbia and the Arctic that had no treaties with the Imperial or Canadian governments. The Métis population on the prairies, descended from European traders and Native women, were not countenanced within the terms of the Act. Thus, the Aboriginal population from a legal standpoint comprised status and non-status (off reserve) Indians, and treaty and non-treaty Indian groups. Native Peoples in the Arctic were determined in law to be "Indian" within the meaning of the *Constitution Act*, but not under the *Indian Act*. It was not until the 1950s that Native Peoples in the Arctic received federal educational and health services, but were subject also to disruption of lifestyle and family through relocation.

In practice, the *Indian Act* has been a paternalistic, bureaucratic and repressive instrument of "white" control over a subject peoples. The state of Canada's Native population is tragic and well known. There are approximately 1,350,00 people of Aboriginal origins, a population that generates dismal statistics on educational achievement, employment, poverty, health, alcoholism, violence, suicide and mortality. Until the 1970s, Native affairs were not prominent on the public agenda because the Native population was small, dispersed, and poorly organized, the people generally possessing low self-esteem induced by the loss of land, livelihood and culture, and reinforced from generation to generation. At the same time, non-Native Canadians generally accepted these conditions as characteristics of a population, without regard to the role played by government policy, especially under the *Indian Act*.

In 1969, the federal Liberal government proposed in a White Paper that the Act be abolished and Indians be integrated into the wider Canadian society. The White Paper was eventually withdrawn, having served unintentionally as a catalyst to mobilize Native groups already upset at the government's program of bilingualism and biculturalism that defined the French and the English as Canada's "two founding peoples." Since the 1970s, federal policy has been directed to give more responsibility for programs and services to Native councils and to settle land claims. The *Constitution Act, 1982* included a definition of Aboriginal peoples and an acknowledgement of existing Aboriginal and treaty rights. The *Indian Act* was subsequently brought into conformity with the Canadian Charter of Rights and Freedoms, notably regarding gender. The constitutional Charlottetown Accord of 1992, which was rejected in a national referendum, would have recognized Aboriginal government as a third order of government, in addition to federal and provincial governments. Native groups participated in negotiating the Accord: the Assembly of First Nations on behalf of Indians under the *Indian Act* (status Indians); the Native Council of Canada for non-status Indians; the Métis National Council of Canada, and the Inuit Tapirisat. When the Accord was defeated, Native leaders and the federal government urged continued negotiations at both federal and provincial levels to institute the intent of the Accord, short of constitutional amendment. Federal responsibilities under the *Indian Act* have been devolved to Native groups in selective provinces. See **Charlottetown Accord (1992)**; **Land claims and settlements (Native; Aboriginal)**; **Native (First Nations) self-government**; **Royal Proclamation (1763)**.

Indirect taxation. Any tax which will likely be passed on by the direct payer and therefore be borne indirectly by someone else. Under the *Constitution Act, 1867*, the federal government has unconditional access to both direct and indirect taxation (s.91:3: "The raising of Money by any Mode or System of Taxation"), and the provinces conditional access only to "Direct Taxation within the Province...for Provincial Purposes" (s.92:2). See **Direct (indirect) taxation**.

Information Commissioner. An officer of Parliament empowered under the *Access to Information Act, 1983* to investigate complaints from individuals denied information by the government and, if necessary, to seek redress through the courts.

Upon denial of a request for information, the government must cite a statutory basis for the denial. In addition to appealing a denial, complaints can be lodged if the government is unresponsive or if there are excessive charges for the information. The commissioner's staff may examine any record except cabinet papers. On finding for a complainant, the commissioner attempts to persuade the relevant government agency to comply and, if access continues to be denied, may appeal to the Federal Court. The commissioner's annual reports to Parliament and addresses by the commissioner and staff to the interested audiences are intended to improve public knowledge about the Act and encourage government bodies to adopt practices consistent with the Act. See **Freedom of information**.

Inner cabinet. A select group of cabinet ministers who have a leading role for the whole cabinet in setting government priorities and decision making. The organization of the cabinet is the prerogative of the head of government, the prime minister or provincial premier, and the notion of an inner cabinet has arisen since the growth in the size of the cabinet, making it an unwieldy executive body. In 1968, Pierre Trudeau was the first prime minister to create a small committee on priorities and planning ("P and P") that constituted his inner circle of key ministers. Subsequent prime ministers have followed suit, either formally through their "P and P," or an even smaller group whose membership by portfolio represents the government's chief policy preoccupations. See **Cabinet; Cabinet organization**.

Inter- (intra-) state federalism. A reference to the relative effectiveness in a particular federal system of the subnational (that is, state or provincial) and national (or central) political institutions in representing regional views and interests. In a federal system characterized by inter-state relations, regional interests are effectively represented by subnational institutions and actors in discussions with political actors at the centre. In a system characterized by intra-state relations, the national institutions at the centre contain effective representatives of regional interests.

In the case of Canada's executive federalism, provincial premiers pose as more effective representatives of local interests than many federal cabinet ministers, members of parliament, or senators from their provinces or regions, and the accommodation of regional interests includes inter-state discussions (sometimes described as diplomacy) among federal and provincial government officials. By contrast, in the United States, state governors are less effective regional political actors than members of both houses of the US Congress. Consequently the US Senate and House of Representatives are the focus of intra-state political accommodation. See **Federalism; Geographic cleavage**.

Interdelegation Reference (Nova Scotia, 1951); ...of legislative power. A Reference in which the Supreme Court of Canada declared the direct delegation of powers between Parliament and the provincial legislatures to be incompatible with the federal constitution (*Attorney-General for Nova Scotia v. Attor ney-General for Canada* [1951]).

The federal Rowell-Sirois Royal Commission on Dominion-Provincial Relations (1940) had recommended a constitutional amendment to permit such delegation of legislative responsibility. In the Interdelegation Reference, the Court declared unconstitutional a Nova Scotia statute which delegated provincial authority to the federal government and anticipated delegation of federal power to the province. Thus, the Supreme Court upheld the "watertight compartment" approach to the division of powers under the *British North America Act* (since 1982, the *Constitution Act*). Subsequently indirect means were tried in order to effect the same outcome as direct delegation of jurisdictional competence. One year after the Interdelegation Reference, the Supreme Court validated the indirect device of parliamentary delegation of powers to a board established by a provincial legislature, rather than to the provincial legislature itself (*PEI Potato Marketing Board v. H.B. Willis Inc.*, 1952).

Constitutional discussions following patriation of the *Constitution Act* in 1982 included possible amendments to the constitution to permit the inter-delegation of legislative power between Parliament and the provincial legislatures upon mutual consent. A joint House of Commons-Senate committee proposal for such an amendment was endorsed by the federal government in 1990. Discussion centred on the likely effect of legislative asymmetry in the federal system and the development of a so-called "checkerboard federalism": whether there should be limits on the interdelegation of legislative power; whether interdelegation should require the approval of more legislatures than those directly affected; whether it should be confirmed periodically, and whether there should be a means of revoking it. See **Judicial Committee of the Privy Council**; **Supreme Court**; **"Watertight compartments" Doctrine (constitution)**.

Interdepartmental committees. An administrative device to achieve co-ordination of government activity. Many government departments have responsibility for programs that bear on related areas of public policy. Thus, governments often create committees of high- and middle-level officials to advise individual ministers or the cabinet on new policy or on improvements in established programs. Some interdepartmental committees are more or less formalized than others. Not surprisingly, these committees are also the site for the protection of departmental jurisdictions and bureaucratic fiefdoms.

Interest groups. Organizations that make demands on political authorities for specific policy outputs, sometimes termed "pressure groups."

Interests that are aggregated in groups are more likely to have political influence than are unaggregated interests. Whether group politics is hostile or not to democratic politics, it is certainly a clear and irreversible feature of the collectivist age. In Canada, there are virtually no residents without an organization whose leadership seeks some protection or enhancement from the government on their behalf. There are many types of interest groups—such as the non-economic and economic, permanent and ad hoc, self-interested and public-oriented, elite- or mass membership-based, regional, national or international, and constantly active or politically latent groups.

The political behaviour of an interest group in Canada often depends on its type and upon the federal and parliamentary nature of the political system. The constitutional entrenchment of the Canadian Charter of Rights and Freedoms in 1982 has also given impetus to some interests and enhanced the political influence of certain organizations pursuing equality rights under the Charter. Some groups—such as the Canadian Bar Association, the Canadian Federation of Agriculture, the Canadian Legion, and the Consumers' Association of Canada—have easy access to the public decision makers who are responsible for formulating policies directly in the areas of these groups' concerns. Indeed, some groups have had at times an occupational affinity with specific political roles. Usually, federal ministers of justice and provincial attorneys-general are lawyers who, in private practice, have been members of lawyers' organizations. Similarly, ministers of finance are usually people who, in their private careers, have been closely associated with organized business groups. At one time, being a medical doctor was thought not just a suitable, but a necessary qualification to be a provincial minister of health. Since the introduction of public medicare, the relationship between provincial medical associations and the provincial bureaucracies may have become more formal and less friendly, but the relationships are still necessarily close.

In contrast to such sectional interest groups are those better described as social movements. These are organizations, linked with others in social movement networks, who are agents of social change as much as, or even more so than, seekers of particular policies or benefits for their members. As social activists, they are interested in altering fundamental societal relationships or attitudes pertaining, for example, to women's rights and gender relations generally, the environment, and community development worldwide. Social movement organizations are reluctant to develop intimate relations with political and administrative decision makers for fear of being "co-opted." Indeed, some see state actors as "guilty" of inappropriate behaviour as much as, or in the cases, for example, of nuclear power development and weak environmental protection regimes, more so than private-sector actors. Consequently, they have a more adversarial relationship with the political authorities, hoping that their various forms of public protest will create favourable public opinion that will force governments to act.

The federal system in Canada makes it necessary for an interest group to select its target and allocate its resources strategically. Some groups will have to operate at both levels, and possibly in all provinces; others may be able to concentrate on one level and in only some provinces. For example, the Canadian labour movement's central body, the Canadian Labour Congress, is a weak federation of provincial groups. This reflects the particular need for effective lobbying for labour's interests at the provincial level, where much of Canada's labour law is enacted and administered. The Canadian Bankers Association, on the other hand, operates in large part at the federal level, as Parliament has jurisdiction over banking. When the insurance industry opposed the introduction of government-operated medical insurance in the 1960s, it had to operate at both levels of government—at the federal level where legislation would allow the federal government to enter shared-cost agreements with the provinces, as well as at the provincial level where the programs would be implemented. Lobbying by the insurance industry against public automobile insurance, on the other hand, has been conducted only at the provincial level, particularly in those provinces where governments were considering the introduction of such programs.

Because parliamentary government in Canada concentrates power in the political and administrative executive, the cabinet and the civil service are the chief targets for interest group activity. If, for example, the group is working against a declared government objective, then legislators, the mass media and the public become the more obvious targets in a campaign which does not appear likely to be successful. Ongoing activity by interest groups may include targeting legislators, party caucuses and the mass media. But this is more to affect the environment for future discussions with government decision makers than to achieve a specific current campaign objective.

The entrenchment of the Canadian Charter of Rights and Freedoms in 1982 has increased the influence of some groups—particularly social movement organizations whose concerns have been "legitimized" by the Charter—and altered the configuration of interest representation and influence. In adjudicating

Charter cases, the Supreme Court has adopted a broad definition of judicial review to ensure Canadians the full benefit of Charter protection. The Charter identifies particular interests in sections 15, 27 and 28, and allows for "appropriate and just" judicial remedies to alleged infringements of Charter rights in section 24:1. In the 1980s, successful Charter challenges in the courts voided, for example, provisions of the Criminal Code regarding therapeutic abortions and statutory prohibitions against third-party, interest group advertising in federal election campaigns, as well as administrative procedures that violated principles of fundamental justice. The Supreme Court has included "sexual orientation" in section 15 as a prohibited basis for discrimination. Though their case was lost, the Supreme Court heard from peace activists opposed to the federal government's agreement with the United States to allow the testing of unarmed cruise missiles over Canada.

There are several indicators of an interest group's day-to-day influence on public decision making through positional politics. Some groups—traditional sectional interest groups more so than social movement organizations—are represented on advisory boards in the public bureaucracy. Formal appearances of major sectional interest groups before cabinet or the government's parliamentary caucus are occasions for the government party to convince those groups of its affinity with the group's interests, and for the group to convince its own members—and public opinion—of its competence and influence on the government. Large private corporations are represented in the Business Council of National Issues which regularly receives invitations to make representations to ministers, officials and legislative committees. Some banks, insurance companies, manufacturing and resource companies, and other government-regulated businesses make a practice of appointing former cabinet ministers, former senior civil servants and current senators to their boards of directors, thus forging a symbiotic relationship between themselves and the public decision makers: interest groups want appropriate government legislation and regulation; governments want assistance from interest groups in developing, legitimating and implementing their policy.

There has been a historic affinity between certain private interests and political parties in Canada. While much of the bargaining between interest groups and governments is secular and accommodative, these historic and current affinities do have some effect on the attitudes of the interest groups toward particular governments. Banks and manufacturing concerns, for example, have long been important financial contributors to the Liberal and Conservative parties; and the cabinets and opposition front benches of these parties have generally been populated with members of parliament integrated in the occupational and social environment of these interests. Given the Conservative party's refusal to merge with it, a strategic objective of the Canadian Alliance, formerly the Reform party, is to encourage the corporate business community to support the Alliance. The Co-operative Commonwealth Federation, precursor of the New Democratic party, was a federation of many groups, including farm and labour organizations. The transformation of the CCF to the NDP in the 1956-61 period was designed to achieve, in part, a larger and more effective affiliation of the Canadian labour movement to the social democratic party. Many NDP candidates and officials have held positions with some trade unions and farm organizations.

Consequences of the replacement of a virtual twenty-one-year-old federal Liberal regime with a Conservative government in 1984 included a cabinet with inexperienced ministers, a proliferation of partisan ministerial aides to counter the influence of officials who had long served under the Liberal government, and of unregulated lobbying firms and lobbyists in Ottawa. Many lobbyists aggressively promoted their personal connections with the new ministerial personalities and the Conservative party, rather than any expertise in policy or in the intricacies of policy making in the public administration. Indeed, during its first several years in office, the government experienced a series of conflict-of-interest scandals, including a judicial inquiry into the behaviour of one businessman-minister and a series of resignations, investigations and proceedings related to others. Consequently, the government proposed legislation respecting both conflict of interest and lobbying. One year after Parliament adopted the *Lobbyists Registration Act, 1989,* 295 firms, many employing a large number of lobbyists, had registered. Lobbyists who are solely employees of single firms or interest groups are also required to register. When the Liberals returned to office in 1993, the legislation was moderately strengthened, but otherwise the lobbying industry accommodated itself to the change of party government, partly through lobbying against even stronger amendments to the law and recruiting personnel with connections to the Liberal party. See **Conflict of interest; Lobby (-ist; -ing);Social movement organizations**.

Intergovernmental committees. Federal-provincial and interprovincial forums in which bargaining takes place in the context of contemporary executive, or administrative federalism in Canada. Executive federalism involves ongoing interaction between the two levels of government and among the provincial governments, especially those in the Maritimes and the prairie West. The bureaucratic process of accommodation has become so important in Canada that some observers have likened the intergovernmental committee system to a fourth branch of government, one that operates largely in private and for which there is no effective legislative oversight.

Federal-provincial committees have become numerous since the 1960s. They have involved increasingly more policy areas at more levels of the public administration, especially as the federal government's involvement in matters of provincial jurisdiction increased. The federal government's greater access to tax revenues has given it the ability to offer money to provinces for programs under provincial jurisdiction (see **Spending power**). Thus, there is federal-provincial consultation on a variety of matters within provincial jurisdiction. At the same time, there are provincial intergovernmental committees whose objective is to pressure the federal government with respect to policy matters.

The highest level of intergovernmental committees involves heads-of-government conferences—for example, the Conference of First Ministers, the Conference of Premiers, the Western Premiers' Conference, and the Maritime Premiers' Conference. Various ministerial conferences comprise second-rank intergovernmental committees, and they are closely associated with committees of senior officials (deputy and assistant deputy ministers). Finally, there is a level involving technical officials charged with making operational the agreements of the higher-level officials.

Many governments have separate departments of intergovernmental affairs. Some provincial premiers were reluctant to establish such structures outside their own office, perhaps much as Canadian prime ministers were once reluctant to relinquish responsibility for foreign affairs to a designated minister. At the federal level, especially given the strength of the sovereignty movement in Quebec, the federal intergovernmental affairs portfolio is held by a person who has the greatest confidence of the prime minister. See **Federalism**.

Interim supply, vote of. A vote by which a legislature authorizes government expenditures prior to the passage of the main estimates. In recent practice at the federal level, the vote on interim supply occurs in the House of Commons in March after the main estimates are tabled and sent to committee for study. The vote of interim supply assumes the main estimates will eventually pass. See **Budget and budgetary process; Estimates**.

International Joint Commission (IJC). A commission established under the Boundary Waters Treaty of 1909, with Canadian and United States sections. The IJC must approve any use, obstruction or diversion of boundary waters affecting the natural level or flow of boundary waters in the other country. It also examines and makes recommendations on the matters referred to the Commission by the two national governments.

Each of the national sections (for a total of two presiding commissioners and four others), is appointed by their respective government, and the Commission is responsible to the national governments. Occasionally, the IJC has been the site for political controversy and high-priority policy implementation. In 1963, the head of the Canadian section, General A.G.L. McNaughton, resigned in order to publicize his disagreement with the Canadian government over the Columbia River Treaty of 1959. In 1978, under the Great Lakes Water Quality Agreement, the two countries gave the IJC responsibility to co-ordinate and monitor programs dealing, for example, with municipal waste treatment. The IJC also plays a similar role respecting air quality under a 1991 Agreement.

Intra (ultra) vires. A phrase which describes the statutes of federal or provincial legislatures as being within (or beyond) their legislative competence described in the *Constitution Act 1867*, as determined through judicial review by the Judicial Committee of the Privy Council (until 1949) and by the Supreme Court. See **Federalism**.

J

Judicial (commission of) inquiry. Investigation by a panel comprising judges and lawyers or a single judge, established by executive order and reporting to a legislature. Such commissions of inquiry may be designated as "royal commissions" and have statutory powers usually associated with courts of law, in order to inquire into and report on specific questions which could give rise to criminal charges. Thus, the commissions may have legal staff and power of subpoena with respect to individuals and documents. Witnesses may be represented by lawyers, and interested parties may also request "standing" in order to comment on procedure and to cross-examine witnesses.

The statutes establishing inquiries and the procedures of the commission are themselves subject to judicial review. For example, in 1978 the Supreme Court of Canada declared that the powers of a commission of inquiry investigating the administration of justice within a province were constitutionally limited. It supported the federal government's opposition to the broad inquiry of a Quebec commission investigating the affairs of the RCMP, a federal police force. Declaring one section of the mandate to be unconstitutional, the Court observed: "Inasmuch as these are the regulations and practices of an agency of the federal government, it is clearly not within the proper scope of the authority of provincial government" (Mr. Justice Louis-Philippe Pigeon). Ruling that the provincial inquiry could not force a federal cabinet minister to appear as a witness, the Supreme Court said that in common law a commission of inquiry has no power to compel the attendance of witnesses and to require the production of documents. Any jurisdiction for such purposes depends on statutory authority, the Court declared, "and it seems that provincial legislation cannot be effective by itself to confer such jurisdiction as against the Crown in right of Canada."

Judicial inquiries may also come into conflict with the government that created them. Again in 1978-79, for example, a federally appointed royal commission of inquiry into certain RCMP activities sparred with the federal government over access to cabinet documents. Nor can judicial inquiries compromise a citizen's right to a fair trial. In Ontario, a judicial inquiry into alleged corruption respecting provincial Liberal party fundraising in the late 1980s was halted by the courts, and likewise an inquiry into a mining disaster in Nova Scotia in 1992, pending criminal investigations, and possible charges and trials. As in the cases cited above, there is often a political as well as a policy need to establish judicial inquiries. Notable federal judicial inquiries in the 1990s involved the non-medical use of proscribed drugs by athletes whose programs were supported by federal funds, and the behaviour of the Royal Canadian Mounted Police toward demonstrators, allegedly under direction from Liberal Prime Minister Jean Chrétien's office, during an Asia-Pacific Economic Cooperation (APEC) meeting in Vancouver. But the most controversial federal judicial inquiry in that decade involved the Liberal government's abrupt termination by executive order of an inquiry into the torture and murder of a Somali teenager by Canadian military personnel and the subsequent behaviour by senior officials, both military and civilian, in the Department of National Defence. See **Royal commission**.

Judicial Committee of the Privy Council (JCPC). Until 1949, the final appeal court for all cases except criminal cases in Canada. As an imperial constitutional court, the Judicial Committee of the Privy Council in London was particularly important in the development of Canadian federalism, essentially enlarging the scope of provincial power at the expense of the broad comprehensive legislative powers of Parliament through its interpretation of the *British North America Act, 1867* (since 1982, the *Constitution Act*).

During this period, the JCPC comprised British privy councillors who had held high positions on the bench and were assisted on occasion by judges from Empire and Commonwealth countries. The Judicial Committee, as an imperial appeal court, did not publish several judgments in a case; rather, it offered only one opinion (in the manner of the Privy Council itself). In 1949, the Supreme Court of Canada became the final court of appeal for Canadian cases.

Since the entrenchment of the Canadian Charter of Rights and Freedoms in the constitution in 1982, the Supreme Court has adopted a broad notion of judicial review in interpreting the contemporary constitution—that is, defining general phrases in the context of contemporary societal need. The JCPC, on the other hand, saw its role as strictly interpreting a British statute, the BNA Act, to preserve a fundamental characteristic of the Canadian union—federalism. At the same time, the JCPC may have been generally unappreciative of the difficulties associated with a federal political system that does not permit easy modification of the constitution as does a unitary state through an Act of a single legislature. The narrowness and inflexibility of judicial review under the JCPC was further reinforced by the single decision of the Court; the expression of one view did not allow for subsequent "distinction" on a case based on a variety of expressed opinions, as in decisions of the Supreme Court.

The JCPC has made some important constitutional judgments: *Russell v. the Queen*, 1882, in which it ruled, in a case involving a federal statute permitting local areas to prohibit the sale of liquor, that the federal government was dealing with "public order and safety" under the "Peace, Order, and good Government" clause (BNA Act, s.91, preamble), an action that took precedence over the provincial jurisdiction of property and civil rights (s.92:13), and thus granted a comprehensive legislative role for Parliament with the preamble to section 91 constituting a residual power clause; *Hodge v. The Queen*, 1883, in which the JCPC began to retreat from approval of the broad exercise of federal power under the "Peace, Order, and good Government" clause, declaring that in one aspect an Ontario statute providing for licensing and control of the sale of liquor locally by provincial authority was constitutional (s.92:8, :9, :15) and that each level of legislature was sovereign and not subordinate to the other (see **Aspect Doctrine**); *Maritime Bank v. Receiver-General of New Brunswick*, 1892, in which the principle of equality was declared among legislatures—in Lord Watson's words, the object of the BNA Act was neither "to weld the provinces into one, nor to subordinate provincial government to a central authority"; *Attorney-General for Ontario v. Attorney-General for Canada*, 1896, also known as the Local Prohibition Case, in which Parliament's power to encroach on provincial jurisdiction enumerated in section 92, using the "Peace, Order, and good Government" clause, was further denied. Having earlier been declared effective when the legislation was of nation-wide importance, the clause was now declared to be only a supplementary statement to the enumerated powers of Parliament which could not take primacy over the enumerated powers of the provincial legislatures. As a result of a reference, *Re Board of Commerce Act and Combines and Fair Prices Act, 1919*, in 1922, and *Toronto Electric Commissioners v. Snider* (1925), the JCPC, under Viscount Haldane, came to look upon Parliament's general power in the preamble to section 91 as an emergency power only. Attempting to reconcile the Judicial Committee's view in 1925 with its view in *Russell v. The Queen* in 1882, Haldane suggested that their lordships at that time must have considered drunkenness to constitute a threat to the nation. In the reference in 1937 concerning the federal *Employment and Social Insurance Act*, part of Conservative Prime Minister R.B. Bennett's New Deal, the JCPC declared the measure unconstitutional, and thus the economic depression insufficient to invoke emergency powers. In effect, "Property and Civil Rights" had become the residual power clause of the constitution, favouring the provinces.

The JCPC eventually denied not only the "Peace, Order, and good Government" clause as a source of comprehensive legislative competence for Parliament, but also "The Regulation of Trade and Commerce" power (s.91:2). Important cases here include *Citizens Insurance Co. v. Parsons and Queen Insurance Co. v. Parsons*, 1881, *Montreal v. Montreal Street Railway*, 1912, *Board of Commerce*, 1921, and a reference in 1937 on the *Natural Products Marketing Act*, another part of Bennett's New Deal.

The decisions of the JCPC were important in delineating jurisdictional responsibilities in a collectivist age. The JCPC, for example, declared the federal role in establishing laws relating to labour and collective bargaining to be restricted to areas in which Parliament had jurisdiction (Snider Case, 1925). Treaty-making power was cited to grant Parliament jurisdiction in the "new" fields of aeronautics and radio, but not to legislate on matters within provincial competence. Parliament acquired jurisdiction through treaty-making power as part of Empire (s.132) in the Aeronautics Reference, 1932; and, in the Radio Case, 1932, through "Peace, Order, and good Government" as a residual power in non-imperial treaty making, there being no specific reference to treaty-making power other than imperial treaties, the obligations for which fell to the federal government, and non-imperial treaties amounted to the same thing. However, the treaty-making powers of the federal government did not give it the power to legislate generally on such labour-related issues as hours of work, holidays and minimum wages (*Attorney-General for Canada v. Attorney-General for Ontario* [Labour Conventions Case, 1937])—also part of the abortive New Deal. By now, the strict "watertight compartments" view of federal-provincial jurisdiction, so called by Lord Atkin in the Labour Conventions Case, was dominant, despite an earlier characterization by Lord Sankey of the BNA Act as a "living tree capable of growth and expansion within its natural limits" which the JCPC did not wish "to cut down…, but rather give it a large and liberal interpretation" (*Edwards v. Attorney-General for Canada*, 1930, the Persons Case in which the use of the male pronoun in the *British North America Act* to describe senatorial qualification was ruled to apply as well to women). By Atkin's "watertight compartment" metaphor, matters assigned to Parliament were the responsibility of Parliament, matters assigned to the provinces were the responsibilities of the provincial legislatures, and this clear-cut distinction would be maintained except for the sole emergency of war.

In cases in 1945 and 1946, the JCPC wove an unsteady pattern in the matter of emergency powers. In 1946 (*Attorney-General of Ontario v. Canadian Temperance Federation*), Lord Simon asserted the Aspect Doctrine in *Hodge v. The Queen*—that the nation-wide importance of the issue (and not an emergency situation) was the litmus test of jurisdictional competence. In 1947 (*Co-operative Committee on Japanese Canadians v. Attorney-General for Canada*), however, the Judicial Committee reasserted the narrow emergency doctrine.

Since 1949, the Supreme Court of Canada has been the final court of appeal, and constitutional development became a matter largely of accommodative bargaining among the federal and provincial governments in the context of Court rulings. However, since 1982 the principle of parliamentary sovereignty within each jurisdiction's legislative competence has been fundamentally compromised by the entrenchment of the Canadian Charter of Rights and Freedoms. Until then, the courts tested legislation against the government-rights-based *Constitution Act, 1867.* Since 1982, legislation and administrative behaviour has also been subject to testing against the citizen-rights-based Charter with the courts as agencies of remedial action. Lord Sankey's "living tree" metaphor in 1930 has in effect been adopted, but in a different context. Sankey was encouraging legislative flexibility between two levels of legislative authority under the constitution. Now, under the contemporary constitution including the Charter, the courts themselves have become active in adjudicating all legislative, executive and administrative action, to provide people with the full benefit and protection of their Charter rights and thereby acquiring a degree of quasi legislative competence themselves. See **Canadian Charter of Rights and Freedoms (1982); Federalism; Judicial review (interpretive; non-interpretive); Supreme Court.**

Judicial review (interpretive; non-interpretive). Judicial judgment on the constitutionality of statutes and administrative behaviour.

Until 1982, Canada's legislatures were supreme within their areas of competence as specified in the *Constitution Act, 1867,* as adjudicated ultimately by the Judicial Committee of the Privy Council until 1949, and the Supreme Court of Canada. In 1982, the constitution was amended to include the Canadian Charter of Rights and Freedoms against which the actions of legislatures, executives and administrative tribunals at all levels of government can be reviewed and tested. It is therefore a matter for the courts to determine the constitutionality of government laws, regulations and administrative procedures, and, in the case of the Supreme Court, to supply an opinion (reference) on the constitutionality of a proposed statute or government action.

With respect to Charter rights, the Supreme Court has adopted a non-interpretive role. That is, judicial rulings are not based on interpretation or understanding of original intent respecting constitutional documents. Instead, the Court's non-interpretive rulings involve a "broad, purposive analysis, which interprets specific provisions of [the constitution] in light of its larger objects" (*Hunter v. Southam,* 1984) to secure the "full benefit" of Charter protection for Canadians (*R. v. Big M Drug Mart,* 1985). The Court is prepared to interpret the Charter permitting "growth, development and adjustment to changing societal needs" (*Motor Vehicle Reference,* 1985), ensuring that legislation complements the "democratic values expressed" in the Charter (*Morgentaler, Smoling and Scott v. The Queen,* 1988). The courts are also available under the Charter for Canadians to engage in remedial litigation, that is, to seek remedy from an alleged infringement or denial of a Charter right "as the court considers appropriate and just in the circumstances" (s.24:1).

Critics of broad, non-interpretive judicial review argue that the non-elected judiciary have effectively become public policy makers. Non-interpretive judicial review is quasi-legislative to the extent that there is less emphasis on rules of constitutional interpretation and more on specifying the meaning of constitutional generalities in a contemporary setting (for example, the phrase "principles of fundamental justice" in s.7), adapting the language of constitutions to changing social conditions (admitting "sexual orientation" into the "Equality Rights" s.15 as a prohibited basis of discrimination). The Supreme Court has established guidelines allowing courts to "read in" words deemed missing from legislation which would otherwise be unconstitutional, as an alternative to striking down the legislation entirely. And though a law be nullified as unconstitutional, its nullification can be suspended to allow the relevant legislature time to amend the legislation, so as not to deprive others who currently receive the benefit of the law.

Parliament and provincial governments can protect their legislation under the Charter in two ways: first, by arguing that, though it violates a Charter provision, it is "saved" under section 1 as a "reasonable" limitation of the relevant Charter right "as can be demonstrably justified in a free and democratic society"; second, by legislative action invoking the "notwithstanding clause" (s.33) that explicitly, but with conditions, allows legislation to "operate notwithstanding a provision" of selective sections of the Charter. See **Canadian Charter of Rights and Freedoms (1982); Judicial Committee of the Privy Council (JCPC); Notwithstanding (*non obstante*) clause (Canadian Charter of Rights and Freedoms, s.33); Supreme Court.**

Judicial system (judiciary). The process by which justice is applied in courts of law. In Canada, the judicial system involves integrated provincial and federal court jurisdictions. Under provisions of the *Constitution Act* (ss.96-101), the federal government appoints and pays superior, county and district court judges in the provinces, as well as federal court judges. The provinces appoint only lower-level provincial court judges, but under section 92:14 are responsible for the administration of provincial courts.

The law which the courts apply is based on legislative statute and on earlier judicial decisions, or precedents. The rule of precedence, or *stare decisis*, requires judges to take account of decisions that have been made in similar cases: individual courts may be guided by their earlier decisions, but are bound by the precedents of superior courts. However, especially with the advent of the Canadian Charter of Rights and Freedoms in 1982, but even before then, the "mechanical deference" involved in the principle of *stare decisis* was being challenged (Chief Justice Bora Laskin, in *Harrison v. Carswell*, 1976) and was finally displaced by judicial activism in a non-interpretive judicial review of the constitution (see **Canadian Charter of Rights and Freedoms [1982]; Judicial review [interpretive; non-interpretive]**).

The legal system in Canada is based on the common law tradition of England and the codified civil law: private law in Quebec is based on the Roman-French civil code, and private law in the other provinces in the English common law tradition; criminal law, which is within the legislative competence of Parliament (s.91:27), is applied uniformly across Canada.

The lower level of courts involves provincial courts, surrogate courts and division courts with civil and criminal jurisdiction. The mid-level includes the supreme courts of the provinces, which include courts of original jurisdiction and courts of appeal. The highest level includes the Federal Court of Canada and ultimately the Supreme Court of Canada. There is also a territorial judiciary in the northern territories. Until 1949, the Judicial Committee of the Privy Council in London was Canada's final court of appeal, except in criminal cases, and effectively a constitutional court (see **Judicial Committee of the Privy Council [JCPC]**).

The Supreme Court and the Federal Court are the major courts of general jurisdiction in Canada. The Supreme Court of Canada, which was established in 1875, comprises nine judges who sit in Ottawa and exercise appellate jurisdiction in both civil and criminal cases. The Supreme Court is also required to consider legislative references and advise Parliament on private bills. The most important references in recent decades concerned Parliament's ability, prior to patriation in 1982, to seek fundamental changes to the constitution by the British Parliament either unilaterally or with minimal provincial support (1980), and the ability of a province to withdraw from Confederation (1998) (see **Reference case [constitutional]**; **Secession Reference**; **Supreme Court**).

The Federal Court of Canada, which was established in 1970, comprises a trial division of eleven judges and an appeals division of fourteen. The Federal Court hears claims against and by the Crown and claims against or concerning officers and servants of the Crown, by individuals seeking relief from decisions of federal boards, commissions and other tribunals. The Court also has certain jurisdiction in disputes between provinces or between Canada and a province (see **Federal Court**).

The appointment of the judiciary in general, and of the Supreme Court in particular, has become an important subject given the increased political aspect of judicial review under the Charter. Apart from the question of appointments as possible manifestations of government patronage, and despite an elaborate, professional process for recommending appointments, debate occasionally focuses on the constitutional monopoly of appointment power held by the federal government and the potential centralist or philosophical judicial bias that might pervade the courts—but especially the Supreme Court. Various constitutional proposals have been discussed since 1982, including the entrenchment of the composition of the Supreme Court subject to amendment with unanimous federal and provincial legislative agreement, and selection of Supreme Court justices acceptable to the federal government from lists submitted by relevant provincial or territorial governments.

Jurisdiction, constitutional. Legislative authority granted under the constitution. In a unitary state, the national legislature is supreme; in a federal state, the constitution enumerates exclusive and concurrent areas of legislative jurisdiction between the autonomous national and subnational legislatures, including residual and emergency powers, subject to judicial review. Federal regimes, such as Canada's, are always subject to federal-provincial jurisdictional disputes, as well as private court action, challenging the jurisdiction of legislatures. See **Canadian Charter of Rights and Freedoms (1982)**; **Division (distribution) of powers**; **Judicial Committee of the Privy Council (JCPC)**; **Judicial review (interpretive; non-interpretive)**; **Supreme Court**.

K

King-Byng Dispute. A constitutional dispute in 1926 concerning the role of the governor general in Canada and crown prerogatives.

Following the federal general election of 1925, the governing Liberals remained in office, but the party had fewer seats in the House of Commons than the Conservatives; a third party, the Progressives, held the balance of power. Eight months later, in order to avoid a vote of censure concerning a scandal in the customs department, Prime Minister William Lyon Mackenzie King asked Governor General Lord Byng for a dissolution of Parliament. Byng refused the request and accepted the resignation of King's government. Arthur Meighen, the leader of the Conservative party that actually held more seats than either of the other parties, accepted Byng's invitation to form a government. Meighen's government, however, lasted only three sitting days before it was defeated in the House. Byng subsequently accepted Meighen's advice for dissolution and, in the election of 1926, the Liberals were returned with a majority. King managed to turn the election campaign, which might have centred on a scandal under his government, into one that focussed on the discretionary power of a non-responsible official exercising an imperial function of his office.

Indeed, the governor general had, and continues to have, the right to grant or refuse the prime minister's request for dissolution, as do the lieutenant-governors in their respective province with respect to the premier. At that time, the governor general, a Briton, not only represented the non-resident head of the Canadian state, but also the British government in Canada. King portrayed Byng's discretionary action as an imperial function rather than the constitutional prerogative of the governor general as the Canadian sovereign's representative. For his part, Byng clearly miscalculated the effect of his exercise of prerogative power. While King's attempt to evade the vote of censure in the House may have been an abuse of power to be checked by the governor general, Lord Byng overestimated Meighen's ability to carry on in a House in which the Progressives held the balance of power. Nonetheless, a governor general can still exercise discretionary power with reference to summoning and dissolving Parliament, and even to request a prime minister's resignation, but only to counter a clear violation of fundamental constitutional principles, and only when there is no reasonable doubt about the justification for such an independent action. See **Crown prerogatives**; **Governor General**.

Kitchen cabinet. An informal and personal group of close advisors to a prime minister or premier.

The term originated with United States President Andrew Jackson who often took the advice of his friends, who met with him occasionally in the kitchen of the White House, over the advice of his cabinet members. The phrase continues to be used in the US, but may have more relevance in Canada where a head of government has much less discretion in the selection of the cabinet and is therefore more likely to gather together personal friends as a kitchen cabinet. For example, both prime ministers Pierre Trudeau and Brian Mulroney came to office with little parliamentary experience or attachment to the caucus they then headed, and suspicious of the permanent senior officials around them in the administration. Nonetheless, constitutional obligations required them to create a cabinet in which the parliamentary caucus was the chief source of cabinet personnel, and with the Privy Council Office the chief source of staff support. Each then used the Prime Minister's Office as a point of entry for trusted friends and colleagues from university, law school and private career—their kitchen cabinet. See **Prime Minister's Office (PMO)**.

L

Labour Conventions Reference (*Attorney-General for Canada. v. Attorney-General for Ontario,* **1937**). A constitutional judgment by the Judicial Committee of the Privy Council that Parliament could not acquire through international obligation legislative powers that it did not possess under the *British North America Act, 1867* (since 1982 the *Constitution Act*).

Though the judgment was a reference to "treaty power," it was also important in the development of provincial authority in significant class-related matters of public policy, that is, labour law. In the particular reference, the Judicial Committee declared unconstitutional three federal statutes which were part of Conservative Prime Minister R.B. Bennett's "New Deal." These dealt with limiting working hours, and establishing minimum wages and holidays from industrial work. The federal government had argued that the legislation was constitutional under section 132 of the Act, in that Canada was carrying out obligations incurred when Canada became a member of the International Labour Organization. The Judicial Committee's earlier decision in the reference on radio communication (Radio Case, 1932) had encouraged the Conservative government to proceed with the labour legislation. According to Lord Atkin, however, the responsibility for a new subject such as radio as a result of a treaty obligation incurred by an independent Canada might fall to Parliament under the residual power of the "Peace, Order, and good Government" clause in the preamble to section 91; however, there was "no constitutional ground for stretching the functions of the [federal] executive...merely by making promises to foreign countries...." The federal government has power to sign treaties, but the ability to implement them depends on subject matter and the division of power under the Act. The Judicial Committee declared the federal "New Deal" legislation unconstitutional as it was intended to be permanent rather than simply a temporary response to the emergency of the worldwide Depression. Thus, labour legislation was protected as a field of provincial jurisdiction under section 92:13 ("Property and Civil Rights in the Province"). Because the federal government cannot use "treaty power" to enlarge its legislative competence in areas allocated to the provinces, it must be careful not to sign treaties which it does not have the power to implement under the division of legislative power in the *Constitution Act*. See **Treaty power**.

Land claims and settlements (Native; Aboriginal). Negotiations since the 1970s between provincial and federal governments and Native groups on comprehensive claims to establish certainty of ownership of land and resources in a way that will allow economic development and environmental protection to the benefit of Native Peoples; and on specific claims of alleged non-fulfilment of treaties or other legal obligations.

The *Constitution Act, 1982* recognized "existing aboriginal and treaty rights" of Indian, Inuit, and Métis peoples, including current and future land claims agreements (Part II). The federal government is responsible for Indian affairs, while the land and resources claimed are under provincial jurisdiction in each province and federal jurisdiction in the territories. In both comprehensive and specific claims, the federal government has assisted Native groups with grants and loans to research and negotiate their claims. Some specific claims on non-fulfillment of treaty or other legal obligations may be resolved administratively; some, on ministerial acknowledgement of a claim, require negotiation and settlement, including financial compensation and land transfer; others involve recourse to the courts. However, there have been disputes over land rights that have involved police and military intervention, and violence, including fatalities (Oka, Quebec, 1990; Ipperwash, Ontario, 1995).

Comprehensive claims recognized by the federal government are those that arise from the traditional occupancy and use of lands by a claimant group (First Nations or Aboriginal community within a geographic area) whose title has not been dealt with in treaty or other legal form, notably in northern Quebec, British Columbia, the territories and Labrador. Treaties otherwise were negotiated before and after Confederation in selective parts of the country. The Quebec government's plans in the 1970s to development the hydro-electric potential of rivers entering James Bay, as well as forestry, mining and tourism in the area, led to negotiations and settlement of land claims, financial compensation, defined Native rights, and a regime for dealing with relations between Native groups and non-Native governments in northern Quebec (James Bay and Northern Quebec Agreement, 1975). Comprehensive claims affected most of British Columbia, as treaties in that province concerned a small portion of southern Vancouver Island and the Peace River area in the northeast. The settlement of comprehensive claims in British Columbia, notably with the Nisga'a (1998), facilitates future investment in the province's mining, fishery and forestry industries. Comprehensive claim settlements have also taken place in Labrador (Newfoundland). Settlements in the Northwest Territories included its division, with the creation of Nunavut in 1999, Canada's only Native-dominated government, in the central and eastern Arctic. In Yukon, agreements might lead to the sharing of the resource revenues and land, resource, fish and wildlife management between the Yukon government and the territory's First Nations.

Specific claims, as opposed to comprehensive claims, involve alleged non-observance of treaty obligations or dissatisfaction with treaties. Over 200 such claims have been settled, with others pending.

Court decisions have been important in the process of negotiating land claims. Aboriginal title was recognized in *Calder*, 1973, respecting the Nisga'a, although the Supreme Court was divided on whether that title had been extinguished. In *Delgamuukw*, 1997, respecting the Wet'suwet'en and Gitksan in British

Columbia, the Court admitted oral history as evidence in the determination of entitlement, granting Natives who had not signed treaties the right to claim Aboriginal title if their ancestors had lived exclusively on the land prior to European arrivals. It admitted the possibility of Crown infringement for valid legislative purposes, but groups with Aboriginal title had to be involved in the process. The Supreme Court has also had a role in determining treaty rights, especially when they conflicted with federal and provincial laws. A Supreme Court ruling in 1999 on fishing rights of the Mi'kmaq in the Maritimes, including a subsequent clarification (*Marshall*), did little, however, to defuse conflict involving Native and non-Native fishers and federal government authority. See **Indian Act; Native (First Nations) self-government**.

Language ombudsman. An informal name for the federal commissioner of official languages, who is responsible for ensuring the recognition of equal status for French and English in the operations of the government of Canada according to the *Official Languages Act.* See **Bilingualism and Biculturalism; Commissioner of Official Languages**.

Language rights. The rights of French- and English-speaking minorities to government services in their language, including education and justice, that is, of the francophone minority in provinces other than Quebec, and in the territories, and of the anglophone minority in Quebec, including the use of English in commerce. The debate over language rights is historic and touches on the substance of Canadian nationality: whether such rights are an intrinsic part of citizenship or are subject to territorial variation across federal and provincial jurisdictions.

In the late twentieth century, language became the chief characteristic and concern of French society in Canada. The debate over language rights focussed on the conflicting policies of the federal government and the government of Quebec, the only North American jurisdiction whose population is predominantly French-speaking. The federal government promotes pan-Canadian minority "personality" rights in a program known as Bilingualism and Biculturalism, including encouragement for provinces to adopt parallel minority rights-based legislation; the government of Quebec, whether of the federalist Liberal party or the sovereignist Parti Québécois, promotes the survival of French through "territorial" laws, limiting the use of languages other than French in the province.

The federal government's commitment to Canada-wide individual minority-language rights was enacted in the *Official Languages Act, 1969* and entrenched in the Canadian Charter of Rights and Freedoms in the *Constitution Act, 1982,* along with minority-language education rights (s.23) and the status of New Brunswick as an officially bilingual province (s.16). Quebec did not endorse the Act. The provincial policy of preferential treatment for the use of French, enacted in the Charter of the French Language (Bill 101) under the Parti Québécois government in 1977, was declared unconstitutional in important respects both before (concerning languages of government and the courts) and after (concerning languages of instruction and commerce) the introduction of the Canadian Charter of Rights and Freedoms. The language policy with respect to commercial signs was reinstated by the Liberal government, invoking the Charter's "notwithstanding" clause (s.33). Bill 178 permitted bilingual signs inside establishments with the French language predominant, but only French-language signs outside. In 1993, Bill 86 amended the provincial language Charter further, without reference to section 33, allowing bilingual outdoor signs as long as French was predominant. See **Bilingualism and Biculturalism; Charter of the French Language (Quebec);** *Official Languages Act* **(Canada, 1969);** **Quebec Protestant School Boards Case** *(A.-G. Quebec v. Quebec Association of Protestant School Boards* **[1984]).**

Leaders' debates (election campaign). Since 1968, televised debates among party leaders during many federal and provincial election campaigns. In federal campaigns, the debates take place separately in English and French.

There are no legal requirements for such debates, but no political party wants to be seen avoiding them. As the least party-controlled aspect of a campaign, relative to advertising and the leader's tour, party strategists weigh the advantages and disadvantages of a debate carefully, negotiating a time and format thought most beneficial to their party. For example, a governing party in the lead in public opinion polls might not be anxious to provide a platform for its opposition and an opportunity to diminish that lead, while the opposition would want an opportunity to challenge the front-running prime minister or premier directly. Third, or minor, parties are generally well disposed to debates as their leaders appear at least for that moment as equals among the major contenders.

When debates are scheduled, party leaders prepare for them assiduously. In addition to opening and closing "set-piece" speeches, close attention is given to possible "one-liners" that might be inserted into the debate to catch an opponent off guard and be the focus of post-debate "sound bites" and "spin" in the mass media. Sound bites comprise the few seconds of exchange that become the highlight of a lengthy debate that are repeated in news broadcasts; spin is the interpretive commentary afterwards, especially focusing on which leaders "won" and which "lost" the debate and the likely effect the debate will have on the election outcome. Parties also prepare for the "sound bites" and "spin," sending forth high-level representatives, or "spin doctors," to shape the discussion and consensus reported in the mass media.

Until the 1980s, it was generally held that the major effect of televised debates among the electorate was to reinforce established partisan preferences. Televised debates during the federal campaigns of 1984 and 1988, however, demonstrated that debates could have an important influence on a campaign. In 1984, with the Liberal campaign already faltering, the Conservative leader, Brian Mulroney, apparently delivered the knockout blow to Prime Minister John Turner over the issue of patronage appointments, reinforcing the Conservative theme that the recent change of Liberal leadership did not amount to change in government. Four years later, Turner effectively challenged Prime Minister Mulroney on the proposed Canada-United States free trade agreement. In this case, however, there was sufficient time remaining in the campaign for the Conservatives to alter their television advertising and campaign tactics, and for third-party business advertising to overcome the Liberal advantage from the debate. In both cases, the lengthy debates were reduced to brief "visuals" and "sound bites" that were replayed and discussed in newscasts and commentaries.

There were no similar knockout blows in either the French- or English-language debates in the 1993 and 1997 elections. In 1993, the reinforcement hypothesis appears to have prevailed, to the advantage of the leading Liberal party and two new parties, the Bloc Québécois and Reform. In 1997, Conservative leader Jean Charest and New Democratic party leader Alexa McDonough were apparently assisted by the debates, but only sufficiently for their parties to regain official-party status in the House of Commons that they had lost earlier. In 2000, the debates were notable for the performance of the Conservative leader, Joe Clark. The Conservatives lost eight seats and managed barely to win official-party status in the House of Commons with 12 seats including Clark's. But his performance in the debates was apparently more creditable especially when compared to Stockwell Day's, the new leader of the Canadian Alliance that failed in its strategic objective of a significant electoral breakthrough in central and eastern Canada. See **Campaign (election)**; **Electoral law (controls; subsidies)**.

Leadership conventions (selection). Meetings of party members to select a parliamentary leader. Leadership conventions are a practice imported to Canada from the United States and adapted firmly, if awkwardly, to the parliamentary system of British origin.

In the US presidential-congressional system, with fixed terms of office for elected officials and therefore known election dates, party conventions to select presidential and vice-presidential candidates are regular quadrennial events, reduced through the primary system to highly orchestrated televised events with predetermined outcomes. In Canada's parliamentary system, however, there is no country-wide contest to fill the "prime ministership" and no fixed term for a government except for the constitutional five-year limit on Parliaments. At one time selected by the parliamentary caucus, leaders have been selected by conventions since the early twentieth century.

Unlike the United States, there are no legal requirements in Canada for the process of leadership selection and provincial and federal parties are free to set their own rules. Until recently, leaders were elected in conventions of party delegates. At the provincial level, several parties conducted balloting of all members by mail and by telephone, and also experimented with weighted balloting according to numbers of members in each constituency, and primaries to determine, in effect, first-ballot results prior to a traditional convention.

Some of these experiences were not successful for technical reasons, but also because they deprived the selection process of drama, and deprived the party of intensive mass media attention to its "renewal." Nonetheless, the federal parties have followed with their own adaptation for choosing a leader. After the Liberal party chose Jean Chrétien as leader in 1990, using the traditional format, the party adopted a format for the future that combines an all-member vote and the convention, with constituency delegates committed to particular candidates selected in proportion to the all-member vote for the candidates in the constituency. In selecting Alexa McDonough as leader in 1995, the New Democratic party was the first federal party to use a combined all-member/convention format. In regional primaries, members' votes determined which candidates would actually contest the leadership in the subsequent convention of delegates. In 1998, Joe Clark was chosen Conservative leader in a process that granted each party member the vote, but weighted the votes such that each constituency had equal influence in the selection process. Also in the late 1990s, the Bloc Québécois selected Gilles Duceppe using an all-member format, and in 2000, the Canadian Alliance selected its first leader, Stockwell Day, in an all-member vote.

The federal Liberal party held the first leadership convention in 1919. The Liberals had held a convention when in opposition in 1893 to boost morale. The leader, Wilfrid Laurier, again in opposition in 1918, announced a convention for similar reasons to be held the following year. However, Laurier died in February 1919, and the parliamentary caucus which would have normally selected a leader decided to hold the convention to "First...draft, discuss, and adopt the platform...; Second...deal with...party organization; Third...select a leader..." (the official call quoted in John C. Courtney, The *Selection of National Party Leaders in Canada* [Toronto: Macmillan Co. of Canada, Ltd., 1973], 64). However, after the selection of William Lyon Mackenzie King in 1919, no Liberal convention was held for any reason until 1949, after King announced his retirement and a successor had to be chosen. King had been prime minister for 22 of those 30 years; thus, on the occasion of his retirement while in office, a party convention for the first time selected not only a new leader but effectively the next prime minister. When King submitted his government's resignation, the governor general asked the convention-selected leader, Louis St. Laurent, to form the next government.

The federal Conservatives adopted the convention model in 1927 and the socialist Co-operative Commonwealth Federation not surprisingly adopted it at the party's inception in 1933. The Ontario Conservatives had selected their provincial leader in convention in 1920. Therefore, by the time Arthur Meighen resigned as federal leader in 1926, the convention model was trumpeted as preferable to selection by a parliamentary "cabal". The convention model by contrast appeared democratic and representative of the party, and the Conservatives could not afford to appear otherwise. As successor to the CCF, there was no question as to how the New Democratic party would select its leader. Although its leaders are chosen by for a fixed term of two years, in practice, leadership changes have occurred only upon the incumbent's retirement.

The traditional convention format was expected to create an impression of openness, liveliness, and ultimately unity behind the new leader. In the traditional leadership convention, delegates cast a secret ballot. If no candidate had a majority of the votes cast, further balloting took place, with the least popular candidate in the previous ballot disqualified and other candidates possibly withdrawing voluntarily, hoping to deliver their supporters' votes to another candidate in subsequent balloting.

Historically, the element of executive control was very strong, especially in the Conservative and Liberal parties. The party officials, the selection of whom the retiring parliamentary leader normally had influenced, were responsible for naming delegates to conventions. Appointed delegates-at-large and ex officio delegates frequently accounted for one-third to one-half of the delegates at federal Conservative and Liberal conventions. At NDP conventions, delegates from affiliated trade unions could usually be relied upon as a conservative brake on any "disturbing" outcomes.

The lack of fixed terms for Liberal and Conservative leaders, the concern of some party activists over leadership-dominated conventions, and possibly the bitter struggle within the federal Conservative party during the final years of John Diefenbaker's leadership in the mid-1960s, led to the development in the 1970s in those parties of rules on leadership accountability. While the precise nature of the instrument of leadership review varies, the intent is to have the leader submit to a periodic vote of confidence at conventions held, for example, within a certain period following a general election. If the leader does not obtain a certain level of confidence, the party executive may then be obliged to call a leadership convention within a specific period. Such a device, then, allows a party, whose leader is selected without a fixed term, to debate the leader's future, which may be appropriate following electoral defeat. A secret ballot on leadership review was conducted at each biennial Reform convention. Its founding leader, Preston Manning, was never challenged during the 1990s. He lost, though, in his bid for the leadership of the Canadian Alliance, successor-party to Reform that retained the Reform party's model of leadership review.

The change in leadership selection format—either to an all-member vote or a combined all-member/convention format—was occasioned by several factors. During the 1980s, there was increased concern about the financial burden of leadership contests and dubious practices surrounding the selection of convention delegates. The Conservative and Liberal parties experienced the appearance of hundreds of "instant" or "one-day" Liberals and Conservatives for delegate selection, some of whom did not qualify for the electoral franchise, and there were media accounts of exorbitant expenditures by some leadership candidates, vote-buying, and the establishment of secret funds to encourage people to become candidates. The NDP, if only out of necessity, was the first federal party to establish rules pertaining to party membership, delegate selection and candidate expenses. It organized pre-convention leadership candidate debates at party expense in various cities across Canada.

Other criticisms of the convention model have included the disproportionate numbers of very young delegates who could be relied upon for displays of enthusiasm and vigour, but perhaps not for the experience and prudence to make such an important decision; the increasingly intrusive nature of media coverage which, while providing the party with an image of youthfulness and vigour suitable for a process of leadership renewal, might also be influencing delegates' decisions for reasons best suited to the requisites of the media than to those of the party; the increasingly "hot-house" environment of the convention floor from ballot to ballot, with exhausted delegates making last-minute decisions under considerable pressure; finally, the requirement that the last-placed candidate be compelled to withdraw could deprive delegates of a "best" second-choice candidate to unite the party after a fractious struggle among first-choice candidates.

Leadership review. See Leadership conventions (selection).

League for Social Reconstruction (LSR). A group of largely university-based intellectuals that existed from 1932 until the Second World War; it was the "brains trust" of the socialist Co-operative Commonwealth Federation, predecessor of the New Democratic party. Modelled on the British Fabian Society, the LSR published pamphlets and articles to educate the public on socialist approaches to the social and economic order. In 1932, members of the LSR met with Labour and some Progressive MPs in Ottawa to pass resolutions leading to the founding of the CCF a few months later.

The CCF's Regina Manifesto, which was published in 1933, was the work of such LSR members as Frank Underhill (historian), F.R. Scott (constitutional lawyer and law professor), and Eugene Forsey (labour and economic historian). In 1935, the LSR published *Social Planning for Canada*, its most thorough critique of Canadian society and the economic order. See **Co-operative Commonwealth Federation (CCF)**; **Regina Manifesto**.

Left, political. See **Class cleavage**.

Legislation. Bills introduced in a legislature. Once introduced, legislation might be removed or withdrawn from consideration, might be defeated, might "die on the Order Paper" when the legislature recesses or is dissolved for an election, might be amended, and might pass the legislature and then be proclaimed as law. When passed, bills become acts of Parliament (or of the provincial legislature) and, upon receiving royal assent, statutes or laws.

Public bills are of a public or general nature and may be introduced by any member of the legislature. However, public bills introduced by private members (that is, legislators who are not in the cabinet) cannot involve the expenditure of money—that being the prerogative of the Crown and its ministers. Also, private members' bills are often introduced for reasons of public education or for personal political reasons, as they are seldom enacted into law (see **Private members' legislation**). Public bills introduced by a member of the cabinet—a minister of the Crown— constitute government legislation and take up the bulk of the legislature's time. Government legislation is either financial or non-financial. Financial legislation, which only a government minister can introduce, deals with the spending of money (supply bills) or with the raising of money (tax measures and ways and means legislation) (see **Budget and budgetary process**; **Estimates**). In the bicameral Parliament, money bills must originate in the elected House of Commons; the power of the Senate to amend them is subject to debate, though it is generally agreed that it cannot increase expenditure proposals. The same legislation must be adopted in both houses in order to receive parliamentary approval; thus, amendments accepted in one house following approval in the other house must be approved subsequently in the other house. Government legislation might involve new programs and the creation of administrative agencies to carry out the objectives of the legislation (enabling legislation), or it might involve amendments to current statutes.

Private bills are non-government legislation designed to alter the law relating to some particular interest, or to confer rights on or relieve the obligations of some person or group of people. For example, bills to incorporate private companies are private bills. In practice, such bills at the federal level are usually introduced and dealt with first in the Senate, receiving perfunctory examination by the House of Commons.

Legislation must receive three readings in the legislature. In the Canadian Parliament, public bills and private bills receive different treatment. The following describes procedure for the passage of most government legislation in the House of Commons (otherwise, see **Private bills; Private members' legislation**). The minister sponsoring the legislation introduces the bill, moving that it receive first reading. The House usually approves first reading automatically and the bill is then printed and distributed. Subject to the negotiation of the schedule of the House among each party's House leader, the minister later moves that the bill be given second reading and referred to a committee of the House. The vote on second reading represents approval in principle and is preceded by extensive debate. At the committee stage, a legislative committee examines the bill clause by clause and may call witnesses to testify in public for or against the legislation. This stage might take weeks and involve considerable debate among the parties, which are represented in committee roughly in proportion to their representation in the House. Following hearings on the measure, the committee prepares its final report, including suggested amendments to the legislation. At the so-called Report stage, the House can debate the bill further. This provides the opposition with another opportunity to prolong debate and upset the government's timetable, if not its legislation, subjecting the bill to time-consuming standing or recorded votes in the House on proposed amendments. The government might be tempted to invoke closure at some stage, allocating time for debate and bringing the measure finally to a vote. After all amendments are voted on, the minister's motion that the bill (as amended) be "concurred in" is voted. After the Report stage, usually at the next sitting, the minister moves third reading. Debate at this stage is limited. If the measure receives approval on third reading, it goes to the Senate for consideration and passage. If the Senate alters the legislation, the House must concur in the changes or the legislation may not proceed to the governor general for royal assent. A prolonged stalemate in the House or between the House of Commons and the Senate could result in the bill dying on the Order Paper, either at the end of a session or upon dissolution of the legislature for an election. Upon receiving royal assent following parliamentary enactment, the law is then proclaimed, taking effect immediately or at a later date. See **Closure; House of Commons; Standing (select, special, joint) committees (of the House and Senate)**.

Legislative Assembly. The official name for the elected legislatures of all Canadian provinces except Ontario, Nova Scotia, Newfoundland and Quebec. The legislatures of the first three are called the House of Assembly, and the legislature of Quebec, the National Assembly.

Legislative override. See **Notwithstanding (*non obstante*) clause (Canadian Charter of Rights and Freedoms, s.33)**.

Legislative process. The consideration of bills by a legislature, which may result in their passage, or enactment, to become law. The process takes place within a centuries-old framework of parliamentary privilege developed in Great Britain, involving respect for the institution of parliament, precedent and individual parliamentarians' privileges and immunities; however, daily business involves the ever-present and often-heated adversarial contest of wills among government and opposition parties, leading to the next election. On the passage of legislation, see

House of Commons; Legislation; Legislature. On pre-legislative activities to encourage or discourage certain legislation, see **Budget and budgetary process; Interest groups; Lobby(ist; -ing); Social movement organizations.** On post-legislative activities that in turn might lead to pressure for further legislative proposals, see **Judicial review; Policy (making-analysis; public); Regulatory agencies (regulations).**

Legislature. That part or branch of government that has the power to enact or amend laws. A legislature may be elected (as are the House of Commons and all provincial legislatures in Canada), or appointed, as is the Canadian Senate. In a less formal but still effective sense, some administrative bodies perform quasi-legislative functions through regulations adopted under enabling legislation passed by a legislature. Because of the extensive nature of judicial review under the *Constitution Act*, including the Canadian Charter of Rights and Freedoms, some observers say that the courts in Canada have acquired a quasi-legislative role. See **Delegated power; House of Commons; Judicial Review (interpretive; non-interpretive); Legislation; Senate.**

Letters Patent (1947). The prerogative instruments defining the office of governor general which Canada's non-resident sovereign makes applicable to each governor general through the commission of appointment.

In addition to prerogative power, the governor general also has statutory constitutional power described in the *Constitution Act, 1867* and power assigned in other statutes exercised on the advice of the federal cabinet. The Letters Patent delegate the sovereign's prerogative powers with respect to Canada to the particular person appointed governor general on the advice of the federal cabinet, effectively the prime minister. There remains a distinction between prerogative powers exercised by the governor general as the Crown's representative in Canada and those exercised by the sovereign on Canadian advice. The prerogative powers of the governor general include the power to summon, prorogue and dissolve Parliament, and the power to appoint or dismiss ministers, including the prime minister. The governor general may also deputize people to act for the governor general. See **Governor General.**

Liberal party. The federal Liberal party of Canada originated in the reform politics of mid-nineteenth-century Canada. In response to the dominant Tory element, the Reformers in Upper Canada or Canada West (now Ontario) and the Maritimes joined with the anti-clerical *Rouges* of Lower Canada or Canada East (now Quebec) in an uneasy alliance. The alignment was notably unsuccessful until the late-nineteenth century. The Liberal party lacked much French-Canadian support because of its extreme anti-clerical element in Quebec and its rural anti-Catholic, Protestant element elsewhere. Led by Alexander Mackenzie, the party came to office in 1873, in the wake of a financial scandal involving the Conservative party. It left office five years later, in the wake of an economic depression and under a wave of popular support for the Conservative's National Policy of railway construction, immigration and tariff increases.

Since 1896, however, the Liberal party has been pre-eminent in federal politics. Considerable credit for the change in party fortunes usually goes to Wilfrid

Laurier, leader from 1887 to 1919. In contrast to the dour quality of Liberal leadership before him, Laurier's style was one of moderation and "sunny ways." Since then, the Liberals have had only six leaders, all of whom became prime ministers. Three came into the position of prime minister when they assumed the leadership (Louis St. Laurent, Pierre Trudeau and John Turner), while the other three eventually became prime ministers after serving initially in the opposition (William Lyon Mackenzie King, Lester Pearson and Jean Chrétien).

Laurier's success, and that subsequently of his party, may be understood in terms of earlier Liberal failure and Conservative success on bicultural and class strategies. The Liberals under Laurier developed a French leadership that was integrated in Quebec society and an English leadership that was at least sympathetic, if not purposively accommodative, to the contemporary political needs of French Canada. In federal elections since 1896, the Liberals have led the Conservatives in popular vote in Quebec in all but the 1958, 1984, and 1988 elections. Three of the six leaders since Laurier have been French Canadians, while no French Canadian has formally led the Conservative party, although Jean Charest was designated interim leader following the election debacle of 1993 in which he was one of only two Conservatives elected and the leader, Prime Minister Kim Campbell, was defeated in her own riding. When the Liberal party's popularity in Quebec has slipped, the chief beneficiary has usually been not the Conservatives, but a more effectively *nationaliste* party such as the Nationalistes, the Bloc Populaire and the Ralliement des créditistes, and recently the Bloc Québécois. In the 2000 election, for example, the Liberal party led in popular vote in Quebec for the first time since 1980, ahead of the second-place BQ, 44 to 40 per cent.

In addition to a *Québec solide*, the Liberals have generally followed the earlier Conservative model of maintaining the goodwill of the economic elite as well as a progressive public image. The sole instances of clear alienation from the business community occurred with Laurier's support for reciprocity in trade with the United States in 1911 and John Turner's opposition to the Canada-US free trade agreement in 1988, and in both cases the Liberals suffered electorally. Since the rise of the industrial trade union movement in the 1920s, with its formal if occasionally tenuous link with the socialist Co-operative Commonwealth Federation, and later the New Democratic party, the Liberals have seemed more right-wing than left-wing in leadership and in economic and social policy, but more progressive in orientation than the Conservatives historically and the Canadian Alliance and its predecessor, the Reform party, more recently. While Liberal governments have introduced redistributive programs, they seem to prefer to maintain a progressive image with non-redistributive social policies such as law reform, internationalist foreign policy and domestic programs to encourage private investment in economically hard-pressed regions. In brief, the Liberal party's success in wooing business support while maintaining popular support is a major key to its predominance since 1896, and having opposition parties positioned markedly both to its left and to its right has been advantageous.

As did the Conservatives in the nineteenth century, so the Liberals in this century have also sought to project an image of their party as the most effective political vehicle of Canadian nationalism. However, especially since the 1940s, but with the exception of the free-trade election of 1988, the Liberals have seemed to identify national interest with the predominant views of the central Canadian economic elite. This patriotic image held as long as elite opinion in central Canada was effectively that of the national economic elite, as long as French Canada's strategy for survival was largely internalized in Quebec and accommodated federally through cabinet portfolios and patronage, and as long as the population of central Canada elected the bulk of members of parliament. A long-term problem for federal Liberals may be that the first two of these conditions regarding the economic elite and francophone Quebec no longer hold, and the last demographic factor is slowly changing. The Canadian West has developed strong, indigenous economic interests at odds with those of central Canada and better reflected in provincial government policy. French-Canadian nationalism is more aggressive than in the past and focuses on the enhancement of the Quebec "state" rather than an Ottawa-centred federation. On the basis of population figures in the 1991 census, the west-coast province of British Columbia, along with Ontario, received additional seats in the House of Commons. The Liberal party's contemporary success arises from its popularity in central Canada, notably in Ontario which comprises approximately one third of the country's population and seats in the House of Commons, but also in Quebec and Atlantic Canada.

Liberalism. Political beliefs associated with the idea of progress achieved through the free play of each person's will to self-aggrandizement.

Liberalism developed in the eighteenth and nineteenth centuries, in the context of political struggles against arbitrary government, notably monarchical and clerical regimes and an associated landed aristocracy. Liberal values were supported by European nationalists and a rising bourgeoisie with wealth based on trade, commerce and industrial capitalism.

A liberal views the state as the instrument to maintain "equality of opportunity." In the nineteenth century, the state's role was to be minimal, but supportive of commercial enterprise unrestricted by monopolies or undue social obligations. In the twentieth century, however, liberals were more inclined to rely upon the social policy and the regulatory power of the state, rather than "free market forces," to achieve this equality. Liberals define citizenship in terms of individual rights and freedoms rather than rights exercised on individuals' behalf by the state. Contemporary liberalism has been more internationalist, and less supportive of the concept of national sovereignty. Having supported movements of national liberation from imperial bonds in the late-twentieth century, liberals are now generally supportive of the pursuit of national interest through multilateral political institutions such as the United Nations and supra-national regulatory bodies such as the International Monetary Fund, the World Bank and the World Trade Organization.

As a broad set of beliefs, liberal ideas are deeply rooted in Canada's political culture and evident in some form in all Canadian federal parties—in the laissez-faire individualism of some Conservatives, and in such populist western movements as the Progressive, Social Credit, Reform and Canadian Alliance parties, in the mild reformism of the New Democratic party, successor to the Fabian socialist Co-operative Commonwealth Federation, and in the Liberal party, architect of Canada's welfare state as the party of power in the twentieth century.

The constitutional entrenchment of the citizen-rights-based Canadian Charter of Rights and Freedoms in 1982, with a broad power of judicial review of legislative, executive and administrative behaviour, highlights the strength of liberalism in Canada. However, the Charter also subjects individual rights to "such reasonable limits prescribed by law as can be demonstrably justified in a free and democratic society" (s.1), permits legislatures to exempt legislation from the Charter (s.33), and allows for affirmative action programs to qualify equality rights (s.15), thus acknowledging other aspects, less individualistic or liberal and more collectivist, of Canada's political culture.

Lieutenant-governor. The representative of the Crown, or head of state, in each of the Canadian provinces.

The lieutenant-governors act virtually always on the advice of their provincial ministers, the Executive Council (provincial cabinet), formally as the lieutenant-governor-in-council. However, the lieutenant-governor can exercise Crown prerogatives with respect to summoning and dissolving the provincial legislature, and appointing and dismissing a government. Because the office of lieutenant-governor is a federal office, under the *Constitution Act, 1867*, they may refuse royal assent to provincial legislation, "reserving" it for consideration by the governor-in-council, the federal cabinet (ss.56, 90). While there are no legal restraints upon the power of reservation, it is not a serious limitation on provincial authorities. The last case occurred in Saskatchewan in 1961 when the lieutenant-governor acted without consulting the federal government. Federal governments since 1970 have considered the power of reservation negotiable in talks on a revised constitution, but it was not removed when the constitution was patriated in 1982.

As federal officers, lieutenant-governors are appointed by the governor-in-council, that is, the federal cabinet and effectively the prime minister, for five-year terms, removable only for cause communicated to the governor general and to Parliament in writing. Parliament sets and pays the lieutenant-governors' salaries (*Constitution Act, 1867*, ss.58-60). Provincial legislatures have always been prevented from legislating with respect to the office of lieutenant-governor (s.92:1 until repealed in 1982). Since 1982, the office of lieutenant-governor (like that of the Queen and the governor general) may be amended only by unanimous consent of Parliament and the provincial legislatures (*Constitution Act, 1982*, Part V). See **Crown prerogatives; Governor General; Reservation (of legislation).**

Lieutenant-governor-in-council. The formal constitutional form through which a provincial cabinet (formally the Executive Council) exercises executive power. The lieutenant-governor appoints the Council by selecting as premier the leader of the party that commands majority support in the legislature and accepting the premier's advice on appointments to the Council, or cabinet. Thus, the lieutenant-governor-in-council is the lieutenant-governor acting on the advice of the cabinet; and the executive instrument of the lieutenant-governor-in-council is the order-in-council, or a minute of the council. The lieutenant-governor does not attend cabinet meetings, but signs the orders or minutes which are sent from cabinet. See **Lieutenant-governor.**

"Living tree" Doctrine (constitution). One of two perspectives in decisions by the Judicial Committee of the Privy Council on the *British North America Act, 1867* (since 1982, the *Constitution Act*).

Expressing a liberal approach to interpreting Canada's major constitutional statute, Lord Sankey wrote that "the Act planted in Canada a living tree capable of growth and expansion within its natural limits. [The JCPC does] not conceive it to be [its] duty…to cut down the provisions of the Act by a narrow and technical construction, but rather to give it a large and liberal interpretation" (*Edwards v. Attorney-General for Canada*, 1930, the Persons Case that determined that the use of the male pronoun in the *British North America Act, 1867* regarding the appointment of senators countenanced the appointment of women [ss.23, 24]).

The liberal approach expressed by Sankey regarding a social issue was distinct from the strict view expressed by Lord Atkin in 1937 with respect to the federal system: "While the [Canadian] ship of state now sails on larger ventures and into foreign waters, she still retains the watertight [federal-provincial] compartments which are an essential part of her original structure" (*Attorney-General for Canada v. Attorney-General for Ontario*, 1937, on declaring unconstitutional aspects of Conservative Prime Minister R.B. Bennett's New Deal legislation).

Since the entrenchment of the Canadian Charter of Rights and Freedoms in 1982, the scope of judicial review (since 1949 solely by the Supreme Court) has been expanded considerably. The Supreme Court adopted a non-interpretive approach of substantive review of legislation similar to Sankey's "living tree" metaphor: "a broad, purposive analysis, which interprets specific provisions of a constitutional document in light of its larger objects" (*Hunter v. Southam*, 1984) to ensure for Canadians the "full benefit of the Charter's protection" (*R. v. Big M Drug Mart*, 1985). See various entries on matters mentioned here.

Lobby (-ist; -ing). Lobby refers to individual or collective action (or lobbying) to influence legislators or other decision makers in the executive and the administration of government.

A lobbyist is a person whose business is to advance the interest of clients or employer in representations to parliamentarians and government officials. In the United States, the weak party system, separation of powers, and the large and diffuse administration make lobbying a crucial and pervasive part of public policy making. By contrast, Canada's disciplined party and parliamentary systems, along with the relative compactness and cohesiveness of the administration, result in less initiative and control by lobbyists than in the United States.

Professional lobbying at the federal level in Canada increased significantly following the election of Brian Mulroney's Conservative government in 1984, the first change in party government in twenty-one years, excepting the nine-month Conservative government of Joe Clark in 1979-80. There already were lobbying firms in existence, assisting private interests in coping with increased regulation in increasingly complex government organizations. Now, however, they were competing with new firms involving people openly declaring their personal connections with the new government and purportedly marketing their influence with ministers and ministerial aides rather than any expertise in policy and the policy-making process in Ottawa. Former parliamentarians, including one-time cabinet ministers and a provincial premier, former ministerial executive aides, and former civil servants joined the "government relations" industry. Meanwhile, those in office realized that there could be an apparently lucrative life after public service in "public affairs consulting."

The aggressive and well-publicized activities of some lobbyists with close ties to the Conservative party and to particular ministers, including the prime minister, and conflict of interest problems in the cabinet itself, led to the *Lobbyists Registration Act, 1989*. In the early 1990s, parliamentarians generally agreed in committee that the Act should be strengthened further to achieve "greater transparency" regarding the activities of lobbyists, and the Liberal government introduced changes to the Act in 1994. Lobbyists are required to register in the Register of Lobbyists, but even considering the amendments of 1994 the requirements remain less restrictive than those in the United States.

The Act recognizes two types of lobbyists: Tier I lobbyists are those who may be hired by clients for a fee. Tier II lobbyists are those who work for a single company, or, since the 1994 amendments, for a coalition of groups and lobby only for that firm or organization. Initially, Tier I lobbyists were required essentially to register the names of their clients and indicate the issue of concern by checking one of several areas listed on a form. Tier II lobbyists needed only to register annually their name, title and employer. Shortly after the legislation was enacted, 295 Tier I firms were registered, many employing a large number of individuals, including, for example, recent senior policy advisors in the Prime Minister's Office and the chief negotiator and deputy negotiator of the Canada-US Free Trade Agreement of 1989. In 1994, there were close to three thousand lobbyists registered with the federal government and many more, usually lawyers who may claim lawyer-client privilege, unregistered. The 1994 amendments require lobbyists to provide more specific information than earlier about their clients and their activities: the names of their clients (if a single corporation, the name of the parent corporation and any subsidiaries that might benefit from the lobbying activity; if an organization, the name of each corporation or group that comprises the coalition); the specific matter, be it legislation, regulation, grant, contract, or any financial benefit, being sought; the government office being lobbied; any moneys being received from the government; whether contingency fees based on success, that can fuel extravagant lobbying activity, are involved; and methods of communication, both public and private. The Registrar of the Registry, who can audit information and issue advisory opinions, had the six-month limitation on proceedings of violations extended to two years. Finally, an ethics counsellor was appointed to investigate any alleged violations of the Act as well as of the government's conflict-of-interest guidelines for ministers, parliamentary secretaries and public officials.

The amendments in 1994, though requiring more information about lobbying techniques and activities, still fell short not only of earlier parliamentary committee recommendations, but also of the Liberal party's campaign promises in 1993. Lobbyists are still not required to divulge their partisan activities, lobbying fees remain fully tax-deductible expenses for lobbyists' clients, and the ethics counsellor is an appointee of the prime minister rather than an officer of Parliament. Indeed, some commentators credit the activities of lobbyists for this legislative shortfall.

If the reports submitted under the requirements of the Act do not tell the full story of lobbying in Ottawa, the public is further assisted by the activity of the Advocacy Research Centre. This private company maintains a website and publishes several titles that provide even more information than the Registry about lobbyists and their activities in Ottawa. In a curious way, though lobbyists have worked strenuously to limit government regulation of their activities, they frequently benefit from learning about their competitors from both the official Registry and the work of the Advocacy Research Centre.

Traditionally the disciplined party and parliamentary systems in Canada have made it necessary for effective lobbying to take place largely within the private confines of the executive and administration. The government is in control of the legislative process and is committed to the passage of legislation once introduced in the legislature. While administrative, regulatory agencies may hold hearings on changes to regulations, it is always best for private interests to understand the mood of the "regulator" so as to have some influence before the hearings and credibility during them. Lobbyists are most effective when they possess specialized information relevant to government policy making and can also assist government decision makers in legitimating and implementing their decisions. Thus, knowledge of, access to, and favourable interaction with senior administrators is crucial to successful lobbying. On legislative changes, a similar relationship with ministerial executive aides is also important. Individual back-bench legislators and party caucuses on either side of the House of Commons are of much less importance as targets for lobbyists, except for possible long-term "political investment" (today's opposition critics or government backbenchers might be tomorrow's ministers) and to affect the general environment which might be relevant to anticipated government action.

Since the entrenchment of the Canadian Charter of Rights and Freedoms in 1982, a number of so-called "single-issue" groups, whose demands have been legitimized with particular reference to equality rights (s.15), have increased in prominence. Many of these rights-based groups (for example, environmentalists, peace activists, women, Natives, multicultural groups, and the disabled) have joined with others in larger social movement organizations and networks to lobby effectively in non-traditional ways, using various forms of public demonstrations and court challenges. While in the short term such tactics can alienate executive and administrative decision makers, the potential for successful court action by these groups compels the political and bureaucratic elites to accommodate this more confrontational style of political representation. As social movement lobbies can influence policies that affect traditional private, sectional interests and groups, these latter groups, for example the pulp and paper, tobacco and financial industries, have also had to augment their traditional "behind the scenes" lobbying of government officials with aggressive public campaigns.

While conflict of interest guidelines affect ministers, parliamentary secretaries and senior officials, a grey area of lobbying involves other parliamentarians. Members of parliament represent constituencies that might contain a dominant private interest or a number of significant interests. When pursuing their constituency service function, some members may in fact be lobbying for a private interest. Because of the tendency of governments to appoint people with significant private business interests to the Senate, attention has been drawn to the activity of some senators, notably on the standing committee on banking, trade and commerce, in establishing at a minimum a favourable legislative environment for business. See **Interest groups**; **Social movement organizations**.

Lord Durham's Report. A report to the British government on the affairs of British North America following the rebellions in 1837 in Upper and Lower Canada (Ontario and Quebec, respectively, after Confederation). The *Report* recommended the reunification of those separate colonies which had been established earlier under the *Constitutional Act, 1791* and the granting of responsible government in the proposed United Province of Canada. The imperial government acted expeditiously on the first recommendation in the *Act of Union, 1840*. However, the second recommendation, which was greeted favourably by the Reformers, was not acted upon.

The most recalled passage from the *Report* bears on the first recommendation: "I expected to find a contest between a government and a people," wrote Durham. "I found two nations warring in the bosom of a single state; I found a struggle, not of principles but of races; and I perceived that it would be idle to attempt any amelioration of laws or institutions until we could first succeed in terminating the deadly animosity that now separates the inhabitants of Lower Canada into the hostile divisions of French and English" (*Report on the Affairs of British North America*, Sir C.P. Lucas, ed. [Oxford: Clarendon Press, 1912], II, 16). Clearly, Durham's expectation was that the political union of the two Canadas would lead to "a complete amalgamation of peoples, races, languages, and laws" (122), an absorption of French society by the British. "I have little doubt," Durham said, "that the French, when once placed…in a minority would abandon their vain hopes of nationality" (307).

On responsible government, Durham wrote: "it was a vain delusion to imagine that…a [legislature], strong in the consciousness of wielding the public opinion of the majority…could look on as a passive or indifferent spectator, while [its] laws were carried into effect or evaded, and the whole business of the country was conducted by [an executive], in whose intentions or capacity it had not the slightest confidence" (76-77). Responsible government, however, did not come to the Province of Canada until 1848, and then by convention after its adoption first in Nova Scotia. See **Bicultural cleavage; Responsible government**.

Lower Canada. A colony in British North America from 1791 (until then Quebec) to 1840 (then Canada East), in which the French-speaking population outnumbered the English-speakers. Under the British *Quebec Act, 1774*, the colony extended west to include land between the Ohio and Mississippi Rivers. Its political system included provisions for freedom of worship and the right of Roman Catholics to hold public office, and for the use of civil law on non-criminal matters unless changed by the colony. In 1791, demands by British loyalists who migrated to Quebec following the American Revolution led to the *Constitutional Act* that divided the colony into Upper and Lower Canada, so named given their relative position in relation to the St. Lawrence River system. This partition allowed for continuation of legal protection for French law and society in predominantly French Lower Canada, while allowing the British majority in Upper Canada the common law and other familiar institutions. Thus, the prospects for French survival, albeit in the context of British colonialism, were enhanced. In 1840, the *Act of Union* reunited the two Canadas once again, this time in a vain attempt to absorb the French into the English-speaking community. See *Constitutional Act, 1791* (**U.K.**); **Lord Durham's Report**; *Union Act, 1840* (**U.K.**).

Lower House. In a bicameral legislature, the chamber with representation more popularly based than the upper house. In Canada's bicameral Parliament, the lower house is the House of Commons, to which members are elected on a modified principle of representation by population, each to represent one constituency, and the support of a majority of whom is necessary for a government to remain in office. The upper house is the Senate. All provincial and territorial legislatures are unicameral. See **House of Commons; Responsible government; Senate; Upper chamber (house).**

M

MHA/MLA/MNA/MPP. Initials designating elected members of provincial legislatures: member of the house of assembly (MHA); member of the legislative assembly (MLA); member of the national assembly (MNA); member of the provincial parliament (MPP).

MP. Initials designating the elected members of the House of Commons: member of parliament. See **Members of parliament (MPs).**

"*Maîtres Chez Nous.*" "Masters in Our Own House," a slogan of the Liberal government of Quebec in the 1960s, expressing the assertive French nationalism and statism of the Quiet Revolution. See **Quiet Revolution.**

Majority government. A government formed by a party that holds the majority of seats in the legislature.

From 1921—when a multiparty system developed in Canada—to 2000, of Canada's twenty-four elected federal governments (that is, excluding Arthur Meighen's governor general-appointed government of 1926, John Turner's of 1984 and Kim Campbell's of 1993), sixteen were majority governments. Nine of the fifteen elected governments from 1957 to 2000 (that is, excluding Turner's and Campbell's), have been majority governments.

The electoral system, gerrymandering and malapportionment have contributed to majority governments in multiparty contests in Canadian federal and provincial elections. The single-member constituency system with simple plurality win tends to result in the most popular party winning a disproportionately larger percentage of seats in the legislature; that is, in multi-party elections, parties with the largest percentage of the popular vote, but usually less than 50 per cent, often form governments with large legislative majorities. The drawing of constituency boundaries historically involved political gerrymandering, and rules which modify the principle of representation by population to favour sparsely populated rural areas over densely populated urban areas also contribute to legislative majorities based on electoral minority support. See **Electoral system; Gerrymander; Malapportionment.**

Malapportionment. A situation in which the population size across electoral districts or constituencies is significantly unequal.

The boundaries of federal constituencies are redrawn following each decennial census in an attempt to deal in part with excessive malapportionment which develops over time because of changes in population growth and movement. Some degree of malapportionment between densely populated urban constituencies and sparsely populated rural and northern territorial constituencies is tolerated. It is argued that effective representation by a legislative member is hampered when constituencies are too geographically large and the distinct interests of rural and far-flung communities would be poorly represented in a legislature if the criterion of representation by population were strictly observed. Thus, by the criterion of "rep by pop," (representation by population) rural and northern populations are overrepresented relative to urban and southern populations—and northern constituencies are still very large nonetheless. In partisan terms, malapportionment favours political parties with a rural base of support, and many provincial party regimes in particular have been deliberately sustained by malapportionment.

The courts have become involved in disputes over electoral constituency boundaries. For some people, section 3 of the Canadian Charter of Rights and Freedoms guarantees voter equality against malapportionment, even against well-established considerations that inevitably lead to under- and overrepresentation. In *Carter v. Saskatchewan (A.-G.)* (1991), the Supreme Court divided 6-3 on an appeal of the Saskatchewan Supreme Court's rejection of nonpopulation considerations in the province's electoral boundaries legislation (Reference re Saskatchewan Electoral Boundaries [1991]). The majority in *Carter* that sustained Saskatchewan's legislation supported a balance of population and nonpopulation factors (distinct community interests: minority representation, cultural and group identity) in drawing constituency boundaries. Dissenting justices on the Supreme Court did not contest the recognition of nonpopulation factors, but opposed the Saskatchewan legislation because it mandated redistribution on rural overrepresentation and urban underrepresentation rather than on voter equality. They argued that the principle of voter equality should be mandated in law, leaving those responsible for drawing the boundaries to limit the application of the principle within reason. See **Electoral system.**

Mandarin(ate). An informal and somewhat pejorative colloquial reference to senior civil servants, implying a high level of cohesiveness, power and privilege allegedly reminiscent of the traditional class of imperial Chinese officialdom.

Mandate. Support for a political program or a specific action, usually issuing from an election victory, or as well from a resolution of a legislature sanctioning government action.

In 1988, for example, the Canada-US Free Trade Agreement was the focus of the federal election campaign. The FTA's passage, obstructed by Liberal senators in the previous Parliament, was quickly adopted in the post-election Parliament as the Conservative government had received a mandate to proceed on the basis of its legislative majority in the newly elected House of Commons. This was an exceptional case, as election campaigns do not usually focus on a single or recognized set of policy issues. Many election campaigns focus on generalized issues such as "leadership" or "the economy." In such cases, the victorious party has received only a general mandate to govern.

In particular instances, though not constitutionally necessary, a government might seek a parliamentary resolution after the fact to mandate, or sanction, a particular policy or decision. In the 1990s, for example, the federal government received such parliamentary sanction or mandates regarding its support for the United States-sponsored Gulf war against Iraq and for military action by the North Atlantic Treaty Organization in the Balkans.

Manitoba Schools Question (and French language rights, 1890). The controversy which followed the abolition of public support for denominational schools, and therefore of predominantly French-language education in Manitoba in 1890 (*Public Schools Act*). Companion legislation abolishing constitutional guarantees on the use of French in government and the courts (Canada, *Manitoba Act, 1870,* s.23) was also adopted at the time (*Official Language Act*).

Because the denominational schools existed before Confederation, they were to be guaranteed under the *British North America Act, 1867,* section 93 (since 1982, the *Constitution Act*). The federal *Manitoba Act, 1870,* confirmed by the British Parliament in 1871 and included as part of the Canadian constitution, contained guarantees for both denominational schools (s.22) and the use of French in government and the courts (s.23).

The courts ruled that the Manitoba *Public Schools Act* was valid, but also that there was a right to appeal to the federal cabinet for a remedial order-in-council under the *British North America Act* (s.93:3). When the provincial government refused the federal Conservative government's request to redress minority rights, Conservative Prime Minister Sir Mackenzie Bowell had a remedial order issued in 1896. When the Manitoba government refused to obey the order or negotiate a compromise, the federal government introduced remedial legislation (in accordance with the *Manitoba Act, 1870* [s.22:3]; *British North America Act* [s.93:4]). The combined opposition of the Liberals and dissident Conservatives prevented passage of the legislation. The Liberals, led by Wilfrid Laurier, a Quebec-based French Canadian, argued that federal action would infringe on provincial rights. When Parliament's five-year term expired, the legislation died. The subsequent election of a Liberal government in 1896, with majority support in Quebec, seemed to affirm the commitment of voters in that predominantly French-speaking province to provincial rights over federal intervention to ensure minority rights in the provinces. Similar attacks on minority French-language education occurred in Alberta, Ontario and New Brunswick in the first fifty years of Confederation.

On the use of French in government and the courts in Manitoba, in 1889 the government passed an order-in-council ending the publication of the *Manitoba Gazette* in French, and the following year the *Official Language Act* of 1890 abolished French as a language of the courts and of the legislature (that is, of the provincial government). In 1985, the Supreme Court ruled the 1890 language law unconstitutional (Manitoba Language Reference). The Court granted them validity ("The constitution will not suffer a province without laws") while they were being translated.

Restrictions on the use of English and on English-language education in Quebec were enacted only after the election of the Parti Québécois in 1976, and were challenged in the courts. In 1982, the constitutionally entrenched Canadian Charter of Rights and Freedoms, which the PQ government of Quebec opposed, included a section guaranteeing publicly funded minority-language primary and secondary educational rights in all provinces "where numbers warrant" (s.23). In 1969, New Brunswick enacted its *Official Languages Act*, had it entrenched in the *Constitution Act, 1982* and moved to improve French-language education for the Acadian population. In Ontario, which has a large and historic francophone population, successive governments have, with some exceptions, expanded access to government and judicial services in French, but shied away from declaring the provincial officially bilingual. See **Bicultural cleavage** and entries on other matters discussed here.

Maritime union. A long-standing idea to amalgamate the provinces of New Brunswick, Nova Scotia and Prince Edward Island.

As a practical matter, union has not been high on the public agenda since the 1860s, when a conference was held in Charlottetown to discuss the matter. A delegation from the United Province of Canada encouraged consideration of a wider union including Canada. Meetings in Charlottetown led to a conference in Quebec on the larger union. Ultimately, a federal union took place in 1867 of the Province of Canada (Quebec and Ontario), New Brunswick and Nova Scotia, with the Maritime holdout, Prince Edward Island, joining in 1873, two years after British Columbia on the west coast. While Maritime union is not now a foreseeable event, some functional interdependence has been achieved as a result of negotiations since the 1960s. For example, the Council of Maritime Premiers was established by statute in 1971, partly as a result of a recommendation of the (Deutsch) Report on Maritime Union in 1965 for amalgamation of the three provinces, but perhaps also to forestall a formal union. See **Council of Maritime Premiers.**

Marketing boards. A reference usually to the co-operative and compulsory marketing of agricultural products in Canada. However, regulatory agencies, such as the federal National Energy Board and the Canadian Transportation Agency, are in part marketing boards although not producer-managed.

The regulation of the marketing of products within a province is a provincial matter (*Constitution Act, 1867*, s.92:13, "Property and Civil Rights in the Province," s.92:16, "Generally all Matters of a merely local or private Nature...," and other sections with particular regard to natural resources), but it comes under federal jurisdiction when the marketing becomes interprovincial or international (s.91:2, "Regulation of Trade and Commerce").

Largely ignored until the 1990s has been the constitutional injunction of section 121 regarding Canada as a common market: "All Articles of the Growth, Produce, or Manufacture of any one of the Provinces shall...be admitted free into each of the other Provinces." In constitutional discussions in the early 1990s, the federal Conservative government pressed without success for the "modernizing" of section 121, including the prohibition of domestic trade barriers with exceptions for reasons of national interest and for programs promoting regional development or equalization, and new powers for Parliament to manage the economic union. Although federal-provincial conferences subsequently affirmed a commitment to reducing provincial barriers to the free flow of goods, services, capital and labour, the greatest challenge to economic protectionism in general, and to marketing boards and agencies in particular, has resulted from international free-trade agreements and subsequent disputes involving Canada, Mexico and the United States, and the General Agreement on Tariffs and Trade (now the World Trade Organization). See **Economic union of Canada; Free trade; "Trade and Commerce" power; World Trade Organization (WTO)**.

Mass media of communication. A reference to television, radio, newspapers, magazines, and film as intermediaries in the political discourse between the public and politicians.

Assuming that these media are not neutral, scholarly inquiries pursue the question of bias on the part of the senders and effects on the receivers of information. The concern is to discover systematic and hence predictable (as opposed to random) patterns of bias or distortion in the transmission of information, and influence subsequently on public attitudes and behaviour.

Investigations of mass media effects in Canada focus largely on television, radio and newspapers, and the class, cultural, geographic and technological biases evident in "agenda setting" (telling readers and viewers what to think about) and "gatekeeping" (telling readers and viewers what to think). Observing that most of the mass media in Canada are in the private sector and subject to ownership by corporate chains and conglomerates, some people identify a right-wing, ideological bias to the media, or at least a conservative bias consistent with profit making. On the other hand, observing the values of the working press, that is, reporters and commentators, others discern a left-wing bias, or at least a critical iconoclasm. Also, there are no national newspapers in Canada similar to those in most European countries, and Canadians tend to read either the English- or French-language daily press, and listen to or watch either, but not both, linguistic news and public affairs programming. Thus the mass media tend to reinforce the geographic and bicultural cleavages in Canada, presenting a regionally and culturally differentiated treatment of issues on the public agenda and occasionally a significantly differentiated agenda. Because the broadcasting component of the mass media comprises large public and private corporations, observers also examine content for evidence of distinctive public-sector and private-sector values in agenda setting and gate keeping. Some people contend that the predominance of television as a medium of communication has reduced political discourse to succinct sound bites, "visuals," and melodrama.

With respect to media effects on individuals, media scholars have also noticed the increasingly sophisticated techniques adopted by party strategists to manipulate public opinion, especially to achieve short-term shifts in opinion during election campaigns. Elections effectively take place on television and comprise advertising, daily reports on the party leaders' activities, and televised leaders' debates. All parties have adopted tactics associated with consumer-testing of products in the private sector in order to develop campaign strategies and day-to-day tactics for television coverage. Consequently, there tends to be a generic quality to party campaigns as well as media coverage, with a tendency of television to demand dramatic and brief daily "sound bites" accompanied by commentary treating campaigns as "horse races" and politics generally as a field of personal rivalries and conflict instead of discussions about preferred choices in public policy.

Recent years have seen important structural changes within the industry generally. The federal government has been hard-pressed to protect the Canadian periodical industry from rulings of the World Trade Organization on so-called "split runs" of popular magazines from the United States that contain little Canadian editorial content, but considerable advertising from Canadian sources that might otherwise patronize Canadian magazines. It has encountered similar difficulties with respect to the Canadian film industry. The mass communication industry has become increasingly controlled by a very few large corporations. Some corporations have sought to divest themselves of many small newspapers in order to concentrate on ventures in electronic publishing, while at least one broadcaster has purchased a number of newspapers and a large telecommunications company has bought a television network and part interest in a major news paper. The television industry is increasingly characterized by so-called specialty channels approved by the federal regulator, the Canadian Radio-television and Telecommunications Commission, and delivered by cable or satellite systems to an increasingly fragmented audience. See **Canadian Broadcasting Corporation (Radio-Canada); Canadian Radio-television and Telecommunications Commission; Leaders' debates (election campaign); Press gallery.**

Means test. An administrative regulation or procedure that distinguishes those who are eligible for a social benefit on the basis of need from those who are not. Thus, the benefit is not "universal" but "needs-based." Tests that require proof of eligibility are generally detested, because they have often required people to make known personal, family and financial affairs, or to arrange personal affairs so as to qualify. Means testing thus also involves high administrative costs. User fees to access public programs may effectively be a means test if level of income determines usage. A more politically palatable way to effect a means test for a benefit is to make the benefit universal but taxable; hence, given a progressive income tax system, the benefit may be recaptured from people with high incomes. See **Clawback.**

Medicare. A popular term for the universal, comprehensive and public medical insurance plans operated by provincial governments on a shared-cost basis with the federal government under the federal *Canada Health Act.* Health care was designated a provincial responsibility under the *Constitution Act* of 1867, a time when the policy field was considered of local concern, also a matter of private charity and therefore not a great burden for the level of government with little access to revenue-generating powers of taxation relative to the federal government. However, by the end of the twentieth century, health care was a major and costly policy field which involved the federal government exercising its spending power to establish country-wide conditions for provincial administration of health care.

Universal, comprehensive and public medicare was first introduced in Canada in the 1960s by the Co-operative Commonwealth Federation government in Saskatchewan. At that time, most doctors in the province withdrew their services and the government brought doctors from elsewhere to provide medical services. The strike was eventually settled, and although the government was defeated in a subsequent election, public medical care insurance was effectively established in Canada. In 1968, a federal *Medical Care Act* set standards by which the provinces, which are responsible for health care, would qualify for federal shared-cost funding. By 1972, all provinces had medicare plans that met the criteria. The universal, comprehensive and single-payer (the provincial governments) system of medical insurance is arguably the most popular public program in Canada.

Because of rising costs, the federal government has sought since the 1970s to reduce its financial obligations while continuing to impose its conditions on provincial administration of medicare. By 1980, some provinces had allowed underfinancing of their medicare plans, leading eventually to the proliferation of user fees and a potentially less-than-universal health care program. In 1984, the federal Liberal government passed the *Canada Health Act,* which effectively abolished extra-billing and user fees by doctors and hospitals. Ontario's compliance with the federal legislation led to an abortive doctors' strike in 1986. Federal under-funding continued despite provincial objections, and in 2000, the Alberta government permitted surgery and overnight accommodation in private clinics, leading people in the industry and among the public to express fears of a potential two-tier health care system based on ability to pay.

Following federal-provincial negotiations in 2000, the federal Liberal government restored funding for provincial health care almost to the level from which it had begun reductions in the 1990s. The intergovernmental agreement acknowledged federal responsibility in a policy field for which the provinces were primarily responsible, and involved both federal and provincial governments in defining and implementing common, verifiable standards of health-care delivery. Despite the opposition of some provinces to federal involvement in that process, it was the minimal demand of the federal government, asserting its responsibility to ensure the proper expenditure of federal money. Apart from confirming the continuing influence of the federal government over provincial programs funded in part by federal transfer payments, these negotiations were conducted in the knowledge of widespread popular support for public health care insurance. In 2001, the federal government appointed a former New Democratic premier of Saskatchewan to examine the future of Canada's public health care program. See **Federal-provincial tax-sharing agreements (fiscal federalism).**

Meech Lake Accord (1987). An agreement on amendments to the *Constitution Act* reached by the eleven federal and provincial heads of government to accommodate Quebec's opposition to the *Constitution Act, 1982* which patriated the constitution with domestic amending formulae and included the Canadian Charter of Rights and Freedoms.

The Accord failed to be ratified by all legislatures within three years of its initial adoption by a legislature, despite last-minute, high-level and high-pressure political negotiations in June 1990. Not only was the failure of the Accord a serious blow to the federal Conservative government that had staked its political future on accommodation with Quebec, but it revived Quebec nationalism that had been politically dormant since the defeat of the sovereignty referendum in 1980. The Accord's defeat also called into question the political and bureaucratic elite-dominated style of executive federalism as a means of achieving political accommodation, especially on something as fundamentally important as the constitution.

The constitutional amendments of 1982 had left Quebec with less power than before. It lost its informal veto over constitutional change, there was no redistribution of federal powers, Quebec legislation—especially its language law— was now subject to challenges under the Charter unless the notwithstanding clause were periodically invoked and, of considerable importance, provincial autonomy with respect to education was compromised by minority-language education rights in the Charter. To add insult to injury, the 1982 amendments represented the "renewed federalism" promised by Liberal Prime Minister Pierre Trudeau during the provincial referendum campaign of 1980 and which very likely accounted for the defeat in that campaign of the Parti Québécois government's proposal to negotiate sovereignty association.

Following the Conservative victory in 1984, Prime Minister Brian Mulroney made Quebec's accommodation to the constitution a matter of priority in a Quebec round of negotiations. The provincial Liberal government of Robert Bourassa, elected in 1985, presented five demands: the recognition of Quebec as a distinct society; a veto on amendments to the constitution; a limitation on federal spending power; a role for Quebec in the appointment of justices on the Supreme Court; and a role in immigration policy. In 1987, an Accord was negotiated at Meech Lake near Ottawa which satisfied the Quebec government, yet apparently maintained the principle of provincial equality. On four of the five issues, the Accord granted similar powers to all provinces: unanimity among the legislatures would be required for any constitutional amendment affecting federal institutions; provinces would be allowed to opt out of new federal-provincial shared cost programs with compensation if they established programs with similar objectives; the federal government would appoint Supreme Court justices and senators it found acceptable from lists of names submitted by the relevant provinces; all provinces were given the right to share immigration powers with the federal government.

The proposal on distinct society agreed to by all heads of government was the most contentious part of the Accord. The constitution was to be interpreted in a manner consistent with the recognition of French-speaking Canadians, centred in but not limited to Quebec, and English-speaking Canadians concentrated outside Quebec but also present in Quebec, as "a fundamental characteristic of Canada," and that "Quebec constitutes within Canada a distinct society." Parliament and the provincial legislatures were "to preserve the fundamental characteristic of Canada" while in addition Quebec specifically was "to preserve and promote the distinct society of Quebec." Nothing in the proposed constitutional amendment was to derogate from the "powers, rights, or privileges" of Parliament, including those relating to language. While none of the amendments was to affect the Aboriginal and multicultural clauses of the *Constitution Act, 1982*, there was no similar provision regarding women's rights.

Debate subsequently centred on the implications of the distinct society provisions and whether they granted Quebec powers not held by other provinces, and would set Quebec legislation regarding the promotion of distinct society above provisions of the Canadian Charter of Rights and Freedoms. There were also objections to increasing the number of constitutional amendments subject to unanimous consent, discrimination against the territories in the unanimity clause and the appointment process regarding the Senate and the Supreme Court, the opting-out clause which critics said would create a patchwork social security system and make new country-wide programs such as child care unlikely. Some also objected to entrenchment of first ministers' conferences including an agenda-setting procedure seemingly controlled by provincial premiers.

All federal parties supported the Accord in ratification by Parliament, and eight provincial legislatures, excepting Manitoba and Newfoundland, eventually approved the Accord. In Newfoundland, the new Liberal government of Clyde Wells rescinded that province's approval. Following federal-provincial negotiations clarifying the Accord in June 1990, the Manitoba delegation, headed by minority Conservative Premier Gary Filmon and including the opposition party leaders, accepted the agreement, while Premier Wells only promised to introduce the Accord in the Newfoundland legislature. In Manitoba, a Cree member, New Democrat Elijah Harper, daily refused unanimous consent for the Accord to be introduced. When he refused consent on the last sitting day before the deadline for the Accord's adoption and the Manitoba legislature adjourned, the Newfoundland government then adjourned that legislature during debate on the Accord, without holding a vote and despite considerable last-minute pressure on Wells by the federal government.

The fallout from the defeat of the Accord was widespread. French nationalist sentiment revived and the political currency of federalism in Quebec fell precipitately. The Quebec government announced that it would only deal unilaterally with the federal government and join multilateral talks only on its terms. Many public-based groups representing labour, women, Native Peoples, the disabled, non-Native Canadians of ethnic origin other than British or French, welfare activists, and cultural nationalists, which opposed the Accord for various reasons, called for fundamental change to the process of constitutional negotiations: the country's constitution and its future was not to be solely the preserve of "eleven middle-aged white men in business suits" meeting behind closed doors. The adoption of the Charter in 1982 had led to increased public support for and political action by "Charter groups" with a vested interest in constitutional negotiations that might affect their new-found political legitimacy. The criticism of executive federalism was intensified following references by supporters during the period of legislative ratification to the Accord as a "seamless web," of which not even a comma could be changed. Some provincial governments had their legislatures adopt the Accord with no committee hearings, while others held only perfunctory hearings. The prime minister also suffered personally from his public reference to his own leadership in the negotiations in which the country's future was subject to his "roll of the dice."

Subsequently, the Quebec government announced another referendum on the province's constitutional future for 1992, the federal government and several other provinces introduced referendum legislation, the federal government established a Citizen's Forum on the constitution, published proposals for parliamentary study, and held several nationally televised forums on the constitution with participation by various public interest group leaders. Thus ensued a so-called Canada round of negotiations. Two months before the Quebec referendum, federal, provincial and territorial government leaders, and Aboriginal leaders negotiated the Charlottetown Accord, which was then submitted to a country-wide referendum. In addition to revisions of the Meech Lake Accord designating Quebec as a distinct society and limiting federal spending power, the Charlottetown Accord proposed radical reform of the House of Commons and Senate, a framework for the implementation of Native self-government, a revised provision on regional disparities, equalization and regional development, and a non-justiciable statement on social and economic policy objectives. However, the Charlottetown Accord was rejected in the referendum. See **Charlottetown Accord (1992)**.

Members of parliament (MPs). Persons elected to the House of Commons in electoral districts, or constituencies. While MPs are probably the most widely recognized link between the public and the federal government, the disciplined nature of the party system makes their actual role in determining public policy at best minimal.

Members of parliament are political representatives of a constituency, but collectively they are not fully representative of the country's population in terms of ethnicity, gender, education and occupation. In terms of social background, Canadians of British or French descent, and high-status Canadians tend to be "overrepresented" among MPs. A discrepancy is also evident regarding gender, with women comprising close to 20 per cent of MPs. A discrepancy is also partic-ularly evident in terms of educational attainment and occupation. In particular, most MPs come from law and education professions and from business. Also, because MPs are elected in constituencies whose boundaries are objectively related to population distribution, most MPs come from the densely populated parts of the country. MPs are also predominantly middle-aged.

Only a few MPs could be described as career professional politicians. Although many may have held party positions prior to their election to the House of Commons, few have had prior experience in elective office at provincial or municipal levels of government. While some MPs hold parliamentary office for lengthy periods, the career of an MP is usually short-lived. Electoral defeat is the most common reason for an MP to leave the House, while diminishing job satis-faction over time with little prospect for advancement to the cabinet, and qualifi-cation for a full parliamentary pension constitute encouragements to retire voluntarily from legislative politics. Government MPs in particular may be offered a post-parliamentary career in public service as a reward for loyal service and an inducement of loyalty from others in the caucus.

MPs do not as a whole have a large personal influence on policy making. The parliamentary system and the disciplined party system necessarily relegate MPs to a predictable and theatrical "reactive" role to government policies which are determined in private by the cabinet and the senior public officials. Government MPs will predictably support the government; opposition MPs will criticize it. Government supporters will claim that their impact on policy deter-mination occurs in the regular private meetings of the parliamentary party caucus, and both government and opposition MPs will assert personal effectiveness in representations to ministers and officials. Since the 1980s, there have been efforts to improve the policy role of MPs by establishing relatively permanent membership on committees, and some private members' bills are also allowed to come to a vote and proceed to committee. Otherwise, the MPs' representative role is more often one of constituency service, redressing constituents' grievances or obtaining service from some administrative body. See **Caucus**; **House of Commons**; **Parliamentary indemnity**; **Parliamentary privilege (immunities)**.

Merit system (in the public service). The principle of recruiting and promoting career civil servants on the basis of objective and published criteria.

Prior to 1918, the federal civil service was based on patronage appointments by the party in power. Since then, the Public Service Commission has been responsible in the main for promotion, recruitment and discipline in the federal administration (except at the most senior levels and in certain crown corporations and agencies). Provisions of the *Official Languages Act, 1969* are an important qualification to appointment and promotion with respect to the merit system. The "free" operations of the merit system tended in the twentieth century to create a unilingual, predominantly anglophone federal administration. Since 1969, apart from providing federal government services in both official languages in selected parts of the country and where numbers warrant service in the minority language, there have been efforts to attract French Canadians to the federal public service and to recruit bilingual candidates to make the federal service in Ottawa functionally bilingual. See **Bilingualism and biculturalism**; *Official Languages Act* **(Canada, 1969)**.

Ministerial responsibility. The principle that cabinet ministers are individually responsible legally, politically and morally to the legislature for actions and policies within their portfolios, and also responsible collectively to the legislature as the government-of-the-day.

These constitutional conventions are central to responsible government, that is, the legislature's "confidence" in the political executive that comprises members from the legislature. The convention that a minister can be questioned only on current and not former responsibilities somewhat insulates particular ministers and the cabinet from opposition criticism. However, the current minister is responsible retrospectively for government activity in the relevant policy area. If a cabinet minister has been derelict, that minister, if abandoned by the prime minister or provincial premier whose party usually dominates the legislature, may be censured by the legislature. In the event of an effective opposition charge against a minister, a "voluntary" resignation from the cabinet is a more likely outcome. Depending on the circumstances, departure from the cabinet may be only short-lived. As long as a majority of legislators, but effectively a prime minister or premier, ignore an evasion of, or delinquency in, ministerial responsibility, there is no way to enforce it, at least until the next election.

The concept of collective responsibility means that charges against one minister are charges against the government, that the government is a single, cohesive administration, and that to remain in office the government must defend its policies and actions in the legislature and retain its confidence. The concept of ministerial responsibility, both individual and collective, in a parliamentary system does not readily distinguish between the political and the administrative. While it may be unrealistic to hold a minister and government responsible for every administrative act in a department, clearly ministers are answerable to the legislature, and implicitly the public, for errors of commission or omission related to government policy or instructions. See **Cabinet**; **Collective (cabinet/ministerial) responsibility**; **Responsible government**.

Ministers (of the Crown). Members of a cabinet, collectively the government- of-the day, whom the governor general (or a provincial lieutenant-governor) appoints on the advice of the prime minister (or provincial premier).

By convention, cabinet ministers must hold seats in the legislature—in the bicameral Parliament, with few exceptions, in the House of Commons. A federal cabinet requires at least one senator—the government's house leader in the Senate without any departmental responsibilities; otherwise, a prime minister might use senatorial appointments to cabinet for some particular representative or policy purpose. (In the 1890s, Conservative senators John Abbott and Mackenzie Bowell each served briefly as prime minister.) Some ministerial appointments represent a prime minister's or premier's attempt to give cabinet representation to a particular group that may be important in electoral calculations. For example, prime ministers usually like to have a cabinet minister from each province and several from particular cities or regions within a province. French Canadians have tended to be prominent in Canadian cabinets, either as prime ministers or as close confidants ("lieutenants") of anglophone prime ministers. Until the 1970s, anglophones monopolized important economic and financial portfolios, and francophones frequently held portfolios such as Justice and Public Works. Some portfolios, such as Agriculture, Fisheries and Oceans, and Transportation, are usually assigned to members from regions particularly sensitive to federal policy in those fields. Some ministers have an occupational affinity with the portfolio to which they are assigned; for example, a lawyer usually holds the Justice portfolio. Prime ministers also like to include representatives from ethnic groups other than British and French, as well as a good proportion of women, without subjecting the government to the cry of tokenism. Cabinet-making is normally fine-tuned to include an anglophone from Quebec, a francophone from outside Quebec, and members of minority ethno-religious communities, such as Aboriginal, Jewish and Asian communities. Fortunate is an ambitious government member of parliament who can satisfy several of these qualifications.

Ministers are individually accountable for policy and administrative action or inaction or in their respective areas of responsibility, and also share responsibility collectively as the government. This constitutional responsibility is effected in the obligation of ministers to have seats in the legislature and to be present to answer questions, defend policy and obtain approval for departmental estimates. Ministers are bound for life by their oath of office as privy councillors not to discuss cabinet matters publicly. They may publicly dissociate themselves from a government policy only by resigning from the cabinet, thereby ceasing to be a minister but remaining bound as a privy councillor never to disclose cabinet confidences.

Theoretically, political parties and the legislature itself are training grounds for future ministers. However, especially following the Second World War, a

frequent route to the federal cabinet of Liberal governments was from the leadership of groups outside the legislature and the party system in business, academe
and public administration. Five of the nine prime ministers from 1949 to 1988
had little parliamentary experience before becoming cabinet ministers— and little
experience, if any, as cabinet ministers before becoming party leader or prime
minister (Louis St. Laurent, Lester B. Pearson, Pierre Trudeau, Brian Mulroney
and Kim Campbell). John Turner, who subsequently served only a few months as
prime minister in 1984, had previous parliamentary experience, but was
advantaged in his leadership bid by having been away from party politics and in
business for about 10 years. Jean Chrétien, whose prime ministerial career from
1993 was more successful, was initially disadvantaged because he remained readily associated with his earlier parliamentary and ministerial experience. Prime
ministers John Diefenbaker (1957-62) and Joe Clark (1979-80) had extensive
parliamentary experience in opposition before assuming office. Appointment
to an administrative office, the Senate, the judiciary, or a business career
commonly follows a minister's exit from the cabinet. It is rare for federal cabinet
ministers to tolerate post-cabinet careers in the backbenches of the government
or the opposition.

Most ministers are heads of particular departments of the government and
are responsible for policy and activity within the particular department or designated government agencies. Other ministers may be ministers with special parliamentary responsibilities, ministers of state responsible for "designated purposes"
or, as an "undesignated" minister, appointed to aid a departmental minister. A
cabinet might also include ministers without portfolio to satisfy some representative or other political requirement. In 1993, Conservative and Liberal governments each reorganized the federal government, reducing the size of the cabinet,
the Liberals creating junior ministers styled secretaries of state, to assist particular
ministers with special interests in their portfolios, but who were not formally part
of the cabinet. See **Cabinet**; **Cabinet organization**; **Collective (cabinet/ministe-
rial) responsibility**; **Executive assistant**; **Inner cabinet**; **Ministerial responsibility**; **Ministers (of the Crown)**.

Ministry. A term that can refer to a particular government department or more
broadly to the government-of-the-day, whose members comprise the political
executive, the cabinet. See **Cabinet**; **Ministers (of the Crown)**.

Ministry (minister) of state. Areas of special ministerial responsibility at the
federal level, each established (and some disbanded) by order-in-council, superseded in 1993 by the designation of junior ministers as secretaries of state, outside
the cabinet proper, to assist ministers in selected areas of their portfolios.

The federal ministry-of-state system for designated purposes was a device
established in 1970 to achieve co-ordinated policy development and implementation across departments, or for someone with ministerial status to carry out a task
for the prime minister, unencumbered with administrative responsibilities. Often
the ministries of state were associated with policy areas to which the government
attached electoral importance. Some, such as the ministry of state for urban
affairs, were short-lived, while others, such as multiculturalism, survived.
Generally these cabinet assignments had no direct control over departments

established by statute, although during the Liberal government of the 1980s an attempt was made to create central agencies out of ministries of state dealing with economic and social development. Conservative Prime Minister Brian Mulroney's government from 1984 to 1993 included numerous ministers of state, for example, for grains and oilseeds, seniors, small businesses and tourism, privatization, youth, and fitness and amateur sport. Many of these responsibilities were held by ministers with departmental portfolios. See **Secretaries of state**.

Minority government. A government formed by a party which holds only a minority of seats in the legislature. Thus, the government's survival depends on the support of another party or some members of another party who then hold the "balance of power."

There have been nine minority federal governments, most occurring between the late-1950s and the late-1970s. The important political difference between a minority and a majority government is the relationship of the cabinet to the legislature. The Liberals under William Lyon Mackenzie King formed two minority governments: one lasted from 1921 to 1925; the minority government elected in 1925 ended the following year in the midst of scandal, with the governor general's appointment of Arthur Meighen's minority Conservative government that collapsed after only a few sitting days. In the minority Parliament of 1957-58, the electoral momentum was with the governing Conservatives. Thus, the government "toyed" with the House of Commons until it felt it propitious to dissolve Parliament in the reasonable expectation of winning a majority. Subsequent minority Conservative (1962-63 and 1979-80) and Liberal (1963-65, 1965-68, 1972-74) governments possessed no such momentum and the House of Commons became an effective forum for policy debate and political accommodation over legislation.

Assuming mutual interests of most parties to sustain a minority government in office, such governments can last as long as party house leaders and party whips then ensure that no vote in the legislature will deny confidence in the government. In 1968, a parliamentary precedent was established regarding "accidental" defeat, a high risk for minority governments. The federal Liberal government was defeated on the third reading of a money bill, clearly a matter of confidence. However, instead of resigning at once, Prime Minister Lester Pearson argued that the defeat was accidental, and insisted privately to the Conservative leader of the opposition, Robert Stanfield, that a winter election in difficult economic times was not in the national interest. Perhaps more significant was the fact that Pearson had already announced his resignation as Liberal leader and the party was in the process of selecting his successor. The House of Commons resumed sitting following Pearson's announced intention to introduce a motion of confidence as the first order of business. When the House met, the government won the vote of confidence and thereby remained in office. By contrast, in 1979 the federal Conservative government lost a very deliberate vote on a New Democratic party subamendment to a Liberal amendment to a government motion approving the budget. Prime Minister Joe Clark might have delayed the vote and negotiated support from the fourth party in the House, the Ralliement des créditistes, but he did not. Clark immediately accepted the vote as want of confidence in the government and advised the governor general to dissolve Parliament and issue writs for an election in early 1980, an election that he lost.

Minority governments, though perhaps relatively short-lived, are not necessarily less productive than majority governments. Indeed, in the 1960s and 1970s, some minority governments pursued very significant policy agendas, for example concerning medicare, bilingualism and biculturalism, and review of foreign investment.

Monarchy (constitutional). A political system headed by a monarch in whose name the government acts, but whose actions are subject to the constitution, in Canada that of a parliamentary democracy. Thus, it is said that the monarch reigns, but does not rule. See **Crown; Crown prerogatives; Sovereign, the**.

Monetary policy. The policy of a national government or central bank in varying the amount of money in circulation and the availability of credit, thus affecting levels of economic activity.

The objective of monetary policy is to pursue economic growth with price stability, that is, with a low rate of inflation. Monetary policy is the ultimate responsibility of the federal government. Major devices to achieve desired policy on money supply, however, are normally under the independent indirect control of the Bank of Canada: interest rates charged by banks and other financial institutions and purchasing or selling of government securities, all designed either to restrict or expand the amount of money in circulation. There is regular consultation between the minister of finance and governor of the central bank. In the event of a disagreement, the government may issue a directive to the Bank; however, a government would presumably want to avoid an ensuing controversy. See **Bank of Canada (central bank)**.

Money bills. Financial legislation that deals with the spending of money (supply) or with the raising of money (tax measures, ways and means). In Canada, only the government can introduce money bills; and in the bicameral Parliament, money bills must be introduced first in the elected House of Commons. Though they must be approved by the appointed Senate, the upper house cannot amend money bills to increase revenue or expenditures. This treatment of money bills reflects the historic relationship between Parliament (especially, the elected lower house) and the Crown, which can raise and spend revenue only with the legislature's approval. The legislative voting of supply (or its denial) is the important foundation of the constitutional convention of responsible government. Responsible government, or the political accountability of the executive to the legislature, is implied in the government's sole responsibility for introducing revenue and expenditure legislation and its necessity to win legislative support for its money bills. See **Budget and budgetary process; Estimates; Legislation; Responsible government**.

***Morgentaler, Smoling and Scott v. The Queen* (1988).** A unanimous decision of the Supreme Court of Canada that struck down provisions in the Criminal Code regarding the voluntary termination of pregnancies as a violation of "liberty and security of the person" guaranteed in the Canadian Charter of Rights and Freedoms (s.7).

Section 251 of the Criminal Code had required the approval of a therapeutic abortion committee of an accredited hospital in order to obtain or perform an abortion. The Court found that the requirement imposed an undue hardship on women that could not be reasonably "justified in a free and democratic society" (s.1). The majority did not judge the issue of abortion, thus leaving Parliament the authority to legislate further in the matter. Some justices made this point clear in their decisions. Only Justice Bertha Wilson argued that the matter was beyond the competence of legislators: that any law pertaining to access to therapeutic abortions inherently violated a woman's right to "security of the person."

Apart from the moral aspect of abortion, the case was important for several reasons. It highlighted concerns expressed before the Charter's adoption about the legitimacy of judicial review in a democratic system like Canada's, whose system of responsible government and the supremacy of parliament values the accountability of legislators for public policy. Judicial review by appointed and tenured judges granted, the case then illustrated comprehensive, non-interpretive review on substantive grounds, including the admission of social and legislative facts on the effect relative to the intention of the legislation. Also, although the Court did not deny Parliament legislative competence, the Court was nonetheless an actor, precipitating the intense political debate that ensued. When, on a vote free of party discipline and resulting in a tie, the Senate subsequently defeated new government legislation that might have survived a Charter challenge, the government abandoned further efforts to legislate. Thus, abortions in Canada became subject not to legislation, but to provincial and territorial government and hospital administration regulations pertaining to availability of the medically insured operation, regulations which could also be challenged in the courts.

Although the action of the Court in declaring legislative policy unconstitutional comes after the fact, rulings such as *Morgentaler* clearly have an inhibiting effect on governments and legislators. Writing in *Morgentaler* but speaking of the role of the Court under the Charter, Chief Justice Brian Dickson said the Court has "the crucial obligation of ensuring that the legislative initiatives of our Parliament and legislatures conform to the democratic values expressed" in the entrenched constitutional document. While the intent of those who framed the Charter might have been otherwise, the Court had earlier determined, in Justice Antonio Lamer's words, that the meaning of the Charter not be "frozen in time to the moment of adoption with little or no possibility of growth, development and adjustment to changing societal needs" (Motor Vehicle Reference, 1985).

The Supreme Court had thus already acknowledged that the possibility of "saving" legislation otherwise violating the Charter with reference to section 1 ("rights and freedoms...subject only to such reasonable limits prescribed by law as can be demonstrably justified in a free and democratic society") or section 7 (depriving a person of their "right to life, liberty and security" only "in accordance with the principles of fundamental justice") enlarged the scope of judicial review. The Court therefore established criteria for such limitations: the objectives of the law must be "pressing and substantial" and the means to achieve the objective represent a minimal violation of rights "rationally connected" to the objective and result in a benefit greater than the cost of the limitation to the individual concerned (*R. v. Oakes*, 1986).

Prior to the Charter, the Supreme Court relied on "adjudicative facts" and tended to reject "social" or "legislative facts" as irrelevant to its decisions. Adjudicative facts refer to events directly pertaining to the parties involved in the legal action, while social or legislative facts refer to information on which policy decisions are based. In examining legislation in the context of Charter rights generally, the Court entertains social and legislative facts. Some questions are beyond the fact-finding capability of the Court, for example, on the effect of cruise missile testing by the United States over Canada in *Operation Dismantle v. The Queen*, 1985: not with the adjudicative fact of executive responsibility for international agreements, but with social or legislative facts regarding threats to "security of the person" from such testing of missiles. But this was not so on the effect of the Criminal Code provisions on access to abortion in *Morgentaler*. In considering the constitutionality of the section of the Criminal Code respecting the procurement and provision of abortions, the Court relied on federal government reports that found that access to abortion was uneven and delayed. Moreover, of crucial importance to the Court, reports connected the delay to "increased physical and psychological trauma" among women seeking the operation whose health the Criminal Code's section on abortion was intended to protect. Thus, the additional responsibilities acquired by the Court under the Charter, including the admission of social and legislative facts on the effects of a section of the Criminal Code relative to its intention, led to a rejection of that section on access to therapeutic abortions as unconstitutional. See **Canadian Charter of Rights and Freedoms (1982)**; **Judicial review (interpretive; non-interpretive)**; **Supreme Court**.

Movement parties. Political parties that were created in society outside the parliamentary environment in times of social stress and crisis when neither of the two major parties, the Conservatives and Liberals, one forming the government and the other the leading opposition party, was seen as acceptable.

Especially in the first half of the twentieth century, such parties were a response to the failure of the established parliamentary parties to deal effectively with serious social tensions associated with immigration and western settlement, and with economic dislocation. Such movements also received support as conservative defenders of a valued lifestyle seemingly being undermined by "outside" forces. While such parties rose in the first half of the twentieth century, the popular attitudes that sustained them continue to be manifested in support for so-called third parties.

In the post-First World War period, the western-based Progressive party was the first movement party to gain significant electoral support, particularly in western Canada, winning the second-largest number of seats in the House of Commons in 1921. Refusing, however, to accept the role of official opposition because of its populist "anti-party" views, it at once began to decline. In the 1930s, the socialist Co-operative Commonwealth Federation and the conservative, populist Social Credit party rose during the Great Depression, also with electoral success largely in the West. In the 1960s, the CCF was transformed into the moderate social democratic New Democratic party, in an attempt to forge electoral success in central and eastern Canada. Many westerners supported the Conservative party for many years during and following its leadership by westerner John Diefenbaker in the 1960s and the gradual dissolution of Social Credit. However, dissatisfaction with the federal government and the Conservative party, particularly among Albertans, led to the formation of the conservative and populist Reform party in the late 1980s. The seeming breakdown of traditional social values and institutions, and recurring opposition to national political organizations that seemed out of touch with western interests spurred support for Reform that formed the official opposition in 1997, but failed to "break through" east of Manitoba. In order to improve its electoral fortunes as a national party, Reform was reorganized as the Canadian Alliance in 2000, but it too failed in the election later that year to make significant electoral gains east of Manitoba.

Movement parties traditionally combine educational and electoral activities, stressing grassroots involvement in party affairs and a desire to alter radically some aspects of the economic and political order. Some movement parties, such as the Progressive, Social Credit, and Reform/Alliance parties, promising systemic political change (for example, less party discipline in the legislature, popular legislative initiatives, recall and referenda) are leader-dominated right-populist parties; others, such as the CCF-NDP, for whom redistributive economic and social issues are important, are democratic socialist, left-populist parties.

The disciplined parliamentary party and federal systems in Canada have encouraged and sustained movement parties. In a parliamentary system in which the government party is normally the one with the largest number of elected members, legislators vote along party lines, suppressing public dissent among sectional representatives who may be in a permanent minority in the government caucus. The rise of third parties in the Canadian West has been caused in part by the central Canadian dominance of the federal Conservative and Liberal parties. Governments in a parliamentary system are formed on the basis of the number of constituencies won in an election. Thus, governments are founded on political support in densely populated parts of country, notably central Canada which has most of the country's constituencies. At the same time, the election of only a handful of members legitimizes a new party by giving it a parliamentary forum in which to criticize both government and leading opposition parties, and a base from which to achieve further electoral gains.

The federal system also legitimizes sectional elites in the provincial political systems who can claim to represent the interests of the region better than the region's members of parliament, including federal cabinet ministers, who are outnumbered by central Canadian MPs in the party caucuses and the federal cabinet. Certainly the appointed Senate, created in part to represent regional interests in Parliament, does not perform that task. Early and sustained success of both the Social Credit and the CCF-NDP, as well as their precursors in various farmer movements, occurred in provincial political arenas in the West and in Ontario. The NDP has remained influential in provincial politics in British Columbia, Saskatchewan, Manitoba and Ontario while its electoral support in recent federal elections has been minimal.

However, the Reform party, led by Preston Manning, the son of a former Social Credit premier of Alberta, focussed attention only on federal politics. Manning can be credited with Reform's creation and electoral success—achieving official opposition status in the House of Commons in 1997—and with the transformation of the party to the Canadian Alliance. But apparently many party members also held him responsible for the party's inability to garner significant support east of Manitoba. In 2000, Manning was defeated in the contest for leadership of the Canadian Alliance by Stockwell Day, a former Conservative cabinet minister from Alberta whom party supporters presumably saw as combining both their social conservative and populist values, and potentially more electoral appeal than Manning to central and eastern Canadians. However, it might very well be the party's and its leader's social conservatism that continued to limit the appeal of the party in the election of 2000. See **Canadian Alliance party; Co-operative Commonwealth Federation (CCF); New Democratic party (NDP); Ralliement des créditistes; Reform party; Social Credit party; Third parties (political).**

Multiculturalism. Policy begun by the federal Liberal government in the 1970s, and continued by the Conservatives, to encourage the expression of the cultural heritage of ethnic groups in Canada, notably other than British and French.

The federal government provided financial assistance for various projects by organized ethnic groups to foster knowledge of their cultural heritage and their contribution to Canada. Originally carried out within the federal portfolio Secretary of State, the Liberal government established a nondepartmental ministry of state for multiculturalism and the Canadian Consultative Council on Multiculturalism, later renamed the Canadian Ethnocultural Council. Multiculturalism was entrenched in the Canadian Charter of Rights and Freedoms in 1982: "This Charter shall be interpreted in a manner consistent with the preservation and enhancement of the multicultural heritage of Canadians" (s.27). The equality-rights section 15 also includes "race, national or ethnic origin" as prohibited bases for discrimination. The Conservatives enacted the *Canadian Multiculturalism Act* in 1988 that established a statutory basis for federal multicultural policy and enumerates implementation measures, including the creation of the Canadian Multicultural Advisory Committee. In 1991, the government created the Department of Multiculturalism and Citizenship, later made part of the Canadian Heritage ministry by the Liberals.

Although the policy of promoting multiculturalism is formally a recognition and encouragement of the cultural mosaic of Canadian society, an important partisan, electoral motive lay behind the developments listed above. The Liberal party in particular was very quick to appreciate the electoral potential of support among immigrant families, especially in the last half of the twentieth century when the Liberal party was usually in office. Immigration prior to the Second World War had come largely from northern and eastern Europe. Soon after, migrant populations tended to come from southern Europe, and later from virtually all parts of the world. In the 1990s, Asia displaced Europe as the primary origin of migrants. Among political parties, only the western-based, right-populist Reform party opposed "official multiculturalism" while the Conservatives, Liberals and New Democrats, acknowledging the growing importance of the "ethnic" factor in Canadian politics, especially in densely populated urban areas in and around Montreal, Toronto and Vancouver, support federal multiculturalism. Although in recent years there had been fewer migrants admitted to Canada than the target number set by the federal government, Reform also argued that the target should be lowered. In 2000, the Canadian Alliance replaced Reform in an attempt to improve its electoral fortunes. Perhaps sensitive to Reform's public image, the Canadian Alliance adopted a more accommodating attitude toward multiculturalism, but fared little better than Reform in the 2000 election.

While support for federal funding of multicultural policies and programs naturally comes primarily from the leadership of minority ethnic groups, there are various sources of opposition to so-called "official multiculturalism." Throughout the twentieth century, francophones were wary of federal immigration policy that would diminish their political influence, if not threaten their cultural survival, as migrants would tend to be socialized into the majority anglophone culture. In the late-twentieth century, the federal government effectively granted Quebec a role in federal immigration jurisdiction, establishing a particular quota of migrants whose initial destination would be Quebec and for whom the provincial government would provide settlement services normally provided by the federal government. There is also criticism from Canadian-born anglophones who argue that multiculturalism has been accompanied by a diminution of their longstanding cultural symbols and practices that "new" Canadians should respect and adopt as part of their identity. And there is even criticism from some people of non-British and non-French background who argue that multicultural policies and programs reinforce ethnic distinctions that constitute barriers to ethnic compatibility within Canada.

N

National Assembly (Quebec). The unicameral provincial legislature of Quebec. From 1867 to 1968, the legislature had been styled the Legislative Assembly. The change of name reflected the assertive nationalism associated with the Quiet Revolution of the 1960s. See **Quiet Revolution**.

National Citizens' Coalition v. A.-G. Canada **(1984)**. A court ruling in Alberta in 1984 that the prohibition in the *Canada Elections Act* of third-party (that is, groups other than political parties) advertising in federal elections was a violation of section 2 ("Fundamental Freedoms") of the Canadian Charter of Rights and Freedoms.

This ruling was the first of several rebuffs in provincial courts to such restrictions. This decision was not appealed to the Supreme Court of Canada and although technically it had effect only in Alberta, the restrictions of the Act were not enforced elsewhere. Federal legislation since 1974 has included controls on party fund-raising, campaign expenditures, and their accounting in order to ensure fairness in federal election campaigns. Third-party expenditures were initially allowed if they were made "for the purpose of advancing the aims of any organization or association other than a political party...." As a result of complaints about individuals and corporations engaged in advertising effectively supporting particular candidates or parties, Parliament adopted legislation in 1983 that limited campaign advertising to registered political parties and their candidates only. The law was immediately and successfully challenged by a conservative lobby group, the National Citizens' Coalition (NCC).

The most controversial consequence of the ruling was intensive third-party advertising on the Canada-United States Free Trade Agreement in the 1988 election. While both supporters and opponents of the Agreement participated, it was the mass media blitz by business supporters in the last few weeks of the campaign that some observers credit for a last-minute surge of support for the successful Conservative government and the Agreement. Third-party expenditures in the campaign were neither controlled nor reported, were estimated to be over $5 million, while the Conservatives reported expenditures were almost $8 million.

The irony of the Court ruling was that the activities of political parties were strictly controlled in federal elections, but not other groups with partisan preferences. Not only did this discrepancy apply to party fund-raising and expenditures, but also to relatively minor restrictions such as the one-day blackout on party advertising prior to election day. Thus, some groups could become surrogates for political parties. The (Pierre Lortie) Royal Commission on Electoral Reform and Party Financing, appointed by the Conservative government after the 1988 election, recommended the formal registration of third parties with restraints comparable to registered political parties. But further amendments to the Act that restricted third-party activity that were even less restrictive than the recommendations of the royal commission were also declared invalid by an Alberta court. However, it could be inferred from the Supreme Court of Canada's decision regarding Quebec's referendum law in 1997, that it would sustain federal restrictions on third-party advertising in federal elections as part of a regime to promote fairness in election campaigns (*Libman v. Quebec [Attorney general]*). In 1999, changes to the *Canada Elections Act* once again included restrictions on third-party advertising nationally and within each constituency. The NCC obtained a court injunction in Alberta against the restrictions in the early stages of the federal election campaign in 2000. However, on a federal government appeal soon afterwards, the Supreme Court overturned the injunction. See **Electoral law (controls; subsidies)**.

National energy policy; program (NEP). Federal policy related to oil supply and pricing, periodically negotiated with the provinces, especially the major oil-producing province of Alberta. Although policy was first established by the Conservative government in 1961, policy in the 1970s and early 1980s under the Liberal government, later dismantled by the Conservatives, became an extremely divisive political issue touching on Canadian federalism and resulting in a constitutional amendment.

For all provinces, resource development generally represents an opportunity for economic diversification, and for those in western and Atlantic Canada, an escape from economic dependency on the central Canadian economy which historically benefited especially from access to cheap energy produced elsewhere. For the federal government, energy policy touches on its commitment to distribute benefits equitably across the country and reduce regional disparities.

National oil policy was first developed when there was an oversupply of cheap oil. Rarely were there disputes between government and industry or between governments. The federal government supported the development policy of the oil-producing provinces and did not oppose the interests of the industry. In the 1960s, the federal government assured sale of domestic oil in Canada west of the Ottawa River and in the United States, with the remainder of Canada supplied by imported oil. In addition, federal and provincial tax concessions to the private, predominantly multinational petroleum industry bolstered the economies of the oil-producing provinces.

This policy, and resource politics generally, changed significantly when world oil prices rose dramatically with the creation of the Organization of Petroleum Exporting Countries cartel in 1973. Political support for the then-minority federal Liberal government was largely in central and Atlantic Canada— energy-consuming regions of the country— at a time when economic nationalism was particularly strong and the democratic socialist New Democratic party had successfully popularized a "corporate welfare bum" theme in the 1972 election. The Liberal government imposed a temporary price freeze in Canada and an export tax on Canadian oil equal to the difference between the domestic and world prices. this prevented "windfall" revenue either to the private oil companies or to the oil-producing provinces. Later, the federal government proposed sharing the additional revenue with those provinces. The federal government also committed itself to the completion of an oil pipeline to Montreal and a guaranteed outlet for domestic oil east of the Ottawa River. A federal-provincial conference in 1974 established the policy of a single price for oil throughout Canada, to be modified by transportation costs and the taxing policies of individual provinces. Canadian oil would be made available at a price below world levels, and the federal government would subsidize the costs of imported oil in part through revenue from the export tax on Canadian oil. In 1975, the now-majority federal Liberal government created Petro-Canada, a crown corporation designed to participate actively at all levels in the petroleum industry, from exploration to retailing, and thus influence private-sector behaviour. Also, Parliament passed the *Energy Supplies Emergency Act* and the *Petroleum Administration Act*, allowing the federal cabinet to fix the price of domestic oil and gas in interprovincial trade in the absence of a negotiated agreement with the producing provinces. The Liberal National Energy Program of 1980 included provisions to "Canadianize" the oil and gas industry, divert a larger share of oil revenue to the federal treasury, and encourage exploration in the federally controlled territories.

Oil policy and other energy and resource questions became the subject of bitter interregional, federal-provincial, and government-industry disputes. Alberta, for example, consistently opposed the export tax on oil and the subsidized domestic price. Nonetheless, the revenue accruing to the oil-producing provinces was so considerable that the federal government periodically revised the formula by which equalization grants to provinces were calculated, especially as Ontario, with one of the highest per capita income levels in Canada, was on the verge of qualifying as a "have-not" province. In 1979, a one-dollar-a-barrel increase in the price of domestic oil was estimated to cost the federal treasury an additional $60 million in equalization payments to all provinces except Alberta, British Columbia and Ontario. Other post-1973 disputes included a federal proposal to end the exemption of royalties paid to provincial governments from corporate income taxable by the federal government.

In 1982, the Liberal government's goal of constitutional patriation with a Charter of Rights and Freedoms was facilitated by agreement to a constitutional amendment, section 92A on non-renewable natural resources, forestry resources, and electrical energy, along with the clarifying Sixth Schedule. The powers of the provinces were broadened, enlarging powers of provincial taxation and legitimizing the right of both levels of government to participate in national resource policy. The constitution thus sets a framework within which the oil- and gas-producing provinces can better pursue their interests and the federal government national interests, including those of energy consumers.

Following its election in 1984, the Conservative government, committed to reduce the level of government involvement in the economy and to respond to western grievances, incrementally dismantled the Liberal National Energy Program and privatized Petro-Canada. Also the Conservative-negotiated Canada-United States Free Trade Agreement of 1988 significantly affected national energy policy by establishing a continental market for energy. Canada cannot discriminate between domestic energy prices and export prices to the US of oil, gas or electricity. See **Natural resources**.

National Housing Act (NHA). Originally the *Dominion Housing Act, 1935,* the often-amended legislation under which the federal government provides funds to assist the housing construction industry, home-buyers, home-owners and renters. Its major areas of responsibility are in: middle- and low-priced private and co-operative, non-profit, and public housing; residential rehabilitation and neighbourhood improvement; elimination and prevention of water and soil pollution; land assembly for new communities; site clearance for areas outside the neighbourhood improvement areas; and mortgage insurance.

The NHA is largely responsible for the postwar creation of the construction industry. Its provisions, administered since 1945 by the Canada Mortgage and Housing Corporation, were designed to complement the private construction industry. However, through housing policy, as well as ownership and control of harbours, railway lands, airport development, military installations and other forms of land ownership, the federal government has acquired a major policy role in urban development, while constitutional jurisdiction over municipalities lies with the provinces (*Constitution Act, 1867*, s.92:8: "Municipal Institutions in the Province). This is not a minor field of federal-provincial tension and partisan political interest, as almost 80 per cent of Canada's population reside in metropolitan areas, and most of that urban population in the three largest metropolitan areas, Toronto, Montreal and Vancouver.

Through CMHC the federal government encourages research in construction materials and effectively sets standards for the construction industry, thus affecting the location and level of economic development in Canadian municipalities and metropolitan areas. Many programs under the NHA involving direct federal assistance to municipalities, the industry, and home-owners take place under bilateral federal-provincial agreements. See **Canada Mortgage and Housing Corporation (CMHC)**.

National Policy (NP). A policy for national development which Sir John A. Macdonald and the Conservative party advocated in the 1870s and 1880s; it involved railway construction, large-scale immigration and western settlement, and an increase in the protective tariff.

The NP is generally credited for the business and popular support that returned the Conservatives to power in the general election of 1878 and re-elected them in 1882. At this time, the Liberal party was politically weak. However, under the leadership of Wilfrid Laurier from 1891, the Liberal party won the election of 1896, adopted Macdonald's development policy, and eventually appropriated the Conservative party's position as Canada's "national" party for much of the twentieth century. As regional consciousness developed and persisted in western Canada throughout the twentieth century, "national policy" became a pejorative term in that region, as federal government policy, for example in trade, transportation and natural resource fields, was more clearly linked to the interests of the central Canadian economy, or "the East."

Nationalistes, the. A political movement in the first two decades of the twentieth century whose most prominent representative as legislator and journalist was Henri Bourassa. The movement articulated the concerns of French Canadians at a time when industrialization, large-scale immigration and Imperial foreign policy, notably support for the war against the Boers in South Africa, posed threats to French-Canadian society. A successful Liberal member of parliament and a likely successor to the party's leader Sir Wilfrid Laurier, Bourassa abandoned the Liberals and his movement eventually constituted an electoral threat to the Liberal party.

In the federal election in 1911, the Nationalistes and the predominantly anglophone Conservatives struck an electoral anti-Liberal alliance in Quebec. In that election, the pro-Conservative sentiment in English Canada, which was generated by business opposition to the Liberal proposal for trade reciprocity with the United States, and the split vote among francophones in Quebec between the Liberals and the Nationalistes, resulted in a majority Conservative government. The Nationalistes thus helped to defeat the Liberals, but they did not hold a balance of power as they had hoped. In that second decade, French nationalist sentiment was fostered by further attacks on French-language rights in education, particularly in Ontario, and in the bitter, polarized bicultural politics surrounding Canada's participation and military conscription in the First World War. In the wartime election of 1917, francophones returned to the Liberal party, while many anglophone Liberals took part in the Conservative-dominated Union government that won the election. Bourassa's influence in politics continued to be reflected in the pages of *Le Devoir*, a newspaper which he established in 1911. See **Fragment (splinter) parties**.

Nationalization. The acquisition by government of ownership rights of private-sector companies.

The nationalization of key sectors of the economy, such as the resource industry, banking, transportation and primary industries, is usually associated with the socialist political agenda of the mid-twentieth century, designed to make government planning in the public interest the fundamental framework for economic activity. However, in Canada non-socialist party governments have also nationalized industries for developmental as well as for social and cultural purposes, for example in the production and distribution of electricity, transportation and cultural industries, including broadcasting, and in the provision of basic health insurance. Since the Second World War, all political parties have acknowledged the so-called managerial revolution, recognizing that management of the economy through regulation may be more effective than through ownership. At the same time, there was an appreciation that public managers were not necessarily more sensitive to the public interest than private ones. Consequently, developmental and social objectives of nationalization may be more effectively achieved with less cost to the public through government regulation rather than ownership of industry. Thus, many parts of the Canadian economy include both private- and public-sector companies regulated by one or more government commissions or agencies established and retained by both socialist and non-socialist party governments. The Canadian economy generally is frequently described as a mixed public-private enterprise economy. See **Regulatory agencies (regulations)**.

Native (First Nations) self-government. The constitutional recognition of the rights of Aboriginal peoples in Canada, including Aboriginal self-government, acknowledging the existence of self-governing Aboriginal, or First Nations prior to European settlement in America and their continued law-making authority.

The demand among First Nations for self-government resulted in the recognition of Aboriginal rights in Part II (s.35) of the *Constitution Act, 1982*. Specifically, "existing aboriginal and treaty rights" of "Indian, Inuit and Métis peoples" were "recognized and affirmed," including "rights that now exist by way of land claims agreements or may be so acquired," and guaranteed equally to men and women (s.35). Section 25 specifically acknowledges Aboriginal "rights or freedoms" recognized by the Royal Proclamation of 1763 and any "that now exist by way of land claims agreements or may be so acquired"; nor are any Aboriginal rights or freedoms impinged upon by the Charter.

Since 1982, attempts to entrench Aboriginal self-government in the constitution have failed, but there have been notable agreements involving the federal and some provincial governments involving self-governance: for example, among Native parties to the James Bay Agreement with the Quebec government in 1984 (*Cree-Naskapi Act*), the *Sechelt Indian Band Self-Government Act, 1986* in British Columbia, and in 1998, the BC government's comprehensive treaty with the Nisga'a. In 1999, the federal Northwest Territories was divided, with the creation of Nunavut in the eastern Arctic, the only political jurisdiction in North America with a predominantly Native population.

As to a constitutionally entrenched right of self-government, the Charlottetown Accord of 1992, defeated in a country-wide referendum, had included recognition of Aboriginal self-government as a third order of government in Canada. In 1987, Native groups objected that the federal-provincial constitutional negotiations that resulted in the Meech Lake Accord did not include their concerns. In Manitoba, Elijah Harper, a Cree New Democratic party member of the Manitoba legislature, denied unanimous consent for the Accord to be introduced for debate and a vote until the period allowed for its adoption expired in June 1990.

In 1991, the federal government proposed entrenching a justiciable right to Aboriginal self-government, with the expectation that the courts would recognize differential circumstances and needs among Native Peoples; and that enforcement not take place for 10 years from the adoption of the constitutional amendment, pending federal, provincial, and municipal negotiations with Aboriginal groups on issues such as land and resources, language, education, the administration of justice, health, and social and economic development. Native groups rejected the proposal, demanding instead an inherent right to self-government and participation on equal footing with the heads of government at subsequent constitutional talks.

In 1992, the Charlottetown Accord, negotiated by Native representatives and federal, provincial and territorial government leaders included agreement that the constitution "recognize that the Aboriginal peoples of Canada have the inherent right of self-government within Canada," and that their governments be recognized "as one of three orders of government in Canada" (Part IV: First Peoples). The Accord was rejected in a country-wide referendum, though not primarily because of the provisions for Aboriginal self-government. However, among Aboriginal groups, there appeared to be serious division over the proposal among treaty Indians, including, for example, opposition from the Native Women's Association of Canada, fearful that women's rights guaranteed under the Canadian Charter of Rights and Freedoms would be jeopardized. Following the public rejection of the Accord, people who had participated in formulating the proposals urged federal and provincial governments to pursue implementation of the Accord regarding First Peoples, notably those sections that did not require constitutional amendment, such as ones regarding the Métis nation.

The Charlottetown Accord had included a "contextual statement" on the legislative authority of Aboriginal governments. The government and Native leaders agreed that justiciability of the entrenched right be delayed for five years without prejudicing the right and that the Canadian Charter of Rights and Freedoms apply to Aboriginal governments as to federal and provincial governments, but in a manner "appropriate to the circumstances of Aboriginal peoples." The Accord encouraged the non-Native governments and Native Peoples (Inuit, Indian, and Métis) to negotiate in good faith to conclude agreements on the relationship among the three orders of governments and outlined a process of negotiation, including a dispute settlement mechanism. The Accord committed Aboriginal governments to social, economic and cultural policy objectives, including reducing "disparities in opportunities" and public services between Aboriginal and other Canadians and the other two orders of government to assist "with fiscal or other resources, including land"; to affirmative action programs respecting languages and cultures; and to gender equity. It committed the other governments to future conferences on matters related to Native self-government, to an assurance that division of power agreements among them would not derogate from the rights of Native Peoples and their governments, and that future constitutional amendments that directly refer to Aboriginal peoples should have their consent. The five westernmost provincial governments agreed with the Métis National Council to negotiate binding and enforceable agreements on Métis issues including self-government, land and resources, jurisdiction in programs and services for Métis, and cost-sharing agreements. Finally, the Accord countenanced guaranteed Aboriginal representation in the Senate with a possible double majority requirement in matters "materially affecting Aboriginal people."

As noted above, Aboriginal rights regarding land and governance have been pursued through various legislative, administrative and judicial processes. In

addition to examples cited above, the federal Department of Indian Affairs delegated its responsibilities in Manitoba at the request of local First Nations governments, under an agreement negotiated in 1994 with the Assembly of Manitoba
Chiefs, with further negotiations in other provinces possible. In 1997, the federal
government agreed with the Mi'kmaq in Nova Scotia to transfer authority over
education. Generally, Native authorities now deliver many services of federal
responsibility involving, for example, education and culture, policing, health care
and social services. The courts have also been a site for the pursuit of Native
claims. In *Sparrow* (1990), the Supreme Court upheld a British Columbia decision, affirming section 35 rights in the *Constitution Act, 1982* against provincial
legislation, in this case fishing rights of the Musqueum. Also in *Sioui* (1990), the
Supreme Court upheld a Quebec court decision affirming a treaty between the
British and the Hurons signed three days before the fall of Quebec in 1760, granting "free exercise of their Religion [and] their customs," in this case fishing and
cutting wood for a purification ritual in provincial parks, contrary to provincial
law. In 1999, the Supreme Court ruled in *Marshall* that treaty rights of the
Mi'kmaq in Atlantic Canada allowed them fishing rights, subject to conservation
measures, though the ruling and a subsequent clarification did not settle the ensuing dispute over fishing rights involving Native and non-Native fishers and the
federal government. Also in 1999, the Supreme Court further affirmed Aboriginal
rights pre-existing European settlement in *Delgamuukw*, admitting oral history as
evidence in a case acknowledging rights of the Gitksan and Wet'suwet'en in
British Columbia.

One can only speculate to what extent these events might have been
spurred on by violent conflicts involving death in Oka, Quebec in 1990 and
Ipperwash, Ontario, five years later. In Oka, the death of a police officer accompanied an armed stand-off between Mohawk warriors and Quebec Provincial Police,
following a decision by municipal authorities to expand a golf course on land
claimed by Mohawks as traditional, sacred land. Sympathetic Natives blockaded
roads through a nearby reserve leading to and from Montreal, and cars carrying
Aboriginal families were stoned. The QPP were eventually bolstered by the
Canadian Armed Forces. In another dispute over land claims, an Ontario
Provincial Police officer killed an unarmed Native demonstrator at Ipperwash in
1995, a matter Natives consider still unresolved. There are also occasions when
mistreatment of Natives, or of botched investigations involving Native victims, by
provincial police authorities become major items in the country's newspapers
and newscasts.

Responding to the failure of the Meech Lake Accord and the later armed
confrontation at Oka, the federal Conservative government established the
(Dussault-Erasmus) Royal Commission on Aboriginal Peoples in 1991. In its final
report, the Commission made recommendations in four areas: Aboriginal-non-
Aboriginal relationship based on mutual respect and reconciliation, Aboriginal
self-government within Canada, Aboriginal economic self-sufficiency, and self-
healing from the effects of neglect and maltreatment by non-Aboriginal authorities. The federal government's immediate response was an apologetic statement of
reconciliation and a statement of renewal. See **Indian Act; Land claims and settlements (Native; Aboriginal).**

Natural resources. Commodities involving "Lands, Mines, Minerals, and Royalties," which, within the provinces, are under provincial jurisdiction (*Constitution Act, 1867*, s.109), but, before section 92A was adopted in 1982, inter-provincial and international marketing of natural resources was solely within the federal domain ("The Regulation of Trade and Commerce," s.91:2). Other relevant sections pertaining to provincial jurisdiction include: 92:5 ("The Management and Sale of the Public Lands belonging to the Province..."); 92:13 ("Property and Civil Rights in the Province"); and 92:16 ("Generally all Matters of a merely local or private Nature in the Province"). The federal government is prohibited from taxing public land and property owned by the provinces (s.125).

Conflicts related to jurisdictional competence have historically involved conflicts between resource-rich provinces and the federal government acting on behalf of the "national interest," notably people and economies in relatively resource-poor and high resource-consuming regions. The eastern provinces and British Columbia always had jurisdiction over their resources upon Confederation, but when the prairie provinces were created from federal territory (Manitoba in 1870; Alberta and Saskatchewan in 1905), natural resources remained in the hands of the federal government until 1930, purportedly to assist western development. Of contemporary importance are resources such as oil, gas and water, which are related to energy, and which, before the adoption of section 92A, involved serious regional, federal-provincial, and government-industry conflict. Provincial jurisdiction historically meant the power to determine the manner in which the resources were developed and to determine the prices that would be charged for the resources in the province. With its "Trade and Commerce" power, however, the federal government could still establish conditions under which the resource commodities (once they were made available) moved beyond a province in interprovincial and international trade. Thus, the volume, price and means of transportation of oil and natural gas in cross-border trade, for example, were subject to federal control. The federal government could also use its declaratory power (s.92:10[c]) or emergency powers under the "Peace, Order, and good Government" clause (preamble, s.91) effectively to nationalize a resource industry. In 1967, the Supreme Court declared offshore mineral rights on the west coast to be under federal jurisdiction, thus giving the federal government an advantage in negotiating with provinces on the east coast.

With the steep rise in world oil prices in the 1970s, occasioned by the Organization of Petroleum Exporting Countries cartel, the debate over natural resources and energy policy was so divisive as to have partisan reverberations in western Canada decades later. The oil-producing provinces of Alberta, notably, and Saskatchewan hoped to use revenue from oil to diversify their economies. The national economy's manufacturing sector was located chiefly in central Canada, whose economy and society had always had access to an abundant supply of cheap energy. The federal government has historically defined "national policy" in terms of the prosperity of manufacturing and responded politically to opinion in densely populated Ontario and Quebec. It also felt obliged to develop a resource policy that protected the poorer Atlantic region from the significant impact of oil price increases. In addition to questions of jurisdiction, the distribution of wealth, regional disparities and equalization agreements, the debate over national oil and energy policy in the 1970s and 1980s touched on foreign ownership in the Canadian economy, the appropriate role of the state in economic enterprises, the rights of Native Peoples, conservation of energy and preservation of the environment.

As part of constitutional patriation in 1982, the *Constitution Act, 1867,* was amended with the addition of section 92A on non-renewable natural resources, forestry resources and electrical energy, and an accompanying schedule. The amendment essentially grants additional revenue-raising and resource management powers to the provinces, including marketing outside the province of origin. The additional revenue powers include many choices, but preclude an export tax. The new management powers are held concurrently with the federal government. A producing province cannot discriminate among other provinces in pricing exports and, in cases of conflict with federal laws, paramountcy remains with the federal government. Exports from Canada remain the jurisdiction of the federal government, though those to the United States are regulated by provisions of the Canada-United States Free Trade Agreement of 1989. See **National energy (oil) program (NEP)**.

New Deal (R.B. Bennett's). Labour-related and agricultural marketing legislation that Prime Minister R.B. Bennett's Conservative government proposed in 1935 during the Great Depression to "ensure a greater degree of equality in the distribution of the capitalistic system" (Speech from the Throne).

The legislation, styled "New Deal" after United States President Franklin Roosevelt's program, was announced in the final year of the Parliament elected in 1930. It is usually cited as an unsuccessful, last-minute attempt to save the government from almost certain electoral defeat. Some people have interpreted it in part as an example of Red Tory politics in Canada. Bennett announced the program in radio speeches written by close aides and without the knowledge of most of the cabinet.

Following the election of 1935, Liberal Prime Minister William Lyon Mackenzie King referred several of the New Deal measures to the courts to test their constitutionality. In 1937, the Judicial Committee of the Privy Council invalidated statutes respecting hours of work, holidays, minimum wages (*Attorney-General for Canada v. Attorney-General for Ontario* [Labour Conventions Case]), and unemployment insurance (*Attorney-General for British Columbia v. Attorney-General for Canada*). The judicial decisions involved narrow interpretations of: federal power to implement treaties (*Constitution Act, 1867,* s.132); federal emergency powers under the "Peace, Order, and good Government" clause (s.91; preamble); and federal power in "Trade and Commerce" (s.91:2). Concomitantly, the judicial decisions strengthened provincial legislative competence under "Property and Civil Rights in the Province" (s.92:13). The view of the Judicial Committee at the time was expressed in Lord Atkin's metaphor describing Canada's federal system as a ship with "watertight compartments" of federal and provincial jurisdiction to be steadfastly maintained despite the "larger ventures" and "foreign waters" on which "the ship of state now sails" (Labour Conventions Case). See **Judicial Committee of the Privy Council**; **Judicial review**; **Red Tory(-ism)**.

New Democratic party (NDP). Founded in 1961, the social democratic successor to the socialist Co-operative Commonwealth Federation (CCF).

The New Democratic party's program was founded on the Winnipeg Declaration of 1956 that advocated a relatively mild reformism dedicated to improving the quality of life through government regulation of the economy. The organization of the NDP was designed to facilitate greater involvement in the party by trade unions and to increase electoral support among the younger, upwardly mobile population of urban Canada and among French Quebeckers. The party has been more successful than the CCF, but its gains have been in provincial and territorial rather than in federal politics. The party has formed governments in British Columbia, Manitoba, Ontario, Saskatchewan and Yukon, and the official opposition in Alberta. In federal elections, the party has fared better in popular vote percentages than the CCF; however, the NDP has never gained more than 25 per cent of the vote and has failed to become an electoral force in Quebec. From 1972 to 1974, it held the balance of power during a minority Liberal government. Between the elections of 1984 and 1988, the party led in national public opinion polls, but this was more a manifestation of lack of support for the Liberals and Conservatives than firm support for the NDP. In the 1988 election, the party elected its largest cohort of MPs ever, but failed to displace the Liberals as the chief opposition party. In 1993, it suffered its worst defeat, winning 6.9 per cent of the popular vote and only nine seats, less than the minimum required to achieve party recognition in the House of Commons. It regained official-party status in the 1997 election, winning twenty-one seats, including new-found strength in Atlantic Canada, but receiving only 11 per cent of the popular vote. In 2000 its representation was reduced to thirteen with 9 per cent of the national popular vote.

Traditional federal voting habits and the weak perception of the party (compared to that of the Liberal and Conservative parties) on the powerful bicultural cleavage partly explain the NDP's weak federal performance. Also, since the 1960s, the Conservative party and later the Reform party—now the Canadian Alliance—has had the support of many "aggrieved" westerners on the geographic cleavage, a source of political tension from which the NDP (and the CCF before it) had traditionally benefitted. The strongest perception of the NDP is that of a left-wing party on the class cleavage. Class-based issues and support for the NDP, however, tend to be more prevalent in provincial politics—where responsibility for matters such as resource development, housing, medical and hospital insurance, social assistance and labour law assist the New Democratic party in particular provinces. In the 1970s, the federal NDP had hoped to benefit from disaffection with federal wage and price controls policy, resource development and the domination of foreign ownership in the economy.

In the 1980s, public support for traditional state interventionist solutions to economic and social problems flagged in the wake of support for market liberalism and reduced state activity to eliminate budget deficits and reduce the public debt. The laissez-faire liberal agenda of privatization of crown corporations, reduced social expenditures, government deregulation, and encouragement of free trade to improve the competitiveness of Canadian business was ascendant.

By the 1990s, public opinion was less sympathetic to the "neo-conservative" economic agenda, but still not fully supportive of a statist agenda. At the same time, organized labour was divided on whether to continue its support for the NDP. However, both left-wing "interventionists" and right-wing "marketeers" have to accommodate themselves to a public agenda which, in addition to the traditional issues of class, region and culture, now includes citizen-rights demands based on the Canadian Charter of Rights and Freedoms of 1982 and concern for quality-of-life and personal identity issues, for example women's, Native, and gay and lesbian rights, environmental protection, urban community and international development. Some commentators argue that as such concerns are thought to be congruent with left-wing social activism and the grassroots organization of the NDP, the party is well positioned to respond to rights-based and postmaterialist agenda items. However, social movement organizations have generally been reluctant to support any political party. In any event, the NDP's continued weakness federally, and its limited strength even in provinces where it has been well-established, has lead to internal party debate on the future of Canada's political left. See **Co-operative Commonwealth Federation; Movement parties; Postmaterialism**.

Nomination. The formal designation of a person as a candidate for elective office. The *Canada Elections Act* establishes qualifications for candidacy in federal elections: essentially that a person be a Canadian citizen resident in the country, but not necessarily in the constituency for which the person is being nominated. Nomination requires the written support of at least 100 electors resident in the relevant constituency (50 in the case of very large and sparsely populated constituencies) and a deposit of $1,000, half of which is returned upon candidates filing their financial statement and the remainder returned only if a candidate wins at least 15 per cent of the vote in the constituency. Candidates endorsed by the leaders of officially registered parties will have the party name included with their name on the ballot.

Governments are formed following elections, based on the number of constituencies won by candidates put forward by each of the political parties. Therefore most nominees are candidates of established parties registered under the Act. The candidate nomination procedure for each party is regulated by party rules and supervised by party officials. In some constituencies the executive of a party's constituency association may have difficulty finding a candidate. But elsewhere there will be highly competitive nomination contests—usually in constituencies where the party's nominee is expected to win in the general election—and there may be serious internal conflict, including challenges regarding the qualifications of people voting, the conditions under which they might have been recruited to the party, and the manner in which the nomination meeting was conducted. In recent years, such challenges have involved participation by children, the financing of memberships by supporters of particular candidates and participation by so-called one-day party members, conflict among ethnic groups supporting different candidates, and attempts by supporters of single issues to control party nomination meetings. Because the leaders of parties registered with the chief electoral officer legally designate their candidates and official agents, occasionally party leaders reject a nominee, but more often a party's central office is involved "behind the scenes" in the nomination process to ensure a desirable outcome. Because of increased public attention to allegations of abuse, parties have attempted to tighten nomination procedures to minimize internal party fighting and reduce undesirable publicity. However, there has been no move to establish legal procedures for the nomination process, such as recommended in1992 by the (Pierre Lortie) Royal Commission on Electoral Reform and Party Financing.

Non-confidence motion. See **Vote of no confidence (want-of-confidence motion).**

Nongovernmental organizations (NGOs). Transnational organizations that, especially in the current period of globalization, promote interests and policies frequently associated with social interests such as human rights, child welfare and environmental protection. As such, they apply pressure to domestic political and corporate decision makers with reference both to domestic and foreign policy. While there has been conflict between governments in Canada and NGOs (for example with respect to logging practices, the environment and Native rights), there have also been occasions when the Canadian government and NGOs have joined forces in, for example, the international treaty banning land-mines and efforts to eliminate the exploitation of children in workplaces and as soldiers. See **Globalization.**

North American Aerospace Defence Command (NORAD). An integrated United States-Canada continental air-defence system involving military surveillance and warning systems, and anti-submarine defence, to protect the nuclear force of the United States for retaliatory purposes if attacked.

The NORAD agreement, which was designed for protection against the former Soviet Union during the Cold War, was negotiated by the Liberal government in the 1950s and signed by the Conservative government in 1957. The executive agreement, which has been reaffirmed periodically, calls for a joint command headed by an American, with a Canadian deputy commander. It represents a culmination of Canadian military collaboration with the United States which began in 1940 when Canada was at war with Germany, but before the United States formally became an allied belligerent.

The end of the Cold War, following the collapse of the Soviet Union and its military allies in eastern Europe around 1990, called into question Canada's future military role in Europe under the North Atlantic Treaty Organization (NATO) as well as the NORAD agreement. Liberal governments have generally reduced defence spending and preferred to concentrate military resources to protect Canadian sovereignty, notably in the Arctic, and contribute to peacekeeping ventures of the United Nations. While not avoiding peacekeeping operations, the Conservative government from 1984 to 1993 had a decidedly pro-US attitude in foreign and defence policies. Canada was the only NATO country that publicly supported the US invasion of Panama in 1989. In 1990, Canada participated in the multilateral, but essentially US-led Gulf War against Iraq following its invasion of Kuwait (as Canada had under the Liberals participated in a protracted US-led, though formally United Nations-sponsored, war in Korea in the early-1950s).The Liberal government renewed the NORAD agreement in the late 1990s, hoping to have some influence as part of international debate on US policy regarding construction of a new missile defence system. See **North Atlantic Treaty Organization (NATO)**.

North American Free Trade Agreement (NAFTA) (1992). A trade agreement negotiated by Canada, Mexico and the United States in 1992 to create a continental trading bloc to protect national interests yet compete effectively internationally. Mexico initiated talks with the United States in 1990 and Canada joined the negotiations essentially to protect and improve its position under the Canada-United States Free Trade Agreement of 1989, notably regarding the dispute settlement mechanism and protection against US anti-dumping laws and countervailing duties.

The term "free trade" is a misnomer as the agreement essentially creates "managed" continental trade affecting, for example, the automobile, textile, agriculture, financial services and information technology industries. Objections in the United States to the agreement parallelled those in Canada to the FTA of 1989, for example, the loss of US jobs to low-wage labour and lower environmental standards in Mexico; also, Canadian critics of the FTA renewed their earlier concerns, now respecting NAFTA. The North American agreement was approved by the Canadian and US governments following "side agreements" and clarifications concerning environmental protection and labour. The Commission for Environmental Cooperation was established under NAFTA, with headquarters in Montreal, to investigate alleged non-enforcement of laws. The Commission for Labour Cooperation, with headquarters in Dallas, Texas, requires provincial co-operation for full Canadian participation.

Regional trade agreements such as NAFTA must conform to the requirements of the World Trade Organization. For example, in a binding decision in 2000, the WTO ruled that the Canada-US Automobile Trade Pact, which had been in existence since the 1960s, violated WTO regulations. See **Canada-United States Free Trade Agreement (1989)**; **Commission for Environmental Cooperation (NAFTA)**; **Environmentalism**; **Globalization**; **World Trade Organization (WTO)**.

North Atlantic Treaty Organization (NATO). A military alliance involving Canada, the United States and selective European countries, designed for mutual defence against the former Soviet Union and its European allies during the Cold War following the Second World War.

In the early years following NATO's creation in 1949, Canada attempted unsuccessfully to promote non-military functions within the alliance (Article 2). Domestic critics opposed Canada's involvement in NATO as contributing to the Cold War environment, while critics on the other side of the issue have described as insufficient Canada's commitment of forces in Europe and national defence generally. Earlier, federal governments defended Canada's involvement in NATO with reference to maintaining good relations with the United States and opposing the expansion of Communism in Europe.

Conflict within NATO usually centred on disputes between some European powers, notably France, and the United States, although there were tensions among European members, notably between Greece and Turkey. Following the collapse of the Soviet Union and its satellite regimes in eastern Europe, and the expansion of NATO to include some post-Communist countries, Conservative and Liberal governments argued that continued military involvement in Europe was necessary in order to benefit from economic, scientific and technological relations with Europe. That involvement has included NATO military engagements and on-going peacemaking efforts in the Balkans. See **North American Aerospace Defence Command (NORAD)**.

Northwest (Riel) Rebellions. Armed revolts by Métis (people of mixed European and Native origins) and Indians in federal Northwest Territories in the early post-Confederation period.

The first rebellion in 1869-70, the Red River uprising led by Louis Riel, resulted in the declaration of a provisional government of Manitoba, the taking of prisoners and the execution of an officer from Ontario. As an expeditionary force approached Fort Garry (Winnipeg), the insurrection collapsed and Riel fled. Parliament established the province of Manitoba in 1870. Riel was elected to the House of Commons in 1874, but was prevented by other members from taking his seat. He led another rebellion of Indians and Métis in 1885 in an area of present-day Saskatchewan, demanding that the Canadian government grant them recognition and representation as a province, acknowledging their right to the land. Several engagements took place between the rebels and government troops. Riel surrendered, was tried and found guilty of treason, and sentenced to death.

Riel's fate created a political storm between British and French Canadians and religionists in Ontario and Quebec. Anti-Catholic, British Protestants in Ontario demanded his execution while French Catholics saw Riel as a patriot, defending French Catholic communities from English encroachment. Riel refused to plead insanity to avoid the death penalty, although he was portrayed as something of a mystic and possibly subject to periods of mental disorder. Under considerable pressure from his Ontario supporters, Conservative Prime Minister John A. Macdonald, assuming that Quebec's support for his government would hold, refused to stay Riel's execution in 1885. Ultimately the prime minister and the Conservative party could not overcome the bitterness engendered in Quebec. Nor did Riel's death diminish the extreme anti-Catholic, anti-French sentiment among Macdonald's supporters in Ontario. In the federal election of 1887, Conservative representation from Quebec was drastically reduced. In the same year, Wilfrid Laurier, who had publicly sympathized with the rebels, became leader of the Liberal party. These events and others preceded the historic realignment of electoral support among French Canadians from the federal Conservative party to the federal Liberal party in the 1890s. In recent years, some western Canadians have sought to portray Riel and the other rebels as early heroes in an ongoing struggle in the prairie West against central Canadian domination. Riel and the conflict have also been acknowledged as a Native Peoples issue, involving the Métis, whose status was constitutionally recognized in the *Constitution Act, 1982* (s.35:2).

Notwithstanding (*non obstante*) clause (Canadian Charter of Rights and Freedoms, s.33). Section 33 of the Canadian Charter of Rights and Freedoms that allows provincial or federal legislatures to enact legislation that violates, limits, or overrides specific sections of the Charter: fundamental freedoms (s.2), legal rights (ss.7-14), and equality rights (s.15). The notwithstanding clause, or legislative override, does not apply to democratic rights (ss.3-5), mobility rights (s.6), or linguistic rights, including minority-language educational rights (ss.16-23).

The inclusion of section 33 in the Charter in 1982 was a compromise between some provincial premiers, who wanted the principle of parliamentary sovereignty to prevail over otherwise constitutionally entrenched Charter rights, and the Charter's main advocate, Liberal Prime Minister Pierre Trudeau. When expressly invoked, a law operates notwithstanding the circumvented sections of the Charter for only five years, or for a shorter period if specified, subject to legislative debate and reenactment which is also limited to five years.

Section 33 has only been used by provincial governments. The section was invoked first by the Parti Québécois government routinely and symbolically, as that province's National Assembly had not approved the constitutional changes of 1982. A Conservative government in Saskatchewan used it in 1986 to compel striking public employees to return to work. In Quebec, a Liberal government abandoned the routine invocation of section 33, but used it effectively and significantly to protect revised sections of Quebec's official-language policy on commercial signage. The Supreme Court had ruled that while the objective of the law was acceptable, its content was an unjustifiable violation of the Charter's section 2, freedom of expression, and it might also have ruled against the revised sign law. The Court had earlier ruled against the province's language law regarding education, as a violation of section 23 of the Charter which is beyond the reach of section 33. Subsequently, the Liberal government amended the sign law further, without using section 33.

A convention might be developing that the notwithstanding clause not be used. In the late 1990s, the Alberta government briefly considered invoking it in two instances, but did not. One case would have prevented victims of a government sterilization program in the distant past from seeking compensation. The other followed a ruling by the Supreme Court of Canada reading sexual orientation into Alberta's *Individual Rights Protection Act* as a prohibited basis of discrimination. Among federal parties, the western-based and social conservative Canadian Alliance, successor to the Reform party, is the only party that encourages the use of s.33. See **Canadian Charter of Rights and Freedoms (1982);** **Charter of the French Language (Quebec).**

Nunavut ("Our land"). A self-governing territory established in the eastern Arctic region of the Northwest Territories (NWT) in 1999, whose capital is Iqaluit, on Baffin Island. Comprising approximately 2.2 million square kilometres, Nunavut contains about 18,000 people, 85 per cent of whom are Inuit. Thus, Nunavut— "Our land" in Inuktitut—is Canada's first political unit governed predominantly by a Native People.

The division of NWT was narrowly approved in a territorial plebiscite in 1992. It had support of 90 per cent of voters in the eastern Arctic, but was opposed in the western Arctic where the territorial capital, Yellowknife, is located. Opponents in the western region feared loss of jobs from the division, and the Dene population claimed that the proposed boundary of Nunavut included part of their land. Under an agreement between the federal government, which is responsible for territorial government, and Nunavut Tunngavik Inc., Inuit have ownership of one fifth of the land and the right to hunt and fish throughout Nunavut. The federal government agreed to provide $1.14 billion over 14 years and transfer some mineral rights to Nunavut. As in the case of the NWT, Nunavut has a parliamentary system adapted to cultural and geo-political circumstances and needs distinctive to the North.

O

Oakes test (*R. v. Oakes*, [1986]). A ruling in which the Supreme Court established guidelines to effect section 1 of the Canadian Charter of Rights and Freedoms that guarantees rights and freedoms subject "to such reasonable limits prescribed by law as can be demonstrably justified in a free and democratic society."

The specific case involved a reverse onus provision in the federal *Narcotics Control Act* which conflicted with the Charter's section 11, the presumption of innocence until proven guilty in a fair and public trial. In the trial, the accused, found guilty of possession of a proscribed substance, was then obliged to establish innocence of the charge of trafficking, guilt being assumed. Appealing acquittal in the Ontario Supreme Court, the Crown argued before the Supreme Court of Canada that the reverse onus provision of the Act was a reasonable limitation under section 1.

In its unanimous seven-member panel decision that has become known as the Oakes test, the Court ruled that for a limitation of a Charter right to be saved by section 1, it must pass two tests: a sufficient-importance test and a three-part proportionality test. First, the legislature's objective in limiting the right in law must be of sufficient importance; second, the limitation must be rationally connected to the objective, it must be as little restrictive as possible of the right in the achievement of the objective, and the benefit resulting from the limitation must be proportional to the cost of the limitation. Thus the Oakes test "operationalized" section 1 of the Charter which requires the courts to weight the collective right of society against the rights of individual members of that society.

In the particular case, the Court declared that the *Narcotics Control Act* passed the first test—"curbing drug trafficking by facilitating the conviction of drug traffickers" was of sufficient importance. However, the Court declared that the Act failed the first part of the second test—rational connection between limiting the presumption of innocence and curbing drug trafficking. As the Act failed the first part of the proportionality test, the Court did not rule on the remaining two parts. See **Canadian Charter of Rights and Freedoms (1982); Judicial review (interpretive; non-interpretive); Supreme Court.**

Occupational (functional) representation. Electoral representation in legislatures by occupational groups, rather than by conventional political parties.

This anti-party, corporatist notion of representation had support in Ontario and western Canada in the early twentieth century. Advocates of occupational representation saw the conventional disciplined party system as representative only of those business interests that financed the established parties, and not of the electors, particularly in rural areas. However, the United Farmers governments in Alberta, Manitoba and Ontario after the First World War made no serious attempts to reform the system of representation. Support for occupational representation among western Progressives in the 1920s also came to naught. Although the movement elected the second-largest groups of members of parliament in the 1921 election, they declined the official opposition role and subsequently had little influence in the House of Commons. The Social Credit party, whose support was based largely in Alberta from the 1930s to the 1950s, also argued that large, central Canadian financial and manufacturing interests controlled MPs through the disciplined party system. Constituency versus party control over elected MPs, a variation on the anti-party theme, still remains an issue, especially in western Canada, and was an important reason for public support of the populist Reform party in the 1990s, predecessor to the Canadian Alliance. See **Delegate theory of representation**.

October (FLQ) Crisis (1970). The kidnapping for ransom under the threat of death of a British trade commissioner and of a provincial cabinet minister in Montreal by two cells of the Front de libération du Québec (FLQ)—an action which led to the declaration of an "apprehended insurrection" and the invocation of the *War Measures Act* by the federal Liberal government of Pierre Trudeau.

Shortly after the Act was invoked, the Quebec minister was killed by his captors. The police eventually discovered the location of the British official and negotiated his release in return for his kidnappers' safe passage overseas. Judicial proceedings took place against members of both cells, including those in exile, upon their return in 1979. While the Act was in effect, approximately 500 Quebeckers were detained without charge and without counsel, virtually none of whom had any connection to the terrorist organization, but only sympathy with Québécois nationalism. However, these events effectively ended the sporadic terrorist activity which had been directed against the federal government's presence in Quebec. The federal government insisted during this period that, on the basis of provincial government and police advice, the constitutional government of Quebec was seriously threatened. And although public opinion in Canada was largely supportive of the federal government at the time, later the government was criticized for not providing evidence that the eventual location and apprehension of the kidnappers and murderers depended on using the extraordinary powers of the *War Measures Act*. Prime Minister Trudeau's response at the time to his critics was that if he as an innocent person had been detained under the Act, his hostility would have been directed not towards the government, but towards those responsible for the events that had caused the government to invoke the Act.

Prime Minister Trudeau was primarily responsible for the entrenchment twelve years later of the Canadian Charter of Rights and Freedoms to which all government legislation must conform. In 1988, emergency legislation was brought into conformity with the Charter. The *Emergencies Act* replaced the *War Measures Act*, distinguishing public welfare, public order and international and war emergencies, but in all cases with automatic expiry of the invocation if not renewed. The *Emergencies Act* requires government explanation and lists specific types of regulations appropriate to different emergencies, applies them to relevant parts of the country, and provides for more effective parliamentary supervision during the emergency, an appeal procedure for compensation, a parliamentary review of the exercise of emergency powers, as well as a government report following the termination of the emergency. See *Emergencies Act* **(Canada, 1988; emergency powers)**; *War Measures Act* **(Canada; emergency powers)**.

Official agent (party; candidate). Under election finance legislation, the person designated responsible for maintaining proper accounts of candidate and party finances. Federal legislation, for example, allows for limited tax credit for financial contributions to registered parties and their candidates. It also defines and limits election expenses, requires the filing of returns accounting for election contributions, including services, and expenses, and allows for the some reimbursement of candidates' expenses. Official agents for the parties and their candidates are legally responsible for adherence to the law. See **Electoral law (controls; subsidies).**

Official Languages Act **(Canada, 1969).** The federal statute establishing French and English as the official languages of Canada, under which both languages have equal status and use in the federal public service, and the federal government supports minority-language, French or English, communities, and encourages provincial governments to do likewise. The substance of the Act was entrenched in the Canadian Charter of Rights and Freedoms in 1982 (ss.16-22), along with the designation of New Brunswick as a bilingual province. The Act created the office of the commissioner of official languages (language ombudsman), to ensure compliance with the Act within the federal public administration.

The Act was the chief recommendation of the (Dunton Laurendeau) Royal Commission on Bilingualism and Biculturalism in 1967. The most contentious issue for the Liberal government at the time was the impact of the Act on the federal public service. The *Official Languages Act* represents the individual rights-based, or personality strategy of the federal Liberal government to make French Canadians feel "at home" across Canada, as opposed to the territorial rights-based approach that would leave the matter of language rights to be determined by each province. The chief example of the territorial rights-based approach is found in Quebec's Charter of the French Language, designed to protect French as the dominant language of the provincial government, economy and society, which has generated considerable controversy both in and outside the province. See **Bilingualism and biculturalism; Canadian Charter of Rights and Freedoms (1982); Charter of the French Language (Quebec); Commissioner of Official Languages.**

Official opposition. The party which usually holds the second-largest number of seats in the legislature and represents the likely alternative to the government-of-the-day should it resign following defeat in the legislature, or at the time is the likely alternative were the government party to be defeated in the next election. As the leading opposition party to the government, it is sometimes designated as "Her Majesty's Loyal Opposition" to "Her Majesty's Government."

However, there have been notable exceptions in the House of Commons. In 1921, the Progressives elected the second-largest number of members, but they refused to accept the role of official opposition which fell then to the third-ranking Conservatives. Though the Liberals elected fewer members than the Conservatives in the 1925 federal election, the Liberal government remained in office briefly with the support of the third-ranking Progressives; thus, the Conservatives were the official opposition although they had the largest caucus. In 1993, the Bloc Québécois formed the official opposition, but, with electoral strength solely in Quebec, it could not win an election.

All parties other than the government party are generally known as "the opposition," but the official opposition party holds specific resource and procedural advantages over the other opposition parties. At the federal level, for example, the leader of the official opposition has a publicly owned and subsidized residence, and receives the salary of a cabinet minister. The office and party of the leader of the official opposition receive more money for research purposes than the other opposition parties; and, of great importance in parliamentary debate, the official opposition party's questions, motions and amendments to government motions, and its replies to ministerial statements, take precedence in debate over those of the smaller opposition parties.

Official-party (recognized party) status. Under standing orders of the House of Commons, a designated number of seats that a party caucus must hold in order for its members to be recognized in House proceedings, including committee membership, and for the party to receive public funding for research and party offices such as the leader, House leader, whips and caucus chair.

Although general elections involve the election of legislators, House business is subsequently conducted on the basis of party organization. For several elections, twelve members has been the minimum requirement for a party to be recognized in the Commons. Otherwise, members of a party with fewer than twelve MPs will normally not be recognized in Question Period, not be allowed to comment in the House on ministerial statements, not be recognized in general debate and not allowed to introduce amendments to government bills including non-confidence motions. Nor will members of parties not officially recognized be given membership on House committees. Without House recognition, such parties will also be deprived of public funding that recognized parties receive to assist in their legislative duties. Otherwise, such party members do have access to the mass media outside the chamber itself.

In 1993, the Conservative and New Democratic parties both failed to win sufficient seats to obtain official party status and were thus virtually invisible in the 1993-97 period. Both parties regained recognition in elections in 1997 and barely so in 2000.

***Official Secrets Act* (Canada, 1939).** Federal legislation that prohibits specific behaviour "prejudicial to the safety or interests of the State..," or "that is calculated to be or might be or intended to be directly or indirectly useful to a foreign power...": spying; communication or attempted communication with an agent of a foreign power; "wrongful" possession, communication, or retention of information; reception of information communicated wrongfully unless contrary to one's desire, and retention of that communication; unauthorized use of uniforms; falsification of reports, forgery and personal misrepresentation; unauthorized possession of any government die, seal or stamp or any resemblance of one "calculated to deceive," or dealing in such items; interference with police or military personnel guarding a "prohibited place"; harbouring anyone whom one has reasonable grounds for believing has committed or is about to commit an offence under the Act; attempting, or soliciting or inciting others to commit an offence, or committing an act preparatory to committing an offence under the Act.

Some sections of the Act under which charges might be laid do not require the demonstration of prejudice, but permit conviction if "from the circumstances of the case, [a defendant's] conduct or his known character as proved, it appears that his purpose was... prejudicial...." An offence is also committed if a government employee, a person contracted with the government or subcontracted, "fails to take reasonable care...or endangers the safety of" information. In a case involving "great emergency[that necessitates] immediate action," RCMP superintendents and superior officers may authorize search and seizure operations "if necessary by force" which normally require approval by a justice of the peace. The Act also allows for trials on charges under it to be held *in camera*, though sentencing upon conviction would take place in public. If a company or corporation is convicted, all directors and officers are deemed guilty unless proved that the offence "took place without [their] knowledge or consent." There are several such "reverse onus" provisions in the Act where an offence will have been considered one "for a purpose prejudicial to the safety or interests of the State, unless the contrary is proved."

Since the adoption of the Canadian Charter of Rights and Freedoms in 1982, the Act has been susceptible to a successful constitutional challenge in the courts. Especially its provisions respecting the search and seizure of evidence, *in camera* trials and reverse onus of proof are apparent violations of several sections of the Charter. Under these circumstances, successful prosecutions might be pursued through public trials on "ordinary" Criminal Code provisions concerning theft and possession of stolen property as well as normal procedures for the gathering of evidence. See **Canadian Charter of Rights and Freedoms (1982)**; **Freedom of information**.

Ombudsman. A public officer, appointed by and responsible to the legislature, who investigates and reports on citizens' complaints about actions by the public administration. The concept, originally established in Scandinavia, has spread to many Western parliamentary democracies, where offices have been established with varying powers. Canada's first ombudsman was appointed in Alberta in 1967 and ombudsmen now exist in most provinces. At the federal level, there are commissioners for official languages, human rights, privacy, information, the military and air travellers, operating effectively as ombudsmen under the terms of their respective statutes.

One-party (single-party) dominance. A phrase denoting a party system with several parties, but with one party being historically dominant. For example, the House of Commons contained four party caucuses from 1935 to 1957, but Liberal majorities dominated the House of Commons during that period, having governed through most of the first and third decades of the twentieth century. Except for minority Liberal governments (1963-65; 1965-68; 1972-74) and a nine-month Conservative government (1979-80), Liberal majorities otherwise dominated the House from 1963 to 1984. Liberal majorities were elected in five-party Parliaments in 1993, 1997 and 2000.

One-party, or single-party-dominant, systems have occurred frequently at the provincial level. For example, the Conservative party retained power in Ontario's three-party system from 1943 to 1985, and Social Credit in British Columbia from 1952 to 1991, with a three-year break in the 1970s. However, the oldest one-party-dominant provincial system is Alberta's. There, the United Farmers dominated a provincial multi-party system from 1921 to 1935, Social Credit from 1935 to 1971, followed by the Conservative party into the twenty-first century. See **Party system**.

Opening of Parliament (of the legislature). Ceremonies and procedures at the beginning of a newly elected Parliament or a new session of a Parliament (in the provinces, the opening of the legislature). Prior to a new Parliament and following their summons to Ottawa by the governor-in-council, elected members of parliament sign the roll and take an oath of office administered by the clerk of the House of Commons. Also prior to a new Parliament, members of parliament elect a Speaker, and the Mace, the symbol of the Speaker's authority, is placed on the table in front of the Speaker's chair. At the opening of a new Parliament or a session of Parliament, the governor general causes MPs to be summoned to the bar of the Senate to hear the Speech from the Throne. In addition to senators, members of the Supreme Court and the diplomatic corps are in attendance. The governor general's Speech from the Throne (in Quebec, the premier's "Inaugural Address") is a government-drafted review of the state of public affairs and an outline of the government's program, usually stated in general terms, for the next session of the legislature.

Operation Dismantle v. The Queen, **(1985).** A decision by the Supreme Court that a federal government agreement with the United States to permit unarmed cruise missile testing over Canada did not violate "the right to life, liberty and security of the person" guaranteed under section 7 of the Canadian Charter of Rights and Freedoms.

Operation Dismantle argued that the testing of cruise missiles to establish their effectiveness over terrain similar to that of the Soviet Union heightened international tensions and the possibility of nuclear war involving Canada, thus jeopardizing Canadians' section 7 rights.

This early Charter decision was important in at least two respects. It established, first, that such cabinet or executive agreements were subject to judicial review under the Charter; second, the Court indicated that it was prepared to entertain "social" or "legislative," in addition to "adjudicative," facts in its fact-finding capacity regarding challenges under the Charter. The Court has deemed this necessary in determining the "principles of fundamental justice" according to which a person can be deprived of section 7 rights or determining whether rights limitations can be "saved" under section 1 ("reasonable limits…as can be demonstrably justified in a free and democratic society"). Adjudicative facts are those events between parties in the action; legislative or social facts refer to patterns of behaviour relevant to policy decisions. The chief justice argued in this case that it was "simply not possible for a court, even with best available evidence, to do more than speculate upon the likelihood of the Federal Cabinet's decision to test the cruise missile resulting in an increased threat of nuclear war." See **Canadian Charter of Rights and Freedoms (1982); Judicial review (interpretive; non-interpretive); Supreme Court.**

Opposition days. In the House of Commons' calendar, 25 days extending over three supply periods during which opposition motions rather than government business are debated. On Opposition days, that are associated with supply periods to fund government expenditures, the opposition can introduce motions forcing the government to debate matters on which the opposition thinks it can embarrass the government. Opposition days, therefore, are part of the overall opposition role of criticizing government policy. The limited number of Opposition days, and therefore the choice as to which matters are to be debated, are shared among the opposition parties. Otherwise, the parliamentary timetable is dominated by the government's agenda. See **Budget and budgetary process.**

Opposition parties. Parties in the legislature that do not constitute the government-of-the-day. Normally, the opposition party with the most seats is designated the official opposition. The historic origin of Parliament as a check on the prerogative powers of the Crown is exemplified in the opposition's constitutional obligation to hold accountable the government, appointed usually from the largest party in the elected House. The rights and obligations of opposition parties in Canada are formalized in the respective Standing Orders or procedures of the provincial legislatures and the two houses of the Parliament of Canada. See **Official opposition.**

Opting-out formula. See **Contracting (opting) out.**

Order of Canada. A system of honours for Canadian civilians established in 1967, the centenary of Confederation, to recognize meritorious service to the country or to humanity generally. A comparable order of military merit for members of the armed forces was created in 1972. Controversies have arisen from time to time as a result of three levels of membership in the Order of Canada: Companion, for national and international achievement and pre-eminence; Officer, for national achievement, and Member for regional achievement. Members may use the initials CC, OC and CM, respectively, after their names, but otherwise there are no attendant rewards or privileges. Members can be "promoted" in the levels of membership. Non-Canadians are eligible to receive honorary membership. The governor general makes the awards on the advice of an advisory council chaired by the chief justice of the Supreme Court of Canada, which considers nominations from the public. Several provinces also have a comparable system of honours.

Order (Notice) Paper. The common name for *Order Paper and Notice Paper*, the daily agenda of the House of Commons, and for similar publications in provincial legislatures. The Senate's Order Paper appears as a section of its *Minutes of the Proceedings of the Senate*. The Commons' Order Paper includes all items that may be considered during the day, that is, government business, private members' business, and questions. Notices include items which members wish to introduce, including questions, private members' business, the production of papers, and notices respecting the report stage of legislation. Items that remain on the Order Paper, or the legislative agenda, when Parliament or a provincial legislature is dissolved for an election are said to have "died on the Order Paper." Business that remains unfinished at the end of a session can be held over to the next session.

Order-in-council. A recorded executive or legislative action determined by the cabinet and proclaimed in the name of the governor-in-council (lieutenant-governor-in-council at the provincial level), a statutory instrument.

Federal executive actions by order-in-council include appointments of senators, diplomats, and certain judges and senior officials. Some dismissals may also be effected by executive order-in-council. The disallowance and reservation of provincial legislation, and the power of clemency, are other federal executive acts effected by order-in-council. Legislative actions of federal and provincial cabinets by order-in-council constitute delegated legislative power, which exists only when permitted under specific statutes. Such orders-in-council are legion; they range from matters of administrative routine to major political acts, such as the invocation of the *Emergencies Act* by the governor-in-council and the reversal or modification of major decisions by administrative regulatory agencies. Federal orders-in-council are published in the *Canada Gazette* and selectively examined by a joint Senate-House of Commons committee on the scrutiny of regulations as part of the surveillance function of Parliament.

Organic law. A statute which is considered one of several laws that comprise the constitution, not because they are entrenched or difficult to amend, but because of their important purpose and content. Thus, for example, federal statutes that established the Supreme Court of Canada, created new provinces, and defined citizenship and the electoral laws can be cited as part of Canadian organic law. Indeed, the federal *Supreme Court Act* has been entrenched in important respects in the *Constitution Act, 1982* (ss.41, 42) and federal Acts establishing the provinces and British statutes applying to Canada were included in the Schedule of the *Constitution Act, 1982* ("Modernization of the Constitution"), clearly defining them as constitutional documents. The organic law also includes comparable provincial statutes, provincial and federal orders-in-council concerning constitutional matters which might be passed from time to time.

Organization of American States (OAS). A regional organization founded in 1890 as the Pan-American Union, renamed in 1948, including virtually all nation-states in the western hemisphere, including Canada since 1990.

For most of this time, the organization comprised independent, republican states led by the United States, institutionalizing the principles of the US Monroe Doctrine. Ostensibly the unilaterally declared Doctrine promised mutual assistance in repelling European threats to the independence of member states; however, the effect was to leave the states of Central and South America subject to US influence. Canada remained outside the Organization, not so much because it was a constitutional monarchy, but largely to minimize conflict with the United States which frequently used the OAS as an agency through which to pursue its foreign policy objectives, notably since the 1960s against Cuba, but also elsewhere in the Caribbean and Latin America. Canada was also spared problems associated with recognizing and dealing with repressive military regimes in the hemisphere.

Canada joined the OAS in 1990, by which time English-speaking Commonwealth states in the Caribbean were already members, and at a time when the government had negotiated a free-trade agreement with the United States and there was talk of a trilateral agreement with Mexico. But this was also during a period when the OAS had become of residual value to the United States. For example, the United States was instrumental in the destabilization and eventual military overthrow in the 1970s of Chile's democratically elected Marxist government, including the summary execution of President Salvadore Allende. The United States invaded Grenada in 1983 to overthrow a pro-Cuba regime, and Panama in 1989 to overthrow the government of Manuel Noriega and take him to the United States for trial on drug and related charges. Nor did the United States pay much heed to multilateral attempts by other governments at this time to resolve violent conflicts in several Central American states in which it was indirectly participating.

Member-states of the OAS have various policy concerns. Most Latin American states are concerned about having their international debts renegotiated or written off, while some Caribbean members pursue benefits associated with ties to the European Union. The Canadian government's declared initial objectives on the OAS in the 1990s included reform and strengthening of the Organization to promote democratic development and respect for human rights, contribute to economic growth, and to deal with problems such as environmental protection, women's issues, and the international drug trade.

P

Pairing. An agreement between a legislator of the government party and a legislator of an opposition party that, for a specified period, neither will vote in a party-based division of the legislature. Thus, both legislators may be absent from the House without the relative strength of government and opposition being affected. Pairing, which the party whips supervise, is important during minority governments or when governments are in power with slim majorities, to avoid an unintended defeat of the government.

Parachuting (candidates). The designation by a party leader of the party's candidate in a constituency rather than the candidate's selection by the party's local constituency association.

Federal and provincial electoral laws require that candidates be resident in the jurisdiction, but not necessarily in the constituency in which they are candidates. Parachuted candidates usually have tenuous links, if any, with the constituency, but are people whom a party leader in particular wants to be elected: in the case of a likely governing party, a likely member of the cabinet; in the case of all parties, someone who is thought to be an electoral asset to the party, beyond the constituency. Party leaders normally seek the compliance of any local party organization, perhaps arguing that the leader-designated candidate's value to the party, if both candidate and party are successful, will somehow rebound to the benefit of the constituency. But the practice can engender opposition from local party notables. Parachuting may occur when there is a weak local organization, but especially when the constituency is safe, that is, the constituency is likely to be won by the party parachuting the candidate irrespective of the candidate.

Parliament of Canada. The Crown, the Senate and the House of Commons (*Constitution Act, 1867* [s.17]). Until 1982, within the powers granted to it under the Act, Parliament was supreme—that is, composed of the executive and the legislature, it was beyond interference by any body. Since the patriation of the constitution with the Canadian Charter of Rights and Freedoms in 1982, all legislation in Canada must conform to the Charter's provisions as determined by the courts.

The Parliament is bicameral, comprising an appointed upper house and an elected lower house. The Senate is the upper house whose members are appointed effectively by the prime minister; members may remain in office until 75 years of age. This lack of popular legitimacy has meant that the Senate is relatively inactive, although it is organized on partisan lines and can be an arena of partisan debate, amending, occasionally defeating, but more likely simply delaying legislation adopted earlier in the lower house. The elected lower house, the House of Commons, can last five years from the day of the return of the election writs, although in times of threat to national security, its life may be extended if not opposed by more than one third of its members (Charter, s.4); but the Crown's representative, the governor general, can dissolve Parliament and issue writs for a new election before the term expires (*Constitution Act, 1867*, s.50). Parliament must also meet for at least one session each year at the summons of the governor general (Charter, s.5).

Within the constitutional limits of the five-year term and one annual session, the governor general summons, prorogues sessions and dissolves Parliament on the "advice" of the prime minister, who, along with other cabinet ministers, must have seats in Parliament and must maintain the confidence of the House of Commons to remain in office. Acts of Parliament require the approval of both the House of Commons and the Senate, followed by royal assent, before becoming effective (excepting that the Senate can exercise only a suspensive veto on constitutional amendments, including those affecting the Senate itself). Unlike the House of Commons, the Senate is not a chamber of confidence.

While the prerogatives of Parliament are considerable, the reality is that of an institution whose members' behaviour, especially in the House of Commons, is determined by political party organization and subsequent government and opposition partisanship. Canada's federal and provincial legislatures operate on the basis of responsible government: the executive, that is, the cabinet and the public administration, initiates public policy and the role of the legislature is to debate and approve government revenue and expenditure items, exercise a surveillance function, and hold the government accountable for its policy and actions. See **Cabinet; Crown; Crown prerogatives; Governor General; House of Commons; Parliamentary privilege (immunities); Senate.**

Parliamentary-cabinet system. A system of responsible government like Canada's in which the executive and the legislative functions are combined in one institution, called Parliament (or the provincial legislature). Cabinet ministers, the political executive whom the Crown's representative appoints, must have seats in the legislature and retain the support of the House of Commons (provincial legislatures) on major legislation, notably money bills.

In Canada, the Crown's representatives (the governor general and the provincial lieutenant-governors) are largely a formal executive with few prerogative powers—the Crown, or head of state's representative acting virtually always on the advice of the political executive, the government, but retaining important prerogative powers regarding the appointment of governments and the dissolution of Parliament for elections. By contrast, the constitution of France includes a parliamentary-cabinet system, but also an elected president with considerable power. Instead of a parliamentary-cabinet system, the United States has a congressional-presidential system under a constitution which enshrines the separation of powers. See **Constitution Act, 1867 and subsequently amended; Crown prerogatives; Responsible government.**

Parliamentary indemnity (salaries, allowances, and budgetary allocations). A traditional term for financial remuneration (now recognized as salaries) for members of parliament, senators and provincial legislators. Indemnity implies that legislative work is a part-time activity performed by people who would otherwise be engaged in private occupations, and who should be compensated for the loss of private income due to their legislative duties.

Members of parliament and senators receive a sessional allowance and an additional tax free expense allowance, indexed to the cost of living. In 2000, MPs received an annual sessional allowance of $68,200 and a tax-free expense allowance of $22,500. Some MPs also receive supplementary allowances for additional responsibilities, from prime minister ($74,100) to deputy government whip and opposition party whips ($7,800). Cabinet ministers, House speaker and deputy speaker, official opposition leader, other party leaders and house leaders also receive supplementary allowances. The prime minister and the leader of the official opposition each have publicly owned and subsidized residences in Ottawa. Senators received a sessional allowance of $66,900 and a tax-free expense allowance of $10,500.

MPs and recognized political parties receive additional funds and services. In 2000, annual office budgets of $190,000 for MPs included salaries for staff. In addition to their offices on Parliament Hill and in their constituency, members also receive printing, translation, telephone, mail and travel subsidies to facilitate communication with constituents. Political parties that have a minimum number of members—currently twelve—receive funds for research purposes and for the operation of their leadership offices: leader, house leader, whip, caucus chair.

Parliamentarians can also qualify for parliamentary pensions, upon leaving the House after serving six years. The pension plan is contributory, and in the 1990s the Liberal government established an age qualification to begin receiving the pension and introduced a prohibition on "double-dipping" by former parliamentarians subsequently appointed to a salaried and pensionable government position. Nonetheless, of all parliamentary allowances, the pension plan remained controversial despite the obvious personal and financial costs of holding public office that caused even some Alliance MPs who earlier had refused to participate in the so-called "gold-plated plan" to change their mind.

Parliamentary privilege (immunities). Rights that the federal Parliament, the provincial legislatures and each legislator individually possesses; these are rights with which no other body can interfere and without which legislators could not carry out their functions. The principle of parliamentary privilege in Canada derives from customary privileges acquired by the British Parliament as a defence against interfering monarchs, known collectively as the *lex et consuetudo Parliamenti*, asserting control over its own business and its members. Today this means protection against citizens or organized interests that might challenge, threaten, intimidate, or otherwise interfere with members, thus violating their ability to act freely as legislators and ultimately violating their privileges.

Canada's *Constitution Act, 1867* recognizes parliamentary privilege (s.18); an amendment in 1875 granted Parliament the powers, immunities and privileges possessed at that time by the British Parliament. Thus parliamentary privilege is established by constitutional statute in Canada, comparable to that existing in Britain by common law.

The privileges of individual legislators are designed to prevent interference with the conduct of parliamentary duties to speak and act freely without fear of disagreeable consequences. They include: immunity from arrest or imprisonment as a result of civil action while the legislature is in session; immunity from actions for libel for content of speeches in the legislature and publications prepared under the authority of the legislature; and exemption from jury duty during a session. Anyone who threatens, assaults or bribes or attempts to bribe a legislator breaches parliamentary privilege. Another parliamentary privilege is the right of committees to summon and hear witnesses under oath. Such witnesses may be extended the privileges of legislators.

The collective privileges of a legislature involve the maintenance of order and discipline. It is the Speaker's responsibility to compel obedience from legislators themselves. If repeated demands for order or for the withdrawal of offending remarks fail to bring a legislator to heel, the Speaker can "name" the offending legislator; that is, the Speaker will call the legislator by name, rather than "honourable member," and have the sergeant-at-arms escort the member from the legislative chamber. Disciplinary measures range from suspension for the day to expulsion from the legislature.

In Canada, legislators' allegations of the breach of personal parliamentary privilege by another member or the mass media are usually frivolous partisan sallies not involving real threats to the legislature or its members. However, serious allegations of breach of privilege by members of the public would be treated as a judge would treat contempt of court. Acting as a court, the legislature can compel people to appear before the bar of the House to explain their behaviour, and it can punish such individuals by public reprimand or by imprisonment during the session of the legislature.

Parliamentary secretaries. Government members of parliament appointed by the prime minister for short terms and without statutory powers, to assist cabinet ministers in their work. Parliamentary secretaries receive an allowance supplementary to their basic compensation as MPs.

An appointment as parliamentary secretary gives a backbench MP some executive and administrative experience, and allows the prime minister and senior ministers to gauge the abilities of such MPs. Also, the appointment of parliamentary secretaries can make the government appear more representative of particular interests and help to keep ambitious backbenchers occupied. While parliamentary secretaries might see themselves as putative cabinet ministers, the practice of Liberal Prime Minister Jean Chrétien was to rotate the positions regularly.

Parliamentary secretaries rather than their ministers usually address the House of Commons in scheduled debates on adjournment. The parliamentary secretary can also act on behalf of the minister outside the legislature—for example, receive deputations from the public and fulfil public engagements. However, parliamentary secretaries are not part of the cabinet and do not take the Privy Council oath. Thus they are not to have access to confidential cabinet documents and information. Therefore, in terms of a working relationship with a minister, a parliamentary secretary, though an MP, may have a less effective working relationship with the minister than the minister's personally selected political staff. See **Executive assistant, ministerial (exempt staff)**.

Parti Québécois (PQ). A nationalist and moderately social democratic party in Quebec, created in 1968 from a union of several *indépendantiste* groups, with its major objective to establish "sovereignty association" (that is, nation-state status for Quebec in association with the government of Canada), or sovereign status for Quebec. PQ governments are credited with improving the probity of Quebec's politics, introducing many social reforms and generally raising the self-esteem of French Quebeckers.

Forming a government first in 1976 under its initial leader, René Lévesque, the PQ passed the Charter of the French Language (Bill 101), but lost its first referendum on sovereignty association in 1980, in which most francophone voters apparently voted No, but then won re-election in 1981. The federal government, having promised "renewed federalism" during the referendum campaign, patriated the constitution in 1982 despite the PQ government's opposition, including, for example, entrenchment of minority-language education rights—education until then a prerogative of provincial governments except regarding denominational education (*Constitution Act, 1867*, s.93)—and a general amending formula that did not include a veto for Quebec (*Constitution Act, 1982*). Following its defeat in 1985 and Lévesque's retirement, the PQ, led successively by Pierre Marc Johnson and Jacques Parizeau, retained its membership-based policy-making process and financing, and was returned to office under Parizeau in 1994. Following the defeat of a second referendum in 1995, in which the question of Quebec's sovereignty was also linked with Canada, Parizeau resigned. He was succeeded as leader and premier by Lucien Bouchard, until then the leader of the federal Bloc Québécois, who led the party to power again in 1998.

The PQ's electoral successes appear to reflect the lack of voter respect for incumbent Liberal governments as well as the vagaries of the electoral system, more so than public support for the party's sovereignty project. This was particularly evident in 1994 when the party won thirty seats more than the Liberals, but with an almost equal share of the popular vote (44.7% to the Liberal's 44.3%). Nonetheless the PQ government proceeded with the second referendum on sovereignty, this time narrowly defeated but apparently carrying majority support among francophone voters. In 1998, the party was returned to office with 1 per cent less of the popular vote than the Liberals, led by Jean Charest, former leader of the federal Conservative party. In 2001, Lucien Bouchard resigned and was succeeded unopposed as party leader and premier by Bernard Landry.

Since its inception, especially when it has formed the government, the party's leadership has moderated the extreme policies of *les purs et les durs* among party activists. The PQ's initial electoral success in 1976 is credited to the weakness of the incumbent Liberal government and to a tactical decision of the PQ leadership to separate the question of sovereignty from voting for the party in the election. The referendum question in 1980 sought only a mandate to negotiate sovereignty association and a promise of another referendum on the outcome, a strategy designed to attract support from those who wished only for a renewed federalism—so-called "soft nationalists."

In 1992, it was revealed that Claude Morin, Quebec's deputy minister of intergovernmental relations in the late 1960s and 1970s and the PQ's minister of intergovernmental affairs from 1976 to 1981, had received money from the RCMP for information. Payments had ceased, but meetings with the RCMP continued when Morin became the ranking cabinet minister after the premier, responsible for constitutional negotiations. (For an account, see *The Globe and Mail*, May 8, 1992, A1 and A3, and May 9, A1 and A6.) Until this revelation, discussion of the PQ's weakness in the early 1980s had focused on Liberal Prime Minister Pierre Trudeau's tactics to outmanoeuvre Lévesque's PQ government in its relation to the other provinces.

PQ defeats in 1985 and 1989, the dormancy of the sovereignty movement in both the 1980s and late-1990s—following a period of heightened nationalist sentiment after the defeat of the constitutional Meech Lake and Charlottetown accords in 1990 and 1992, respectively—and the more conservative economic and social policies of the PQ government under Bouchard, were attributed generally to the growth and ascendancy of a francophone business class and the greater security of French as a working language in Quebec. Nonetheless, PQ leaders must at least appear to be "keeping the faith." During the election campaign in 1998, Bouchard promised a third referendum, but only when success was likely. Since then, the federal Liberal government has pursued both conciliatory and confrontational strategies with the PQ government—so-called "Plan A" and "Plan B": on the one hand, having Parliament adopt a resolution recognizing Quebec as a distinct society, in the manner of the Meech and Charlottetown accords, and devolving Parliament's veto on constitutional change in the general amending formula to various regions, including Quebec; on the other, subjecting the matter of provincial separation from Confederation to a ruling by the Supreme Court of Canada, and then enacting the so-called Clarity bill, setting conditions for the federal government's response to future referenda in Quebec on sovereignty. See **Charter of the French Language (Quebec); Clarity bill (on secession from Confederation);** *Constitution Act, 1867* **and subsequently amended; Referendum; Secession Reference; Sovereignty association.**

Party discipline. A requisite of responsible parliamentary government that legislators, elected as party candidates, act in concert as united party caucuses during the term of the legislature and thus be held publicly accountable in the next election.

The matter of discipline is particularly important for the government party which must retain the support, or confidence, of the legislature to remain in office, and more so if members of the government party comprise only a minority of legislators. In addition to constitutional convention, however, discipline arises from the influence that party leaders have over the future political careers of their supporters. This influence is actual in the case of the prime minister and his party, and includes post-political career prospects in public service. A leader's influence over the caucus is less actual and more prospective in the case of large opposition parties. But even in the case of opposition parties, leaders manage their caucus members' role in House procedures and debate, in committee assignments, and in perquisites such as travel abroad.

Party discipline under the convention of responsible government is strictly observed in Canadian legislatures relative to the British House of Commons, where government legislation can be defeated without necessarily requiring the government to resign. The British experience may be attributed to the relatively large number of members of parliament in the British Commons which makes it difficult for the government whip to enforce discipline, and to the relatively large number of safe seats which allows sitting members to be more independent of mind. In recent years, Canadian MPs of all parties have individually supported greater personal latitude in committee deliberations and free votes in the House. The populist Canadian Alliance, like its predecessor the Reform party, in particular argues that legislators should be free of party discipline to support the apparent majority view of their constituents. However, during the 1990s, Reform MPs did not appear to exercise much independence from the party whip, and the leader applied sanctions to some who did.

Apart from ensuring a more coherent process of electoral accountability, party discipline also protects legislators from the pressures of special-interest groups that may be well organized in their constituencies. The experience in the United States Congress, with weak party discipline, suggests that lobbyists representing special interests would soon fill any political vacuum left by party whips in Canada's legislatures. See **Caucus; Responsible government; Whip (party).**

Party system. The totality of relationships among political parties and the public in communities of particular interests and as individual voters.

The conduct of electoral competition among organized parties to obtain political power in legislative and executive institutions, and in the subsequent political debate and enactment of public policy in those institutions through a party system, constitute the hallmark of pluralist, parliamentary democracies. Authoritarian regimes, including military dictatorships and totalitarian states, that are notable for the banning of parties and party competition, nonetheless often seek legitimacy through a pseudo-party system involving one party or a purported coalition of parties for national unity, but without effective legislative institutions.

Party systems are often described in terms of the number of parties. Thus, Canada is said to have had a federal one- or single-party-dominant, multi-party system since 1921. Provincial party systems in Canada vary from the historical single-party dominant system of Alberta to a competitive three-party system in Ontario.

Analyzed in research studies and the final report of the (Pierre Lortie) Royal Committee on Electoral Reform and Party Financing in the early 1990s, the federal party system in Canada is often characterized as having three periods of development: the pre-mass democratic and rural post-Confederation period when patronage was the glue that held together cliques of parliamentary notables; a post-First World War period when an increasingly large and enfranchised population expressing sectional economic and regional interests led to brokerage politics, ministerial governments, the rise of third parties and extra-parliamentary party organization; and a late-twentieth century period when television and computer-based information technology gave rise to leader-oriented personality politics and parties dominated by leadership entourages.

Passage of legislation. The process by which a bill, once introduced in Parliament or a provincial legislature, is approved and becomes an act of the legislature. See **Legislative process**.

Patriation of the constitution. The transfer of power to amend the Canadian constitution from the British Parliament to Canadian institutions—Parliament and the provincial legislatures. Patriation was achieved in 1982, following the British Parliament's enactment of the *Canada Act, 1982* which included the *Constitution Act, 1982*, which itself contained several amending formulas involving only the Canadian Parliament and provincial legislatures, and a declaration that no British statute enacted afterwards would have effect as Canadian law.

The *Constitution Act, 1982* was proposed to the British Parliament in a request from the Canadian government accompanied by a resolution of Parliament which had the support of all provinces except Quebec. Earlier attempts to patriate the constitution had been thwarted by the lack of unanimity among the eleven governments on an amending formula and the unwillingness or inability of the federal government to act unilaterally. Several formulas for a Canadian amendment procedure—notably the Fulton-Favreau Formula (1964) and the Victoria Charter (1970)—were advanced; but none received the support of all governments, and notably not of Quebec.

The basic Canadian constitutional statute, before 1982 called the *British North America Act, 1867* and now the *Constitution Act, 1867*, was an Act of the British Parliament which had been amended from time to time by the British Parliament on a request from the Canadian government, accompanied by a parliamentary resolution. In 1949, the Act was so amended to allow the Canadian Parliament to amend "the Constitution" except where it affected provincial jurisdiction, language and education rights, and the requirements that Parliament meet at least once a year and that a House of Commons not last more than five years (then s.91:1, repealed in 1982; replaced by ss.4,5 of the Canadian Charter of Rights and Freedoms in the *Constitution Act, 1982* regarding federal and provincial legislatures). The amendment of 1949 thus established a distinction between sections to be amended on a resolution of the Canadian Parliament only and those to be amended on an address by the Canadian Parliament with, by convention, the consent of the provinces. There was debate about whether Parliament could amend Canadian constitutional statutes, such as the federal act establishing the Supreme Court of Canada, without provincial support. In 1979, the Supreme Court ruled on a reference that Parliament could not unilaterally amend the BNA Act with respect to the role of, and representation in, the Senate—changes which would fundamentally alter the constitution.

In 1980, the federal Liberal party led by Pierre Trudeau won a majority in an unanticipated election that followed the Liberal government's election defeat in 1979, its replacement by Joe Clark's minority Conservative government, Trudeau's announced retirement, the defeat of the Clark government and Trudeau's rescinding of his retirement. The election victory provided Prime Minister Trudeau and his government with renewed vigour. Heading the agenda was constitutional patriation, eventually including several domestic amending formulas; a Charter of Rights and Freedoms entrenching not only standard liberal freedoms, but also the government's policy on bilingualism and biculturalism, minority-language educational rights in the provinces, gender and other recognized "equality" interests, affirmative action programs for these interests, and multiculturalism; federal equalization payments to qualified provincial governments; and recognition of Aboriginal rights. The patriated constitution also contained a revised section 92 enhancing the role of provinces in the management of natural resources. At one point in the process the federal government submitted a request to the British Parliament, including a parliamentary resolution, which was supported only by Ontario and New Brunswick. When the British Parliament balked, the prime minister submitted a constitutional reference to the Supreme Court which ruled that, while the request was legally constitutional, it was not in accordance with the convention of substantial provincial support. Further negotiations resulted in the *Constitution Act, 1982* described above achieving the support of all provinces except Quebec and taking effect April 17, 1982.

Quebec's reconciliation to the constitution, a major objective of Prime Minister Brian Mulroney's Conservative government after its election in 1984, was to have been achieved with the Meech Lake Accord of 1987. It was approved by the Quebec National Assembly, but died in 1990, lacking legislative approval in Manitoba and Newfoundland. Following wide-ranging consultations, federal, provincial and territorial government leaders, and representatives of Native groups negotiated the Charlottetown Accord in 1992. It was subsequently defeated in a country-wide referendum, achieving majority support of voters in only three Atlantic provinces and the territories and a slim majority in Ontario. Approximately 57 per cent of Quebec voters opposed the Accord. For French nationalist critics, it represented "less than Meech." It also received only minimal support in western Canada. See **Administrative (executive) federalism; Charlottetown Accord (1992); Charter groups; interests; *Constitution Act, 1867* and subsequently amended; Fulton-Favreau Formula (1964); Meech Lake Accord (1987); Victoria Charter (1971).**

Patronage. The appointment of individuals to honorific or authoritative public positions, or the granting of government business to an individual or a group, on a discretionary basis.

In a pejorative sense, political patronage usually refers to discretionary acts without reference to competition and merit, perhaps even lacking merit. Such acts of patronage by the government-of-the-day constitute rewards for past service and an incentive or example to others of benefit to be derived from loyal service to the government party. While patronage may be recognized as an essential lubricant of the political process, there is reasonable debate about whether it is in the public interest for it to extend to large contracts without tendering, or to appointments to the judiciary and boards of significant crown corporations and regulatory agencies.

In dispensing patronage, governments seek to avoid negative publicity, but otherwise will trumpet government awards as deserved, of material benefit to a larger community, or as symbolic recognition of the importance of particular groups or interests in the population.

"Peace, Order, and good Government". The phrase in the preamble in section 91 of the *Constitution Act, 1867* generally stating the scope of the Canadian Parliament's legislative competence. A reading of the preamble readily suggests that the intention of the framers of Confederation was to centralize political power in the Canadian federation and to place broad residual and emergency legislative powers in Parliament.

In the process of interpreting the Act, the Judicial Committee of the Privy Council systematically made the "Peace, Order, and good Government" clause supplementary to the enumerated federal and provincial powers. While the decision in *Russell v. The Queen* (1882) upheld the centralist view of Parliament's role, the process of judicial review eventually reduced the clause to a residual power to be exercised by Parliament only in a time of great national emergency. In 1937, the JCPC declared most of Conservative Prime Minister R.B. Bennett's "New Deal" legislation (introduced during the depression of the 1930s) to be *ultra vires*, that is, beyond the jurisdiction of Parliament. "While the ship of state now sails on larger ventures and into foreign waters," Lord Atkin wrote of the Canadian constitution for the JCPC, "she still retains the watertight compartments which are an essential part of her original structure." Thus, "Peace, Order, and good Government" was effectively reduced from a justification for comprehensive residual legislative competence by the Parliament of Canada to a justification for temporary competence only in a national emergency such as war or insurrection. In its place, the Judicial Committee effectively substituted the enumerated head under provincial powers, "Property and Civil Rights in the Province" (s.92:13), as the residual power clause except in dire national emergency.

After the Supreme Court became the final court of appeal in 1949, judicial decisions tended to strengthen the power of the federal government, at least in economic matters. The Court replaced the narrow emergency doctrine of the Judicial Committee with the notion of "inherent national importance" under the "Peace, Order, and good Government" and "Trade and Commerce" (s.91:2) clauses. For example, the Supreme Court permitted the reassertion of federal authority over aviation, the assertion of federal authority over western offshore mineral rights, and federal power to establish mandatory wage and price controls. Settling disputes regarding federal-provincial jurisdiction under the *Constitution Act, 1867* still falls to the judiciary, though challenges to government legislation since 1982 frequently focuses on individual rights under the Canadian Charter of Rights and Freedoms, rather than only jurisdictional rights held between the two levels of government.

The phrase "Peace, Order and good Government" is sometimes referred to in discussions of Canadian political culture, as a counterpart to the constitutional phrase "Life, liberty and the pursuit of happiness" of the United States, distinguishing foundational collectivist, conservative values from the foundational individualist, liberal values of the US. See *Emergencies Act* (**Canada, 1988; emergency powers**); **Emergency power; Judicial Committee of the Privy Council (JCPC); Judicial review (interpretive; non-interpretive); Political culture; Supreme Court.**

Persons Case (*Edwards v. A.-G. for Canada* [1930]) A decision by the Judicial Committee of the Privy Council (JCPC) that women were qualified under the *British North America Act, 1867* to be appointed to the Senate.

Section 24 grants the governor general the power to "summon qualified Persons to the Senate" and section 23 lists formal qualifications using the male form of the personal pronoun. The decision overturned an earlier Supreme Court ruling. Generally the traditional approach to constitutional interpretation limited fact-finding to the wording of relevant statutes, to adjudicative rather than social or legislative facts. In this case, the Judicial Committee allowed that women were "Persons" within the meaning of the Act. Lord Sankey indicated that the JCPC did "not think it right to apply rigidly to Canada of today the decisions and the reasons therefore which commended themselves, probably rightly, to those who had to apply the law in different circumstances, in different centuries, to countries in different stages of development....The British North America Act planted in Canada a living tree capable of growth and expansion within its natural limits." It was not the duty of the JCPC "to cut down the provisions of the Act by a narrow and technical construction, but rather to give it a large and liberal interpretation" at least within "certain fixed limits" of federal-provincial jurisdiction and not impose a "strict construction" on "an Act passed to ensure the peace, order, and good government of a British colony."

There were, however, relatively few such non-interpretive JCPC decisions, especially ones not related to the federal-provincial division of power, inspired by Lord Sankey's "living tree" metaphor. As for the substance of the case, gender equality was entrenched in the Canadian Charter of Rights and Freedoms in 1982 (s.28), along with affirmative action programs designed to improve the conditions of individuals or groups disadvantaged because of several enumerated factors, including sex (s.15:2).

Petition. A request from the public to a legislative body or official to redress a grievance or to seek a particular change in policy. The presentation of policy-related petitions to the legislature by a member is a regular occurrence, acknowledging John Stuart Mill's description of the British House of Commons as "the nation's committee of grievances and its congress of opinions." Historically, redress was sought against the Crown, but today it is sought against governments that act in the name of the Crown. Although the behaviour of provincial legislators and federal members of parliament is largely circumscribed by the disciplined party system, they retain an area of discretion with respect to non-policy representation. Members can readily present policy-related petitions that conform to party policy or at least do not conflict with it. On particular grievances involving constituents, an individual legislator might seek redress through private, personal contacts with relevant officials or publicly through a question to the minister in the legislature, acting as a constituency ombudsman in a non-partisan way. Several provinces have an ombudsman to whose office the public can seek redress from government decisions. At the federal level, there are various commissioners, dealing for example with complaints regarding bilingualism in the public service, privacy, information, corrections, the military and air travel. See **Ombudsman**.

Platform. Policy proposals, often individually termed "planks," announced by political parties prior to or during an election campaign, to which the party is supposedly committed should it form the government.

Platforms of cadre parties, such as the Liberal and Conservative parties, are constructed by the leadership in the context of an imminent election campaign. Policy resolutions of party conventions are, to use a metaphor of Liberal Prime Minister William Lyon Mackenzie King, a "chart and compass" provided to the leadership by party members. Because the leaders of movement parties such as the social democratic New Democratic party and the right-populist Canadian Alliance are restrained by the policy resolutions of their conventions, the leadership carefully manages the nature, specific terms, and interpretation of resolutions that come to a vote.

In all cases, the campaign committees of each party create campaigns around specific themes and issues designed to maximize electoral support. This pragmatism, or opportunism, tends to minimize the importance of the platform and heighten the importance of generalized issues such as "leadership" and "the economy." However, federal election campaigns in the 1980s and 1990s did focus on precise issues, including the constitution, free trade and fundamental changes to the tax system. See **Brokerage politics**; **Cadre parties**; **Movement parties**.

Plebiscite. See **Referendum**.

Plurality. The largest number of votes cast for one candidate in an election, but which is not a majority (at least 50% plus 1) of all votes cast. All provincial and federal elections in Canada operate on the single-member constituency system with plurality win, or first-past-the-post system.

In multi-party elections, it is common for legislators to be elected with a plurality, but not a majority, of the votes cast. As the votes for the defeated candidates do not have any electoral effect, the system results in discrepancies between the percentage of the votes cast for the parties' candidates and the percentage of seats the parties hold in a legislature. Thus governments in Canada are usually formed by parties with a majority of seats in the legislature, but based only on a plurality of the popular vote. Such discrepancies also prevail among the several opposition parties. See **Electoral system**; **Proportional representation**; **Single-member plurality electoral system**.

Policy (**-making; analysis; communities; instruments; public…**). Decisions related to the determination of objectives and the selection of methods to achieve them. Policy objectives or goals may be concrete or abstract, broad or narrow. They may involve a single decision or a set of decisions; action or inaction.

The term "public policy" refers specifically to government decisions. Usually, "public policy"encompasses several decisions related to a general purpose or objective.

Policy making is the process involving various "actors" and institutions by which policies are determined and implemented. In specific cases, this may involve a set of activities including intergovernmental negotiations, cabinet consideration, legislative debate, interest-group lobbying, the regulatory process and judicial review.

Policy communities comprise actors in the policy-making process with an interest in a particular policy field, whether in the foreground ("lead" actors and "subgovernment") or in the background (the "attentive public") of debate.

Policy instruments are the devices and techniques chosen by the government to implement policy that can range in degrees of intrusiveness from moral suasion expressed in a minister's speech to coercion through law.

Policy analysis is a concern of academics to examine policy making and policy output using various models of decision and policy making. Widely used models include the power elite, the pluralist community, Marxist, and state-centred models. The object of policy analysis is to discover "who governs" by understanding "who gets what, why, and how."

Political culture. A set of orientations—that is, attitudes, beliefs and values toward the political process, including laws, institutions and personalities, held by members of a political system.

A political culture is the result of the interplay of historic and contemporary factors in an ongoing process of socialization from childhood through adulthood. It may comprise subsets, or subcultures, based on ethnic, geographic and class differences. Political subcultures that are distinct from the political culture of the larger political community may pose a threat to the integration of the larger community.

Academics have studied political culture in Canada from historical and individual-level, attitudinal perspectives. The former has involved debate on the strength of American liberalism (for example, political equality and majoritarianism) in relation to the values of European collectivism (as in bicultural elite accommodation, a state-centred political economy, including public enterprise and social security, and deference to authority). Individual-level studies have focussed on regional differences among Canadians respecting political efficacy, trust and involvement in politics (the purported civic culture of some regions and the clientelistic culture of others).

Polling (election day). The casting of votes for candidates in a general or by-election at designated polling stations in a constituency.

During the election campaign, voters are officially notified by mail of the date of the election, the location of their neighbourhood polling station and the hours of polling. They are also notified of the time and location of the advance poll at which they may vote if they expect to be absent from their poll on election day. Proxy voting is allowed for voters who cannot come to the polling station for medical reasons. Polling stations are usually located in public places such as schools, libraries and community centres, or private places that are readily accessible to electors. The station is managed by a deputy returning officer, assisted by poll clerks, in the company of designated party scrutineers who confirm the eligibility of the electors, distribute the ballots and monitor their deposition in locked ballot boxes. When the polls close on election night, the boxes are opened and the ballots counted unofficially, both for each candidate and against the total number of ballots distributed, and reported to the returning officer of the constituency. The party scrutineers in the polling stations report the vote count and any alleged irregularities in the conduct of the poll, to their respective headquarters.

Polling (public opinion). The determination of views held by the general public or a specific segment of the public through systematic survey techniques involving a sample of the relevant public.

Public opinion surveys are a mainstay of contemporary politics. Government, political parties, the mass media and interest groups engage to a greater or lesser degree in the regular polling of public attitudes and views relative to their own particular interests. This polling is "scientific," meaning that sophisticated questionnaire construction and testing, interviewer training, sample design and statistical techniques are used to make statements about a larger public. For example, the results of a scientific poll of a small sample of respondents may be said to be representative of a larger public within a specific margin of error. A properly selected sample of, say, 1,200 Canadians may be accurate within a margin of error of plus or minus 3 per cent nineteen times out of twenty. There are, of course, many "unscientific" polls conducted, especially by some media and legislators, from which no inference can be drawn about the larger public; these polls are largely gimmicks.

Especially since the 1970s, reported opinion surveys have become endemic both between, but especially during, election campaigns. In addition to the omnibus or general surveys, campaign themes are "market tested" with focus groups of "targeted" voters prior to campaigns, and daily "tracking" of public opinion through telephones takes place during campaigns. The polling industry is large and several commercial companies are widely known to the public through their name or their leading "pollster." Some firms are closely associated with particular parties or with particular newspaper chains and broadcasting networks.

There is no convincing evidence regarding the impact of poll results on the voting decision one way or another—voting for the apparent winner, the "bandwagon" effect, or otherwise the "underdog" effect. Nonetheless, mass media coverage of election campaigns, which includes reports of their own polls as well as party polls, tends to be of the "horserace" variety, focusing on who's ahead and by how much. There might be comfort in this for the leading party, for which "momentum" in Canada's relatively brief campaigns is crucial, but there are many instances of parties entering a campaign with a lead in the polls, only to lose in the "poll that counts" on election day.

There has been widespread support for the prohibition of the reporting of poll results immediately before election day, similar to bans on advertising. But amendments to the *Canada Elections Act* to prohibit the publication of polls three days prior to federal elections were declared unconstitutional by the Supreme Court of Canada in 1998 (*Thomson Newspaper Co. v. Canada [Attorney General]*). In response, the Act was amended a year later to regulate the publication of election-related surveys during a campaign: anyone who first releases survey results must declare the survey's sponsorship, the agency that conducted it, when and how the sample was drawn, how many people participated and the margin of error; non-broadcasters such as newspapers and Internet sites must publish the wording of the questionnaire and where a copy can be obtained; and like advertising, new survey results cannot be published on election day.

Democratic politics implies government by popular consent, but some commentators fear that Canadians now have government by secret public opinion poll. Opinion surveys associated with private marketing are now used perhaps to change policy, but also to alter public perceptions of parties and governments without changing policy. As mentioned above, political parties employ such techniques as rolling surveys of selected target groups and focus group discussions to determine areas of strength and weakness relative to their opposition. Election campaign strategies and tactics are then designed and tested on these groups, prior to the actual campaign, to establish successfully an emotional bond between the selected public and the "product"—a particular policy position, theme, the party name or its leader.

The volatility of Canadian political public opinion both between and during election campaigns is an important development that has been tracked by opinion surveying since the 1970s. There appears to have been simultaneously a weakening of traditional party identification as a predictor of party support. It is debatable to what extent the widespread "horserace" reporting of surveys before and during election campaigns has been a contributing factor. However, it is evident that the increased use of increasingly sophisticated survey techniques by the parties has led to relatively homogeneous party campaigns treating elections as advertising campaigns leading to a one-day sale of a market-tested product.

Popular vote. See **Electoral system.**

Populism. A term describing a political movement which seeks in general terms to wrest government from the control of a centralized and sophisticated clique and to make it responsive to the needs and interests of "ordinary people." Some politicians may also be described as populists, although their party may not be a populist movement.

Populist movements in Canada have been successful when led by charismatic individuals who could articulate regional grievances and exploit established social and political organizations and new techniques of communication such as radio and television. Examples of such populist movements have been: the various United Farmers parties and the Progressives in the 'teens and the 1920s, the Social Credit party in the 1930s and 1940s, and the Ralliement des créditistes in Quebec in the 1960s, led by Henry Wise Wood, William Aberhart, and Réal Caouette, respectively. In the 1990s, the Alberta-based and populist Reform party led by Preston Manning, son of a former long-serving Social Credit premier of Alberta, successfully challenged the dominance of the federal Conservative party in western Canada. The party's inability to forge support in central and eastern Canada led to its transformation to the Canadian Alliance, with Manning replaced by Stockwell Day, also an Albertan, and a former provincial Conservative cabinet minister. In addition to such social conservative populist movements, western Canada has given rise to left-wing populist movements, notably the socialist Co-operative Commonwealth Federation and its social democratic successor, the New Democratic party.

John Diefenbaker is an example of a populist politician in a non-populist party. Often rebuffed in his leadership ambitions, this long-time Saskatchewan lawyer and member of parliament eventually became leader of the federal Conservative party from 1956 to 1967 and prime minister from 1957 to 1963. He was the first western-based prime minister and the first of ethnic background other than British or French. Though the Conservative party was historically associated with wealthy business interests and their preferred economic and social policies, Diefenbaker's leadership led to the development of a populist constituency for the party in western Canada. The party formed the government under Quebec-based Brian Mulroney in 1984 and 1988 with leading cabinet personalities from western Canada and policy more sensitive to western interests, for example in energy policy and trade. In the 1993 election, however, the Reform party captured that base of support.

Political populism in Canada in the twentieth century has comprised several important elements: a nostalgic view of one's society as expressing traditional, civilizing values associated with personal industriousness, thrift and family attachments, now threatened by "external" cultural values and norms; criticism of industrial or big-business capitalism as harmful to the interests of independent, small-scale commodity producers; and corruption in politics largely found in the control of political parties and institutions by large-scale finance, industrial and manufacturing capitalists. Especially in the first half of the twentieth century, western populism was fuelled by the failure of settlement to match immigrants' high expectations created by the federal government, the dominance of the western economy by central Canadian-based financial, trans-portation and manufacturing companies, and the apparent control of both Liberal and Conservative parties by these interests as evidenced in the policies of the federal government located thousands of miles away. Cross-border influences from agrarian populist movements in the United States also spurred populism in western Canada. Many of these elements help explain the appearance and success in western Canada of the Reform party in the late 1980s and 1990s, although the specifics of the perceived cultural threat were different (generically referred to as "special interests") and there was less ill will toward private-sector enterprise relative to the public sector that was now seen as too large and unaccountable. See **Canadian Alliance party; Co-operative Commonwealth Federation (CCF); Movement parties; New Democratic party (NDP); Progressive movement (party); Ralliement des créditistes; Reform party; Social Credit party.**

Pork barrel. A term to describe political patronage—the "pork"—dispensed by the government party from the public treasury—the "barrel"—to a community or private interests as a reward for, or incentive to provide support to the party in the form of money, organizational resources, or votes. Federal "pork" has traditionally been government jobs or untendered contracts for individuals and firms, and public works such as bridges, post offices, road, airport and waterfront improvements for communities. In an era of complex and costly programs, grants for job retraining and industrial incentive programs, regional development, as well as some federal expenditures related to military defence, may also qualify as "pork." See **Patronage**.

Portfolio. A term used to describe ministerial responsibilities in a cabinet. For example, finance is the portfolio of the minister of finance. Ministers who are appointed "without portfolio" may be fulfilling some honorific or symbolic political obligation in an honorific way, or conducting important government business without the impediment of departmental or administrative responsibilities.

Positive (negative) entitlement. A positive or negative figure indicating whether, in recognized revenue fields, the per capita tax yield in each province is above or below the national provincial average in those fields.

If the total figure of all entitlements is positive (that is, the total provincial tax yield of a provincial government is lower than the national average), the province is entitled to an unconditional equalization transfer payment from the federal government to make up the difference. If the total figure is negative (that is, the total provincial tax yield is higher than the national average), the province is not entitled to a transfer payment. The designation of provincial revenue sources and tax fields as well as the definition of the national provincial average is crucial to the outcome of the calculation, both in terms of which provinces qualify for equalization payments and their amount. See **Equalization grants (unconditional transfer payments); Federal-provincial tax-sharing agreements (fiscal federalism)**.

Postmaterialism. A concept related to increased prominence in Canadian political discourse of quality-of-life and personal identity issues and the growth of single-issue groups, allied in social movement networks, to focus public and government attention on those issues.

Since the 1970s, traditional class-based alliances with materialist concerns such as economic development and individual security have shared the public agenda with postmaterialist group actors and their interests. This agenda includes concerns related to the natural environment, including for example deforestation, the plight of endangered species and global warming, third-world community development, safe urban communities, and minority human rights including those of Aboriginal peoples, women, children, gays and lesbians, and the disabled. Organizations promoting a postmaterialist agenda are described as social movement organizations, often involving people who have not been previously involved in politics, frequently in forms of political action to attract coverage in the mass media and thus influence government through public opinion as well as through direct representation.

Established political institutions in Canada such as political parties that have managed an agenda generated by the traditional interests reflecting the

French-English duality, region and class, now have to respond to these contemporary social movement alliances and their policy challenges. In Canada, judicial review of government activity under the Canadian Charter of Rights and Freedoms since 1982 has provided such groups with another avenue to advance the postmaterialist agenda. See **Social movement organizations**.

Premier. The head of a provincial cabinet, or government, appointed by the lieutenant-governor of the province, whose government remains in office as long as it retains the confidence of the legislature. Thus, the premier is usually the leader of the party that has elected the most members to the legislature. The premier "recommends" the appointment of the cabinet, which acts formally as the lieutenant-governor's Executive Council. The premier's relationship to the lieutenant-governor, the cabinet and the legislature is comparable to that of the prime minister to the governor general, the federal cabinet and the House of Commons. See **Prime minister**.

Prerogative power. Discretionary power, usually with reference to the Crown's relationship to the government-of-the-day and the legislature. See **Crown prerogatives**.

President of the Queen's Privy Council for Canada. A cabinet portfolio with no constitutionally defined role; thus, the prime minister assigns particular responsibilities to this cabinet minister. For example, in the Liberal governments immediately before 1984, the government's House leader, who manages government business in the House of Commons, held the honorific title. Under Conservative Prime Minister Brian Mulroney, the title was held by the cabinet minister designated acting prime minister. In Liberal Prime Minister Jean Chrétien's cabinet, the position was held initially by a minister whose primary responsibility was the reorganization of the federal bureaucracy, and later by the minister responsible for intergovernmental affairs.

The Queen's Privy Council for Canada is, constitutionally, the formal executive body advising the Crown, the effective part of which, however, is the current federal cabinet. The Privy Council Office is the cabinet secretariat whose head, the clerk or secretary to the cabinet, is also designated the prime minister's deputy minister, and the prime minister is the minister responsible to Parliament for the PCO. See **Privy Council for Canada (the Queen's)**; **Privy Council Office (PCO)**.

President of the Treasury Board. The cabinet minister who chairs, and is responsible to Parliament for, the federal Treasury Board. The Treasury Board, the only statutory committee of cabinet, also includes the minister of finance. This cabinet designation of president derives from the Treasury Board's status among cabinet committees as a statutory committee of the Queen's Privy Council for Canada. Until 1966, the minister of finance chaired the Treasury Board, and its staff came from the Department of Finance. In 1966, however, the Treasury Board was established as a separate department of the federal government with its own minister, styled the president, and its own Secretariat. See **Treasury Board**; **Treasury Board Secretariat**.

Press, the. See **Mass media of communication; Press gallery.**

Press gallery. A collective term for journalists and broadcasters who cover the activities of a legislature and government, derived from the area above the Speaker's chair from which journalists traditionally observed the proceedings of the House.

Through a formal organization, correspondents accredited to the press gallery gain access to facilities provided by the Speaker of the legislature to cover political events in and around the legislature on a daily basis. The press gallery is an important link between the politicians and the public. Citizens rely heavily on the mass media of communication for political information, and politicians, for whom public approval is singularly important, use the media to gauge public opinion and foster favourable impressions of themselves and their party. The status of the press gallery is recognized, for example, in its members' confidential access to government documents such as budgets and throne speeches before they are made public. They also have access to areas of the legislative buildings which are normally closed to the public.

Once a small and fairly stable organization of mostly male newspaper reporters, the composition and behaviour of the parliamentary press gallery in Ottawa changed dramatically as it came to terms with television journalism in the 1960s and profound changes in electronic communication technology in the 1980s. The daily deadline of newspaper-dominated political communication gave way to the "instant" 24-hour communication of dramatic conflict- and personality-driven photo opportunities and sound bites from debates in the House of Commons and scrums outside the House following Question Period to more sedate press conferences and scheduled events. In the 1990s, the parliamentary press gallery, now comprising mostly electronic journalists with sound equipment and accompanied by camera crews, contained approximately four hundred, frequently short-term, members. While the number of female journalists has increased considerably, the membership is still predominantly male. Once a high-status assignment in journalism, the parliamentary press gallery may now be more a stepping-stone to international postings, private-sector public relations, media consultancy and lobbying, even employment within government itself which is larger and more concerned with "public relations."

The rise of electronic journalism and corporate conglomerate newspaper chains, with the concomitant reduction in the influence of regional newspapers and their Ottawa correspondents, has tended to homogenize the behaviour of both journalists and their subjects, the political elites. However, differences persist between anglophone and francophone journalists. The francophone members of the parliamentary press gallery address for the most part a Quebec audience, with a focus on issues dealing with Quebec and events at the federal level from a Quebec perspective. Generally unlike their anglophone counterparts, francophone journalists comprise part of a cultural intelligentsia which has contributed in important ways to the political life of Quebec. Henri Bourassa early in the twentieth century and, more recently, André Laurendeau, René Lévesque, Gérard Pelletier, Claude Ryan and Pierre Trudeau, are examples of this Quebec elite for whom politics and journalism were inextricably linked in public debate on the "national question." Francophones constitute a minority of the press gallery, but their influence in Quebec probably outweighs that of their anglophone colleagues in their respective communities. See **Mass media of communication**.

Pressure groups. See **Interest groups**.

Prime minister. The head of the federal cabinet or government-of-the-day, appointed by the governor general, who remains in office as long as the government retains the confidence of the House of Commons. Thus, the prime minister is usually the leader of the party that has elected the most members to the House, and the governor general acts virtually always on the prime minister's advice. The prime minister chooses the cabinet, which acts formally as the Queen's Privy Council for Canada through the governor-in-council.

The power of prime ministers over their colleagues, as well as over the opposition, lies in their relationship to the Crown. The prime minister "advises" the governor general on matters ranging from judicial, administrative, senatorial and diplomatic appointments to the dissolution of Parliament, effectively setting the date for a general election. The prime minister "recommends" appointments to and within, and departures from, the federal cabinet. The prime minister may also organize and allocate responsibilities in the cabinet, the Privy Council Office, and the Prime Minister's Office largely without constraint. In some cases, parliamentary approval may be required for some reorganization, but other changes can be made without legislative approval—through an order-in-council. The prime minister's usually effective control over the majority of members of parliament in the House of Commons, and the normal dormancy of the Senate, ensures parliamentary approval that might be required.

The prime minister has been traditionally termed *primus inter pares*—first among equals. While cabinet ministers may be the prime minister's colleagues, the prime minister clearly has powers as party leader and prime minister which they individually or collectively do not possess. The prime minister is required to appoint to cabinet people who have seats in Parliament, usually the House of Commons. Some appointments to cabinet might be a grudging recognition by the prime minister of the popularity in the party and in the country of personal opponents. But, having appointed and organized the cabinet and the rest of the executive organization, including the Prime Minister's Office, the prime minister determines the cabinet's agenda, chairs its meetings and defines its consensus on issues.

The constitutional conventions of cabinet secrecy and collective ministerial responsibility enhance the prime minister's power over colleagues. Any minister wishing to diverge publicly from the prime minister's declared view of the government's position must first resign from the cabinet. Cabinet resignations can be accompanied by a statement of disagreement with the government's position, but former cabinet ministers remain bound by their Privy Council oath not to disclose cabinet business. This, however, does not entirely prevent unattributed leaks of information to the mass media from "usually reliable sources."

In what has come to be known as executive federalism in Canada, the prime minister can affect the direction of federal-provincial relations. Perhaps here, among provincial first ministers, the prime minister may be more aptly called *primus inter pares*: the provincial premiers holding power in their own right, and not at the behest of the prime minister, but the prime minister always the primary focus of attention in federal-provincial matters. The prime minister calls the meetings of first ministers, manages the prior agenda-setting process, and also chairs, guides and attempts to define the consensus of the meetings. In general, the prime minister influences the pace and quality of federal-provincial relations in a way that can be matched only by some premiers on some issues. While the federal system constrains the prime minister in important respects, the process of federal-provincial consultation, with the prime minister and relevant cabinet colleagues at the centre, sets federal priorities in areas of provincial or intergovernmental jurisdiction. The defeat of the Meech Lake Accord in 1990, which had been agreed to by the eleven heads of government under Prime Minister Brian Mulroney's guidance in 1987, was said by some to have under-mined executive federalism. Consequently, the process of constitutional negotia-tions leading to the Charlottetown Accord, which was defeated in a country-wide referendum in 1992, involved broader public consultation. Nonetheless, constitu-tional amendments and the general working of the federal system still require some form of executive federalism managed by the prime minister at the centre.

A prime minister's personality clearly determines the style and form of the government. Some prime ministers may be more committed than others to specific policy objectives, but usually all are concerned about popularity as time for the next election draws close. The extent of the government's rise or fall in public opinion will have an influence on the prime minister's power. The influ-ence of Prime Minister John Diefenbaker over his cabinet was very different in 1962-63 from what it was in 1957-58. Diefenbaker, who was uncontested from within in 1958, led a cabinet in disarray in 1962-63. Prime Minister Joe Clark attempted unsuccessfully to ignore the political realities of minority government and lasted in office only a few months in 1979-80. He was replaced by Pierre Trudeau, who, after being defeated in 1979 and having announced his resignation after eleven years as Liberal leader and prime minister, then had an opportunity to pursue with single-minded determination the patriation of the constitution with a Charter of Rights and Freedoms. The early years of Brian Mulroney's "brokerage" government from 1984 to approximately 1986 was characterized by lack of control over the agenda and charges of corruption and incompetence involving his ministers, disorder in the Prime Minister's Office, and a precipitous slide in public opinion polls. Later, he established a clear agenda for a reorganized executive, two rounds of constitutional negotiations designed to accommodate Quebec to the constitutional changes of 1982, Canada-United States and North American (with Mexico) free trade agreements and fundamental changes to the tax system. It was something of a personal accomplishment that, despite Prime Minister Mulroney's personal unpopularity by the time of his resignation in 1993, his government remained relatively cohesive. Prime Minister Jean Chrétien's Liberal government, first elected in 1993, and re-elected handily in 1997 and 2000, reflected a personal and low-key approach to government, but one over which the prime minister and his senior aides in the Prime Minister's Office nonetheless exercised strict control. See **Cabinet; Cabinet organization; Prime Minister's Office (PMO); Privy Council Office (PCO)**.

Prime Minister's Office (PMO). The political secretariat or administration that keeps the prime minister informed on political developments in the country, the party and the legislature. There are comparable premiers' offices in the provinces. The PMO maintains contact with ministers, party backbenchers, the party organization and provincial party organizations; it arranges the prime minister's schedule of private appointments, public appearances, correspondence, public statements and relations with the mass media.

The prime minister determines the organization and role of the PMO, and its operations are therefore a reflection of the prime minister's personality and needs. As an important source of political information and counsel as well as a personal public relations bureau, the organization and senior staff of the PMO, headed by a chief of staff or principal secretary, reflects the timely needs of the prime minister and the government.

Especially in his early years as prime minister, Pierre Trudeau used the PMO to bring to Ottawa people in whom he had confidence, but who neither held prominent positions in the Liberal party nor were in parliament and therefore could not be in his cabinet. The PMO then included regional officers who reported on political developments—to the chagrin of some cabinet ministers and backbench Liberal members of parliament, who saw the PMO usurping one of their roles. The senior civil servants in government departments and at the Privy Council Office also perceived the policy role of the PMO as a challenge to their traditional prerogatives. Indeed, some important government policy initiatives, such as a program of economic restraint introduced in the late 1970s, were announced with Trudeau advised solely by the PMO. When he formed a government in 1984, Brian Mulroney, an Ottawa newcomer even more so than Trudeau, also initially created a powerful PMO of personal confidants.

Prime ministers replace the staff and reassign priorities in the PMO as political conditions change. The PMO under the majority government of Trudeau from 1968 to 1972 was very different from the PMO of the minority government years from 1972 to 1974, as electoral considerations became more important than rational management. As already mentioned, Mulroney's slide in public opinion after 1984 led to changes in the PMO. Following re-election in 1988 and the failure of the Meech Lake Accord in 1990, constitutional negotiations determined the composition and activity of the PMO until 1991, when another precipitous midterm slide in public opinion led to new senior staffing and a focus on the next election in addition to further constitutional negotiations. When he became prime minister in 1993, Jean Chrétien initially established a smaller PMO, partly as an example to ministers whose staffs would also be smaller than their Conservative predecessors', and also as a hopeful signal for good relations with senior officials in the public service. In general though, all prime ministers are dependent on political staff in their PMO for daily briefings and advice on policy and personnel, as well as the scheduling of their appointments, movements and public pronouncements. See **Chief of staff (principal secretary).**

Principal secretary. See **Chief of staff (principal secretary).**

Priorities and Planning Committee ("P and P"). See **Inner cabinet.**

Privacy Act, 1983 **(Canada); Privacy Commissioner.** Federal legislation extending protection of individual privacy with respect to personal information held by designated federal government agencies, providing personal access to that information, requesting correction of information, and providing recourse to a privacy commissioner and the courts in cases of noncompliance. The governor-in-council, that is, the cabinet, may exempt certain government databases from the legislation, or personal information that, for example, might be injurious to international and federal-provincial affairs, law enforcement and investigations and personal safety, or is related to security clearance procedures.

The Act establishes the Office of the Privacy Commissioner and outlines its investigative powers, including access to information, excluding cabinet "confidences." The privacy commissioner may also carry out investigations of government institutions to ensure proper collection, retention and disposal of personal information under the law. On application by a complainant or the privacy commissioner following noncompliance, the Federal Court may review the case and issue an order. In recent years, the privacy commissioner's annual reports to parliament have included, in addition to reports on government bodies amassing extensive and cumulative files on citizens, concerns over Supreme Court decisions permitting widespread electronic surveillance by police, biomedical testing in areas such as the transportation industry, prisons, the military and among athletes.

Private bills. Nongovernment legislation introduced by private members to alter the law relating to some particular interest, to confer rights on or relieve the obligations of some person, group of people, or a company. For example, bills to incorporate private companies federally or to alter their charters are private bills. In the federal parliament, most private bills are introduced in the Senate. Bills which must receive the approval of the House of Commons are usually dealt with perfunctorily by that chamber. By contrast, public bills are intended to affect the public generally and include both government bills and private members' bills. See **Legislation**.

Private member. A member of a provincial or federal legislature who is not a cabinet minister. See **Backbencher; Private members' legislation (bills)**.

Private members' legislation (bills). Public, nongovernment bills introduced by legislators who are not in the cabinet.

Private members' bills, which normally cannot involve the expenditure of public money (a prerogative enjoyed only by ministers introducing public government bills), may concern any matter that falls within the jurisdictional competence of the legislature. Private members' bills introduced in the House of Commons that do involve public expenditures require a "royal recommendation" prior to third reading. However, seldom do private members' bills go beyond first reading—introduction and printing stage. Should the bill go further, it will likely be "talked out," that is, it will not be voted upon before the brief time allotted for the debate has ended. It then falls to the bottom of the list of private members' bills. In the House of Commons, up to fifteen private members' bills and fifteen motions can receive greater attention, three hours of debate and a vote for possible study in committee and report back to the Commons. Rarely does a private member's bill make it to the statute books. The little time allotted to the lengthy list of private members' bills in all Canadian legislatures, and governments' reluctance to concede legislation other than their own to be of value, are the chief causes for the fate of most private members' bills.

The importance of private members' legislation is the opportunity it gives backbenchers on both sides to introduce measures they consider important; though not passed by the legislature, the bill in printed form can be distributed to interested groups in the public and to public officials for consideration. Private members' bills bring issues to public attention and maintain them on the public agenda in the hope that eventually a government will commit itself to the measure. Such is the origin, for example, of federal access-to-information legislation and the eventual abolition of capital punishment, both of which were debated in the House of Commons over many years, in the form of private members' legislation.

Privatization. The disposal of crown corporations and other government assets through sale or lease to private interests, the contracting of government services to private companies, and the relaxation and elimination of regulatory controls.

Although privatization has ideological supporters who oppose state intervention in the economy in principle, a trend to privatization in the 1990s was spurred by an economic recession which resulted in a dramatic decline in government revenues, a growing public debt and public opposition to tax increases. The federal Conservative government elected in 1984 supported privatization in principle. In 1986, it established the Office of Privatization and Regulatory Affairs and a cabinet position designated minister of state for privatization and regulatory affairs to oversee the divestiture of corporate holdings which allegedly did not require government ownership to fulfil their public mandate. In 1993, the newly elected Liberal government increased the number of Special Operating Agencies (SOAs), self-contained and independently managed government operations, which could eventually be privatized. Examples of federal corporations privatized since 1984 include Air Canada, the Canada Development Corporation, de Haviland Aircraft, Eldorado Nuclear, Petro-Canada and Teleglobe Canada. See **Special Operating Agencies (SOAs)**.

Privy Council for Canada (the Queen's). The formal executive advisory body to the Crown, established under the *Constitution Act, 1867* (s.11), whose members the governor general appoints on the advice of the prime minister. By convention, however, those members of the Privy Council who actually "advise" the Crown comprise a committee identical to the current federal cabinet. Neither the cabinet, nor the prime minister, are mentioned in the *Constitution Act*. Thus, the cabinet acts formally through orders-in-council and minutes of council in the name of the governor-in-council. Membership is normally for life and allows members to add "Honourable" before, and "P.C." after their names. The Privy Council now comprises several hundred, mostly honorific members. Occasionally appointments will be required for administrative purposes. For example, members of the Security Intelligence Review Committee (SIRC) must be privy councillors. See **Cabinet**.

Privy Council Office (PCO). The prime minister's government department headed by the Clerk of the Privy Council who, since 1940, has been designated secretary to the cabinet. The Privy Council Office is a central executive agency responsible for co-ordinating the activities of cabinet and cabinet committees (except the Treasury Board which has its own secretariat) and for liaison with government departments and agencies on cabinet matters.

The PCO provides secretarial and other support, involving the preparation and presentation of documents, for interdepartmental committees. It ensures conformity of submissions for approval by the cabinet to policy and legal requirements; examines, edits, registers and arranges for the publication of statutory regulations; and it generally advises concerning the prime minister's prerogatives and responsibilities in the organization of the federal government, including the organization of cabinet and the decision-making process, senior administrative appointments that are outside the purview of the Public Service Commission and matters related to security and intelligence. The PCO also assists the prime minister in the setting and managing of government priorities and policies.

In brief, under the clerk and secretary to the cabinet, the PCO is the central link between the political executive—the prime minister and cabinet—and the administrative executive of government, providing logistical support for the cabinet, advice on the organization of government and appointments, advice on intergovernmental affairs, and co-ordinating policy across the public administration. See **Clerk of the Privy Council (secretary to the cabinet).**

Progressive Conservative party. See **Conservative (Progressive Conservative) party.**

Progressive movement (party). A political movement, comprising mostly farmers and small businessmen close to the agricultural community, in the Canadian prairie West in the late 'teens and 1920s. The political disaffection of western farmers increased steadily during the first two decades of the twentieth century. High tariffs that successive federal governments imposed to protect commercial interests, located primarily in central Canada, compounded the natural problems of farm life on the prairies. Through co-operative action, farmers advanced their particular interests, conscious of their political weakness in the disciplined parliamentary party system which made their few members of parliament in Ottawa powerless. The Progressive movement supported various reforms to effect greater constituency or grassroots control over MPs, including recall and referenda. A more radical anti-party proposal involved the replacement of territorially based constituency representation with occupational representation, especially to strengthen the influence of rural communities.

The momentum for independent political action was delayed by the First World War, but resumed soon afterwards. In 1919, the federal Liberal party selected William Lyon Mackenzie King, an Ontario-based former senior public official and later cabinet minister, closely associated with business, to succeed Wilfrid Laurier, and the party reaffirmed its commitment to tariff protection. In 1919, T.A. Crerar, a Liberal, resigned from the federal Union cabinet of Conservative Prime Minister Robert Borden, but to sit with eight other MPs as Independents. A general strike took place that same year in Winnipeg. A coalition of the United Farmers of Ontario, Labour and independent members formed a minority government in Ontario, and the United Farmers of Alberta decided to contest the next provincial election. In 1920, the Progressive party was formed out of what was basically a Manitoba group, led by Crerar and dedicated to parliamentary politics, and a group from Alberta led by Henry Wise Wood that was dedicated to replacing the party system with a form of occupational group representation. In the House of Commons, eleven MPs designated themselves the National Progressive party and chose Crerar as their leader.

In the general election of 1921, the Progressives elected the second-largest group with sixty-four MPs elected from Ontario, Manitoba, Saskatchewan and Alberta. The Liberals, the largest group with 116 MPs, formed Canada's first minority government. However, Wood's anti-party sentiment dominated the Progressive caucus, and the Progressive MPs refused to form the official opposition, the role falling then to the smallest group, the fifty Conservatives. The United Farmers of Alberta formed the government of Alberta that same year. Disagreement persisted among Progressive MPs between those who wished to participate in conventional party politics and those who supported the movement's objective to replace the system. By 1922, Crerar had resigned the leadership and returned to the Liberal party (eventually to be appointed to the Senate) and the federal party/movement was in disarray. In the general election of 1925, the Progressives held a crucial position in another House of minorities, but that Parliament was short-lived. After the 1926 election, the party ceased to be an important organization.

The "shades" of the Progressive party in western Canada continued to be present in federal politics. In the 1930s, some Progressives drifted into alliances that resulted in the formation of the Social Credit party and the Co-operative Commonwealth Federation, later the New Democratic party. After 1940, when John Bracken, a former Progressive premier of Manitoba assumed the leadership of the Conservative party, it was re-named the Progressive Conservative party. John Diefenbaker's leadership of the party from 1956 to 1967 and the persistent central Canadian dominance of federal Liberal leadership and government policy were responsible for the Conservatives benefiting from the populist legacy of Progressivism in western Canada for almost 40 years. However, in the 1993 election, the populist Reform party, originating and based in Alberta, was a major cause of the Conservative government's rout and the party's virtual elimination from the House of Commons. While Reform's western, populist base remained intact following the election of 1997, it did not win seats in central or eastern Canada. Hoping to establish the party beyond the West without diminishing aspects of its populist "Progressive" heritage, Reformers created the Canadian Alliance in 2000. However, that the Alliance fared little better than Reform in the election later that year is attributed in part to the limited appeal in central and eastern Canada of the social conservative aspects of the "Progressive" legacy that would involve less government involvement in social and economic policy and potentially restrictive social policies arising from initiatives and referenda.

"Property and Civil Rights in the Province." An enumerated head, section 92:13 of the *Constitution Act, 1867*, respecting the "Exclusive Powers of Provincial Legislatures" which gained primacy over the "Peace, Order, and good

Government" phrase in the preamble to section 91 as a source of residual power except in extreme national emergencies. When the Judicial Committee of the Privy Council over time made the "Peace, Order, and good Government" clause subordinate to the enumerated powers of the two levels of government—notably in sections 91 and 92—the provinces gained, because 92:13 was capable of inclusive meaning. The Supreme Court became the final judicial arbiter of the constitution in 1949, and it has since tended to sanction the federal government's use of the "Peace, Order, and good Government" and the "Trade and Commerce" (91:2) clauses in matters of "inherent national importance." See **Judicial Committee of the Privy Council**; **"Peace, Order, and good Government"**; **Supreme Court**.

Proportional representation. An electoral system by which political parties hold a percentage of seats in the legislature that approximates their percentage of the popular vote in the previous election. For example, a party that wins 40 per cent of the popular vote would invariably hold close to 40 per cent of the legislative seats under proportional representation (PR). Variants of proportional representation systems, in which electors vote for a list of party candidates in multi-member constituencies, are used in many countries.

Supporters of proportional representation argue that each party's legislative representation should reflect electoral support as accurately as possible. In multiparty systems, PR usually results in no single party winning a majority of seats and governments are subsequently formed through formal or informal coalitions of parties. Critics of proportional representation therefore argue that it legitimizes small parties—including parties of extreme views and policies representing only minor sectarian interests—and grants them disproportionate political power that can lead to legislative gridlock, and at worst a degree of civil unrest.

In Canada, the single-member constituency system with plurality win is the electoral system used in federal and provincial elections. Discussions about PR have arisen, however, because under the single-member plurality system in a multiparty system, there is usually a discrepancy—often a gross discrepancy—between the percentage of votes won and the percentage of seats subsequently held by the parties. Also, the single-member plurality system reinforces regionalism. The system disproportionately rewards parties with concentrated pockets of support over those whose support is more widely distributed. Parties that find it difficult to win seats in some parts of the country and easier elsewhere will tend to perpetuate those sectional strengths and weaknesses in legislative representation and policy preferences, to the detriment of the party system as a device for political integration.

Almost any federal election in Canada since 1921 provides evidence of these "distortions." Following the federal election of 1979, the Conservatives formed a minority government with twenty-two seats more than the Liberals, but with 4 per cent less of the popular vote. The results of the 1993 election illustrate the discrepancies and the bias towards sectionalism. The Liberal party won 60 per cent of the seats (177) with 41.3 per cent of the popular vote; the Bloc Québécois, 18.3 per cent of the seats (54) with 13.5 per cent of the vote; the Reform party, 17.6 per cent of the seats (52) with 18.7 per cent of the vote; the New Democratic party, 3.1 per cent of the seats (9) with 6.9 per cent of the vote; but the Conservatives, only 0.7 per cent of the seats (2) with 16 per cent of the vote. The

Bloc's success was due to its concentrated support in Quebec: 49 per cent of the provincial popular vote. Reform's success was based in the West, notably 52 per cent of the Alberta vote and 36 per cent of the vote in British Columbia. By contrast, the Conservative failure, apart from its low share of the vote relative to the Liberal share, resulted from the diffusion of its support relative to the other parties. Subsequent federal election results included similar "distortions" for similar reasons: for example, in 2000 the Conservatives won 4 per cent of the seats with 12 per cent of the vote while the regionally based BQ won 13 per cent of the seats with 11 per cent of the vote.

Quebec's Parti Québécois is the only party in Canada to win office whose platform included the possibility of introducing a system of proportional representation. While in opposition, it elected seven members to the provincial National Assembly (6% of the MNAs) with 23 per cent of the vote in 1970, and only six members (6%) in 1973, although it obtained 30 per cent of the vote. In 1976, it formed the government, winning 71 seats (65%) while increasing its vote to 41 per cent. In 1979, the PQ government published a green paper on the reform of Quebec's electoral system, including a discussion of PR. However, no changes were enacted, suggesting that once a party benefits from the distortions of the single-member/plurality win system, enthusiasm for PR fades. Indeed, in 1994 the PQ formed a majority government with roughly the same percentage of popular votes than the leading opposition party, the Liberals; in 1998, it was re-elected with a legislative majority although it won fewer votes than the Liberal party.

At the federal level, in 1979 the Task Force on Canadian Unity recommended the introduction of an element of proportional representation into the federal electoral system. Discussions since then on a reformed Senate have included the possibility of senatorial elections through some form of proportional representation by party lists. See **Electoral system; Single-member plurality electoral system**.

Prorogation of Parliament. The formal termination of a session of Parliament by the governor general, acting on the "advice" of the prime minister. Prorogation brings all parliamentary business to an end. Bills remaining on the Order Paper normally "die," possibly to be reintroduced as new items in a subsequent session. Because of this, sessions are frequently "adjourned" for a break, rather than prorogued. Otherwise a government motion is required to allow a bill introduced in a previous session to be re-introduced in its existing stage from the previous session. On the "advice" of the prime minister, the governor general may proclaim the dissolution of Parliament following the prorogation of any session within the five-year term of the House of Commons. However, a request for prorogation and dissolution following only a brief first session of a Parliament might, under some circumstances, result in the exercise of the Crown's prerogative to deny such a request. See **Crown prerogatives; King-Byng Dispute**.

Provincial autonomy (rights). The scope of independent, legislative competence enjoyed by the provincial legislatures in the Canadian federation under the distribution of powers outlined in the *Constitution Act, 1867* and adjudicated by the courts.

Provincial regimes have jealously guarded their rights and sought to enlarge them since Confederation. Governments of Quebec, the only predominantly francophone province, have always defended provincial rights for cultural reasons, but many anglophone provinces have also had provincial rights-oriented governments. The careers of many provincial premiers (perhaps beginning with Oliver Mowat of Ontario in the early decades of Confederation) have been constructed on opposition to the federal government. Many Alberta governments have fought provincial elections against "the feds," as though the federal government rather than other provincial parties were their electoral opponents. Federal party leaders have also come to power as proponents of provincial rights. Wilfrid Laurier in 1896, John Diefenbaker in 1957, Joe Clark in 1979, and Brian Mulroney in 1984 came to power opposing government parties long associated with centralization and insensitivity to provincial interests. Since Confederation, many federal political parties have arisen, notably in Quebec and western Canada, when the two dominant parties, the Conservatives and Liberals, have seemed indifferent to provincial interests in those parts of Canada.

Debate over provincial autonomy and rights has involved not only jurisdictional disputes but also the financial arrangements within the federation. The extensive power of taxation constitutionally granted Parliament has resulted in the exercise of so-called spending power and federal intrusions into areas of provincial jurisdiction, notably in education, health care and income maintenance. Moreover, the uneven distribution of resources among the provinces makes the taxation power of some provinces less valuable in revenue yield than others. This leads to some provincial support for federal spending power, especially among poorer provinces that benefit from federal unconditional equalization grants and regional development programs in a variety of policy fields. Thus provincial governments frequently disagree when attempting to forge a united position against "intrusive" activity of the federal government. See **Division (distribution) of powers; Federal-provincial tax-sharing agreements (fiscal federalism); Judicial Committee of the Privy Council (JCPC); Supreme Court.**

Provincial governments (legislatures). Autonomous subnational units in the federal union of Canada under the *Constitution Act, 1867* and subsequently amended. The Act describes the provincial constitutions and distributes legislative powers between the provincial legislatures and the federal Parliament. The constitutional statutes of provinces which joined Confederation after 1867 are listed in a Schedule to the *Constitution Act, 1982*, which also grants provinces the right to amend their constitutions except respecting the federal office of lieutenant-governor (s.45; originally 92:1 of the Act of 1867). Judicial rulings on federal-provincial disputes determines respective areas of federal and provincial jurisdiction under the Act. Since 1982, the actions of provincial legislatures and administrations, as well as Parliament, have also been tested against the entrenched Canadian Charter of Rights and Freedoms.

Proponents of Confederation in the United Province of Canada agreed to a federal state in part to gain support among Maritime colonies for a union. Though initially intended to be inferior to Parliament, the provincial legislatures acquired equal constitutional status with the federal parliament through judicial review. The principle of constitutional equality among provinces has also been established, although the special character of Quebec was recognized in special obligations respecting minority language and educational rights in that province, the recognition of the Civil Code and the minimum requirement of three justices from Quebec on the Supreme Court, and opting-out provisions with compensation which Quebec alone exercised regarding some federal programs.

The argument for provincial equality and the contrary argument for Quebec's distinctiveness are both based on versions of Confederation as a compact. In one version, the provinces are said to be inheritors of the role of the colonies who were original parties to Confederation; in the second, Confederation is said to have been a compact between two founding cultural groups, the English and the French. The general constitutional amending formula adopted with the consent of all legislatures except Quebec in 1982 requires a resolution of Parliament (not necessarily with Senate support) and of two-thirds of provincial legislatures having at least 50 per cent of the population of all the provinces, with provisions for provincial dissent and exclusion with compensation in certain cases. Thus, provincial unanimity on constitutional change is not required in all cases and Quebec does not possess a constitutional veto. Constitutional negotiations since 1982, designed to accommodate Quebec to the patriated constitution, have foundered largely on constitutionally defining Quebec's distinctiveness and a role for its legislature and government respecting Quebec as a distinct society.

See various entries related to the constitution and constitutional development, and federalism, including judicial review, and federal-provincial fiscal arrangements. See also **Provincial autonomy (rights)**.

Public Accounts Committee. A standing committee of the House of Commons that is responsible for post-auditing government expenditures, primarily through an examination of the auditor general's annual report to Parliament. Provincial legislatures have committees to perform a comparable task.

As in other House of Commons committees, membership is roughly proportional to party representation in the House, but unlike other parliamentary committees, an opposition member of parliament chairs this committee. In addition, the auditor general and the auditor general's staff assist the committee in its post-audit scrutiny. The auditor general's report and presentation to the committee are often more effective in attracting public attention than the committee's own report later to the House. The auditor general is an independent officer of Parliament, while the committee's activity is naturally partisan. The auditor general's report is often the subject of parliamentary questions and debate and is widely reported to the public in the mass media prior to its "study" in committee. See **Auditor General**.

Public bills. Bills introduced in a legislature either by the government or a private member that are intended to be of general application to society. Government-sponsored public bills comprise most of the legislation introduced and are referred to as government bills, while those sponsored by private members are called private members' bills. Public bills may deal with any matter that falls within the competence of the legislature, but normally only government bills may involve the expenditure of money, and revenue bills are solely the prerogative of the government. See **Legislation**; **Private member's legislation**.

Public opinion. Views of individuals reported in aggregate terms. There may be as many opinions on a given issue as there are people willing to offer one. However, views are usually "reduced" to those of "publics." For example, on the question of access to therapeutic termination of pregnancy, there is a public that is opposed to abortions, a public that supports ready access to abortions, and a public that supports restricted access. The essence of democratic governance is to respond to conflicting and competing opinions prudently and to be accountable to the public in a subsequent election.

Public opinion formation involves a complex interaction of interpersonal and impersonal networks involving family, neighbourhood and workplace acquaintances, social group leaders and the mass media of communication. Because opinions are changeable, politicians and others survey public opinion regularly on issues and personalities, either to modify a particular policy or to determine how better to alter public perceptions and obtain public support for a policy, personality or group. See **Lobby (-ist; -ing); Policy (-making; analysis; communities; instruments; public...); Polling (public opinion).**

Public service (administration). The public bureaucracy, also referred to as the civil service, which is characterized in Canada by large, well-defined hierarchical administrative units; it is staffed in large part by career officers ("civil servants") who work under an oath of secrecy. The federal public service includes several types of institutions. These are: government departments headed by deputy ministers and their assistants; several types of crown corporations; and central structures such as the Privy Council Office, the Treasury Board Secretariat, and the Public Service Commission. Regulatory agencies, such as the Canadian Radio-television and Telecommunications Commission and the Canadian Transportation Agency, are also part of the public service. Provincial public bureaucracies contain similar organizations. The scope of activity and size of the public service is so large that the term "administrative state" may be an apt description of government in Canada in addition to such terms as cabinet or parliamentary government.

Theoretically, the public service is subject to general legislative authority and specific cabinet direction in applying and enforcing current policies and developing new policies. However, because of the large size of the public service, there are concerns about its independence in terms of actual policy determination and the lack of effective cabinet control of policy implementation and financial expenditures. Since the late 1960s, the organization of the political executive—the cabinet and the Prime Minister's Office—has been designed to counterbalance the independent policy-making tendencies within the federal public service. Also, since the late 1980s, there have been concerted efforts by federal and provincial governments to restructure and reduce the size of their respective public administrations, in part to achieve efficiency and economy, but occasionally to effect an "anti-public sector" disposition of the governing party.

In carrying out administrative duties under delegated authority, public officials often exercise considerable discretion in departments and regulatory agencies. In recent years, the enactment of access-to-information and privacy legislation, including information and privacy commissioners with power to seek redress in the courts on noncompliance, and the establishment of ombudsmen in some jurisdictions, reflect recognition of the growth and power of the administrative state. In 1971, the Exchequer Court was reconstituted as the Federal Court, as a tribunal to hear appeals allowed by law from the decisions of federal agencies, boards and commissions. The courts also protect Canadians from administrative abuse through the adjudication of administrative behaviour under the Canadian Charter of Rights and Freedoms.

Until the early-twentieth century, federal politicians treated the public administration as a pork barrel with which to reward friends and supporters. As the business of government became more complex, the merit principle was introduced and eventually entrenched by the mid-century—without eliminating entirely the scope for patronage appointments and other rewards. Later reforms focused on the need for a representative bureaucracy, as recruitment and promotion led to a public service predominantly of anglophone men of European descent. Also, the policy-making echelons of the federal public administration tend to be populated by long-term residents of central Canada, even the area of the capital region itself. These factors, along with high educational attainment, gave rise to a widespread notion of the federal government as an elite institution at the senior levels, removed from the day-to-day interests and concerns of a more diverse and widespread population.

Since the 1960s, restrictions on political activity by most federal and provincial public officials have been eliminated and collective bargaining rights for public-service unions introduced. Public service unions, once virtually non-existent, are now among the largest unions in Canada. This has led to increasingly complex industrial relations in the public sector with frequent disputes involving various forms of industrial action by public employees.

Public Service Commission. The federal agency responsible to Parliament that staffs a large part of the federal public service under the *Public Service Employment Act, 1967* with the objective of maintaining a competent public service of qualified people.

The Commission, appointed by the governor-in-council, or cabinet, recruits people to, and promotes and dismisses people within the public service. In practice, the Commission sets the rules for staffing to enforce the merit principle and delegates authority for most appointments to departments. It hears appeals on staffing decisions, investigates and rules on allegations of discrimination and political partisanship, and operates staff development programs. The creation of its predecessor, the Civil Service Commission, in 1908 introduced the principle of merit into a service that had been run on a partisan patronage basis. Comparable commissions exist in all the provinces.

The Public Service Commission's jurisdiction does not include many senior civil servants who hold their positions at the "pleasure" of the government-of-the-day, and many federal departments, crown corporations and other government bodies have the authority to hire personnel themselves. Also, the Treasury Board, which represents management in the negotiation and administration of collective agreements with civil servants, is responsible for some personnel management policy and for administrative efficiency. See **Public service (administration)**.

Q

Quasi-judicial decisions. Decisions made within the public administration based on discretionary power held under delegated legislative authority, and that have the force of law. Judicial decisions in the courts are based on law, including strict observance of rules of evidence and procedure. Quasi-judicial decisions are based on considerations of public policy and the public interest.

The chief advantage of quasi-judicial power is the flexibility possessed by expert decision makers in the administration of complex regulatory matters. Thus, administrative boards, agencies and commissions, assisted by their staffs, make policy, gather evidence on its implementation and adjudicate on cases under the policy. Such power raises concerns regarding arbitrariness and threats to the rule of law. The legislatures, ombudsmen, various parliamentary commissioners and the courts remain, however, as overseers of the administrative process and the exercise of quasi-judicial power. See **Canadian Charter of Rights and Freedoms (1982)**; **Delegated power; Regulatory agencies (regulations)**; **Rule of law.**

Quebec Act, 1774 (U.K.). A British Act pertaining to the ceded French colony of Quebec. The Act defined the territory of the conquered colony and the rights of its subjects. It extended the western boundaries to include land between the Ohio and Mississippi Rivers, granted freedom of worship to Roman Catholics, and sanctioned the retention of French civil law until altered by the colony. Criminal law remained British.

The Royal Proclamation of 1763 had called for the establishment of a legislative assembly (in contemporary terms, an elected lower house). However, the political assertiveness of colonial assemblies to the south, coupled with doubt that the French majority in Quebec wanted an assembly, led instead to a provision in the Act for only an appointed legislative council (in contemporary terms, an appointed upper house) The *Quebec Act* thus opposed the trend toward representative government in British North America.

On the other hand, the tolerance of the Act towards French-Canadian society was both culturally and politically astute. When the American Revolution took place a short time after its enactment, Quebeckers remained loyal, or at least neutral during the Revolution. The westward expansion of Quebec under the Act was itself a threat to American expansion. The influx of loyalists to Quebec (including areas now in Ontario) during and after the Revolution led to the replacement of the *Quebec Act* with the *Constitutional Act* in 1791. See **Constitutional Act, 1791 (U.K.).**

Quebec Conference (Resolutions) (1864). A conference of colonial representatives from Canada, Nova Scotia, New Brunswick, Prince Edward Island and Newfoundland. It endorsed the principle, agreed upon a few months earlier at Charlottetown, of a federal rather than a unitary union of all the colonies under the Crown. As a counterweight to centripetal forces, the new constitution would have a strong bicameral Parliament and inferior provincial legislatures. The

Conference, which lasted only three weeks, resulted in seventy-two resolutions outlining such a union, including a resolution to obtain "the sanction of the Imperial and Local Parliaments" for the union.

The consensus achieved at Quebec, however, did not last. Only the Canadian legislature approved the resolutions and requested the British government to implement them. Prince Edward Island and Newfoundland repudiated the proposed union. The government of New Brunswick was defeated on the question in an election, and the Nova Scotia government simply reaffirmed its support for Maritime union, to avoid a similar fate. The Canadians, however, convinced the British government of the value of the union, which in turn applied pressure to bring about partial Maritime approval and participation. At a conference in London in 1866-67 attended by delegates from Canada, New Brunswick and Nova Scotia, the Quebec Resolutions were revised and some substituted. The London resolutions were the basis for the *British North America Act*, which came into effect on July 1, 1867—since 1982, the *Constitution Act*—Canada's fundamental constitutional statute.

Quebec Protestant School Boards Case (*A.-G. Quebec v. Quebec Association of Protestant School Boards* [1984]). A leading decision of the Supreme Court among several regarding minority-language education rights under the Canadian Charter of Rights and Freedoms, enacted two years earlier. This decision declared elements of Quebec's Charter of the French Language that restricted access by anglophones to primary and secondary school education in English, to be a violation of the Canadian Charter of Rights and Freedoms ("Minority Language Educational Rights" [s.23]) that could not be "saved" by section 1 ("subject only to…reasonable limits…as can be demonstrably justified in a free and democratic society"). The legislative override (the "notwithstanding" or "*non obstante*") clause (s.33) cannot be used regarding section 23.

Provisions in the Canadian Charter of Rights and Freedoms respecting minority-language education rights qualified provincial jurisdiction in education (*Constitution Act, 1867*, s.93) and were a direct challenge to the Quebec language law. And while the Charter's immediate effect was to deny the Quebec law its effectiveness, it also permitted francophone minorities elsewhere to seek remedial court action in their respective provinces under enforcement section 24. Thus the courts have also ruled on specific government obligations respecting minority-language education rights (*Marchand v. Simcoe Board of Education* [Ontario, 1986], *Lavoie v. Nova Scotia* [1988] and *Mahé v. Alberta* [1990]). In the latter case, the Supreme Court of Canada held unanimously that section 23 should be broadly interpreted because its purpose was to prevent the assimilation of minority-language groups, anglophones in Quebec and francophones elsewhere. See **Canadian Charter of Rights and Freedoms (1982); Charter of the French Language (Quebec); Language rights; Remedial decree (litigation).**

Quebec sign law. A reference to provisions of Quebec's Charter of the French Language regarding languages used on commercial signs. Quebec's sign law was the subject of criticism as a violation of freedom-of-expression rights in the Canadian Charter of Rights and Freedoms (s.2). The Supreme Court of Canada ruled that the objective of "marked predominance" of one language over others was valid, but not through an outright prohibition of signs in languages other than French (*Quebec v. Ford* [1988]).

The provincial government created a Canada-wide political controversy when it subsequently invoked the notwithstanding clause of the Charter (s.33) to protect from further Charter challenges a revised, but still discriminatory version of its sign law allowing only the French language on outdoor signs. In 1993, however, the law was further amended to allow signs in other languages along with French as the predominant language. Court rulings in Quebec have since sustained those provisions against appeals that the French language was sufficiently secure in Quebec to obviate the necessity of the law. See **Canadian Charter of Rights and Freedoms (1982)**; **Charter of the French Language (Quebec)**; **Language rights**.

Queen, the. See **Crown**; **Sovereign, the**.

Question period. The occasion in the proceedings of the legislature when the government is required to respond to oral and written questions from private members, usually opposition legislators. The time devoted to questions varies in legislatures. In the House of Commons, for example, there is a daily forty-five-minute period for oral questions asked without notice, while responses to written or starred questions are tabled and printed in Hansard.

The oral question period often highlights dramatically the principle of responsible government, or executive accountability to the legislature. Both opposition members and government ministers prepare carefully for the event, which is supposed to focus on urgent matters and elicit information from the government. The opposition's objective is to embarrass the government by forcing it to respond to interrogatory charges defined on the opposition's terms. The government's objective, by contrast, is to respond succinctly without appearing too disdainful. No debate is permitted during the period, but the "supplementary questions" allow a member an opportunity to cross-examine a minister who has evaded the question or to enter a brief retort in Hansard. The Speaker occasionally recognizes a government backbencher who may put a soft, "planted" question to a minister or pursue some constituency interest. In the first case, the minister's response can effectively be a ministerial announcement that, as a response to a question, precludes opposition replies.

The effectiveness of question period for the opposition is measured by the amount of interest aroused in the press gallery on particular questions. Dramatic exchanges between government and opposition are well suited to the requirement of television news for personality conflicts and brief "sound bites." Following question period, the mass media pursue some matters in interviews with government and opposition MPs during "scrums" in the lobbies. If the public show an interest in a certain line of questioning, the opposition will continue its attack on the government in subsequent question periods, for which the relevant minister will have senior civil servants prepare responses for anticipated questions.

The question period is one of few occasions in a legislature when the opposition should have a tactical advantage over the government. While the questions may elicit information, the potential loser in the exchange is the government if ministers seem to be evasive or ignorant. With the support of the senior officials, however, a minister should be well prepared for questions from an opposition member who has presumably much less access to information. Question period generally keeps a government attentive, and occasionally matters of ministerial or administrative recklessness are exposed.

Quiet Revolution. A popular term for the totality of events in Quebec in the 1960s, when the provincial strategy for the survival of French society changed from a traditional, conservative and defensive nationalism to a modern, aggressive nationalism, with the government of Quebec as the chief instrument of *épanouisement* and *survivance*.

The Quiet Revolution is associated in particular with the Liberal government of Jean Lesage from 1960 to 1966 and with the slogan "Maîtres chez nous." The return to office of the more conservative Union Nationale from 1966 to 1970 did not reverse the direction of change. Numerous "separatist" movements came into being, and in 1968 several merged to form the Parti Québécois under former Liberal minister René Lévesque. The Parti Québécois eventually displaced the Union Nationale. The Quiet Revolution, initially associated with wresting economic control from the anglophone minority, became a broader *nationaliste* stream with strong federalist and *indépendantiste* cross-currents.

While the Quiet Revolution led to new demands upon the federal government and applied new strains to Confederation, its effect within French society in Quebec was both dramatic and profound. These included the growth and increase in post-secondary educational institutions, including an expanded curriculum notably in business administration and the social sciences, expansion of the public sector, an intellectual renaissance in the arts, growing militancy of trade unions, and the decline of the Roman Catholic Church as a social and political force.

The federal government's response to the Quiet Revolution is associated primarily with Lester Pearson's Liberal government from 1963 to 1968 and Pierre Trudeau's first government from 1968 to 1972. The federal government acceded to Quebec's concerns about financial and administrative autonomy in the formula for contracting, or opting out of, shared-cost federal-provincial programs. It promoted constitutional reform and a policy to increase bilingualism in the federal public service and to strengthen the position of French minorities outside Quebec. The federal policy of "bilingualism and biculturalism" and co-operative federalism was, however, opposed by the *indépendantiste* element of Quebec society, seeking at a minimum enlarged provincial authority to protect French language and culture through collective legislative action in Quebec and at a maximum the independence of Quebec. See **Bilingualism and biculturalism; Parti Québécois (PQ)**.

Quorum. A specific number of members of a legislative body required to be present before it can meet and conduct business. In the legislatures and their committees, the government party whip and deputy whips are responsible for ensuring that enough government members are available to establish a quorum should the opposition try to embarrass the government by challenging the existence of a quorum and forcing the legislature or committee to adjourn. The quorum for Parliament established under the *Constitution Act* is twenty members for the House of Commons, including the Speaker (s.48), and fifteen senators including the Speaker for the Senate (s.35).

R

Racism. The belief that differences among people in ability and character are rooted in "racial" or ethnic origins, and that some races are therefore superior to others; or more generally, prejudice against persons because of their "racial" or ethnic background. Racism is explicitly prohibited under the Canadian Charter of Rights and Freedoms and various federal and provincial human rights Acts, with commissions to deal with complaints of racial and other forms of discrimination. Various private-sector groups also exist to combat racism.

Historically, racism in Canadian politics was associated with discriminatory treatment by European whites, first, of Native Peoples and later people of African and Asian origins, but also within the European population, with the Anglo-Saxon and Protestant bigotry of the Orange Order directed against francophones and Catholics, as well as immigrants from central and eastern Europe. Racist movements in this century include the Klu Klux Klan in Saskatchewan in the 1920s, which promoted the traditional views of the Orange Order (selective immigration, Protestantism, and "British" patriotism), and fascist organizations in the 1930s inspired by the contemporary movements in Germany and Italy. The best known, but still small, indigenous fascist movement was the National Social Christian Party in Quebec. Jews were the object of fascist hatred in the 1930s, when "casual" intolerance towards Jews and nativism generally was widespread. Casualness about anti-Semitism and electoral concerns to maintain the favour of voters in the tradition-bound Catholic society of Quebec led Liberal Prime Minister William Lyon Mackenzie King's government to adopt a studied indifference to the plight of Jewish refugees in Europe. After war was declared in 1939, fascist movements were suppressed; approximately 1,500 Germans, German Canadians, Italians, and Italian Canadians were interned. At the same time, however, although there appeared to be no "fifth-column" organizations among Canadians of Japanese origins, approximately 20,000 such Canadians on the west coast were dispossessed of their property and transported to detention camps in the interior of British Columbia.

Immigration from the Caribbean region has become significant since the 1970s and, in the 1980s, for the first time Asia ranked ahead of Europe as an origin of immigrants. As a result, contemporary political action against racism in Canada has been occasioned by tensions arising from the increased cosmopolitanism of Canadian society, especially in large urban areas. Action includes the creation of a framework of law and commissions to prohibit and combat racism, the constitutional requirement for "the preservation and enhancement of the multicultural heritage of Canadians" (Canadian Charter of Rights and Freedoms, s.27), the negotiation of constitutional status, including self-government, for Native Peoples, and formal apologies with or without compensation to groups such as Canadians of Japanese origin who suffered past official mistreatment. The Canadian Charter of Rights and Freedoms makes racial and other forms of discrimination illegal, and allows for affirmative action programs designed to improve conditions of individuals or groups disadvantaged because of race and other designated conditions (s.15). The federal Criminal Code has also been amended to prohibit the dissemination of hate literature.

Political debate on the increasing ethnic and racial diversity of the Canadian population covers a wide spectrum of issues and opinion. Debate over immigration and refugee policy can engender views at least tinged with racist attitudes. However, some Canadians are genuinely concerned that traditions related to the Anglo-French heritage are threatened with extinction in the name of "inclusiveness." See **Multiculturalism**.

Radio-Canada. The French-language section of the Canadian Broadcasting Corporation, a federal crown corporation, with production facilities located primarily in Montreal.

French-language radio and television services are also available in Quebec and selectively elsewhere in Canada on private networks centred in Quebec (TVA), provincial public broadcasters (Radio-Québec and TVOntario), an international francophone satellite service on cable (TV5), specialty channels on cable (for example, the House of Commons, the Quebec National Assembly in Quebec, sports, weather, and popular music), and community stations, including a designated local community channel on cable-distribution systems. See **Canadian Broadcasting Corporation (Radio-Canada; CBC)**.

Radio Reference Case (1932). See **Treaty power**.

Ralliement des créditistes. The Quebec section of the federal Social Credit party, which experienced its greatest electoral successes in the 1960s and outlived the western-based anglophone section of the federal party electorally. The party grew increasingly weaker during the 1970s, finally failing to win a seat in the 1980 election. Despite national pretensions, the federal Social Credit party in the 1970s was the Quebec organization.

Social Credit emerged in Quebec in the 1940s as the Union des électeurs. In 1962, when Social Credit could elect only two members of parliament each from British Columbia and Alberta, the Ralliement (led by Réal Caouette) won twenty-six seats in Quebec, second in the province to the Liberals' thirty-five. Like Social Credit earlier in the West, the Ralliement under Caouette was an indigenous and populist movement, responding to the economic and social grievances among a rural and small-town population. The existence of the *créditiste* MPs from Quebec was based largely on their personal appeal and the weakness of the Conservative and New Democratic parties in Quebec as alternatives to the dominant Liberal party.

After 1962, friction developed not unexpectedly between the Quebec and western sections of the federal party, whose formal leader was one of the western MPs. Many of the western and Quebec MPs were unilingual English- and French-speakers, respectively. Eventually, the federal Conservative party displaced the Social Credit party in the West, leaving the Ralliement as the major electoral force in the party. The Ralliement alternated between alliance and separation from the few remaining anglophone Social Crediters. In 1979, under Fabien Roy, the party won six seats with 14 per cent of the popular vote in Quebec. In 1980, it gained 5 per cent of the popular vote in Quebec and elected no candidate. See **Populism**; **Social Credit party**; **Third parties (political)**.

Ratification. The power to accept or reject agreements reached by others, usually a legislative power over the executive. Failure to vote on ratification implies defeat of the agreement.

Since 1982, various amending procedures in the Canadian constitution each required some degree of legislative ratification. In 1990, the proposed constitutional Meech Lake Accord failed for want of unanimous approval of the eleven legislatures. Support voted earlier in the Newfoundland legislature was later rescinded and no vote took place subsequently there or in the Manitoba legislature before the deadline for ratification. The constitutional Charlottetown Accord of 1992 included proposals for the Senate to ratify appointments of the federal government such as governor of the Bank of Canada and the heads of selected cultural institutions and regulatory agencies. The Accord was defeated in a country-wide referendum (opposed by a national majority of voters and by six provincial majorities, including Quebec), effectively a ratification procedure, although it was not clear before the vote how the results would be interpreted by the federal and provincial governments.

Treaty-making power in Canada, including ratification, is an executive prerogative. However, a wise political strategy includes parliamentary discussion and approval, especially if the treaty, such as the Canada-United States Free Trade Agreement of 1989, is controversial. The implementation of treaties or other international agreements may involve federal or provincial legislation. For example, the federal Conservative government of John Diefenbaker negotiated and signed the Columbia River Treaty with the United States in 1960 without an explicit agreement with the government of British Columbia. As a result, the treaty could not be implemented until the successor Liberal government of Lester Pearson reached an agreement with BC and negotiated a protocol with the United States. In this case, the federal government also allowed a parliamentary committee to hear witnesses both for and against the treaty before approving it.

Readings. Three stages of legislative approval required for the passage of bills. The parliamentary tradition of three readings is intended to ensure careful consideration of legislation. See **Legislation**.

Recall. A device by which electors can remove someone from elective office during their term of office. The recall is associated with the delegate theory of representation, to ensure that legislators, once elected, faithfully represent constituents' interests and views.

Recall was supported particularly by the various provincial United Farmers parties, the Progressive movement, and the Social Credit party in the early twentieth century. Manitoba experimented with recall, and Alberta had a *Recall Act* until 1937, when, with the Social Credit premier experiencing a recall movement in his own constituency, the government had the legislature rescind the legislation.

British Columbia allows for recall, but the requirements are complex: a member must have been in provincial office for eighteen months after the election, and 40 percent of voters who were eligible to vote earlier and remain eligible must petition within a sixty-day period, with spending limits on subsequent campaigns.

While ostensibly designed to hold legislators accountable to their constituents, there are concerns that recall campaigns could be mounted by well-organized and financed special interests, that minority legislatures in particular would be particularly susceptible to further instability, and that the principle of accountability so clearly established through disciplined parties would be weakened. See **Delegate theory of representation**.

Reciprocity. A term used in the nineteenth and early-twentieth centuries to describe free trade, the elimination of protective tariffs, customs duties and other restraints on trade between countries.

The termination by the United States of a reciprocity agreement between the British North American colonies and the United States respecting primary products in 1866 was an economic encouragement for Confederation. The issue of protection versus free trade traditionally distinguished the federal Conservatives from the federal Liberals, although the differences were sometimes more symbolic than real. The Conservatives were associated with protection largely as a result of the National Policy under John A. Macdonald in the 1880s. The Liberals at that time and later were associated with reciprocity and free trade, and supported a limited agreement with the United States that resulted in electoral defeat in 1911. Reciprocity was popular in western Canada, where protective measures against imports from the United States were seen to benefit Canadian business interests in central Canada to the detriment of western consumers.

The "reciprocity issue" was renewed when the federal government negotiated a free-trade agreement first with the United States in the late-1980s and then with the US and Mexico in the early 1990s. On these agreements, the traditional party roles were reversed. A Conservative government negotiated the agreements and the Liberal opposition strenuously opposed the Canada-US Free Trade Agreement, and less so the subsequent North American Free Trade Agreement. The regional and national arguments generally remained constant in the 1911 and 1988 elections. However, an important difference was the forceful opposition of the business elite to reciprocity in the earlier period, but its enthusiastic support for free trade in the later period. In the early-twentieth century, Britain was the major source of foreign investment in the Canadian economy, largely portfolio investment, or loans; by the late-twentieth century, most foreign investment was American and involved equity, or ownership, of Canadian businesses. See **Canada-United States Free Trade Agreement (1989)**; **North American Free Trade Agreement (NAFTA) (1992)**.

Reconstruction party. A political party created in 1935 by H. H. Stevens, formerly a prominent minister in Prime Minister R. B. Bennett's Conservative government. Stevens was concerned about the level of profits being made during the depression, especially by retail stores and packing houses. His frequent attacks on business when in cabinet resulted in rebukes from the prime minister. Stevens resigned from the cabinet and was appointed to head the Royal Commission on

Price Spreads and Mass Buying. Later, when Prime Minister Bennett seemed reluctant to deal with the royal commission's recommendations for coping with unfair competition and profiteering, Stevens resigned from the party and formed the Reconstruction party—whose platform comprised the recommendations of his royal commission.

The party contested only the election of 1935, when it received 8.7 per cent of the popular vote—almost as many votes as the Co-operative Commonwealth Federation (CCF) and twice as many votes as the Social Credit party (both of which were also contesting a federal election for the first time). The party, however, won only one seat, Stevens', while the CCF won seven seats and the Social Credit, seventeen. The fate of the Reconstruction party demonstrates the bias of the electoral system against parties with diffused national support. The party had won over 10 per cent of the vote in each of Nova Scotia, New Brunswick and Ontario, but failed to win any seats in those provinces. See **Electoral system; Fragment (splinter) parties; Single-member plurality electoral system**.

Recorded (standing) vote. A division of the legislature on a question called by the Speaker, requested by a minimum number of legislators as provided in the Standing Orders, or rules, of the legislature.

In recorded votes in the House of Commons, members rise when the Speaker calls first for those in support of, and then opposition to, the question, and resume their seats when the clerk calls their name for the printed record in Hansard. Because of the disciplined party system, members of a party caucus almost always rise unanimously in their support or opposition to the question. Following the division, the clerk announces the result. Again, given the disciplined party system in Canadian legislatures, the outcomes are usually predictable.

The process is time-consuming and therefore most questions are decided by a voice vote with the Speaker declaring the government position to have carried. Recorded votes are taken on legislation considered important by opposition parties, to prolong debate and bring public attention to the question. In rare instances of free votes, that is, when the party whips are relaxed, standing votes are recorded, first in support and then in opposition to the question, by rows, first to one side of the Speaker and then to the other. Voting by electronic means was one of several reforms to these procedures discussed by MPs after the 2000 election.

Red Tory (-ism). A description of those whose sympathy for collectivist public policy associated with state intervention in the economy and society seems to be based, not on liberal notions of equity or the egalitarian values of social democracy, but on a traditional conservative or Tory value of obligation inherent in a hierarchical society which is necessary for the preservation of the social order.

The concept of Red Toryism was popularized in the 1960s following publication of George Grant's *Lament for a Nation* (Toronto: McClelland and Stewart, 1965), a polemic on the disintegrative influence of North American liberalism on traditional societies and their values. Academics and others subsequently argued whether the existence of a "Tory tinge" in English-Canadian political tradition, combined with the traditional collectivism of French society, made the political culture of Canada fundamentally or only superficially different from that of the United States. The Tory values of collectivism are alleged to be responsible for the greater legitimacy of the political left and the relative weakness of market-oriented individualism in Canada compared to the US.

Since Confederation, both Liberal and Conservative governments in Canada have generally introduced government programs involving state enterprise and regulation of the economy, and major redistributive social programs. The failure of the generally anti-government and social conservative Reform party to entice the Conservative party into a merger to "unite the right" in 1999-2000 might in part reflect differences between social conservatives and traditional conservatives. See **Class cleavage**; **Political culture**; **Redistributive policy**.

Redistribution (electoral...of seats). The periodic redrawing of federal and provincial constituency boundaries to take into account population growth and shifts that have taken place since the previous redistribution. Redistribution takes place every decade and usually results in the creation of additional constituencies, the reduction of seats in some parts of a jurisdiction, and an increase elsewhere. The process is therefore replete with territorial and partisan political significance and potential for political conflict.

The courts have also become involved in disputes over electoral constituency boundaries in several provinces. For some people, section 3 of the Canadian Charter of Rights and Freedoms would guarantee voter equality against malapportionment—that is, that constituencies should have approximately the same number of voters regardless of traditional considerations of geography and community attachments. The Supreme Court of Canada divided 6-3 on an appeal of the Saskatchewan Court of Appeal's rejection of nonpopulation considerations in the province's electoral boundaries legislation (Reference re Saskatchewan Electoral Boundaries [1991]). The majority on the Supreme Court sustained Saskatchewan's legislation that included a balance of population and nonpopulation factors (distinct community interests: minority representation, cultural and group identity) that achieved "effective representation" in drawing constituency boundaries. Dissenting justices on the Supreme Court did not contest the recognition of nonpopulation factors, but opposed the Saskatchewan legislation because it premised redistribution on rural overrepresentation and urban underrepresentation rather than on voter equality. They held that voter equality should be mandated in law, leaving those responsible for drawing the boundaries to limit the application of the principle within reason. See *Electoral Boundaries Readjustment Act* (**redistribution**).

Redistributive policy. Public policy designed either to re-allocate wealth on an egalitarian basis (for example, in a progressive system of taxation) or to minimize its importance in obtaining a particular benefit (for example, public education or health care). Redistributive issues are class-related, with supporters of redistribution on the left of the class cleavage, and those opposing redistribution on the right.

Debate in the twentieth century, and especially since the economic depression of the 1930s, has focused on the role of the state or public sector in appropriating private wealth for reinvestment as "social capital" and regulating the market economy to achieve basic standards of human welfare, reasonable living and working conditions. One means of doing this is through the tax system, while others include the statutory power of government to nationalize certain industries or to create public corporations to compete with private companies, to regulate business activity through regulatory bodies, and to manage the economy generally through monetary as well as fiscal policies.

By the end of the twentieth century, serious criticism had developed concerning the size of government involvement at all levels in the Canadian economy. This criticism was particularly powerful because it included left-wing critics who conceded that there was no necessary connection between the increased size and activity of the public sector since the Second World War and the distribution of personal wealth in society. Discussion of poverty in Canada has traditionally focussed on territory and "have-not" regions. Since the 1990s, attention has also focussed on population groups such as Native Peoples, the elderly, and the young, notably women and children in single-head families. See **Class cleavage**.

Reference case (constitutional). A judicial decision on the constitutionality of legislation or proposed legislative action referred to a provincial court of appeal by a provincial government or to the Supreme Court of Canada by the federal government. Provincial governments can appeal provincial reference cases to the Supreme Court of Canada.

The reference procedure is used variously by governments to transform debate on policy to debate on law, perhaps to evade political responsibility, to confer constitutional legitimacy on government policy, or to deny constitutional legitimacy to a policy it opposed.

An important and recent federal reference to the Supreme Court of Canada concerned the ability of a province to secede unilaterally from Confederation and the position of international law on the matter (Secession Reference, 1998). Other examples of important federal references include the Labour Convention Reference (1937) on federal "new deal" legislation, the Alberta Press Bill Reference (1938) on provincial Social Credit legislation, the Anti-Inflation Board Case (1976) on federal wage and price control legislation, on the ability of Parliament alone to amend the Senate (1979) and of the federal government to seek patriation of the constitution with limited provincial support (1981). The federal government also used the reference procedure with respect to negotiating offshore mineral rights with the provinces.

A recent example of provincial use of the reference involved the Supreme Court's confirmation in 2000 of the constitutionality of federal gun control legislation. The Alberta government had appealed the decision of the province's Court of Appeal upholding the federal legislation, and was joined in its unsuccessful appeal to the Supreme Court as intervenors by several other provincial and territorial governments as well as private parties. It could be said that the provincial and territorial governments knew Alberta's case was weak, but that the reference procedure was used to satisfy local public opinion that they had opposed the federal legislation as much as possible. See some of the reference cases mentioned above in other entries; also, **Canadian Charter of Rights and Freedoms (1982); Judicial Committee of the Privy Council (JCPC); Judicial review (interpretive; non-interpretive); Supreme Court.**

Referendum. A means by which a policy, constitutional question, or proposed legislation can be put to electors to register their approval or disapproval. This direct-democracy device runs counter to the principle of responsible government, with the political executive, or government-of-the-day, accountable to a representative legislature for all public policy.

In the United States, whose constitution enshrines separation of powers rather than responsible government, many state legislatures and municipal councils use referendums to settle policy and constitutional questions; and citizens have the right to petition for a referendum on a legislative enactment or on the failure to enact legislation. The popular demand for a referendum is called an initiative. In Canada, British Columbia provides for initiatives that, if successful, require government legislation or a referendum.

Canadians have only limited experience with country-wide referendums. The Progressive party in the early twentieth century supported the institution of the referendum in the American manner, and currently the Canadian Alliance, in the populist Progressive tradition, favours referendums and initiatives. Three national referendums have been held in Canada, in 1898, 1942, and 1992 (under enabling legislation), on prohibition, conscription and constitutional reform. In the referendum in 1942—actually defined as a plebiscite—the federal Liberal government of William Lyon Mackenzie King sought support to be relieved of its anti-conscription election pledge two years earlier. A seriously divisive issue, the referendum was designed to satisfy pro-conscription Canadians (predominantly anglophones), without necessarily committing the government to conscription, thus allaying the fears of anti-conscription Canadians (including most francophones). The referendum on the constitutional Charlottetown Accord in 1992, though advisory to the federal and provincial governments, was held in view of widespread criticism of the elitist nature of constitutional negotiations that led to the ill-fated Meech Lake Accord of 1987 and the indication earlier that Quebec's Liberal government would hold a provincial referendum on Quebec's future in Confederation.

Although the referendum in 1992 was the first country-wide vote on constitutional change, there had been earlier provincial experiences. Referendums were held in Newfoundland in 1949 on its future, including union with Canada. With different options proposed, Newfoundlanders barely rejected Confederation in the first referendum and accepted it in the second. In 1980, Quebeckers defeated a Parti Québécois government referendum seeking a mandate to negotiate sovereignty association with the rest of the country and promising a further referendum on the outcome. In 1994, the PQ returned to office promising a provincial referendum on sovereignty. Quebec's enabling legislation of 1978 required the creation of two umbrella committees by members of the National Assembly to control participation and expenditures during the referendum campaign. Also in 1978, the federal Liberal government countered with legislation, which subsequently died on the Order Paper, to allow for non-binding national or provincial votes on questions related to "political and judicial institutions and processes." According to the government, the bill was designed, not in response to Quebec's proposed referendum, but as part of a constitutional amending formula should one or more provincial governments oppose an amendment. The federal legislation did not propose umbrella committees as in the Quebec legislation, but it would have restricted private spending in a campaign, placed no restrictions on federal and provincial political party involvement, and provided for partial public reimbursement to parties and registered referendum committees for expenses.

Following the criticism of the private executive process of constitutional negotiations associated with the ill-fated Meech Lake Accord, several provinces introduced legislation to allow for referendums on constitutional amendments, notably Quebec, British Columbia and Alberta. The federal Conservative government followed suit, essentially to grant itself the option of holding one possibly to preclude several provincial referendums on differently worded questions. Unlike the earlier legislation, the federal legislation in 1992, following a court decision which declared restrictions on non-party advertising in federal elections unconstitutional, did not include organizational or financial restrictions. The country-wide referendum on the Charlottetown Accord was held under federal law throughout Canada, except Quebec, on the same day as the Quebec provincial referendum under its law, using the same question. Alberta and British Columbia treated the federal referendum as their own.

Although there was no prior agreement on how to interpret the results on the Charlottetown Accord, it appeared that the provincial governments would accept the results in their respective provinces. In the event, the Accord was clearly rejected: by a country-wide majority of voters (55.4%) and by a majority of voters in all provinces except New Brunswick, Newfoundland, Prince Edward Island, Ontario (where 49.8% voted "yes"), and the territories. Following the campaign, several criticisms of the referendum included the difficulty of defending a comprehensive set of compromise proposals against those who selectively opposed elements of the Accord and who were not obliged to present a comprehensive alternative, the tendency of some voters to treat the referendum as a "mid-term" vote of confidence in their federal and provincial political leadership, and the prospect of political leaders being less prepared in the future to compromise on constitutional matters that would be subject to a popular vote.

Reform party. A social conservative populist movement party founded in Winnipeg in 1987, with its primary leadership and popular support base in Alberta, but also elsewhere in western Canada and to a lesser extent in Ontario and the Maritimes. In the late-1990s, the Reform leadership under Preston Manning failed to convince the Conservatives party leadership to merge with Reform in a so-called "unite the right" strategy. In 2000, the Reform party became the Canadian Alliance party, with Manning defeated by Stockwell Day, a former Alberta cabinet minister, as the first leader.

As a movement party, Reform gave prominence to grassroots membership opinion, and the party's policies were those adopted at biennial party conventions, or Assemblies. However, as a populist party its public image was projected chiefly by the personality of Manning, and his careful articulation of deeply felt public grievances against federal policy on biculturalism (including what was felt to be Quebec's undue influence in federal government), multiculturalism and immigration; excessive and wasteful government spending, high levels of taxation, and deficit financing; a generalized and widespread public cynicism about politicians in all established parties and the disproportionate influence of so-called "special interests" relative to that of "ordinary Canadians." Like earlier populist movements originating in western Canada—and particularly the Alberta Social Credit party which was led for several decades in government by Manning's father, Ernest—the Reform party and Manning himself constituted an anti-party led by an anti-politician who would "do politics differently." Reform's proposals for parliamentary reform included such familiar populist devices as recall of legislators, binding referendums and popular initiatives.

Though created initially to articulate grievances and garner support among western Canadians, Manning's longer-term objective was for Reform to develop support in Ontario and Atlantic Canada, with little attention paid to Quebec. The party, clearly propounding western interests under the slogan, "The West wants in," won no seats in the 1988 election, but later won a federal by-election in Alberta, garnered an appointment to the Senate through an unusual election procedure in Alberta, and in the early 1990s received as much as 15 per cent support in national opinion surveys. However, most of that national support remained concentrated in western Canada among disaffected supporters of the Conservative party and government. The West had been an important base of support for the federal Conservatives since the late 1950s, but in the 1993 election, the Reform party succeeded in depriving the Conservatives of that support. With 18.7 per cent of the popular vote, the Reform party elected fifty-two seats, all but one in the West, while the Conservatives, with 16 per cent of the vote won only two seats, one each in Ontario and New Brunswick. Reform won twenty-two of Alberta's twenty-six seats with 52 per cent of the provincial vote and twenty-four of British Columbia's thirty-two seats with 36.4 per cent of that province's vote. Shortly after the election of the large parliamentary wing, the party exhibited tensions evident in other movement parties, that is, conflict among members of parliament whose legitimacy was based in their constituency elections and the leader and the extra-parliamentary wing, notably the Executive Council acting in the name of the party's Assembly. Although the Reform party formed the official opposition in 1997 in a five-party House of Commons, it did so with only 19 per cent of the popular vote and all of its sixty seats in western Canada.

Having failed to "break through" east of the Manitoba-Ontario border, Manning pursued his "unite the right" strategy, shepherding the Reform party's transformation to the Canadian Alliance, but failing to achieve a merger with the Conservative party and losing the contest for leader of the Alliance in 2000. See **Canadian Alliance party; Movement parties; Populism; Third parties (political).**

Regina Manifesto. The founding document of the Co-operative Commonwealth Federation (CCF), adopted in Regina in 1933, advocating government ownership of basic industries and economic planning to create "democratic self-government, based on economic equality."

The Manifesto declared that "the principle regulating production, distribution and exchange will be the supplying of human needs and not the making of profits. We aim to replace the present capitalist system, with its inherent injustice and inhumanity, by a social order…in which economic planning will supersede unregulated private enterprise and competition…." The document asserted that no CCF government would "rest content" until it had "eradicated capitalism and put into operation the full programme of socialized planning…." The members of the League for Social Reconstruction drafted the document, and the CCF executive revised it before it was adopted by the party. In 1956, the party began to shift to a more moderate, socialist position. The Winnipeg Declaration of 1956 eschewed talk of the eradication of capitalism and emphasized government planning and regulation to pursue the party's egalitarian goals. The CCF was subsequently reorganized in 1961 as the New Democratic party. See **Co-operative Commonwealth Federation (CCF); League for Social Reconstruction; New Democratic party (NDP).**

Regional disparities. The variations in levels of natural, industrial and personal wealth in different regions of Canada. These disparities, especially as they are defined in spatial terms, have fostered the development of a powerful geographic cleavage in Canadian politics. For example, in the early half of the twentieth century in the prairie West, the combination of geographic- and class-related discontent led to the development of indigenous mass political movements. Federal-provincial tax-sharing agreements since the Second World War have been designed to "equalize" the per capita revenue of provincial governments in Canada in order to provide comparable levels of public services to the population. In 1982, federal government regional economic development policy to reduce disparities in opportunities and federal equalization payments for provincial public services were entrenched in the constitution.

Earlier, federal regional development policy included programs under the *Agricultural Rehabilitation and Rural Development Act, 1961*, the Fund for Rural Economic Development (1966), and the *Regional Incentives Development Act, 1969*. The federal and provincial governments signed comprehensive general development agreements in the 1970s to co-ordinate federal programs for the development of particular provinces and regions under the aegis then of the federal Department of Regional and Economic Expansion, later renamed Regional Industrial Expansion. From 1980 to 1984, two central agencies, the Ministry of State for Social Development and the Ministry of State for Economic and Regional Development, played key roles in regional development policies. By 2000, there were separate economic development offices for most regions, each with a regional minister responsible—the Atlantic Canada Opportunities Agency, Western Economic Diversification, Economic Development Agency of Canada for the Regions of Quebec, and Federal Economic Development Initiative for Northern Ontario. In addition, Human Resources Development Canada (HRDC), a separate federal department, oversees a multi-million dollar job-grants program.

Debate persists over federal development strategy in so-called "designated regions" as well as the HRDC's job-grants program. Apart from complaints that the programs constitute mammoth handouts for electoral purposes, there are significant policy issues: Should efforts be designed primarily for "prosperity of place" or "prosperity of people"? For example, is the commitment of public capital and the direction of private capital into low-income regions a better strategy than the promotion of labour retraining and subsequent emigration to high-productivity areas of the country? To what extent and cost should national public enterprises and regulatory agencies be compelled to sustain regional development objectives? See **Federal-provincial tax-sharing agreements (fiscal federalism); Geographic cleavage.**

Regional government. A form of local or municipal government, usually result-ing from the amalgamation and/or federation of established area municipalities. Municipal government is an area of provincial responsibility (*Constitution Act, 1867* [s.92:8]) and forms of regional municipal government may vary widely within a province. The purpose of regional government is to establish an equitable tax base and distribution of municipal public services over a wide area, while disturbing the established sense of community as little as possible. The formation of regional governments facilitated the interests of property development and other related business by eliminating or weakening small municipalities and rural townships, and establishing regional authorities with overall planning and economic development responsibilities, including public-sector investment in infrastructure.

Regionalism. A term used objectively to indicate distinctive areas within a larger spatial unit, and normatively to indicate a positive or negative impact of such distinctiveness in the larger unit. In Canada, for example, the country is divided into several regions for purposes of representation in the Senate under the *Constitution Act*; the provinces are autonomous political units in the federal state which may individually or collectively constitute regions; and several provinces contain regional municipalities. On a normative level, governments have sought to overcome socio-economic regional disparities, while in cultural terms region-alism has tended to be viewed as a positive force. See **Cultural duality**; **Geographic cleavage**; **Political culture**; **Regional disparities**.

Regulation 17 (Ontario, 1913). A provincial regulation which severely restricted the use of the French language in Ontario's public schools, making English effec-tively the only language of instruction after Year Three. This anti-French measure was particularly objectionable because there were sizeable French communities in the province, especially in the Ottawa Valley along the Ontario-Quebec border, including Canada's capital city. The dispute over Regulation 17 was one of several disputes in the late-nineteenth and early-twentieth centuries over minority rights in education which were "protected" in the *British North America Act, 1867* (s.93) (since 1982, the *Constitution Act*) but had been under attack since passage of the *Public Schools Act* in Manitoba in 1890. The *Constitution Act* addresses Protestant and Roman Catholic minority rights in education. However, the Canadian Charter of Rights and Freedoms of 1982 includes educational rights defined in terms of English and French linguistic minority populations in the provinces (s.23). See **Language rights**; **Manitoba schools question (and French language rights, 1890)**; **Quebec Protestant School Boards Case (*A.G. Quebec v. Quebec Association of Protestant School Boards* [1984])**.

Regulatory agencies (regulations). Public bodies established and operated under authority delegated by a particular statute to establish, supervise and administer public policy. Enabling legislation usually states the intent of public policy in broad terms, leaving it to the agency to formulate specific policy in the form of regulations, or subordinate legislation.

A regulation or order enacted by a regulatory agency has the force of law. Thus, some agencies sit as courts of record, examining witnesses under oath, compelling the production of papers and enforcing the agencies' orders. Federal agencies in important policy fields include the Canadian Radio-television and Telecommunications Commission, the Canadian Transportation Agency and the National Energy Board. A relatively minor agency in terms of policy fields, but one that attracts considerable public attention is the National Parole Board. Parliament has a joint Senate-House committee on the scrutiny of regulations to examine the subordinate legislation of federal regulatory agencies. However, the committee cannot examine fully the output of the regulatory apparatus of the federal executive and administration.

The delegated power which regulatory agencies possess is quasi-judicial— that is, decisions are based on considerations of public policy and public interest by an agency which combines executive, legislative, administrative and adjudicative functions. The fact that agencies can establish and enforce regulations, and exercise quasi-judicial functions, creates considerable scope for abuse of delegated power. Particular statutes set out the right of appeal to the courts or the cabinet of the decisions of each regulatory agency. The procedures of regulatory agencies are subject to court challenge under the Canadian Charter of Rights and Freedoms. For example, in a case involving the determination of refugee status, the Supreme Court ruled that "utilitarian considerations" and "administrative convenience" of the Immigration and Refugee Board were insufficient grounds, according to "principles of fundamental justice," on which to deny "the right to life, liberty and security of the person" (s.7), in this case the right to an oral hearing respecting a refugee claimant (*Singh v. Minister of Employment and Immigration* [1985]). See **Delegated power; Quasi-judicial decisions; Rule of law; Singh Case (*Re Singh and Minister of Employment and Immigration* [1985]).**

Remedial decree (litigation). Action in the courts (litigation) and judicial rulings (decrees) that impose obligations on governments to achieve a remedy for the denial or infringement of a constitutional right protected by the Canadian Charter of Rights and Freedoms.

The effect of such litigation and decrees is the judicial alteration of public policy and thereby an active political and social role for judges. In addition to the power of judicial nullification of legislation that conflicts with the constitution in the *Constitution Act, 1982* (s.52:1), the Charter grants courts the power to remedy an infringement or denial of a guaranteed right or freedom as the court "considers appropriate and just in the circumstances" (s.24:1). Thus, judges can impose obligations on relevant public authorities regarding public policy.

Perhaps because remedial action regarding education rights has been part of the Canadian constitution since Confederation (see **Remedial legislation**), the area of public policy most affected by this form of judicial activism has been minority-language education rights guaranteed under the Charter (s.23). Courts have imposed obligations on education authorities in several provinces respecting facilities, funding and administration of French-language education (*Marchand v. Simcoe Board of Education*, Ontario, 1986; *Lavoie v. Nova Scotia*, 1988; *Mahé v. Alberta*, 1990).

Remedial litigation and decrees have also dealt with infringements or denials of equality rights under the Charter (s.15). The Supreme Court of Canada has established guidelines for reading "missing words" or additional provisions

into legislation. In some cases, the Court suspends nullification of an unconstitutional Act, to ensure that benefits of the Act are not denied and to give the relevant legislature time to amend its legislation and any ensuing regulations. This
practice has occurred, for example, in matters related to the definition of the
family law involving adoptive and natural parental rights and single-sex unions.
See **Canadian Charter of Rights and Freedoms (1982)**; **Judicial review (interpretive; non-interpretive)**; **Supreme Court**.

Remedial legislation. Legislation that the federal cabinet can introduce on its
own, or in response to a formal appeal, to protect denominational schools established in a province at the time of union. The *Constitution Act, 1867* gave
provinces the right to legislate on education (s.93). Remedial legislation, however,
represented an explicit limit on provincial rights.

Remedial legislation introduced by the federal Conservative government to
deal with the anti-French and anti-Catholic Manitoba *Public Schools* Act of 1890
failed to pass in the face of Liberal opposition and dissident Conservatives. The
Liberals nonetheless appeared to win on the issue in Quebec in the 1890s, as
defenders of provincial rights.

The Canadian Charter of Rights and Freedoms adopted in 1982 protects
the education rights of French- and English-language minorities. In 1984, the
Supreme Court struck down the provisions of Quebec's Bill 101 which restricted
access to English-language education in the province as a violation of the provincial minority-language educational rights entrenched in the Charter (s.23). In
1986, 1988 and 1990, the courts were used to assert francophone rights under
section 23 of the Charter in Ontario, Nova Scotia and Alberta, respectively. In the
1990s, following resolutions of the Newfoundland and Quebec legislatures and
Parliament, the *Constitution Act* was amended, abolishing the denominational
basis of public education in those provinces. See **Charter of the French Language
(Quebec)**; **Manitoba schools question (and French language rights, 1890)**;
**Quebec Protestant School Boards Case (*A.G. Quebec v. Quebec Association of
Protestant School Boards* [1984])**.

Renewed/Restructured federalism. Terms used in the late-1970s and 1980s to
describe various options for constitutional reform essentially in opposition to the
sovereignty-association proposals of the Parti Québécois. The federal Liberal
government described its proposals in the constitutional amendment bill of 1978
as "renewed federalism." In 1979, the federal Task Force on Canadian Unity
described its proposals as "restructured federalism." In the Quebec referendum
campaign of 1980 on sovereignty association, the federal government promised
"renewed federalism." Various proposals by the Liberal party of Quebec under
Claude Ryan from 1977 and Premier Robert Bourassa from 1985 were generally
referred to as "renewed federalism." During the debate on sovereignty in 1995,
federalists, notably Quebec Liberal leader Daniel Johnson, supported "flexible
federalism." Federal Liberal governments in the 1960s described their approach to
federal-provincial relations as "co-operative federalism" and in the 1990s as
"collaborative federalism." See **Federalism**; **Sovereignty association**.

Representation by population. The determination of representation in a legislature according to the size of the population. In the *Union Act* of 1840, which reunited Upper and Lower Canada in the Province of Canada, Canada West (Upper Canada, later Ontario) had equal representation in the assembly with Canada East (Lower Canada, later Quebec), although Canada East had a larger population. The phrase "Rep by Pop" was a political slogan of Reformers such as George Brown in Canada West in the 1850s, when the census of 1851 showed that the population in Canada West had become larger than in Canada East.

The principle of representation by population is modified in Parliament by concerns over representation of territory and of minority francophone and anglophone cultural interests. At the time of Confederation, the *Constitution Act* established representation by population in the House of Commons by province, using Quebec's predominantly francophone population as a base to calculate the number of seats each province would have, with no province having fewer members of parliament than its number of senators ("proportionate representation": ss.51-52). Proportionate provincial "Rep by Pop" in the House of Commons is matched with a permanent sectional balance in the appointed Senate, which includes an equal number of twenty-four senators from Quebec, Ontario, the three Maritime provinces combined, and the four western provinces combined (ss.21, 22, 40) (as well as representation from Newfoundland and the territories). Twenty-four was a deliberate choice of number, as representation in the Senate from Quebec, the only majority-francophone province, was related specifically to the twenty-four electoral constituencies of Lower Canada, to ensure minority representation in the upper house from then predominantly anglophone parts of the province. Federal legislation—successive *Representation Acts*—contains the formula for the redistribution of seats in the House of Commons following each census.

Representative government. A political system that includes an elected assembly. In North America, the phrase is usually a reference to early forms of government in British colonies settled largely by Britons, in which legislative power was shared between an elected assembly and an appointed body, but executive power was divorced from the legislature and held by the appointed governor and an appointed Executive Council. Thus representative government existed where there was a British-appointed governor and his appointed Executive Council (cabinet), an appointed Legislative Council (upper house) and an elected Legislative Assembly (lower house).

The first representative assembly was elected in Virginia in 1619. In what is now Canada, representative government was established first in Nova Scotia in 1749 and in Prince Edward Island in 1773. New Brunswick was separated from Nova Scotia and granted representative government in 1784. The *Quebec Act* of 1774 required the governor of that colony to establish an appointed legislative council but not an elected assembly, which was, considering the largely francophone population and the trouble brewing in colonies to the south, "at present inexpedient." Provisions for elected assemblies eventually came with the creation of Upper and Lower Canada by the *Constitutional Act* of 1791. Newfoundland first achieved representative government in 1832. The west coast colonies of Vancouver Island and British Columbia had some form of representative government periodically from 1856, but the principle was not firmly established until Confederation in 1871.

Though government was representative, a governor's appointed Executive Council was not accountable, that is, not responsible to the elected Assembly. The Executive Councils of Upper and Lower Canada, for example, were drawn from society's elite (known respectively as the Family Compact and the Chateau Clique). Representative government acquired significant meaning in British North America with the development of responsible government in 1848, which required the governor to select executive advisors, or ministers, from those who had seats primarily in the legislative assembly and who had to retain its support, or confidence, in order to remain ministers of the Crown. See **Responsible government**.

Representative theory of representation. A theory of representation according to which legislators are elected as trustees to represent views that, following debate, they hold to be in the general interest, regardless of the particular interests of their constituency or the views of the majority of their constituents. Thus a legislature is a supreme assembly of representatives from all regions of the province or country freely debating and determining public policy according to their independent judgment. This is counter to the delegate and occupational group theories of representation, and against such populist inhibitions on legislators and parliaments as recall and referendums.

In practice, the disciplined party system compromises the representative theory. Most candidates for election to the House of Commons and the provincial legislatures stand on behalf of political parties, and they can be relied upon to support their party if elected. It was this reality, combined with the insensitivity of the established parliamentary parties' leadership to the interests of western Canadians, that gave rise to the delegate and occupational group theories of representation in Canada in the early twentieth century and to demands for the introduction of such devices of direct democracy as recall and referendums. See **Delegate theory of representation; Recall; Referendum**.

Reservation (of legislation). Powers exercised in the early years of Confederation by the governor general to reserve certain classes of parliamentary bills for the "Queen's Pleasure" (that is, for approval or disallowance by the British government); power similarly possessed by the provincial lieutenant-governors, under the *Constitution Act*, to reserve provincial bills for the pleasure of the governor-in-council (that is, the federal cabinet) (ss. 56, 90). The imperial conference in 1926 and a conference in 1929 formally terminated this British role in the dominions, although the federal power remains "on the books."

Federal reservation and disallowance powers were consistent with the intentions of the founders of Confederation to create a centralized federal union. However, the trend of federal-provincial relations in the twentieth century, assisted by judicial decisions, was in the opposite direction. In a reference sought by the federal government in 1938, the Supreme Court declared the federal powers of reservation and disallowance to be unimpaired (Disallowance and Reservation Case). However, constitutional negotiations since the 1970s have included federal government offers to abolish its powers of reservation and disallowance. See **Disallowance**.

Residual power. A comprehensive grant of legislative authority to one particular level of government in a federation, exclusive of those areas to which authority has been explicitly assigned.

In Canada, the founders of Confederation clearly intended Parliament to possess residual power as the preamble to section 91 of the *Constitution Act, 1867* allows Parliament to legislate "for the Peace, Order, and good Government of Canada, in relation to all Matters not coming within the Classes of Subjects...assigned exclusively to the Legislatures of the Provinces." The Act then lists federal powers under enumerated heads "for greater Certainty, but not so as to restrict the Generality of the foregoing...."

Through judicial review, the Judicial Committee of the Privy Council (JCPC) elevated the enumerated head outlining provincial jurisdiction with respect to "Property and Civil Rights in the Province" (92:13) to a position superior to that of the preamble to section 91. Incrementally, the JCPC viewed the "Peace, Order, and good Government" clause as an emergency power clause or as a source of residual power only in new policy fields not foreseen in the 1860s, such as radio broadcasting for which legislative competence was granted to Parliament in 1932. The Supreme Court, which became the final judicial arbiter of the constitution in 1949, has generally broadened the federal government's use of "Peace, Order, and good Government" in matters of "inherent national importance." See **Judicial Committee of the Privy Council (JCPC)**; **"Peace, Order, and good Government"**; **"Property and Civil Rights"**; **Supreme Court**.

Resolution (of the House) (Motion). An opinion expressed by the legislature on its adoption by a majority of members present. Only cabinet ministers may introduce resolutions or motions whose effect would involve supply or the raising or spending of money. Government and opposition backbenchers introduce motions, like private members' bills, to publicize a policy idea and encourage public support. Opposition motions imply criticism of government policy and highlight an alternate course of action. The government can encourage its backbench supporters to introduce resolutions or motions that do the opposite, to highlight division within an opposition party's ranks on some policy. See **Private members' legislation**.

Responsible government. The requirement by convention of the Canadian constitution that to remain in office within a parliamentary term, a government must retain the support of the legislature. Thus, the governor general (lieutenant-governors in the provinces) normally appoints as prime minister (premier) the acknowledged leader of the largest party represented in elected legislature. Having been asked to form a government, the prime minister (premier) will recommend the appointment of party supporters in the legislature as cabinet ministers—the effective part of the Queen's Privy Council for Canada (the lieutenant-governor's Executive Council).

An incumbent prime minister or premier whose party does not command a majority in a newly elected House nonetheless has the right to remain in office and seek its confidence. If a government is defeated in a confidence vote, the governor general will either ask another party leader to form a government and seek the confidence of the House or dissolve the legislature for an election.

The advent of responsible government in British North America is associated with Lord Durham's concurrent governorship of Upper and Lower Canada, New Brunswick, Nova Scotia, Prince Edward Island and Newfoundland, following unrest in the colonies in the 1830s. In his report to the Imperial government, Durham recommended responsible government—the retention of appointment to the Executive Council conditional on the continued confidence of the Legislative Assembly (lower house)—as appropriate for all the colonies. The possible conflict between a governor's instructions from the British Colonial Office and the advice of the colonial government would be resolved by an appropriate division or distribution of responsibilities between the colonial and imperial governments. Durham reported in 1839, and responsible government eventually came by convention to Nova Scotia, New Brunswick and the United Province of Canada in 1848, and to Prince Edward Island in 1851. Responsible government was established in British Columbia upon entry into Confederation in 1871. Newfoundland first achieved responsible government in 1855 and the prairie provinces previously governed as part of federal territories acquired responsible government upon acquiring provincial status in Confederation (Manitoba, 1870; Alberta and Saskatchewan, 1905). See **Lord Durham's Report**.

Returning Officer (RO) and Deputy Returning Officers (DROs). The principal electoral officer in a constituency, responsible for the direction and supervision of the administration of a general election or by-election, and the deputies, appointed by each Returning Officer. The Returning Officer is responsible for the availability of the list of eligible voters and its revision; the establishment of polling stations; the administration of advance polls and the polling on election day; the official reporting of the vote; and the care of both cast and unused ballots. Political parties and the public may call upon the Returning Officer for clarification of the provisions of the *Elections Act*.

Each Returning Officer appoints deputy returning officers who, assisted by poll clerks, administer the election in the polling stations in the constituency. Where one location might contain several polling stations, the RO will appoint a central poll supervisor to oversee the deputies at each poll. The deputies are immediately responsible for their polling station, for the initial unofficial count of the ballots when the polls have closed, and for the secure delivery of the ballots to the Returning Officer. In the case of close elections or allegations of impropriety, the Returning Officer or a candidate may apply for a judicial recount. At the conclusion of the election process, each Returning Officer returns the election writ to the chief electoral officer, certifying the results.

Riding. An informal term for a legislative constituency or electoral district. See **Constituency (riding)**.

Right, political. See **Class cleavage**.

Rowell-Sirois Royal Commission on Dominion-Provincial Relations (1937-40). A royal commission that the federal government established unilaterally to examine and make recommendations on the division of legislative powers and the financial relationship between the federal and provincial governments. Its evidence and report constitute an important study of the basis of Confederation that set the stage for major restructuring of federal-provincial relations following the Second World War.

The Commission examined the division of legislative responsibilities, including access to revenue and regional, economic and social disparities within the country. In brief, it recommended a transfer of functions and a shifting of taxation power to the federal government and the creation of federal grants to the provinces on the basis of need, to equalize the tax revenues of the provinces. Thus, every province could "provide for its people services of average Canadian standards and…thus alleviate the stress and shameful conditions which now weaken national unity and handicap many Canadians…without resort to heavier taxation than the Canadian average, to provide adequate social, educational, and developmental services" (*Report of the Royal Commission on Dominion-Provincial Relations*, 2 [Ottawa, 1940], 125, 86). Specifically, the Commission recommended that the provinces give up personal income and corporation taxes and succession duties, and that the federal government "respect" the provinces' remaining revenue sources, assume all provincial debts, and accept responsibility for relief of the unemployed and a proposed old age pension. The federal government would pay an "adjustment grant" to "have-not" provinces, based on a formula reviewed every five years.

The Rowell-Sirois report was presented to Parliament in 1940 and discussed at the Dominion-Provincial Conference in 1941. Its proposals generated provincial opposition at a time when there was a more immediate need to prosecute successfully the Second World War. However, many of its proposals were effectively introduced on a piecemeal basis under the wartime and postwar leadership of the federal government. Canada thus began an era of centralized political leadership and federal-provincial fiscal arrangements. See **Federal-provincial tax-sharing agreements (fiscal federalism)**.

Royal assent. Approval by the Crown's representative (the governor general, or the lieutenant-governor of a province) given to legislation passed by the legislature. The date on which royal assent is given is endorsed on every Act, becomes part of the Act, and is the date on which the Act takes effect unless other provisions for its proclamation are contained in it. There is statutory provision for royal assent in sections 55-57 and 90 of the *Constitution Act, 1867*. By the Statute of Westminster (U.K., 1931), imperial reservation and disallowance is no longer effective, but the statutory power of the governor general to withhold royal assent to federal legislation remains. By convention, however, royal assent to federal legislation is a formality. Since the 1970s, federal governments have proposed in constitutional negotiations to abolish the federal power relating to the royal assent of provincial legislation by lieutenant-governors (federal reservation and disallowance powers). See **Crown prerogatives; Disallowance; Reservation (of legislation); Responsible government**.

Royal Canadian Mounted Police (RCMP). The federal law-enforcement agency created in 1873 that enforces criminal and provincial law in all provinces and territories except Quebec and Ontario which have provincial police forces. The RCMP is a civil force, trained and organized in a paramilitary fashion. The principal officers are appointed by the governor-in-council, or federal cabinet. They include a commissioner and four deputy commissioners. In 1984, responsibility for security services was transferred from the RCMP to the newly created Canadian Security Intelligence Service (CSIS). The RCMP Public Complaints Commission and the RCMP External Review Committee were also established in the 1980s.

In 1978, a federal royal commission was established under Judge David McDonald to investigate allegations of wrongdoing by the RCMP during the 1970s. Matters referred to the McDonald Commission included: a break-in at Parti Québécois headquarters and the theft of membership lists and financial documents (1973); four hundred break-ins without warrants by the criminal investigations branch, mainly in British Columbia (from 1970); penetration of a faction of the New Democratic party (1970-73); the electronic surveillance of at least one member of parliament (1977); extensive unauthorized mail openings (1950s-76); the burning of a barn in Quebec (1972); theft of dynamite (1972); use of forged documents (1971); widespread monitoring of election candidates (since the 1950s); and the use of violence in recruiting informants (early 1970s in Quebec). Some of these matters were also investigated in the late 1970s by a Quebec inquiry (Keable Commission). Also under investigation in Ontario (Krever Commission) was access to confidential files (widespread since 1970). In the matter of a break-in at a news agency in Montreal in 1972, an RCMP officer was found guilty and given an unconditional discharge. In some of these cases, the extent of RCMP knowledge and authorization was undetermined; in others, senior personnel either were or were not informed, but apparently authorized some of the activities. In 1992 it was revealed that the surveillance of the *indépendantiste* movement in Quebec in the 1970s and 1980s included payment for information from a deputy minister, later minister of intergovernmental relations.

One of the objectives of the McDonald inquiry was to ascertain the degree of ministerial involvement. There was liaison among the Royal Canadian Mounted Police, senior civil servants and three solicitors general during this period. It appears, however, that communications were characterized partly by distrust between the civilians and the police officers. There also appeared to be a desire on the part of the police to protect their "cabinet boss" from having embarrassing information, and an equal desire on the ministers' part not to have it. While RCMP officers testified to the McDonald Commission that they had informed their ministers of various activities, the three former solicitors general each testified that they had not been informed. In 1977, the solicitor general told the House of Commons that steps were being taken to bring the security service division of the RCMP within the law and under cabinet control. Two years later, however, the head of security service told the McDonald Commission that there were still no "formalized briefings or range of specifics to be brought to the attention of a new…minister." A chief recommendation of the McDonald Commission was the creation of a separate civilian organization for security services.

The creation of the civilian security organization and of the RCMP Public Complaints Commission resulted from the McDonald and other inquiries into the RCMP. The Commission, composed of full- and part-time members, is appointed by the federal government in consultation with ministers responsible for policing in the relevant province or territory. The Commission reviews and inquires into public complaints about the RCMP and may itself initiate investigations and hold public hearings. Commission reports go to the solicitor general who is the minister responsible for the RCMP, the RCMP commissioner, the complainant, and officers whose behaviour has been reviewed. The RCMP External Review Committee is an independent quasi-judicial body appointed by the federal government to review cases referred by the RCMP commissioner on internal grievance cases including discipline, demotion and discharge. The Committee's role involves regular and civilian employees of the RCMP whose employment is outside the jurisdiction of the Public Service Staff Relations Board.

Despite the foregoing, the RCMP is held in considerable public esteem, especially in western Canada. First as the North-West Mounted Police, the RCMP was closely associated with European settlement from the late-nineteenth century when the region was federal territory, and is currently more visible in the West and Atlantic Canada as provincial police forces. See **Canadian Security Intelligence Service (CSIS)**.

Royal commission. An inquiry into some special matter of public interest, in the case of federal commissions under the *Inquiries Act* or another statute. Not all commissions of inquiry, as they are generally known, are designated "royal"; but, apart from the prestige afforded by the name, any other commission of inquiry may have as much authority.

A royal commission may comprise one or several members, empowered to hold public hearings and call witnesses, and some have extensive research programs and published studies as supplements to their reports. While commissioners may be appointed on the basis of their expertise and background in the area of investigation, governments are also careful to choose people who are likely to be sympathetic to their general aims.

Some recommendations of royal commissions may have fairly immediate impact in terms of government legislation; others may help to create a climate of public opinion favourable to the implementation of comparable legislative proposals later. A commission might be established to allay public concern on a particular matter, giving the impression of government attention to it without actually acting on the matter. The appointment of a royal commission at least signals a government's interest and concern.

Important federal royal commissions since the mid-twentieth century have included the Rowell-Sirois Royal Commission on Dominion-Provincial Relations (1937-40), the Glassco Royal Commission on Government Organization (1960-62), and the Laurendeau-Dunton Royal Commission on Bilingualism and Biculturalism (1963-67). In the 1980s, the Macdonald Royal Commission on the Economic Union and Development Prospects for Canada, though established by a Liberal government, reported during a Conservative government. Its major recommendations supporting free trade with the United States and government policy to make Canadian business more competitive internationally suited the government's agenda. Later, the Conservative government established the Lortie Royal Commission on Electoral Reform and Party Financing following criticisms of the electoral process, including behaviour in the government party. In 1996, the Dussault-Erasmus Royal Commission on Aboriginal Peoples issued its report, calling for a new relationship between Aboriginal and non-Aboriginal people based on equality, respect, reconciliation and self-determination for Aboriginal peoples through self-government.

Royal Commission on Bilingualism and Biculturalism (1963). A federal commission of inquiry formed by the Liberal government of Lester B. Pearson in 1963 to investigate the status of French Canadians and the use of French in Canada. The co-chairs were André Laurendeau, editor of the Montreal daily *Le Devoir*, and Davidson Dunton, president of Carleton University. The Commission was appointed during the period of the Quiet Revolution in Quebec, when French society was undergoing important internal changes and expressing a more assertive nationalism than in the past. The Royal Commission also sponsored a considerable amount of social science research into questions related to culture, language, the economy and government.

There was little surprise about, and all-party support for, the Commission's major recommendation that English and French be declared the official languages of the federal government and administration. The Commission also recommended that provincial governments extend their services, notably to francophone minorities in predominantly anglophone provinces. On language, the *British North America Act, 1867* (since 1982, *the Constitution Act*) then only required the use of French and English in Parliament, the Quebec legislature (that is, the government), and the federal and Quebec courts (s.133). This individual-rights approach to language rights with respect to government service was adopted in the federal *Official Languages Act* of 1969, the core of Liberal Prime Minister Pierre Trudeau's program of bilingualism and biculturalism. In 1982, this policy was entrenched in the Canadian Charter of Rights and Freedoms (ss.16-22), along with the designation of New Brunswick as a bilingual province. The legislature and courts of Quebec remain bilingual under section 133 of the *Constitution Act*, and minority-language provincial educational rights are entrenched in section 23 of the Charter.

While the leadership of the Conservative, Liberal and New Democratic parties have been unanimously supportive of the "B and B" (bilingual and bicultural) objectives, there has been less sympathy at the public level in English-speaking Canada and increasingly so among francophones in Quebec. Notably in western Canada, but also in rural areas and small cities in Ontario and in parts of New Brunswick, there was increasing opposition to "official bilingualism," manifested in support for the Reform party, which was formed in the late 1980s, and for other regional parties such as the Confederation of Regions party in New Brunswick, and in some resolutions of municipal councils in the 1990s. In Quebec, many nationalists, adopting a territorial-rights approach rather than an individual-rights approach to the protection of the French language, would prefer the provincial government to have greater power to preserve and promote the French language in the province even if this meant less provincial support elsewhere for francophone minorities. See **Bilingualism and biculturalism**; **Charter of the French Language (Quebec)**; *Official Languages Act* **(Canada, 1969)**; **Parti Québécois (PQ)**.

Royal Proclamation (1763). Instructions received by the colonial governor of Quebec from the British government, effectively the constitution of the colony following its cession by the French. In establishing the British Crown's sovereignty, the Royal Proclamation acknowledged Indian rights, including land rights. Subsequently, various treaties and agreements were concluded involving the cession of Indian lands in return for money and benefits, such as rights to conduct traditional economic activities on crown land. The Canadian Charter of Rights and Freedoms acknowledges the Royal Proclamation as an effective constitutional document regarding Aboriginal rights and freedoms (s.25).

The British government also intended to promote British settlement and assimilation of the French population. Thus the Royal Proclamation instructed Governor Murray in 1763 to establish a representative legislature ("a General Assembly of the Freeholders") "so soon as the Situation and Circumstances...will admit thereof" similar to other American colonies. The British government, however, changed its mind as the approximately nine thousand French Roman Catholics were by their religion denied the vote, with the franchise then held by the approximately six hundred British Protestant settlers whose aggressive mercantile interests were creating friction with the disenfranchised majority. In addition, the British felt that, given the current political mood in colonies south of Quebec, popular colonial assemblies were considered a source of rebellious sentiment.

Governor Carleton, Murray's successor, planned to use Quebec as a base of military operations against any revolution in the American colonies. Carleton convinced the British government to reverse its assimilationist policy as a French population loyal to the Crown would be essential to British interests in the event of revolution in other American colonies. In 1774, the Royal Proclamation of 1763 "found upon Experience to be inapplicable to the State and Circumstances of the Province," the *Quebec Act* extended the boundaries of Quebec, established freedom of worship for Roman Catholics, allowing them to be appointed to a legislative council, and retained French civil law in non-criminal matters. See *Indian Act*; **Native (First Nations) self-government**; *Quebec Act, 1774* **(U.K.)**.

Rule of law. The principle of "legal equality, or the universal subjection of all classes to one law administered by the ordinary courts" (A.V. Dicey, *Introduction to the Study of the Law of the Constitution* [10th ed.; London: The Macmillan Company, 1961], 193). The exact meaning of the rule of law is not stated in statutory form, but it is a customary principle of the constitution; it restricts arbitrary authority and requires the law of government to be stated precisely and to be subject to adjudication by the courts. The practice of parliamentary delegation of discretionary executive and legislative authority, especially since the 1940s, tended to remove officialdom from such judicial scrutiny. However, protection afforded by the Canadian Charter of Rights and Freedoms (1982) includes judicial review of the exercise of discretionary power under enabling legislation, including subordinate legislation by government tribunals and regulatory agencies. See **Canadian Charter of Rights and Freedoms (1982)**; **Delegated power**; **Regulatory agencies (regulations)**.

***Russell v. The Queen* (1882).** A decision by the Judicial Committee of the Privy Council (JCPC) upholding the comprehensive legislative power of Parliament under the "Peace, Order, and good Government" preamble in section 91 of the *British North America Act, 1867* (since 1982, the *Constitution Act*).

Specifically, the federal *Temperance Act* provided for local prohibition subject to local option. The ruling was an early (and soon to be undermined) decision upholding the comprehensive legislative authority, or residual power, of Parliament. One year later, the JCPC ruled that the Russell Case was not relevant, when it adjudicated another case involving the liquor trade and established the so-called Aspect Doctrine. Eventually, the Judicial Committee restricted application of the "Peace, Order, and good Government" clause to temporary national and residual power in areas not designated a provincial responsibility in the BNA Act. Attempting to reconcile its view in 1925 of Parliament's power under the "Peace, Order, and good Government" clause with the decision in *Russell v. The Queen*, Viscount Haldane wrote that in 1882 the JCPC must have considered drunkenness a pestilential "menace to the national life"— though the Act in question provided for local option (*Toronto Electric Commissioners v. Snider*, 1925). In 1949, the Supreme Court of Canada became the country's highest court, and it has tended to sanction broader legislative jurisdiction for Parliament using a test of "national importance." See **Aspect Doctrine; Judicial Committee of the Privy Council (JCPC); Judicial review (interpretive; non-interpretive); Residual power; Supreme Court**.

S

Safe seat. An electoral district or constituency that has elected the candidate of the same political party over an extended series of elections with overwhelming margins of support, thus a safe seat for that party.

Scrutineer. A representative or agent of a candidate who is allowed to oversee the administration of a polling station on election day, including the unofficial count of ballots, in a general or by-election. Typically, urban constituencies have approximately 200-250 polling stations. Each candidate in a constituency is allowed to designate one person to be in attendance at each polling station during the poll and the count, to ensure proper procedures are followed and to report the unofficial count to the party.

Secession Reference. A ruling by the Supreme Court of Canada in 1998 on questions put to it by the federal Liberal government regarding the secession of provinces from Confederation (*Reference re the Secession of Quebec*), and the basis subsequently for the government's Clarity bill in 2000.

The Reference, part of the government's response to the narrow defeat in 1995 of the second referendum in Quebec on sovereignty association, posed three questions: could Quebec declare unilateral independence under the Canadian constitution; could it do so under international law; and in the event of a conflict between domestic and international law, which takes precedence? The Parti Québécois government of Quebec refused to participate in the Court's hearing on the Reference. Its position was argued by a Court-appointed "friend of the court."

First the Court held that its jurisdiction as a "general court of appeal" in the *Supreme Court Act* allowed it to give advice on these questions that related to the *Constitution Act* "touching on the future of Canadian federalism" and, in so doing, did not "usurp any democratic decision that the people of Quebec may be called upon to make" in the future.

The Court replied No regarding the first two questions, and saw no conflict between domestic and international law. No province has the right of unilateral secession under the Canadian constitution, nor does international law grant Quebec such a right because it "does not meet the threshold of a colonial people or an oppressed people [who] have been denied meaningful access to government to pursue their political, economic, cultural and social development," though the ultimate success of an unconstitutional, unilateral declaration of secession "would be dependent on recognition by the international community, which is likely to consider the legality and legitimacy of secession having regard to the…conduct of Quebec and Canada…."

On unilateral secession, the Court said: "Democracy…means more than simple majority rule…. [It] exists in the larger context of other constitutional values…that include federalism, democracy, constitutionalism and the rule of law, and respect for minorities." Secession can be achieved only with "principled nego tiation with other participants in Confederation within the existing constitutional framework." The justices observed that "the continued existence and operation of the Canadian constitutional order could not be indifferent to a clear expression of a clear majority of Quebeckers that they no longer wish[ed] to remain in Canada." Thus, a "clear majority vote in Quebec on a clear question in favour of secession would confer democratic legitimacy" on the secession movement that would have to be recognized by "the other participants in Confederation."

The Court left it to "the political actors" to determine what constituted a "clear majority on a clear question" as well as "the content and process of negoti-ation," but its ruling was relevant to the ongoing public debate over the size of a majority needed in a referendum on secession and objections that the questions in the referendums of 1980 and 1995 linked sovereignty to a partnership with the rest of Canada, thus confusing the issue.

Sovereignists took comfort in the Supreme Court's acknowledgment of the potential legitimacy of the secessionist movement, and the federal government enacted the Clarity bill in 2000, setting conditions under which the House of Commons would respond to future referendums on secession, in the context of the Court's ruling. See **Clarity bill (on secession from Confederation); Sovereignty association**.

Secrecy. A dominant feature by convention, but reinforced by statute, of the oper-ation of cabinet government and the public administration in Canada. All members of the Queen's Privy Council for Canada (effectively the federal cabinet) are bound by oath to "keep close and secret all such matters as shall be treated, debated, and resolved on in Privy Council, without publishing or disclosing the same or any part thereof, by Word, Writing or any otherwise to any Person out of the same Council, but to be such only as be of the Council." Similar oaths pertain to provincial Executive Councils, or cabinets. Thus, all documents which may be construed as relevant to treatment, debate and resolution by cabinet are confidential. Upon entering the federal or provincial public service, employees swear not to disclose without authority or make known matters that come to their attention during employment.

All citizens are subject to various provisions of the Criminal Code of Canada dealing with offences such as breach of public trust, theft and treason. The federal *Official Secrets Act* is the major statutory device that describes the offence of possessing or communicating "documents or information" entrusted in confidence, or possessing information while believing it to be illegally obtained. The Act provides for public or secret trials and punishment by fine and/or imprisonment. Since 1983, a federal *Access to Information Act* has required the government and administration to respond to requests for information and established an information commissioner to take court action if necessary on behalf of the applicant. However, there are broad categories of exemption as well as statutory exemptions. See **Freedom of information**; *Official Secrets Act* (**Canada, 1939**).

Secretariat. The executive/administrative staff of a government body that has an integral role in the development and implementation of policy, although ostensibly having only an advisory and administrative support role to the particular government body. The senior officials of such secretariats are among the most influential of government officials. At the federal level, for example, the Privy Council Office and the Treasury Board Secretariat are central executive/administrative secretariats for the cabinet and the Treasury Board, respectively. See **Privy Council Office (PCO)**; **Treasury Board Secretariat (TBS)**.

Secretaries of state. Offices within the federal ministry, most held by ministers who are not full members of the cabinet. Partly to distinguish his government from Conservative Prime Minister Brian Mulroney's, but also in response to a general anti-government public mood and following emulating the short-lived example of Conservative Prime Minister Kim Campbell, Liberal Prime Minister Jean Chrétien initially appointed a cabinet of twenty-three ministers in 1993, approximately one half the size of Prime Minister Mulroney's cabinet. However, Prime Minister Chrétien also established secretaries of state, in effect members of the ministry, but not necessarily with full cabinet membership. Unless they also held cabinet portfolios, the secretaries of state were designated to assist full cabinet ministers in aspects of their portfolio responsibilities.

In 2000, members of the Chrétien ministry were designated secretary of state for various regional development agencies (that is, the Economic Development Agency for the Regions of Quebec, for Western Economic Diversification, the Atlantic Canada Opportunities Agency and Federal economic Development Initiative for Northern Ontario); for Children and Youth; Asia-Pacific; Latin America and Africa; Multiculturalism; Status of Women; International Financial Institutions; Rural Development; Science, Research and Development; and Amateur Sport.

Secretary to the Cabinet. See **Clerk of the Privy Council**.

Sections 91 and 92 (*Constitution Act, 1867*). The sections of the *Constitution Act, 1867* and subsequently amended (before 1982, the *British North America Act*) that, in addition to some others, outline in large part the division (or distribution) of legislative powers between Parliament (section 91) and the provincial legislatures (section 92).

The adjudication by the courts of legislation enacted under the authority of these two sections determines the scope of legislative power (and implicitly political power) of the two levels of government. In particular, debate has centred on the extent of emergency and residual power resting with the federal government as a result of the "Peace, Order, and good Government" clause in the preamble of section 91, and the scope of provincial competence under the enumerated head "Property and Civil Rights in the Province" in section 92:13. The courts have also adjudicated the scope of federal authority under section 91:2, "The Regulation of Trade and Commerce," and section 91:27, "The Criminal Law...." Since 1982, judicial review has also included testing legislation, including subordinate legislation or regulations of government agencies, against provisions of the constitutionally entrenched Canadian Charter of Rights and Freedoms.

Legislative competence established in 1867 in sections 91 and 92, but also section 93, is also the source of intergovernmental tension over federal spending power and federal-provincial fiscal arrangements. The federal government, for example, has unlimited taxation power (s.91:3) while provincial taxation power is restricted (s.92.2). Yet the provinces are responsible for policy fields considered minor in the late-nineteenth century, but major since the mid-twentieth century, notably health, income maintenance and post-secondary education (s.92.7 and s.93). See **Constitution Act, 1867 and subsequently amended; Federal-provincial tax-sharing agreements (fiscal federalism); Judicial Committee of the Privy Council (JCPC); Judicial review (interpretive; non-interpretive); "Peace, Order, and good Government"; "Property and Civil Rights in the Province"; Spending power; Supreme Court; "Trade and Commerce" power.**

Security Intelligence Review Committee (SIRC). A federally appointed committee created in 1984 to monitor the activities of the Canadian Security Intelligence Service (CSIS), handle complaints about the behaviour of CSIS, and act as an appeal board regarding security clearances and a review board on matters dealing with immigration, citizenship and security. Theoretically SIRC, which reports annually to Parliament, acts as an independent civilian review agency of CSIS, Canada's civilian security organization. Parliamentarians and others have generally criticized SIRC for ineffectiveness as an oversight body, recommending that it be replaced by a parliamentary committee. See **Canadian Security Intelligence Service (CSIS); Communications Security Establishment (CSE); Royal Canadian Mounted Police (RCMP).**

Senate. The upper house of the Parliament of Canada, whose composition, appointment procedures and legislative competence have been the focus of public displeasure and intergovernmental constitutional negotiations.

The governor general, acting on the "advice" of the prime minister, appoints senators who remain in office until seventy-five years of age unless they resign or become disqualified. Representation in the Senate is based on regions, and is intended to balance the weight of representation from densely populated central Canada in the elected lower house, the House of Commons. The Senate's regional divisions as defined in the *Constitution Act* are: Ontario (24 senators); Quebec (24); the Maritime provinces (24); the western provinces (24); Newfoundland (6); Yukon (1); Northwest Territories (1); and Nunavut (1), with provision for four or eight more members representing equally the first four divisions (ss.22, 24).

Liberal prime ministers have had more opportunities than Conservatives to appoint senators, resulting in a Liberal majority for most of the twentieth century. Conservative Prime Minister Brian Mulroney thus used the power to make additional appointments in 1990 to ensure passage of legislation introducing the Goods and Services Tax (GST), a value-added, or consumption tax, against concerted Liberal opposition.

There are formal (in accordance with the *Constitution Act*) and informal qualifications for appointment to a seat in the upper chamber. To qualify formally, one must be a Canadian, at least thirty years old, hold residence in the relevant division, and hold unencumbered real property worth at least $4,000. A senator is disqualified by failure to attend two consecutive sessions, loss of Canadian citizenship, ceasing to meet the residence and property qualifications, being adjudged bankrupt, or upon conviction of a criminal offence. No one can hold a seat in the Senate and the House of Commons concurrently. However, a crucial qualification for a "summons" to the Senate is the favour of the prime minister. With few exceptions, Senate appointments are rewards for service to the party in power, and represent a publicly remunerated office from which some senators continue to perform important organizational, fund-raising, and election campaign activities for their party.

Though it possesses legal powers almost as great as the House of Commons, and is designated the upper chamber signifying its traditional link to the Crown as opposed to the Commons' link to the electorate, the Senate is inferior to the Commons. For example, revenue (money) bills must be introduced by the government in the Commons. Perhaps more significantly, the Senate is not a chamber of confidence. That is, the government is responsible only to the Commons; a defeat in the Senate does not require the government to resign or for Parliament to be dissolved and a general election held. Also, since 1982, constitutional amendments requiring a resolution of both houses of Parliament can be effected by the House of Commons alone if, after 180 days of adoption by the House, the Senate has not adopted such a resolution and the Commons adopts the resolution again. This provision thus allows for important changes to the Senate itself without its approval.

In the 1890s, two senators—Sir John Abbott and Sir Mackenzie Bowell—served briefly as prime minister, but in recent history, there have rarely been ministers in the Senate other than the government leader who is responsible for guiding government legislation through the Senate. On some occasions, however, a prime minister might appoint senators to cabinet for significant purposes. In forming his cabinet in 1980, Prime Minister Pierre Trudeau included one senator from each of the three westernmost provinces following an election in which no Liberal candidates were elected in those provinces. In 1979-80, Prime Minister Joe Clark had several senators with important portfolios in his cabinet. This was done to satisfy a need for French-Canadian representation in his cabinet, and included one candidate who had failed to win a seat in the Commons in the election. A chief constitutional negotiator for Prime Minister Brian Mulroney in the 1980s and 1990s was a senator whom he appointed to his cabinet.

Like the House of Commons, the Senate is organized into government and opposition ranks, with some independents, and must approve legislation on three readings. The House of Commons must concur in any amendments made by the Senate to legislation it has already approved. Though created in part as a moderating influence in the legislative process, the contemporary Senate, especially when a majority were members of the government party, did little to frustrate the government. However, after the election of the Conservative government in 1984, the Liberal majority in the Senate did hold up important government legislation, contributing, for example, in its refusal to consider the Canada-United States Free Trade Agreement, to the government's decision to dissolve Parliament for an election in 1988. Also, the GST would not have been adopted without the appointment of additional senators in 1990 to support the measure. When the Liberals returned to office in 1993, the party positions in the Senate were reversed. The Conservatives, now having a majority, used their dominant position to delay passage of, and even defeat, some Liberal government legislation. Even when they eventually regained their majority in the Senate, the Liberal government had to remain concerned about the possibility of "independent" behaviour by some Liberal senators.

Supporters of the Senate see its current value in the legislative process mainly in the "pre-study" of proposed legislation before its actual introduction to Parliament, and in its longer-term examination of particular policy areas. There is a standing joint Senate-House of Commons committee which scrutinizes statutory and other regulatory instruments. The Senate is also known for the examination of government policy and legislation and for private bills pertaining to business and finance in its very active committee on banking, trade and commerce. However, many senators—and particularly those on the banking committee—hold positions with private companies, or are connected with law firms that represent clients who do business with the government. Consequently, there have been reasons to cite some senators for "informal" conflict-of-interest, if not formal conflicts following the enactment of the *Lobbyists Registration Act* in 1989.

Finally, despite non-partisan senatorial investigations of public policy and recent episodes of partisan activism, the Senate's public image remains that of a largely lazy body of recipients of party patronage now retired at public expense. A recent resignation of one inactive senator and prosecutions of two others, one on charges of influence peddling and the other on charges arising from political activity prior to appointment to the Senate, obviously has done additional harm to the reputation of the upper house.

The question of Senate reform has been one of several permanent items in constitutional negotiations for several decades. In the 1990s, it was the focus of interest in western Canada in particular, where regional representation in federal institutions is an important issue and where demand for a "Triple-E" Senate originated. Supporters of "Triple-E" wanted a Senate similar to the United States Senate, in which provincial representation would be equal, senators would be elected, and the legislative role would be as effective as that of the House of Commons. However, francophone Quebeckers were concerned about the totality of representation in Parliament from the only province with a francophone majority. Also, public opinion in some provinces, particularly in Atlantic Canada, expressed concern that an effective Senate might prevent adoption of federal legislation which would benefit that region.

A fundamental reform of the Senate, along with an enlarged House of Commons, was an important part of the Charlottetown Accord negotiated in 1992 by federal, provincial, and territorial government leaders and Aboriginal representatives. Although the Accord was defeated in a country-wide referendum, its proposal for Senate reform is worth presenting as an example of a complex response to demands for a Triple-E Senate. Under the Accord, the Senate would have comprised equal numbers of provincial senators (6), and territorial senators (1), elected directly or indirectly by the provincial or territorial legislatures. The Quebec senators were expected to be chosen by Quebec's National Assembly, effectively the government. There would additionally have been guaranteed Aboriginal representation. Although it would not become a confidence chamber, the Senate would have become more effective, with power relative to four categories of legislation: supply bills (revenue and expenditure items); legislation materially affecting French language or culture (so designated by the initiator subject to appeal to the Speaker with protection for francophones); fundamental changes to tax policy related to natural resources; and other legislation. The Senate would have been obliged to dispose of legislation adopted by the House of Commons within thirty sitting days of the Commons, except for supply bills which would be subject to a thirty-day suspensive veto (that is, would be enacted if, following defeat or amendment in the Senate, they were adopted again by the Commons). Legislation affecting French language or culture would have required a double majority in the Senate (that is, a majority of senators voting and a majority of senators personally designated French-speaking voting) and not be subject to a Commons override, effectively a francophone veto. The Senate would have had the power to defeat legislation on tax policy affecting natural resources by a majority vote. Defeat of "ordinary" legislation would have resulted in a joint sitting of the two chambers with a parliamentary majority deciding the issue (effectively a Commons override only if the government had a sizeable majority in the enlarged Commons and/or opposition support). Any ordinary bill initiated in the Senate and defeated in the House would also have been disposed of in a joint sitting. Otherwise, the legislative powers of the Senate would have remained the same, notably regarding its role in Parliament's approval of constitutional amendments. However, under the Charlottetown Accord, the Senate would have also acquired a constitutionally entrenched power to ratify the federal government's appointment of the governor of the Bank of Canada, the heads of "key" federal cultural institutions and regulatory boards and agencies.

Senior civil servants. A common term for the high-level policy makers and advisors in the public service of Canada and the provinces. While there is no precise definition for the term, deputy ministers and those with deputy minister rank, assistant deputy ministers, and directors in government departments are usually considered to be senior civil servants; chief officers of important crown corporations and members of important regulatory agencies may also be termed senior civil servants. The government-of-the-day effectively appoints most senior civil servants. Some are easily removed; others are career officials, whose appointments are "protected" by a public employment statute, or they are officials with term appointments who can be removed before their terms expire only by a vote of the legislature.

The phrase is sometimes used pejoratively. Because of the tendency of long-term party rule in some Canadian jurisdictions, senior civil servants individually acquire permanency, and collectively acquire considerable influence over their ministers in the cabinet. Their full-time devotion to administration and their control over information flow give them advantages in influencing their "political masters." Ministers are part-time administrators, given their important political duties in the cabinet, the House, their party and their constituency, and often hold their portfolios for reasons other than their personal expertise in the policy field of their department, and only for a relatively brief period of time.

Separate schools (parochial, dissentient). Tax-supported denominational primary and secondary schools, usually a reference to those operated by the Roman Catholic Church in predominantly Protestant provinces, but including schools in predominantly Catholic Quebec run by Protestant school boards. Historically, the issue of denominational schools also involved French- and English-language minority groups in the provinces.

The *Constitution Act, 1867* gave jurisdiction in education to the provinces, but it protected "Separate or Dissentient" systems of education established before union from prejudicial provincial action. The Act provided for an appeal from any "Protestant or Roman Catholic Minority" to the governor-in-council, or federal cabinet, on any prejudicial decision and for "remedial Laws" by Parliament (s.93). Nonetheless, since the controversy over Manitoba's *Public Schools Act* in the 1890s, federal governments have preferred to leave disputes over the provincial denominational schools to the directly interested parties in the provinces and the courts. In the 1990s, Quebec and Newfoundland obtained constitutional amendments to eliminate the denominational basis of their provincial education systems.

In 1982, education rights based on provincial minority French and English languages were entrenched in the Canadian Charter of Rights and Freedoms in a section (s.23) beyond the reach of the legislative override, or "notwithstanding" clause (s.33). In 1984, the Charter was used to void restrictions in Quebec on access to English-language primary and secondary education and later to obtain francophone minority rights in several anglophone provinces. See **Charter of the French Language (Quebec); Manitoba Schools Question (and French language rights, 1890); Quebec Protestant School Boards Case (*A.-G. Quebec v. Quebec Association of Protestant School Boards* [1984]).**

Separation of powers. A constitutional division of political functions which distinguishes legislative, executive and judicial duties, founded on the concern that these functions not be assigned to a single body, but rather to several bodies in a system of checks and balances. Institutional specialization can be created through different procedures for selection and different terms of office, with each body having constitutional authority to check the behaviour of the others.

Separation of powers is an essential feature of the United States constitution. The President, the Congress and the Supreme Court, each acting in its own sphere, can check the others, the first two through vetoes of each other and the Court through judicial review of legislation under the Bill of Rights. The United Kingdom, by contrast, has a parliamentary-cabinet system of responsible government, with judicial review circumscribed by the principle of parliamentary supremacy. Canada combines a system of responsible parliamentary government—like the UK, though in a federal union—but with a broad scope for judicial review of all government legislation and administrative law under an entrenched Canadian Charter of Rights and Freedoms—as in the US. See **Constitution Act, 1867 and subsequently amended; Judicial review (interpretive; non-interpretive); Responsible government; Supremacy of Parliament.**

Separatism. The term commonly applied to provincial secession from Canadian Confederation associated with various movements in Quebec originating in the 1960s, some of which merged to form the provincial Parti Québécois (PQ) in 1968.

The strategists in the PQ prefer using the more positive "independence" and later the more complex and perhaps more strategically appealing "sovereignty association." Public opinion polls suggest that Quebeckers are more favourably disposed to the PQ's secessionist project when it is linked to a continued association with Canada. In the early 1970s, a vote for the PQ was considered to be a vote for separation; but prior to its successful 1976 election, the PQ differentiated between electoral support and the question of independence to be voted on later in a referendum. In 1980, the PQ lost a referendum in which it had sought a mandate to begin negotiations, but was re-elected in 1981.

The PQ government opposed the patriation of the constitution in 1982 because, among other matters, the general amending formula did not include a veto for Quebec. The PQ government was subsequently defeated by the Liberals, and the separatist movement remained dormant until the defeat of the constitutional Meech Lake Accord in 1990. The PQ opposed the Charlottetown Accord in the 1992 referendum as "less than Meech." In the 1993 federal election, the federalist Liberal party led by Jean Chrétien formed a majority government, but the new *indépendantiste* Bloc Québécois won fifty-two seats in Quebec, sufficient to form the official opposition. Promising another referendum on sovereignty, the PQ was returned to office in 1994 with a thirty-seat margin over the Liberals based on a virtually equal share of the popular vote (44%). In a referendum in 1995, the sovereignty-association option was barely defeated, but unlike the outcome in 1980, a majority of francophone voters apparently supported it. In 1998, the PQ was re-elected, promising a third referendum. In anticipation of another referendum, the federal Liberal government sought constitutional advice in a reference on secession to the Supreme Court of Canada, and Parliament adopted its Clarity bill in 2000 based on the judicial ruling. See **Charlottetown Accord (1992); Clarity bill (on secession from Confederation); Meech Lake Accord (1987); Parti Québécois (PQ); Secession Reference; Sovereignty association.**

Shadow cabinet. A collective term for the critics in each of the opposition parties in the House of Commons and provincial legislatures, particularly those of the official opposition, the largest opposition party, who would likely be in the cabinet should their party come to power. In small opposition parties, members may be designated critics for several portfolios. Largely because of the smaller number of members of parliament and of provincial legislatures, and the desire of party leaders to maintain flexibility, the shadow cabinet is not as formalized in Canada as in the United Kingdom.

Shared-cost programs. Public programs provided by one level of government, usually the provinces, using money from both federal and provincial governments. Shared-cost programs especially benefit those provincial governments with jurisdiction over major social policy fields but lacking the financial resources to provide adequate services in those fields. Lacking jurisdictional competence, but possessing a comprehensive power of taxation relative to provincal power, exercises spending power involving the federal government in areas of provincial jurisdiction to maintain country-wide standards of public service. Such programs began in the early twentieth century with federal support for provincial old-age pensions and unemployment assistance. The bulk of shared-cost programs now is directed to hospital and medical insurance, post-secondary education, and income maintenance under the Canada Health and Social Transfer (CHST).

The current system originated with the Wartime Tax Agreements of 1941. Later, agreements were periodically renegotiated as the federal *Federal-Provincial Fiscal Arrangements and Established Programs Financing Act*. In the 1960s, Quebec "opted out" of certain shared-cost programs and received financial compensation under the *Established Programs (Interim Arrangements) Act*. In 1977, the federal government terminated the costly shared-cost programs, by which it paid 50 per cent of provincial expenditures in hospital and medical insurance and in post-secondary education. Instead, the federal government granted equalized tax point abatements and block funding unattached to particular programs. Ill-fated constitutional proposals in the 1980s and 1990s included proposals to constrain federal spending power, an outcome not necessarily sought by provincial governments in less advantaged parts of the country. In 1995, Established Programs financing, involving education and health care, and the Canada Assistance Plan, involving income maintenance, were replaced with a single federal transfer, the CHST. See **Canada Health and Social Transfer (CHST); Contracting (opting) out; Federal-provincial tax-sharing agreements (fiscal federalism); Spending power.**

Singh Case (*Re Singh and Minister of Employment and Immigration* [1985]). An early decision of the supreme Court of Canada that tested the procedures of a federal administrative agency against "the principles of fundamental justice" guaranteed in the Canadian Charter of Rights and Freedoms (s.7). Specifically, the procedure did not offer a refugee claimant an oral hearing, although a committee had available a sworn transcript of an earlier meeting between the claimant, accompanied by a lawyer, and an immigration officer. A decision rejecting the claim could result in the claimant meeting with an appeal board if the board thought there was a "reasonable" chance for the decision to be reversed.

The federal government sought to "save" the case by arguing that the procedure was a "reasonable" limit "prescribed by law" that could be "demonstrably justified" (s.1). The Court held that financial costs, "administrative convenience," and "utilitarian considerations" were insufficient justification to compromise the integrity of administrative fact-finding in adversarial hearings. Moreover, it was not sufficient for administrative tribunals simply to follow procedures established by statute. "Fundamental justice" required that even procedures established in law must satisfy independent standards. Two years later, in *R. v. Oakes*, the Court specified guidelines for applying section 1: a provincial or federal government must demonstrate that the objectives of the restrictive measure are "pressing and substantial" and involve only a minimal restriction that is rationally connected to the objectives, and will result in a benefit greater than the cost of the limitation. See **Canadian Charter of Rights and Freedoms (1982)**; **Judicial review (interpretive; non-interpretive)**; **Oakes test (*R. v. Oakes* [1986])**; **Supreme Court.**

Single-member plurality electoral system. The electoral system currently used in all provincial and federal elections in Canada, also known as the "first-past-the-post" system. The winner in each constituency is the candidate who receives at least one vote more than any opponent. Thus, when there are more than two candidates, the winner often has a plurality, but not a majority, of the votes cast. The votes of the defeated candidates have no electoral effect; and when such constituency results are aggregated, a discrepancy exists between the popular vote percentages for the parties and their percentage share of seats in the legislature. Such systemic discrepancies are occasionally significant and lead to demands for some form of proportional representation. See **Electoral system**; **Proportional representation**.

Social Credit party. A social conservative, populist movement party that originated in the Canadian West in the 1930s. It was most successful in Alberta and British Columbia, but had a following as well in Quebec, particularly in the 1960s. The movement was successful in part because of the populism of its leaders—individuals in sympathy with dominant regional cultural values of their respective time who could effectively articulate the economic and social grievances and interests of their region. The party, however, could never integrate these several regional support bases, specifically the West and Quebec, into a national political force. The party was electorally successful in provincial politics in Alberta until the 1970s and remained a major force in British Columbia politics until the early 1990s, while in Quebec it maintained only nominal representation in the House of Commons and minor activity in provincial politics through the 1970s.

The Social Credit party began in Alberta, a province with a history of militant agrarian activism, under the leadership of evangelist William ("Bible Bill") Aberhart. It defeated the United Farmers of Alberta in 1935 and remained in power in Alberta—for many years under the leadership of Aberhart's evangelist-politician protegé Ernest Manning—until 1970. It then formed the official opposition to the Conservatives with a handful of seats and later fell behind the New Democratic party. In the late 1980s, Manning's son, Preston Manning, established and led the federal Reform party from Alberta apparently with the same populist appeal of his father and Aberhart in the Social Credit party. However, Preston Manning deliberately kept the populist and social conservative Reform party out of provincial electoral politics, to focus party resources instead on the federal arena. In the 1993 federal election, Reform won fifty-two seats, all but one in the West, and contributed significantly to the Conservative government's historic defeat. Failing to extend its electoral support significantly east of Manitoba in

1997, Manning sought unsuccessfully to merge Reform and the Conservative party. Instead, Reform became the Canadian Alliance and Manning lost the leadership to Stockwell Day, a former Alberta cabinet minister. The Canadian Alliance continued, though, to project the same social conservative and populist views of Reform, and prior to it, of Social Credit.

Secondary to the charismatic, populist leadership in explaining the success of Social Credit were its formal monetary theories. The theory of Social Credit was the so-called "A + B Theorem" of Major C.H. Douglas, a British army engineer. According to Douglas, there is always a discrepancy between the costs of production and the purchasing power of individuals. The Social Credit party promised to supplement individuals' purchasing power through direct grants. The Supreme Court, however, ruled the provincial government's attempts to effect Social Credit legislation in Alberta in the 1930s to be unconstitutional. Subsequently, the party became a populist, conservative party. Prosperity following the Second World War, occasioned in particular by the discovery of oil in the province, reinforced the position of Social Credit as the party of government and administration in Alberta.

In British Columbia, the party came to power in 1952 under the leadership of W.A.C. Bennett, a high-spirited, small-town businessman who had failed earlier to win the leadership of the provincial Conservative party. Bennett and the party held office until 1972. Under the leadership of his son, Bill, the party returned to power in 1975 and remained there, later under William Vander Zalm, for sixteen years. In 1991, Vander Zalm resigned the leadership of a divided party. Social Credit fell to minor-party status and elected members later drifted away, some identifying themselves as Reformers. From 1935 to 1958, Social Credit had minor representation from Alberta and British Columbia in the House of Commons, being eliminated in John Diefenbaker's Conservative landslide in 1958. In 1962, the party—which had an organization in Quebec since the 1940s called the Union des Électeurs—elected twenty-six members of parliament under the leadership of Réal Caouette, a dynamic, small-town businessman. The Quebec members and the four western Social Credit MPs elected in 1962 were never integrated; as the western party finally disappeared from the House, the Ralliement des créditistes membership in the House of Commons also dwindled, eventually to five MPs in 1979 and finally no seats in 1980. See **Canadian Alliance party; Populism; Ralliement des créditistes; Reform party; Third parties (political).**

Social movement organizations. Differentiated but interconnected groups and networks that, as sponsors of "new" social meaning and action, act on both government and society, promoting discourse on innovative values and a rethinking of basic relationships. Examples of the discourse of social movement organizations include attitudes related to the environment and consumption, the family, gender and gender relations, race and ethnic relations, human rights and the rights of children, the elderly and the poor in particular, and the power of multinational corporations in a global economy.

Like traditional interest groups, social movements seek to influence public policy, but unlike traditional interest groups, social movements do not seek to do so in a collegial, mutually accommodative relationship with political parties and public officials. As social as well as political actors, social movements temper collaborative arrangements with government and use various tactics of direct action to draw public attention to, and encourage public support for, their objectives. Although social movements predate the introduction of the Canadian Charter of Rights and Freedoms in 1982, its equality rights section 15 and sections 27 and 28 on multiculturalism and gender, respectively, have constitutionally legitimized some social movement interests. See **Canadian Charter of Rights and Freedoms (1982); Globalization (globalism); Interest groups; Postmaterialism**.

Social Union Framework Agreement (1999). A federal-provincial agreement on the funding of joint programs, including a continuing role for the federal government, with Quebec dissenting. With the federal government's post-Second World War "entanglement" in policies of provincial jurisdiction through various conditional shared-cost programs, including notably health care, post-secondary education and income maintenance, combined with a contemporary desire to remain involved but with a smaller financial commitment, the Social Union Framework was intended to establish rules for future joint relations on social policy.

In general, the federal government promised not to introduce new programs that entailed transfers to provincial governments without the support of a majority of the provinces. It would, however, retain the right to make transfers to individuals which, incidentally, would be direct and visible federal benefits to Canadians unlike indirect federal transfers through provinces. The agreement encouraged the elimination of discriminatory provincial employment requirements and residency requirements regarding access to social benefits, increased public accountability and visibility for intergovernmental transfers, improved federal consultation with the provinces on funding changes in transfers for social programs, and notice regarding any new federal transfer programs for individuals.

The Agreement applies to Quebec, although the sovereignist Parti Québécois government dissented from it. This aspect of so-called "collaborative federalism" by the federal Liberal government followed an agreement in 1994 on internal trade and was concurrent with the federal government's introduction of a national child benefit and a millennium scholarship fund. Critics of the Agreement, especially in Quebec, argued that it further legitimized federal spending power in social policy and allowed for change without the consent of Quebec. Not surprisingly, "centralist" critics argued that the federal government had granted too much to the provinces while supporters argued that the Agreement struck an acceptable balance between federal involvement and provincial autonomy. See **Canada Health and Social Transfer (CHST); Federal-provincial tax-sharing agreements (fiscal federalism); Spending power**.

Socialism. A cross-national set of values according to which economic production, distribution and exchange should be controlled through public ownership and regulation to achieve egalitarian goals, rather than permitting individual aggrandizement through minimally regulated economic competition. Thus, the full development of individual personality would be achieved in harmony with others and would be enhanced in the attainment of the common good.

Socialism comprises many "schools" and political groupings. In the late-nineteenth and early-twentieth centuries, the Canadian left included many sectarian groups. In 1921, the Communist party of Canada was founded on the Leninist model, appropriating for itself the role of official interpreter of the ideas of Karl Marx. The party existed as a sometimes legal, sometimes proscribed organization, remaining loyal to the policies of the Communist party of the Soviet Union and undergoing the tensions and schisms that Communist parties experienced elsewhere outside the Soviet bloc until the demise of Soviet Union itself in 1991.

Many democratic socialists—advocating gradualist, democratic and parliamentary means to achieve socialist objectives—eventually joined forces in the Commonwealth Co-operative Federation (CCF) in 1933. The CCF was an intellectual force as well as a political movement, especially evident in the output of the League for Social Reconstruction. As a political force, it formed the government of Saskatchewan for almost two decades from 1944 and became an important electoral factor in Ontario and British Columbia. However, it was never a strong federal force except as its policies might have been taken over by other parties in office when the CCF showed signs of becoming popular.

During post-Second World War prosperity, the CCF underwent a transformation similar to that experienced by other western socialist parties. In the 1950s, the ideological rhetoric of the CCF and its policies of nationalization were exchanged for a more moderate brand of socialism, emphasizing public planning through the managerial and regulatory powers of government. The New Democratic party (NDP) issued forth from this process in 1961, modelling its policies less on those of the British Labour party, which had been an important model for the CCF, and more on Scandinavian social democratic parties. The NDP has remained influential in Ontario, Saskatchewan and British Columbia, forming governments in those provinces concurrently in the early 1990s; it developed strength in Manitoba and Yukon, forming governments there, and became an opposition force to some extent in Nova Scotia. In federal politics, the party has remained a relatively minor force, winning no more than 25 per cent of the popular vote in general elections, perhaps having its greatest influence on policy during the minority Liberal government of 1972-74. Its weakest federal performance has been in recent elections, losing official-party status in 1993, though regaining it with minimal popular support in later elections.

However limited the electoral success of socialists in Canada, the redistributive social policies associated with the movement and promoted by the CCF-NDP have been adopted by other party governments. Indeed, many Canadians who would not think of themselves as socialists point to the social security system, including such federal-provincial shared-cost programs as publicly administered health care, as an important feature distinguishing Canada from the United States. Despite occasional grumbling from some revenue-rich provincial governments, governments are now constitutionally committed to promoting economic development and individual well-being, reducing economic disparities, and providing essential public services to all Canadians, in part through federal equalization payments to provincial governments (*Constitution Act, 1982*, s.36).See **Co-operative Commonwealth Federation (CCF); New Democratic party (NDP); Red Tory (-ism).**

Sovereign, the. The person on whom the Crown is constitutionally conferred, symbolizing Canada's status as a constitutional monarchy and the incumbent's status as Canada's head of state in whom formal executive power is vested. Canada's Sovereign is the same person as the British Sovereign, resident in London. Therefore, in large part the Sovereign's executive authority in Canada is delegated to a representative, the governor general, whom the Sovereign appoints on the prime minister's recommendation.

On the prime minister's recommendation, the governor general appoints the Sovereign's Privy Council for Canada, "to aid and advise in the Government of Canada" (*Constitution Act, 1867*, s. 11), the effective part of which is the federal cabinet. There are also Executive Councils, effectively the provincial cabinets appointed by each provincial lieutenant-governor on the advice of the provincial premier.

At the time of Confederation in 1867, the convention of responsible government was already established in the participating colonies; that is, the governor general and lieutenant-governors were obliged to appoint "advisors" who had the confidence of their legislatures, and who would, in almost all matters, accept their minster's "advice." All legislation must receive royal assent and be proclaimed to be effective. Judicial functions are conducted in the name of the Sovereign. Command of Canada's military is also vested in the Sovereign. Canada's honorary awards are conferred in the Sovereign's name. The Sovereign is also recognized as the head of the Commonwealth, a voluntary association of independent states, formerly British colonies or trusts, and associated states. See **Crown prerogatives**; **Governor General**; **Letters Patent**; **Lieutenant-governor**.

Sovereignty association. The objective of the Parti Québécois (PQ) in restructuring Quebec's relationship with the rest of Canada—to achieve national sovereignty in an economic association with Canada.

Sovereignty association was defined first at a convention of the Parti Québécois in 1979 and later refined in a government white paper, *Quebec-Canada: A New Deal—the Quebec Government's Proposal for a New Partnership between Equals: Sovereignty-Association*. The PQ had won election in 1976, promising a separate vote on sovereignty. A government-sponsored referendum seeking a mandate to negotiate sovereignty association was defeated in 1980, but the PQ government was re-elected the following year. Out of power, the PQ opposed the constitutional Meech Lake Accord in 1990 and the Charlottetown Accord of 1992, characterizing it as "less than Meech." The *indépendantiste* Bloc Québécois won fifty-four seats in the 1993 federal election and formed the official opposition. One year later the PQ returned to office in Quebec, promising to hold another referendum on sovereignty. The PQ's thirty-seat margin over the Liberals was based on a virtual equal share of the popular vote (44%). The sovereignty association option was narrowly defeated in the second referendum in 1995 (50.6% "No") with a 92 per cent voter turnout, though in this vote a majority of francophone voters apparently voted "Yes." The PQ was re-elected again in 1998, though it received a smaller share of the popular vote than the federalist Liberal party. PQ Premier Lucien Bouchard promised a third referendum, but only when success appeared likely. At the federal level, the BQ lost its official opposition status to the Reform party in 1997, and the Liberal government responded to close results of the second referendum and the possibility of a third with its so-called Plan A and Plan B: on the one hand, encouraging the predominantly anglophone provinces to accommodate themselves to some constitutional "distinct-society" designation for Quebec, but also to set conditions for recognizing the validity of future referendums in Quebec on sovereignty association. See **Bloc Québécois; Clarity bill (on secession from Confederation); Parti Québécois; Secession Reference**.

Speaker (of the legislature). The presiding officer of a legislative chamber.

The elected members of parliament choose a Speaker for the House of Commons from among themselves prior to the opening of Parliament following each general election and for the duration of that Parliament (*Constitution Act, 1867*, s.44). Until 1986, the prime minister nominated (seconded by the leader of the opposition) a member of parliament—usually a government MP—who assumed the position by acclamation. Since then, the Commons has effectively chosen its Speaker by secret ballot, announced by the Clerk of the House without identifying vote totals. The Speaker presides at sittings of the House (s.46) and, following the Standing Orders, or rules, of the House, enforces those rules and maintains the rights and privileges of the House and its members. Most procedural rulings of the Speaker are not subject to appeal. The Speaker is also responsible for the internal management of the House, including the estimates of House operations, and sits with government and opposition MPs on the Board of Internal Economy to control the financial and administrative affairs of the House. On the prime minister's nomination, the House elects various deputies who serve in the chair during the term of the Parliament. Although assisted in rulings by the Clerk of the House and legal officers, the Speaker nonetheless must be familiar with the rules and precedents, and retain the respect of members. Because of this, and because a constituency is denied an active participating MP while the person is Speaker, there have been suggestions that the position be a permanent appointment not contingent on holding elective office to the House of Commons.

The appointment and functions of speakers of the provincial legislatures are similar to those of the Speaker of the House of Commons. However, respect for the position and the decorum of the legislature will vary according to provincial custom. The governor general—but effectively the prime minister—appoints the Speaker of Parliament's upper house, the Senate (*Constitution Act, 1867*, s.34), who usually serves for the term of the Parliament. The duties of the Senate's Speaker are similar to those of the Speaker of the House, but because the Senate is much less a site of extensive partisan debate, the position is less demanding. See **House of Commons; Parliamentary privilege (immunities)**.

Special Operating Agencies (SOAs). Self-contained operating units within the federal public service, operating relatively autonomously in government departments, which have the potential for being financially self-sufficient. The approximately 19 SOAs include the Canada Communication Group, the public information agency of the federal government, the Passport Office and the Translation Bureau. The creation of SOAs was part of restructuring and rationalizing within the federal administration begun under a Conservative government and continued under the Liberal government elected in 1993.

Special status. An objective sought in a new constitution recognizing that Quebec, the historic homeland of most French-speaking Canadians and the only jurisdiction in North America with a French majority, should have legislative powers in addition to those assigned to the provinces generally, in order to preserve the French culture.

The demand is associated initially with the provincial Liberal government of Jean Lesage during the Quiet Revolution of the 1960s. However, the Lesage government spoke of *statut particulier* only in 1965, during its last year in office. This could be read either as a reference to recently acquired status as the sole province having opted out of federal-provincial shared-cost programs with financial compensation, or as a generalized demand for jurisdiction not shared with the other provinces. Later premiers Daniel Johnson, Sr. (Union Nationale, 1966-70) and Robert Bourassa (Liberal, 1970-76) walked the fine line between the "older" Quebec demands for a revised federalism and "new" demands for a constitution recognizing the existence of two nations. The election of the Parti Québécois in 1976 placed sovereignty firmly on the agenda and, following the return of the Liberals to office under Bourassa in 1985, the provincial government sought the agreement of the federal government and the other provinces to constitutional recognition of Quebec as a "distinct society," with legislative jurisdiction to "preserve and promote the distinct society of Quebec..." (Canada Clause, Charlottetown Accord, 1992, after the Meech Lake Accord, 1987). See **Charlottetown Accord (1992)**; **Distinct society clause**; **Meech Lake Accord (1987)**; **Quiet Revolution**; **Sovereignty association**; **Two nations (*deux nations*)**.

Speech from the Throne. The governor general's address in the Senate, before senators, members of parliament and the judges of the Supreme Court, that opens sessions of Parliament. In all provinces but Quebec, the lieutenant-governors read the Speech from the Throne to the provincial legislatures. In Quebec, the premier delivers an Inaugural Address in the National Assembly in the presence of the lieutenant-governor. The prime minister's (premier's) advisors actually compose the Speech which generally reviews the state of public affairs from the government's perspective and provides a general outline of its legislative priorities in the coming session. At the next sitting of the legislature, a general "throne speech debate" takes place on a government motion commending the governor general (lieutenant-governor) for the address. Opposition amendments to the motion constitute want-of-confidence motions which the government must win in order to stay in office.

Spending power. Given its greater constitutional powers of taxation and therefore its capacity to acquire revenue relative to the provinces, the federal government's ability to make payments to people, institutions and provincial and municipal governments, notably in policy fields in which Parliament does not have the constitutional power to legislate.

Spending power grants the federal government a leading role in establishing conditional federal-provincial shared-cost programs to achieve national standards of public service regardless of the constitutional division of legislative jurisdiction in the federation. Confirmed by the Supreme Court, federal spending power is based in the broad powers of taxation given Parliament (*Constitution Act,* s.91:3, "The raising of Money by any Mode or System of Taxation") and the right to make laws relating to "The Public Debt and Property" (s.91:1A). By contrast, provincial governments have powers only of "Direct Taxation within the Province in order to the raising of a Revenue for Provincial Purposes" (s.92:2).

Especially since the Second World War, federal spending power has involved the federal government in areas of provincial responsibility in a number of ways, notably shared-cost programs such as post-secondary education and health care, but also in a variety of bilateral programs in such areas as labour training, culture, forestry, mining, housing, municipal and urban affairs, tourism and recreation. Through spending power, the federal government indirectly sets provincial, even municipal, spending priorities and standards for programs in areas of provincial jurisdiction. Since the 1960s, other provinces have joined in Quebec's traditional opposition to the federal government's intrusion into provincial affairs. Not all provinces feel as strongly as some about the exercise of federal spending power, as successive federal governments, including those sensitive to provincial concerns, have maintained an obligation to ensure comparable levels of basic public services across the country and a reduction in regional economic and social disparities. In 1999, the federal government and nine provinces, with Quebec dissenting, signed the Social Union Framework Agreement to establish rules on the use of federal spending power in social policies that touch on provincial jurisdictions. See **Charlottetown Accord (1992); Conditional grants; Federal-provincial tax-sharing agreements (fiscal federalism); Meech Lake Accord (1987); Social Union Framework Agreement (1999).**

Standing (select, special, joint) committees (of the House and Senate). Various small committees of a legislature, including permanent or standing committees named according to major policy fields, committees to deal with specific legislation, some to examine specific problems in certain policy fields, joint standing and special parliamentary committees of both houses, and others to deal with matters such as public accounts, miscellaneous private bills, procedures and organization, and privileges and elections.

Most of the standing committees of the House of Commons, with approximately fifteen members, are named for major government departments and policy areas, such as Agriculture and Justice. They examine the estimates of those departments and legislation emanating from them, hearing from ministers, senior officials and representations from private organizations and individual witnesses. Other important standing committees include Public Accounts and Elections, Privileges and Procedure. Special committees are created to examine a policy area in which the government intends to legislate. There are also joint House-Senate committees, notably the joint committee on the scrutiny of regulations, and special joint committees on the constitution.

Membership on committees of legislatures is roughly proportional to party representation in the legislature. The chairs of all House committees, except the Committee on Public Accounts, are usually members of the government party. Though chairs are ostensibly elected by the committee, the government may occasionally be more directly involved than simply leaving the matter to its majority members. Though there will be differences in style from chair to chair and committee to committee, generally the chair is simply a presiding officer not exercising any extraordinary control over the committee. Although the proceedings of committee meetings appear less formal and party-disciplined than the legislature, partisanship is never far below the surface. Employees of the legislature serve as staff to the committees and their role is essentially supportive of the whole committee. Neither the chairs nor the staff have roles and influence comparable to their counterparts in the congressional committee system in the United States. Special House or parliamentary committees, such as those on the constitution in 1991-92, can recruit academics and others to their staff and hold hearings across the country.

The major function of legislative committees is to scrutinize government legislation, including supply and ways and means legislation. Such committees usually meet only in the capital city. Thus, parliamentary committees and those of large provinces effectively restrict their reservoir of potential witnesses to representatives of organized or well-financed groups that can afford travel to the capital, or employ or retain permanent lobbyists there. The committees decide whom to call as witnesses and, following testimony, what recommendations to submit to the legislature in the form of amendments to bills. Witnesses tend to be public officials, interested private-sector representatives, and academics. On estimates, the witnesses called to support departmental estimates are ministers and officials in their departments who have already managed the onerous hurdles within the executive apparatus of interdepartmental and cabinet committees, including Treasury Board and its Secretariat; and they now have the support of cabinet and government backbenchers in the House. At this stage, however, the minister and accompanying officials are operating for the first time in public, and the committee can be a forum for general criticism of government programs as well as a rare occasion for holding ministers accountable for every estimated expenditure in their departments. Since the late 1980s, parliamentary committee hearings have been selectively recorded and broadcast on the parliamentary channel of cable television systems, when the proceedings of the Commons are not being televised.

The ability of committees to perform legislative, surveillance and audit functions effectively depends on the independence and competence of their members and the size and expertise of their staff. Committee activity, like that of the House itself, cannot be entirely removed from the partisan context of debate. A more effective committee system would require legislators interested in long-term committee membership; willing to devote more time to policy areas and questions which might be of little, if any, direct relevance to the interests of their constituents; prepared to spend less time on constituency matters; willing to work largely without public attention, as committee hearings receive much less attention from the mass media than do debates in the House, interviews in the lobby, and news conferences; and perhaps most important, to act independently of their party whip. See **Estimates; House of Commons committees**.

Standing Orders. The codified rules of procedure of the legislature, enforced by Speaker.

In the House of Commons, for example, the Speaker, the deputy speaker, and the deputy chairman of committees enforce the *Standing Orders of the House of Commons*, interpreting them on the basis of precedents in Canada and occasionally of other parliaments, notably of the Westminster Parliament of the

United Kingdom and of other Commonwealth countries whose parliamentary traditions also derive from the so-called "Mother of Parliaments." However, as the legislature is the master of its own affairs, it can revise its standing orders.

Disputes usually arise in the context of heated partisan debate, but the disciplined party system in Canadian legislatures also assists the Speaker in enforcing the rules. Each party's House leader and whip arrange the business of the legislature as best they can, frequently in a highly charged partisan atmosphere. The revision of Standing Orders themselves often becomes a matter of partisan debate—as changes which the government proposes, while designed to make the legislature more "efficient," usually mean less time for the opposition to debate government measures.

Stare decisis. The rule of precedent in judicial decisions. By convention, lower courts are bound by decisions of higher courts in deciding similar cases, while a court may depart from its own precedents. The constitutional entrenchment of the Canadian Charter of Rights and Freedoms in 1982 has reduced the rule of *stare decisis* in judicial review. Precedents are still cited and respected. However, judicial activism associated with substantive review of legislation and administrative behaviour under the Charter has led to judicial interest in so-called legislative facts and the identification of justice with the court's appreciation of "democratic values" expressed in the Charter (*Morgentaler, Smoling and Scott v. The Queen*, 1988) whose meaning should permit "growth, development and adjustment to changing societal needs" (*Motor Vehicle Reference*, 1985). See **Canadian Charter of Rights and Freedoms (1982); Judicial review (interpretive; non-interpretive).**

State, the. A political community exercising control over specific territory. The state expresses itself chiefly through a political regime or government which includes a public administration, a judiciary, and police and military organizations. Its chief functions are to manage conflict associated with the allocation of resources within the territory, to pursue its own interests in relation to other states, and to protect itself from both internal and external threats, preferably through legitimate and non coercive means. International law is based on the sovereignty of states. In recent years, state sovereignty has been challenged by two streams of globalization: multinational corporations seeking to enhance their freedom to operate independently of state controls and nongovernmental organizations seeking to establish a supra-national regime of laws to regulate the behaviour of both states and private corporations. See **Globalization (globalism).**

Statistics Canada. A federal agency established in 1918, responsible for the census of Canada and for collecting, analyzing and publishing statistical information relating to social, economic, industrial, commercial, agricultural, and financial activities and conditions in Canada. Statistics Canada is also responsible for collaborating with other government departments for the publication of statistical information based on government activities, and for developing integrated social and economic statistics pertaining to Canada and each of the provinces and territories, in accordance with scientific standards and practices. Statistics Canada disseminates some information without cost and also provides specialized information on a fee-for-service basis.

Statute (Act). Styled a bill when introduced, legislation that has passed three readings in each parliamentary chamber (or a provincial legislature) and received royal assent. In bound form, federal statutes are known as *Statutes of Canada* and legislation amended since original passage is periodically published in updated form as *Revised Statutes of Canada (R.S.C.)*. See **Legislation**.

Statute of Westminster (U.K., 1931). An Act of the British Parliament giving effect to resolutions of the imperial conferences of 1926 and 1930. It formalized the national independence of the dominions (Canada, Australia, New Zealand and South Africa) and created the constitutional basis of the contemporary Commonwealth.

The Statute of Westminster gave statutory sanction to a resolution of the imperial conference of 1926 that "They [Great Britain and the dominions] are autonomous Communities within the British Empire, equal in status, in no way subordinate to one another in any aspect of their domestic or external affairs, though united by a common allegiance to the Crown, and freely associated as members of the British Commonwealth of Nations...." The Act declared that the *Colonial Laws Validity Act* (by which dominion legislation was void if it conflicted with British statutes) no longer applied to the dominions; that the British Parliament would not invalidate future acts of dominion parliaments; that no act of the British Parliament would affect a dominion unless it had requested and consented to it; that dominion parliaments could enact laws with extra-territorial effect; and that the *Colonial Courts of Admiralty Act* (1890) and the *Merchant Shipping Act* (1894) no longer applied to the dominions.

At Canada's request, a clause exempted the *British North America Act* to prevent amendments solely by the Parliament of Canada. Through an amendment of the BNA Act in 1949 by the British Parliament, the Canadian Parliament acquired the power to amend the Act, on a request to the British Parliament, except sections regarding provincial jurisdiction, constitutional guarantees on education and the use of French and English, and the requirement for an annual session of Parliament and its five-year term. In 1982, the constitution was patriated with amendment procedures involving only Canadian legislatures and renamed the *Constitution Act*. See **Commonwealth (The British...of Nations);** *Constitution Act, 1867,* **and subsequently amended**.

Statutory instrument. Any order, rule, regulation, tariff, commission, warrant, resolution, proclamation, or other government device that has the power of law. Such instruments are the subordinate legislation of executive and administrative bodies exercising delegated legislative authority.

Federal instruments are published in the *Canada Gazette,* but there remains the question of adequate legislative scrutiny of delegated legislation. At the federal level, the joint Senate-House of Commons committee on the scrutiny of regulations is responsible for ensuring that statutory instruments do not exceed authority delegated by Parliament. As such instruments constitute the effective laws of a modern administrative state and number in the thousands as well as being constantly subject to change, this committee cannot effectively scrutinize all subordinate legislation. The Federal Court, which hears appeals of administrative decisions, assists consequently in the development of administrative law. See **Delegated power; Federal Court; Regulatory agencies (regulations)**.

Subordinate legislation. Rules, regulations, orders and any other statutory instruments enacted by executive and administrative bodies under enabling legislation passed by Parliament or a provincial legislature. Most legislation is enabling legislation which grants discretionary authority to an administrative body to effect regulations that have the force of law. See **Delegated power; Regulatory agencies (regulations); Statutory instrument**.

Sunset laws. Statutory provision for a law to expire at a given time, subject to re-enactment. Such stipulations are supported by those who feel that the public sector is too large, but who do not wish to oppose some innovation at least for a short period, and who also do not have confidence that legislators will later terminate a program or administrative body supported either by vested private interests or widespread public opinion.

An important example of a sunset law in Canada is the legislative override of specific sections of the Canadian Charter of Rights and Freedoms. Section 33 of the Charter was a concession to those supporting the principle of the supremacy of Parliament (the legislature). Section 33, the so-called "non obstante" or "notwithstanding" clause, allows legislatures to adopt legislation that admittedly violates fundamental freedoms (s.2), legal rights (ss.7-14), and equality rights (s.15) of the Charter. However, the override "shall cease to have effect" five years after it comes into force unless it is re-enacted; and any re-enactment also has a five-year limitation. See **Notwithstanding (*non obstante*) clause (Canadian Charter of Rights and Freedoms, s.33)**.

Supplementary estimates. Government requests to the legislature for additional funds to meet financial needs purportedly unforeseen when the main estimates were drawn up and presented earlier. These estimates are usually tabled late in a parliamentary session and final supplementary estimates at the end of a fiscal year. See **Budget and budgetary process; Estimates**.

Supply bill. The informal name for an appropriation measure, that is, government legislation to appropriate funds to finance specified government operations according to the estimates. In Parliament, the government may introduce supply bills only in the House of Commons. Following legislative approval and royal assent, government departments and agencies may spend money only for purposes authorized by the legislature. See **Budget and budgetary process; Estimates**.

Supply period (allotted days; Opposition days). Time allocated in the legislative timetable for the debate of supply bills, to approve appropriations for government expenditure. In the House of Commons, there are twenty-one days in the three supply periods during which opposition motions take precedence over all government business. On these so-called allotted days, or Opposition days, the opposition introduces a motion of non-confidence in the government. Such days are rare occasions in the House timetable when the opposition can determine the subject of debate on which the government must defend itself.

Supremacy of Parliament. The principle that legislative power rests with a sovereign legislature.

Until 1982, the supremacy of the Canadian Parliament and provincial legislatures was restricted only by the adjudicated distribution of legislative powers under the *British North America Act, 1867,* as amended. Disputes over jurisdictional competence were resolved by appeal to the Supreme Court and, until 1949, the Judicial Committee of the Privy Council in London. In 1982, the constitution was patriated as the *Constitution Act* with a Charter of Rights and Freedoms, against which all legislation can be tested in the courts irrespective of the distribution of legislative authority. As a concession to supporters of the principle of the supremacy of Parliament, the Charter allows for a conditional legislative override of important sections of the Charter (s.2, fundamental freedoms; ss.7-15, legal rights; s.15 equality rights). However, the override must be re-enacted after five years. Otherwise legislation violating the Charter can only be "saved" in the courts if it constitutes "reasonable limits" that can be "demonstrably justified in a free and democratic society" (s.1). Any legislation enacted in compliance with the *Constitution Act* can be subsequently amended or rescinded by the legislature. See **Canadian Charter of Rights and Freedoms (1982);** *Constitution Act, 1867,* **and subsequently amended.**

Supreme Court of Canada. The superior court of Canada, established by federal statute in 1875. In addition to being the court of appeal from all other courts in Canada, the Supreme Court of Canada exercises an important political role through decisions on constitutional references and litigations on constitutional matters. The Supreme Court hears appeals selectively from provincial courts of appeal in civil and criminal matters, and appeals from decisions of the appeals division of the Federal Court of Canada on cases involving administrative law. Cases heard by the Supreme Court involve predominantly constitutional and criminal law. Until 1949, the Judicial Committee of the Privy Council (JCPC) in London exercised final appellate powers except in criminal cases.

The governor-in-council (that is, the federal cabinet) appoints all nine justices, designating one as the court's chief justice and the others as puisne ("ranked after") judges. A judge retires automatically upon reaching 75 years of age and can be removed by the governor-in-council only on a joint resolution or address of Senate and the House of Commons. Three of the nine judges must be from the Quebec bench or the bar, thus learned in the province's Civil Law. By custom, three justices come from Ontario, two from the West and one from Atlantic Canada. An appointee must be, or have been, a superior court judge in a province or a barrister with at least 10 years' experience. The Supreme Court sits in Ottawa, hearing appeals for which it has granted leave or on constitutional cases referred to it by the federal government or on appeal by provinces on decisions on their references to their provincial court of appeal. When hearing appeals on cases originating in Quebec, at least two of the sitting judges must be from that province. Five judges constitute a quorum, allowing therefore a majority of three from Quebec to sit on cases involving civil law. All nine justices will participate in important constitutional questions.

The Supreme Court has always been an important constitutional actor, but especially so following the entrenchment of the Canadian Charter of Rights and Freedoms in 1982. Until then, and like the JCPC until 1949, the Court's judicial review function essentially involved distinguishing federal and provincial legislative competence under the *British North America Act*, with due regard for precedents. Especially after 1949, observers sought to determine patterns on decisions relating to federal-provincial power, especially in the determination of federal jurisdiction under the "Trade and Commerce" clause (s.91:2), and the effectiveness of federal emergency and residual powers under the "Peace, Order, and good Government" preamble to section 91. The Supreme Court publishes separate concurring decisions and dissenting opinions. Thus, the court can be analyzed judge by judge and case by case.

With the development of executive federalism in the 1960s and ongoing negotiations of constitutional reform, governments used the Court to achieve political advantage in intergovernmental negotiations. For example, the Court confirmed Parliament's jurisdiction over western offshore mineral rights, but denied Parliament the power to amend unilaterally the *British North America Act* with respect to the role of, and representation in, the Senate. When the British government balked at a parliamentary resolution to patriate the constitution in 1981-82 with the support of only two provinces, the federal government referred the matter to the Court. It ruled that though the action was constitutionally legal, it was a violation of constitutional convention. The federal government resumed negotiations with the provinces, achieving the support of all but Quebec for the *Constitution Act, 1982*, patriating the constitution with an entrenched Canadian Charter of Rights and Freedoms. As part of its strategy in response to a likely third referendum in Quebec on sovereignty association, the federal government received a Court ruling regarding secession from Confederation on the basis of which Parliament enacted the so-called Clarity bill in 2000, legislation that itself could be the subject of judicial review.

Since 1982, the scope of judicial review has widened as a result of the Court's willingness to grant Canadians the "full benefit" of the Charter through a so-called "non-interpretive" approach, adopting a "broad, purposive analysis, which interprets specific provisions of a constitutional document in light of its larger objects" (*Hunter v. Southam*, 1984). At the same time, Canadians, both individually and as organized interests, have realized the political importance of a citizen-rights-based constitution. So-called Charter interests and groups have developed and linked together in broader social movements to pursue political objectives through the courts in addition to the traditional legislative and administrative processes. The country's traditional elites of federal and provincial governments, their administrations and dominant interest groups, who have never shied from pursuing their interests in the courts, have thus been joined by other groups that some commentators have termed the "Court party."

The Court decided early on that it would review legislation on substantive grounds to ensure "accordance with the principles of fundamental justice" (s.7), so that the meaning of the Charter would not be "frozen in time to the moment of adoption with little or no possibility of growth, development and adjustment to changing societal needs" (*Motor Vehicle Reference*, British Columbia, 1985). The Court accepted, perhaps reluctantly, the "crucial obligation of ensuring that the legislative initiatives of our Parliament and legislatures conform to the democratic values" of the Charter (*Morgentaler, Smoling and Scott v. The Queen*, 1988). To this end, the Court has broadened its fact-finding capacity to include social and legislative facts, in addition to traditional historical or adjudicative facts, in hearing Charter cases on legislation and executive and administrative decisions of governments at all levels. For instance, it upheld the federal government's agreement with the United States allowing the testing of unarmed cruise missiles over Canada, in part because it was not possible, "even with the best evidence available, to do more than speculate upon the likelihood [of the agreement] resulting in an increased threat of nuclear war" and hence a threat to Canadians' "right to life, liberty and the security of the person" (s.7) (*Operation Dismantle v. The Queen*, 1985).

However, the Court accepted as important evidence reports commissioned by the federal government that indicated to the Court's satisfaction that provisions of the Criminal Code permitting therapeutic abortions required observance of a procedure that created "many potential barriers" so as to be "practically unavailable" to many women, thus imposing "serious delay causing increased physical and psychological trauma to those women who [meet] its criteria." The federal criminal law respecting abortions was therefore a denial of section 7 rights of the Charter and unconstitutional (*Morgentaler et al.*, 1988). On administrative tribunals, the Court has ruled that financial cost and administrative convenience cannot be cited to justify procedures that, given the possibility of error, represent a denial of "fundamental justice" (*Re Singh and Minister of Employment and Immigration*, 1985). On warrants for search and seizure of property, the Court ruled that only someone capable of acting judicially—not administrators who hold investigatory and enforcement powers— can issue warrants, and then only on "probable" rather than "possible" grounds and specifying the details of the search (where, when, by whom and for what purpose) (*Hunter v. Southam*, 1984). These rules affect police authorities as well as administrative tribunals and consequently the admissibility of evidence in court under section 24.

The Charter allows for violations to be "saved" under section 1, as "reasonable limits prescribed by law as can be demonstrably justified in a free and democratic society," that is, justified before the courts. Recognizing that this involves the judiciary directly in political discourse, the Supreme Court has established guidelines for "saving" violations: limitations are permissible if the objectives of the challenged law are "pressing and substantial," the means to achieve its effect involve a minor constraint on otherwise protected rights and freedoms and are rationally linked to the objectives, and will result in benefit greater than the cost of the limitation (*R. v. Oakes*, 1986).

The Court has also ruled on traditional constitutional matters, now involving provisions of the Charter. For example, having declared in 1979, before enactment of the Charter, that provisions of Quebec's Charter of the French Language respecting government and the judiciary to be a violation of section 133 of the *British North America Act,* the Court ruled against provisions regarding access to primary and secondary education in English under section 23 of the Charter in 1984 (*A.-G. Quebec. v. Quebec Association of Protestant School Boards*).

The Court has also developed even further as a political institution in the context of remedial decree litigation under the Charter. Section 24:1 allows anyone whose Charter rights and freedoms have been infringed or denied to "apply to a court of competent jurisdiction to obtain such remedy as the court considers appropriate and just in the circumstances." In 1990, the Supreme Court ruled that the francophone minority in Edmonton (and by implication elsewhere) should have administrative control over curriculum, instruction and buildings (*Mahé v. Alberta*). In this and other cases respecting minority-language education rights, the Court was in effect issuing remedial decrees placing "positive obligations on government to alter or develop major institutional structures" (Chief Justice Dickson, in *Mahé*) (re ss.23 and 24:1).

In 1992, the Supreme Court established guidelines that would allow the courts to "read into" legislation missing words or new provisions that otherwise lacking would make the legislation unconstitutional (*Schacter v. Canada [Employment and Immigration Commission]*). Conferring benefits on people otherwise excluded by the legislation, which the courts determine are a constitutional right rather than simply a benefit for a social purpose, the courts can avoid declaring the legislation unconstitutional and thus denying benefits to people receiving them, by nullifying the invalid section of the law, but suspending the invalidity and allowing the relevant legislature time to amend the legislation. The ruling had to do with a section of the federal *Unemployment Insurance Act* dealing with differential parental leave benefits for natural parents and for adoptive parents. Increasingly, however, gay and lesbian rights have been "read into" family law and human rights codes, given the Charter's section 15 on equality rights. The Supreme Court has effectively ruled that, as section 15 is concerned with equality rights, the prohibited bases for discrimination enumerated in the section are essentially illustrative and do not comprise the totality of constitutionally prohibited bases for discrimination.

Clearly, because the Charter is a political document, the Supreme Court's political role has increased in importance since 1982 in direct and indirect ways: directly, as citizens continue to exercise their Charter rights in the courts; indirectly as governments and administrators determine future policy and decision making in anticipation of possible litigation. Also, public attention has turned to the matter of appointment power: should the federal government share the power of appointment with relevant provincial governments; should Parliament have a role in ratifying the appointments; should the Court be enlarged to lighten the burden on the nine justices?

More than before, the Supreme Court is subject to scholarly examinations. There have been several studies of judicial review under the Charter, focussing on the decisions of individual justices, the categories of Charter cases (fundamental freedoms, democratic rights, equality rights, and so forth), the object of cases (legislation, regulations and so forth), the source of the case (federal, provincial), and their outcomes, including individual voting patterns, inter-agreement levels among justices, and attitudes toward narrow or broad Charter interpretation among those concurring with and those dissenting from Charter decisions.

Constitutional discussions in the 1980s and 1990s included changes regarding the Supreme Court. For example, in both the ill-fated Meech Lake and Charlottetown constitutional accords of 1987 and 1992, the federal government would have appointed judges from lists submitted by the relevant provincial and territorial governments, with provision for interim appointments if a list were not forthcoming or the names were unacceptable to the federal government. See **Canadian Charter of Rights and Freedoms (1982); Judicial review (interpretive; non-interpretive).**

Surveillance (function of Parliament). Maintaining the constitutional principle of responsible government, the chief function of Parliament (and provincial legislatures) is constantly to scrutinize government policy and behaviour, holding the executive accountable to the legislature. Short of voting no confidence and forcing the government's resignation and possibly a general election, various procedural devices of surveillance include exchanges during question period, debate on supply motions (especially so-called Opposition days in the House of Commons), emergency debates and general debates (for example, on the Speech from the Throne, the budget and departmental estimates). The surveillance function of Parliament is also seen in the detailed examination of government bills and statutory instruments in committees. See **Estimates; House of Commons; Question period; Responsible government; Standing (select, special, joint) committees (of the House and Senate).**

Suspensive veto. The power to oppose and delay the passage of legislation for only a limited time.

   The Canadian constitution contains a traditional, now irrelevant example, as well as an important contemporary example of a suspensive veto. Traditionally, the governor general had the prerogative power to "reserve" legislation received for royal assent "for the Signification of the Queen's Pleasure," that is, of the British government (*Constitution Act*, ss.56 and 57; and ss.61 and 90 for the lieutenant-governors of the provinces, for the "Signification of Pleasure" by the federal government). By statute, the governor general no longer does so; neither do the lieutenant-governors, by convention.

   An effective contemporary example involves Parliament's role since 1982 in amending the constitution. Most of the amending procedures require a resolution of the bicameral Parliament, that is, a similar resolution adopted by both houses. However, the Senate can exercise only a suspensive veto. It can only delay parliamentary approval of an amendment by not adopting, or even defeating, a resolution approved by the House, and requiring the House to adopt the resolution again after 180 sitting days for the amendment to have the approval of Parliament without authorization by the Senate (*Constitution Act, 1982*, s.47). Such was the case in the 1990s, following the defeat in the Senate of a constitutional amendment adopted by the House of Assembly of Newfoundland and the House of Commons eliminating the denominational basis of the province's education system. See **Senate; Veto**.

T

Tariff (non-tariff barriers). A tax levied on imports to protect domestic industry, labour and agriculture from external competition. Protectionist measures also include so-called non-tariff barriers, such as excessively restrictive health and environmental laws regarding the importation of goods from abroad.

Traditionally, tariffs were applied to protect so-called infant industries in early stages of development. The National Policy initiated by the federal Conservative government in 1879 included protective tariffs. The policy continued under the Liberals from 1896, although earlier they had championed free trade with the United States. Canadian goods also benefited from British Imperial preferential treatment of goods imported from Commonwealth and Empire states until the United Kingdom entered the European Economic Community in the 1960s. Because many countries including Canada are exporting countries, there has been a desire among industrialized countries since the Second World War to reduce barriers to international trade under the General Agreement on Tariffs and Trade (the GATT)—now the World Trade Organization (WTO). The world comprises several trading blocs, involving freer trade within blocs centred on Europe, Japan and the United States. Following unsuccessful attempts by the federal Liberal government to forge a "contractual link" with Europe in the 1970s, the Conservative government of the 1980s committed Canada's economic future to a North American trading bloc through a free trade agreement with the United States and later with Mexico as well.

In the twentieth century, Canada's tariffs and the Imperial preferences eventually resulted in the creation of a miniature replica of the United States economy, as branch plants of foreign (predominantly US) firms were established within the national and Imperial barriers. By and large these Canadian firms were intended to satisfy the local market and were not committed to further research and development. Thus, from an international perspective, some were small and inefficient. At the same time, primary resources were exported to the manufacturing sectors of other countries. People in the eastern and prairie regions of Canada have historically complained about national tariff policy which benefited the protected manufacturing core in central Canada at the expense of Canadians living elsewhere who did not benefit from freer international trade. The postwar development of the oil and gas industry in western Canada also pitted regional support for free trade in those primary products against the national policy of the federal government.

Although Canada constitutes an economic union, provincial jurisdictions have established various non-tariff barriers to achieve local objectives similar to the purpose of national tariffs. The *Constitution Act, 1867* prohibits barriers to the movement between provinces of "Articles of Growth, Produce, or Manufacture" (s.121) and the Canadian Charter of Rights and Freedoms of 1982 includes mobility rights "to pursue the gaining of a livelihood" subject to provincial affirmative action programs to deal with high unemployment (s.6). Over the years, various non-tariff barriers erected by provincial governments have included the marketing of agricultural products, preferential labour hiring laws and professional accreditation procedures, and regulations regarding securities, investment funds, land ownership, environmental protection, purchasing practices and the retailing of goods and services. While all provincial governments are in some sense protectionist, Quebec in particular was reluctant to abandon any tools then available to the government of the only predominantly French-speaking jurisdiction in North America to strengthen the economic union of a predominantly anglophone Canada. While pursuing its North American free-trade objectives, the federal Conservative government in the 1990s was less successful in convincing provincial governments to adopt a more effective constitutional provision on the economic union. However, restrictive provincial and federal barriers are increasingly under attack from other national governments as violations of regulations of the WTO. See **Economic union of Canada; Free trade; World Trade Organization (WTO).**

Task force. An informal term designating either an independent investigative body established by a government to obtain information and make recommendations on policy matters, or a small working group established to advise a larger or higher-level group of decision makers. The use of independent task forces is one way of obtaining nongovernment advice for possible implementation in legislative form.

A task force is a less formal body than a royal commission, but with a staff and budget to carry out research and possibly hold public hearings. The effectiveness of a given task force is a function of its terms of reference, members and financial resources, but also of the relevance of its recommendations to the electoral future of the government. Generally the work of independent task forces is easier to ignore than the reports of higher-profile royal commissions, and their appointment may be only a dilatory or symbolic government response to a problem. For example, the Task Force on Canadian Unity of 1978-79 co-chaired by former Ontario Conservative premier John Robarts and former federal Liberal minister Jean-Luc Pépin made recommendations that were not entirely in accord with the views of Liberal Prime Minister Pierre Trudeau. The government, however, pursued others in constitutional negotiations leading to the patriation of the constitution in 1982 (*A Future Together: Observations and Recommendations* [Ottawa: The Task Force on Canadian Unity, 1979]). In 1986, Conservative Prime Minister Brian Mulroney established a ministerial Task Force on Program Review. It engaged several study teams of private- and public-sector personnel to investigate the effectiveness of government operations and used their published reports as a basis for its recommendations to the cabinet.

Tax abatement and Tax points. Federal tax abatement involves withdrawal by the federal government from a tax field, and a tax point is a percentage point of personal income taxes. The federal abatement of tax points occurs in a province whose government has "opted out" of a conditional federal-provincial cost-sharing program in order to finance a similar program itself.

In the *Established Programs (Interim Arrangements) Act, 1965,* the federal government gave provinces the opportunity to opt out of certain shared-cost programs and pursue similar provincial programs without financial penalty. Only Quebec exercised the option, and the federal government compensated Quebec through the abatement of tax points. Abatements of equalized tax points were the basis of negotiated federal transfer payments in the federal *Federal Provincial Fiscal Arrangements and Established Programs Financing Act* of subsequent years, and now of the Canada Health and Social Transfer. See **Canada Health and Social Transfer (CHST); Federal-provincial tax-sharing agreements (fiscal federalism).**

Tax expenditures. Potential public revenue foregone through tax-incentive programs. Governments use such policies, notably to business but also to individuals, to direct private spending in particular ways. Such incentives, for example tax "holidays," credits and deductions, constitute indirect public spending or public subsidies. Popular with individuals and companies that benefit from them, their existence and dollar value in terms of public revenue foregone are relatively unknown to those who cannot take advantage of them. See **Budget and budgetary process**.

Tax rental agreements (payments). Early federal-provincial agreements under which the provincial governments might abandon, or "vacate," their power to levy taxes in such fields as corporate and personal income tax and succession duties to the federal government in return for financial compensation, or "rent." Under the Wartime Tax Agreements of 1941, all provinces entered agreements to abandon the fields until 1946 in return for a calculated tax rental payment. A tax rental payment scheme existed until 1957, after which there were periodically negotiated "tax-sharing agreements," enacted as the federal *Federal Provincial Fiscal Arrangements and Established Programs Financing Act*, now the Canada Health and Social Transfer. See **Canada Health and Social Transfer (CHST); Federal-provincial tax-sharing agreements (fiscal federalism)**.

Territorial governments. Governments in the territories of Canada that do not have provincial status—Yukon, Northwest Territories and Nunavut. Each comprises an elected representative assembly and responsible government, but which, especially in NWT and Nunavut, operate with more collegial and less adversarial party systems consistent with the customs and practices of their predominantly Native populations. Unlike provinces that are autonomous political jurisdictions, territories are constitutionally subordinate to the federal government. The establishment of new provinces and the extension of existing provincial boundaries into the territories can be accomplished using the general amending formula of the *Constitution Act, 1982* with no allowance for provincial dissent (s.42.1,c,f.)

Third parties; Third-party campaign advertising. In a legal context, third parties are individuals or groups, that is, parties, not directly involved in a matter, but with sufficient interest to receive standing in a court case or before a judicial inquiry. In electoral politics, third-party campaigning refers to advertising by individuals or groups other than registered political parties, candidates of registered parties and their agents in election and referendum campaigns.

At one end of the legal spectrum, third parties are prohibited from advertising in provincial elections and referendum campaigns in Quebec. At the other end, there have been several court decisions, beginning in Alberta in 1984, that declared sections of the federal *Canada Elections Act* prohibiting third-party advertising in support of particular parties or candidates to be a violation of fundamental freedoms guaranteed in the Canadian Charter of Rights and Freedoms (s.2). In 1999, possibly encouraged by a recent ruling by the Supreme Court of Canada that sustained the principle of such restrictions in a decision regarding Quebec's referendum legislation, the federal government once again enacted restrictions on third-party advertising in federal election, and once again they were challenged in court. During the federal election of 2000, the Supreme Court of Canada lifted an injunction that had been granted by an Alberta court against the restrictions. Without judging the constitutionality of the restrictions on third-part advertising, in an 8-1 decision the majority cited a "rule against granting the equivalent of final relief in interlocutory challenges to electoral statutes, even in the course of elections governed by those statutes" (*A.-G. of Canada v. Stephen Joseph Harper*, 2000). See **Electoral law (controls; subsidies)**.

Third parties (political). Political parties other than the Liberal and Conservative parties, that have come into existence since Confederation. Although they effectively displaced one or both of the "old" parties in some provincial party systems in most of the twentieth century—notably in the western provinces—with the exception of the Progressives in 1921, none other did so in federal politics until 1993 when the Bloc Québécois and the Reform party won the second- and third-largest representation, respectively, in the House of Commons while the New Democratic party, a long-standing third political party, lost its official-party status.

Various explanations exist for the rise of third parties in Canada. An institutional explanation focuses on such contributing factors as the parliamentary, federal and electoral systems. The parliamentary system contributes because the focus of general elections is the numerous constituency contests, and the election of only a few members gives some legitimacy and credibility to new movements. Under the rules of the House of Commons, a group with at least twelve members of Parliament receives public funds for a leader's salary, additional office space, research facilities and staff, and procedural recognition in question period and during debate, for example, to introduce resolutions and motions and respond to ministerial statements. The disciplined parliamentary party system contributes indirectly because it demands conformity from backbenchers, thus potentially alienating regional representatives who cannot alter the policy of established parties to suit the interests of their region, and resulting in popular support for new political forces. The electoral system contributes because it disproportionately rewards parties with concentrated sectional support. The federal system contributes because small movements articulating regional or localized grievances may be more successful in provincial than in federal elections, and may eventually form provincial governments and exercise considerable influence in federal-provincial relations.

Structural factors related to the economy, society and culture comprise another explanation. Changes that heighten class, regional, or ethnic concerns may contribute to the success of new parties. Finally, in the constant jockeying for electoral advantage, established parties may ignore some long-standing or newly emergent interest, allowing a new party to take over the vacant "issue space."

Examining the rise of the Ralliement des créditistes in Quebec in the 1960s, Maurice Pinard suggested that third parties develop in times of social or economic discontent when a single party has dominated electoral politics in a large area for a long time. Thus, the long period of Liberal dominance in federal politics led aggrieved rural Quebeckers to conclude that the alternate parliamentary party, the Conservative party, was not a credible choice. The third-party

Ralliement, an indigenous populist movement led by Réal Caouette, provided such an alternative (*The Rise of a Third Party: A Study in Crisis Politics* [Englewood Cliffs: Prentice-Hall, 1971]). Pinard's explanation seems to apply also to the case of the Social Credit party ousting the United Farmers of Alberta in 1935. However, C.B. Macpherson suggested that the one-crop agricultural economy of the prairies at that time created a "colonial" society in relation to central Canada and resulted in widespread electoral support for a party representing the interests of the single-class society in Alberta and a "quasi-party system" (*Democracy in Alberta: Social Credit and the Party System* [Toronto: University of Toronto Press, 1953]). Examining the Co-operative Commonwealth Federation in Saskatchewan, Seymour Martin Lipset argued that the one-crop agricultural economy there led to the creation of co-operative organizations and a class of experienced and relatively well-off activists who transferred their experience and energies to the CCF. Consequently, the CCF became a successful and entrenched political party in that province (*Agrarian Socialism: The Co-operative Commonwealth Federation in Saskatchewan* [Berkeley: University of California Press, 1950]).

Following the 1921 election, the western-based Progressive party held the second-largest number of seats, but because it rejected the role of official opposition, the third-place Conservatives were able to maintain their strategic parliamentary role against the Liberal government. The success in the 1990s and 2000 of the Bloc Québécois and Reform/Alliance parties can be analyzed with respect to all explanations mentioned above. See entries on political parties named here and different elements of the political system.

Throne Speech (Debate on the...). A speech by the governor general (lieutenant-governor in the provinces), opening a session of Parliament (provincial legislature), followed by a general debate in the House on a government motion commending the speech. In Quebec, the debate is on the premier's Inaugural Address.

The speech, written by the government, generally outlines the state of national or provincial affairs and the government's legislative program for the legislature. Debate lasts several days, with the opposition parties moving amendments, in effect confidence motions, referring to some deficiency in government policy. Apart from the initial remarks by the parties' chief speakers which attract the attention of the mass media, the debate is a rare opportunity for backbench members to address the House on matters of importance to them and their constituents, if not the national media. The debate ends with votes on opposition amendments to the government motion and on the motion itself, each constituting a vote of confidence in which the disciplined party system almost always ensures the government's success.

Tory. Currently, a popular reference to the Conservative party and its supporters (more so in central Canada and the Maritimes than in the West). Historically, in pre-Confederation British North America, Tories were generally in favour of maintaining the power of the colonial governor and the appointed and non-responsible Executive Council against encroachments by the representative legislative assembly. They would also be well represented in the appointed colonial upper chamber, the Legislative Council. Because Tories are often associated with the privileged colonial elites of church, state and society, the term is also used pejoratively to refer to upper-class privilege. Privilege was supposed to be accompanied, however, by the observance of social responsibilities and obligations.

Contemporary reference to "Red Tories" are to those Conservatives whose sense of obligation extends beyond personal charity to support government measures to deal with social problems, especially as they might pose a larger threat to social order. Such "conservatives" are distinct from the so-called "neo-conservatives" who wish to minimize the role of the state in economic life and "social conservatives" who wish likewise, but who want the state to enforce a strict code of behaviour on individuals. See **Red Tory (-ism)**.

"Trade and Commerce" power. Legislative jurisdiction granted Parliament under the *Constitution Act, 1867* (s.91:2), and, as a form of residual power, one way by which the federal government has sought to enlarge its legislative competence. Historically, the Judicial Committee of the Privy Council (JCPC) denied section 91:2 as a source of broad legislative power, but after 1949 the Supreme Court, then the final court of appeal, tended to be more accommodating to federal arguments for jurisdiction under the "Trade and Commerce" power.

From its earliest adjudication of "Trade and Commerce" power, the JCPC was careful not to allow it to become effectively an emergency or residual power clause. It felt that if the framers of the constitution had intended it to be so, then the subsequent enumeration of other matters in section 91 would have been unnecessary. Thus, the "Trade and Commerce" head was not to permit federal interference in the business or trade "in a single province" (*Citizens' Insurance Co. v. Parsons*, 1881) that "would seriously encroach upon the autonomy of the province" (*Montreal v. Montreal Street Railway*, 1912). In adjudicating federal "Trade and Commerce" power, the JCPC distinguished between goods in intraprovincial trade and those in interprovincial and international trade and the result made effective legislation by governments at both levels difficult.

Following the abolition of appeals to the JCPC, the Supreme Court was relatively flexible in accommodating the federal constitution to contemporary need. On marketing, for example, the Supreme Court declared interdelegation of powers between Parliament and a provincial legislature unconstitutional, but it permitted the delegation of power from one level to a regulatory body of another level (Nova Scotia Interdelegation Case, 1951; *PEI Potato Marketing Board v. Willis Inc.*, 1952). In the 1950s, the Supreme Court introduced the notion of the "flow of trade," to replace the difficult categories of intraprovincial and interprovincial and international trade, thus at least recognizing the need for federal-provincial co-operation (*Reference Re Farm Marketing Act [Ontario]*, 1957). Such "co-operation," allowing a federal role, had implications for provincially owned natural resources, clarified in the constitutional amendment of section 92.A in 1982. Generally, the Court has interpreted "Trade and Commerce" power according to a "dimension" doctrine respecting the national importance of the matter being legislated, and supported provincial legislation intended to have effect only in the relevant province though there might be an incidental extra-provincial effect. For an opinion in 1971 by Justice Bora Laskin (later chief justice) that reviews the adjudication of the "Trade and Commerce" power, including the Judicial

Committee's attenuation of federal power and the Supreme Court's generally restorative decisions, see *Attorney-General for Manitoba v. Manitoba Egg and Poultry Association*, 1971, the so-called Chicken and Egg Reference. See **Interdelegation Reference (Nova Scotia, 1951); Judicial Committee of the Privy Council (JCPC); Supreme Court.**

Transfer payment. Any payment from one level of government to another (usually from the federal to the provincial governments), or from a government to an individual. See **Canada Health and Social Transfer (CHST); Canada (Quebec) Pension Plan (CPP, QPP); Conditional grants (special-purpose transfer payments); Equalization grants (unconditional transfer payments); Federal-provincial tax-sharing agreements (fiscal federalism); Unconditional grants (general-purpose transfer payments).**

Transferable vote (preferential ballot). An electoral system no longer used in Canada that allows the voter to rank candidates in single-member constituency elections according to preference. Instead of marking the ballot in favour of a single candidate, the voter ranks candidates 1, 2, 3, and so forth. Should the count of first preferences not result in a candidate having a majority of the votes cast (that is, at least 50 per cent plus one), the least popular candidate is dropped from consideration and the second choices on ballots which listed that candidate as first choice are counted. This process continues until one candidate has a majority of the votes. The transferable vote, or preferential ballot, was used in provincial elections in Manitoba and Alberta in the early part of the twentieth century. It was also used in the British Columbia general election in 1952.

Treasury Board. A statutory federal cabinet committee (that is, formally a committee of the Queen's Privy Council for Canada), chaired by a minister designated president of the Treasury Board and including notably the minister of finance.

The Treasury Board and its Secretariat, headed by the secretary/comptroller general, constitutes an important central executive agency in the federal government. The Treasury Board is responsible for the management of the federal public service, including financial management. Over-seeing a rolling multi-year expenditure planning cycle, it is responsible for annual recommendations to cabinet on the selection of programs and projects, and the appropriate allocation of funds to achieve government objectives. In its management role, the Treasury Board has powers under the *Financial Administration Act* for administrative policy for financial management in the public administration, and for matters related to personnel, office space, supply and contracts for services. The Treasury Board also negotiates for the government in collective bargaining arrangements with public service unions and associations. See **Auditor General; Budget and budgetary process; Comptroller General of Canada; Estimates; Treasury Board Secretariat; (TBS).**

Treasury Board Secretariat (TBS). An important central staff agency in the federal government whose powers are based in the authority of the Treasury Board, the only statutory committee of cabinet.

The TBS assists the Treasury Board in the determination of program priorities and review of expenditures, administrative policy and organization of the public service, financial administration, personnel management, staff relations, federal property management and transactions, and official-languages policies in the public service. On program determination and expenditure review, it implements the budgetary process (when program forecasts are reviewed and an expenditure plan is established) and recommends estimates or expenditure plans eventually for cabinet approval and submission to Parliament. It then oversees the implementation of approved expenditure plans to ensure that intended results are achieved.

The TBS also deals with administrative management to ensure effective government operations and personnel management. The Secretariat advises Treasury Board on the management of real property, including land use and the capital plans. It oversees the implementation of federal official-languages policy in the public service. The TBS negotiates and administers collective bargaining agreements on behalf of management with employees of the federal government. In 1993, the Office of Comptroller General was subsumed within the Treasury Board Secretariat and the secretary designated as comptroller general. See **Budget and budgetary process; Comptroller General of Canada; Estimates; Treasury Board.**

Treaty power. The authority of the federal government to enter into international commitments, tempered by the federal-provincial division of legislative power.

The need to recognize the conditional nature of federal power arises because the *Constitution Act, 1867* grants treaty powers to the "Parliament and Government of Canada...for performing the Obligations of Canada or of any Province thereof, as Part of the British Empire..." (s.132). As Canada developed an international personality separate from that of the Empire in the twentieth century, the Judicial Committee of the Privy Council (JCPC) was obliged to clarify federal treaty power. It ruled that, if section 132 did not apply, the power of the "Parliament and Government of Canada" depended on the division of legislative powers between the two levels of government. Thus, there was no such thing as "treaty legislation," that is, legislative scope for the federal government in an area of provincial jurisdiction simply because the federal government committed Canada in a treaty to legislative action.

In the 1930s, the federal government acquired jurisdiction in aeronautics and broadcasting, policy areas unforeseen by the framers of Confederation in the 1860s: in the Aeronautics Case, 1932, through an Imperial treaty, but in an aside Lord Sankey wrote that legislation dealing with air transportation would have been *intra vires* under the "Peace, Order, and good Government" preamble of section 91 as the legislation was on a matter of "such dimensions as to affect the body politic of the nation"; and in the Radio Case, 1932, in which Lord Dunedin wrote that, as an independent dominion, the federal government acquired treaty power under the "Peace, Order, and good Government" clause, as a residual power, since legislative authority in empire treaty making was treated as a separate section apart from sections 91 and 92 and that a non-Imperial treaty "comes to the same thing." (In 1952, the Supreme Court upheld federal jurisdiction in air transportation and navigation although the British Empire treaty on which the *Aeronautics Act* had been based was replaced by the non-Imperial Chicago

Convention. The Supreme Court noted Lord Sankey's "dimensions" doctrine in affirming federal jurisdiction through the "Peace, Order, and good Government" clause [*Johannesson v. Rural Municipality of West St. Paul*].)

However, the JCPC denied Parliament scope in labour legislation by virtue of the federal government incurring an obligation by treaty. In the Labour Conventions Case, 1937, Lord Atkin wrote that while the federal government had the full power to make treaties, there was "no existing constitutional ground for stretching the competence of the Dominion Parliament...to keep pace with enlarged functions of the Dominion executive...merely by making promises to foreign countries...."

Since the 1960s, the federal government has accepted some provincial involvement in international meetings and in the negotiation of conventions and treaties, to ensure their implementation. Earlier, in 1961, a federal Conservative government had signed the Columbia River Treaty with the United States regarding upstream dam construction on the Canadian portion of the river. However, its implementation was delayed until the successor Liberal federal government and British Columbia reached an agreement in 1963, necessitating then a negotiated protocol between Canada and the United States. The treaty involved the development of a natural resource (a provincial responsibility under s.92:5) in a project which the federal government was unwilling to declare "to be for the general Advantage of Canada or for the Advantage of Two or more of the Provinces" ("declaratory power," 92:10 [c]). Although the ratification of international treaties is a function of the Crown, federal governments usually apply good political sense and refer them to Parliament for public debate and approval. See **Judicial Committee of the Privy Council (JCPC); Ratification.**

Triple-E Senate. A characterization of a reformed Canadian Senate that would be "Elected, Effective and Equal."

The Senate is the appointed upper house of Parliament, possessing almost the same legislative power as the lower house, the House of Commons, with proportionate representation by regions, but lacking in popular legitimacy. Representation based on population and the disciplined party system in the House of Commons render regional representation from less populated parts of the country weak in numbers and voice. Consequently, demands for Senate reform have arisen, especially in western Canada, to make the upper chamber a truly federal institution where sectional interests could be better addressed than in the House of Commons, the majority of whose members are elected from central Canada. Thus, it is argued, senators should be elected, with equal representation from the provinces and with effective legislative power.

The failed constitutional Meech Lake Accord of 1987 would have required the federal government to appoint senators from lists of nominees proposed by relevant provincial governments. The Charlottetown Accord of 1992, rejected in a country-wide referendum, included both Senate and House reform that would have allowed for a Senate with equal representation from each province and some representation from the territories. Effectiveness was defined variously according to several classes of legislation, but the House of Commons would remain the only chamber of confidence. Senators would also have acquired the power to veto the government's nominee to head the central bank and other unspecified "key appointments," such as the heads of cultural institutions and regulatory boards and agencies. To stress the role of senators as publicly vocal regional representatives, they would not have been eligible for appointment to the cabinet. See **Charlottetown Accord (1992); Senate**.

Two nations (*deux nations*). A phrase denoting the view that Canada comprises "two founding nations," one French- and one English-speaking. Debate over the concept focuses on special legislative powers sought by Quebec as the only predominantly francophone jurisdiction in Canada.

Formally, Quebec has special status respecting the civil law in the province, the requirement that both English and French be used in government and the courts in Quebec (though New Brunswick became constitutionally bilingual in 1982), and the statutory requirement in the federal *Supreme Court Act* for representation from the Quebec bar or bench on the Supreme Court. Informally, Quebec achieved "special status" in 1965 under the federal Liberal government's *Established Programs (Interim Arrangements) Act*. All provinces were given the option of withdrawing from federal-provincial shared-cost programs without incurring financial penalties, but only Quebec accepted the offer. Also, the federal Liberal government in the 1970s allowed provincial governments to participate in international conferences on matters related to provincial jurisdiction as long as Canada retained a single international personality. Thus, in 1971, Quebec and the federal government concluded an agreement on participation in the international francophone Agency for Cultural and Technical Co-operation. Under the agreement, Quebec ministers or officials may attend Agency conferences to express Quebec's point of view on matters within provincial jurisdiction.

Provincial parties in Quebec continue to press for "self-determination" for Quebec either in the form of "renewed" or "restructured" federalism proposed by the Liberals, or in sovereignty or "sovereignty association" proposed by the Parti Québécois. In 1982, Quebec opposed the patriation of the *Constitution Act* because of the amending formula and the Canadian Charter of Rights and Freedoms. A subsequent Quebec round of constitutional negotiations resulted in the Meech Lake Accord under which Quebec would have been granted four of its five demands by their extension to all provinces. The fifth demand agreed to was the constitutional recognition of Quebec as a "distinct society" with a legislative and executive role to "preserve and promote the distinct identity of Quebec." The eventual failure of the Accord in 1990 led to renewed debate and negotiations resulting in the Charlottetown Accord of 1992 which included a Canada Clause defining Quebec as a distinct society "which includes a French-speaking majority, a unique culture and a civil law tradition," and affirming Quebec's role "to preserve and promote the distinct society of Quebec." See **Quiet Revolution; Renewed/restructured federalism; Sovereignty association; Special status**.

Two-party system. A party system in which there is long-standing electoral competition between only two major parties. The use of this or other phrases to describe the competitiveness of a party system is somewhat arbitrary—except with reference to those countries where only one party is permitted by law.

Distinctive regional political cultures and federalism have resulted in an extremely fragmented party system in Canada. The Atlantic provinces have the most traditional two-party system, although in some of them "third parties" have occasionally been competitive. Party systems elsewhere in Canada may be described either as competitive multi-party systems or as one-party dominant multi-party systems. Moreover, numbers aside, parties dominant or competitive in one part of the country can be non-existent elsewhere. See **One-party (single-party) dominance; Party system; Third parties (political)**.

U

Ultra (intra) vires. A phrase that describes a statute of federal or provincial legislatures as beyond (within) their legislative competence as determined through judicial review of the *Constitution Act* with final appeal to the Judicial Committee of the Privy Council until 1949, and later only to the Supreme Court of Canada. See **Judicial Committee of the Privy Council (JCPC); Judicial review (interpretive; non-interpretive); Supreme Court.**

Unconditional grants (general-purpose transfer payments). Federal grants to provincial governments that are not designated for any specific expenditure program. The statutory subsidies originally provided for in the now-spent section 118 of the *Constitution Act, 1867* were, in effect, unconditional grants (see the notes pertaining to section 118 in the consolidated text of the Act). Currently, however, most unconditional grants are made under the equalization program which was entrenched in the *Constitution Act, 1982.* "Have-not" provinces qualify for unconditional federal transfer payments "to ensure that provincial governments have sufficient revenues to provide reasonably comparable levels of public services at reasonably comparable levels of taxation" (s.36). See **Conditional grants (special-purpose transfer payments); Equalization grants (unconditional transfer payments); Federal-provincial tax-sharing agreements (fiscal federalism).**

Unicameral legislature. A term denoting one chamber in a legislative system as opposed to two (bicameral). All the provincial legislatures in Canada are unicameral, while the federal Parliament is bicameral by virtue of having a lower house, the House of Commons, and an upper house, the Senate.

Union Act, 1840 **(U.K.).** The imperial statute which reunited Upper and Lower Canada in 1840, forming the United Province of Canada, until Confederation in 1867.

Following the rebellions of 1837 in Upper and Lower Canada, the British government suspended the colonial constitutions and dispatched Lord Durham as governor to report on conditions. His two main recommendations were the unification of the Canadas in order to assimilate the French population and the granting of responsible government to encourage popular support. However, the *Union Act* provided only for unification. Responsible government came later by constitutional convention. The Act provided for a British-appointed governor, a Legislative

Council (upper house) appointed by the Crown for life and an elected Legislative Assembly (lower house) of eighty-four members equally divided between Canada East (Lower Canada) and Canada West (Upper Canada). The Act consolidated the revenue of the two colonies and initially only English was recognized as an official language of government. The constitution thus favoured the initially less populous and financially less well-off, predominantly anglophone Canada West, and was clearly intended to achieve the assimilation of the French community.

Eventually the conventions of domestic politics subverted the assimilative purposes of the union, brought about responsible government, but also a political deadlock that led to the Confederation project. Governments of the Province of Canada included dual leadership—anglophone and francophone—from each of the Canadas, a double-majority convention that required support for the legislative leadership from both sections, hence bicultural legislative accommodation, and eventually the recognition of French as an official language of government. As for responsible government, it was politically impossible for the governor to choose an Executive Council without considering the opinions of the Assembly, but there was no obligation to alter the Council as the Legislative Assembly wished. In 1848, a legislative want-of-confidence vote following an election in Nova Scotia had led to the Executive Council's resignation under Governor Sir John Harvey, and thus the introduction of responsible government in British North America. Two months later, under the governorship of Durham's son-in-law Lord Elgin, a defeat of the Executive Council on a non-confidence motion in the Assembly of the United Province of Canada resulted in a change of government, the first instance of responsible government in that colony.

As a result of the balancing of sectional and cultural interests, the governance of the Province of Canada eventually led to a political deadlock. In 1839, Lord Durham had rejected the union of all British colonies as premature. However, by the 1860s there were separate and shared reasons for the colonies as well as the Imperial government to reconsider the matter. In the 1860s, the Canadian leadership prevailed on the leadership of the Maritime colonies to discuss the confederation of British colonies which was partially effected in 1867. See **Confederation; Lord Durham's Report; Responsible government**.

Union government. A wartime coalition federal government that was formed in 1917, won a general election later that year, and remained in office until 1920. Although the coalition included anglophone Liberals, it was essentially a Conservative administration created by Prime Minister Robert Borden, who had been in office since 1911. It ceased when Liberals departed, Borden resigned and Conservative Arthur Meighen formed a government.

This was a time of intense French-English discord as francophone members of parliament sat as a distinct minority on the opposition side in the House of Commons, facing an anglophone government of Conservatives and Liberals intent on introducing military conscription for a war generally opposed by French Canadians. Apart from the difficulty of discerning a Canadian interest in the First World War, French Canadians were concerned that their cultural survival would be jeopardized by consigning a generation of young men to a European slaughter.

The Union government has been the only coalition government in Canadian federal history, other than the Confederation alliance in 1867, although from time to time minority governments have remained in office through informal alliances with opposition parties.

Unitary state (legislative union). A political system in which legislative authority derives from a single parliament. By contrast, a federal system involves the division of legislative powers between autonomous levels of legislature and government which may also entail concurrent legislative powers, as outlined in a written constitution with appeal on disputes to the judiciary.

The United Kingdom is an example of a unitary state, and Canada is an example of a federal state, both otherwise with similar systems of responsible parliamentary government under a Crown. Colonial leaders meeting in Charlottetown and later in Quebec City in 1864 to discuss union of the British North American colonies opted for a centralized federal state, a compromise between supporters and opponents of a legislative union, or unitary state.

United Farmers of...(Alberta, Manitoba, Ontario). Associations of farmers and rural interests that contested elections and formed governments in several provinces in the early twentieth century. Their success, however manifested later in different parties, shattered the national two party system and established "third parties" as competitive regional forces.

The Alberta group was the most successful, holding office in that province from 1921 to 1935. The movement supported the notion of occupational or functional group representation in legislatures rather than the conventional party system. Provincial party supporters elected Progressive members to the House of Commons during the 1920s, and in the 1930s participated in founding the Co-operative Commonwealth Federation, precursor to the New Democratic party, with others participating in the eventual success of the Social Credit party in Alberta in 1935. In Ontario, the United Farmers formed a provincial government from 1919 to 1923, with the support of Labour and Independent members. In Manitoba, the United Farmers formed a government in 1922, but were later absorbed by the Liberals, who remained in office as the Liberal-Progressive party until 1958. See **Third parties (political)**.

Upper Canada. A colony in British North America from 1791 to 1840.

Under the *Quebec Act* of 1774, the colony of Quebec extended west to include land between the Ohio and Mississippi rivers. The political system included provision for freedom of worship for Roman Catholics and for the use of the civil law on non-criminal matters unless changed by the colony. The American Revolution resulted in the migration of Loyalists to the Maritime colonies and Quebec. In Quebec, loyalist settlement took place notably on the south shore of the St. Lawrence River and around Lake Ontario and Lake Erie.

The loyalist newcomers to Quebec insisted, however, on living under entirely English law with representative institutions. Thus, in 1791, the *Constitutional Act* divided Quebec into Upper and Lower Canada, creating representative institutions for both colonies and allowing for the maintenance of French civil law in Lower Canada (later Canada East and Quebec). One of the earliest acts in Upper Canada (later Canada West and Ontario) was the introduction of English common law in civil matters.

By the 1830s, demands in the representative assemblies for control over the executive through responsible government led to unrest in both Upper and Lower Canada. Following unsuccessful rebellions in both Upper and Lower Canada in 1837, and agitation in the Maritime colonies, the British government sent Lord Durham as governor to investigate conditions. Durham recommended responsible government for the colonies and the reunion of the two Canadas in order to assimilate the French population of Lower Canada. In 1840, the *Union Act* reunited the two colonies once again as the United Province of Canada, without mention of responsible government, in order to achieve assimilation. See *Constitutional Act, 1791* **(U.K.)**; **Lord Durham's Report.**

Upper chamber (house). In a bicameral legislature, the chamber which usually represents regional or sectional rather than majoritarian interests. It is less immediately accountable (if at all) to the electorate than the lower house, and is theoretically a conservative, moderating influence on the lower house.

In Canada's bicameral Parliament, the upper house is the Senate, to which the governor general "summons" people (on the prime minister's "advice") to represent regional divisions as specified in the *Constitution Act, 1867* (ss.21-36). Elsewhere, upper houses may be elected for longer terms and from larger constituencies than representatives in the lower house, with only partial election at a given time and hence staggered terms (for example, the United States Senate); elected concurrently with elections to the lower house, but on a different electoral system (for example, the Australian Senate); appointed to represent state or provincial governments (for example, the Federal Republic of Germany's Bundesrat); have representation based on life appointments and selectively on heredity (for example, the British House of Lords).

Constitutional negotiations in Canada since the 1970s have focused in part on proposals for reform of the Senate. See **Senate**.

Urgent business (emergency debate). Provisions in the rules of a legislature for the opposition to request debate on an urgent matter that has arisen unexpectedly and cannot otherwise be considered during normal House business.

In the House of Commons, the opposition can request the Speaker's approval for an emergency debate. If the ruling is favourable, the debate begins in the evening and, despite time limits on members' speeches, can last far into the night. Requests by the opposition for the debate and the debate itself attract the attention of the mass media and can be an effective way to convey criticism of the government. Even if the Speaker denies a request for an emergency debate, the request and subsequent discussion might draw public attention to some alleged government failure. See **House of Commons**.

V

Veto. The power to overrule a decision of another person or body, from "I forbid" in Latin.

In the Canadian constitution, there are several forms of veto. The royal prerogative of reservation and disallowance of legislation exists in Canada by constitutional statute: lieutenant-governors in the provinces retain the constitutional authority to reserve legislation for consideration by the governor-in-council, that is, the federal cabinet. The federal government also has the legal power to disallow provincial legislation within one year of its passage (*Constitution Act, 1867*, ss.56, 57, 61, 90). The governor general had the authority to disallow federal legislation or reserve it for the Queen's consideration, that is, the British government's, until the Statute of Westminster of 1931. In effect, then, the federal government has legal constitutional authority to veto provincial legislation, but by convention does not (the last case being in 1943).

The courts can nullify legislation, including the subordinate legislation (or rules and regulations) of executive and administrative bodies, either through a constitutional reference or litigation, declaring it either *ultra vires*, beyond the jurisdictional competence of the relevant legislature in Canada's federal system, or a violation of the provisions of the Canadian Charter of Rights and Freedoms.

The procedures adopted in 1982 for amending the constitution involve a variety of vetoes, including the general amending formula requiring a resolution of Parliament and two-thirds of provincial legislatures representing at least 50 per cent of the population of all the provinces. Thus Parliament and combinations of provinces (possibly comprising regions) can exercise a veto on constitutional change, or a province affected by certain amendments could dissent and receive compensation (*Constitution Act, 1982*, ss.38, 40). In specific respects in which the constitution requires the unanimous consent of Parliament and the provincial legislatures, all legislatures have a veto (s.41). Finally, where the consent of Parliament is required in sections 38 and 41-43, the Senate exercises only a suspensive veto (s.47). See **Canadian Charter of Rights and Freedoms (1982)**; ***Constitution Act, 1867*, and subsequently amended; Judicial Committee of the Privy Council (JCPC); Senate; Supreme Court; Suspensive veto.**

Victoria Charter (1971). The agreement reached in Victoria, British Columbia, among the Canadian heads of governments (including initially Liberal Premier Robert Bourassa of Quebec) to patriate the constitution; it was subsequently rejected by Quebec. In many respects, the Victoria Charter contained elements in the *Constitution Act, 1982*, which patriated the constitution, but without the support of Quebec. The Victoria Charter comprised a domestic amending formula and an entrenched bill of rights, provincial consultation on federal appointments to the Supreme Court, entrenchment of federal equalization payments to fiscally hard-pressed provinces and minority-language rights.

Quebec rejected the Charter, as it had the earlier Fulton-Favreau Formula in 1964, because of the provisions regarding the federal role in matters of social policy. In 1982, the constitution was patriated by a parliamentary resolution to the British Parliament supported by the Canadian Parliament and all provincial legislatures except Quebec's. Two rounds of constitutional negotiations leading to the Meech Lake (1987) and Charlottetown (1992) Accords, each an attempt in part to accommodate Quebec to the constitution, failed. See **Canadian Charter of Rights and Freedoms (1982); Charlottetown Accord (1992); *Constitution Act, 1867*, and subsequently amended; Fulton-Favreau Formula (1964); Meech Lake Accord (1987).**

Vote of no confidence (want-of-confidence motion). A vote in the House of Commons or a provincial legislature on an opposition motion amending an important government motion, or a vote on the main motion itself, the loss of which represents defeat for the government in the House.

The constitutional convention of responsible government requires that when a government loses the confidence of the elected House, the prime minister (or provincial premier) either advises the governor general (or provincial lieutenant-governor) to dissolve Parliament (the legislature) and issue writs for an election, or resigns. If the prime minister (premier) resigns, the governor general (lieutenant-governor) asks someone else to form a government and seek the confidence of the House. In the bicameral Parliament, the appointed Senate is not a chamber of confidence.

In Canada's federal and provincial legislatures, the norm is for votes to be matters of confidence unless, in rare instances, party leaders remove the whip, allowing members to vote as they wish. When the government party controls more than half of the representation in the legislature, votes will predictably favour the government. Especially in the context of minority governments, there have been suggestions for a narrow definition of confidence measures. Similar demands come from those who feel that, whether the government commands majority support or not, legislators should be less constrained by the discipline of their party whip. For example, confidence could be specifically limited to the motion on the Speech from the Throne, the budget, estimates, and legislation that the government designates on introduction as a matter of confidence. See **Confidence (of the House; Chamber of…)**; **Responsible government**.

Voters list. See **Enumeration (of voters)**.

W

War Measures Act (**Canada; emergency powers**). A federal statute adopted in 1914, which served as Canada's emergency enabling legislation under the "Peace, Order, and good Government" provision in the preamble of Section 91 of the *British North America Act, 1867* (since 1982, the *Constitution Act*) until it was superseded by the *Emergencies Act* in 1988.

Under the *War Measures Act*, the cabinet had to report the proclamation of an emergency immediately to Parliament if it was in session; otherwise, within fifteen days of the opening of the next session. When introduced, ten members of either the House of Commons or Senate could move revocation and force a debate. The Act was in effect during the First and Second World Wars. During the wars, normal parliamentary procedure was suspended, the economy was effectively nationalized and censorship was imposed. The Act was also used to register, imprison, or deport "enemy aliens." In the Second World War, Canadians of Japanese origin had their property confiscated and were interned under the Act.

Liberal Prime Minister Pierre Trudeau invoked the Act in peacetime during the "October Crisis" in 1970. Declaring the existence of an apprehended insurrection, the government invoked the Act following the kidnapping and holding for ransom of a British trade official and a Quebec cabinet minister in Montreal by two cells of the Front de libération du Québec. The minister was later murdered. Public order regulations made the FLQ, successor organizations, and any other organization which advocated force or illegal activity as a means of changing government to be illegal and specified indictable offenses for people associated with them. Police and the military were given extraordinary powers of search and arrest, and provincial attorneys-general had the power to enforce a three-week detention before a specific charge was required under the regulations. The federal government asserted that the regulations, though national in scope, had particular reference for Quebec only, and that the provincial government remained chiefly responsible for activities during the emergency under the "normal" powers of the *British North America Act* (s.92:14, "The Administration of Justice in the Province..."). Subsequent debate focused on whether the extraordinary powers granted police under the Act in 1970 had been needed in the eventual apprehension of the kidnappers, including those who murdered the cabinet minister after the Act was invoked.

After 1982, all legislation, including emergency legislation, had to conform to the Canadian Charter of Rights and Freedoms. The *Emergencies Act*, which replaced the *War Measures Act* in 1988, distinguishes several types of emergencies, with orders and regulations appropriate to each, and requires parliamentary approval and an ongoing, though secret, parliamentary review of regulations as well as a report to Parliament within a year of the expiry of the emergency declaration. See *Emergencies Act* **(Canada, 1988); October (FLQ) Crisis (1970).**

War-crimes legislation (trials). Amendments to the Criminal Code in 1987 permitting prosecutions in Canada for war crimes and crimes against humanity committed outside the country, both prior and subsequent to the enactment of the amendments.

Under the Criminal Code, a war crime is "an act or omission" committed during an international military conflict, regardless of the law that prevailed in the place and at the time of the alleged crime, but which was a offence against "the customary international law or conventional international law applicable in international armed conflicts." A crime against humanity is "murder, extermination, enslavement, deportation, persecution or any other inhumane act or omission that is committed against any civilian population or any identifiable group of persons," again regardless of the law in the place at the time, but which contravened "customary international law or conventional international law" or constituted a crime "according to the general principles of law recognized by the community of nations." An act or omission involves "attempting or conspiring to commit, counselling any person to commit, aiding or abetting any person in the commission of, or being an accessory after the fact." Although the motivation for war-crimes legislation and trials arose from concern that Canada was a haven for Nazi war criminals from the Second World War, Canadian immigrants can also be prosecuted on allegations arising from contemporary behaviour in their country of origin.

Following unsuccessful criminal prosecutions, the federal government resorted to quasi-judicial procedures regarding the violation of immigration regulations, in order to deport alleged war criminals, procedures that can be appealed to the Federal and Supreme courts.

***Wartime Elections Act* and *Military Voters Act* (Canada, 1917).** Two federal statutes involving the Union government's manipulation of the franchise to ensure victory in the wartime election of 1917. Both Acts enfranchised some women for the first time and disenfranchised some voters. The *Wartime Elections Act* gave the vote to wives, widows and other close female relatives of servicemen overseas, but disenfranchised conscientious objectors, men born in enemy alien countries, and others of European birth speaking an enemy alien language who had been naturalized since 1902. The *Military Voters Act* enfranchised all Canadian men and women on active service and it created a floating vote, allowing the military vote to be cast in constituencies which might be suggested to the voters on election day for maximum advantage to government candidates in close contests. The newly enfranchised voters were expected to vote for the pro-conscription government led by the Conservative prime minister, Robert Borden, while the disenfranchised might have voted Liberal. The Liberal party was led by Wilfrid Laurier, who opposed conscription and refused to join a coalition government.

Wartime Tax Agreements (1941). Agreements by which the provinces "vacated" and "rented" the personal income and corporation tax fields to the federal government until 1946 in return for a rental payment for lost revenue. The federal government also encouraged the provinces not to levy succession duties. The rental payment was based on revenue yields in the abandoned fields in 1941 or on total costs of servicing the provincial debt. British Columbia, Manitoba, Ontario and Quebec opted for the former, and remaining provinces the latter method of calculating the rental payment. The federal government deducted provincial succession duties from the rental payment to those provinces that opted for the servicing of the debt. The Agreements became the basis for later periodically negotiated federal-provincial fiscal arrangements. See **Canada Health and Social Transfer (CHST); Federal-provincial tax-sharing arrangements (fiscal federalism).**

"Watertight compartments" Doctrine (constitution). A metaphor used by Lord Atkin, thus indicating a narrow interpretation by the Judicial Committee of the Privy Council (JCPC) of federal and provincial legislative competence under the *British North America Act, 1867* (since 1982, the *Constitution Act*).

Dealing with the treaty power of the federal government in the Labour Conventions Case (*Attorney-General for Canada v. Attorney-General for Ontario*, 1937), the JCPC said that "the competence of the Dominion Parliament [could not be] enlarged to keep pace with enlarged functions of the Dominion executive...merely by making promises to foreign countries...." "While the ship of state now sails on larger ventures and into foreign waters," Lord Atkin wrote of the Canadian constitution, "she still retains the watertight compartments which are an essential part of her original structure." Despite some broader interpretations of the BNA Act, as illustrated in Lord Sankey's "living tree" metaphor in the Persons Case of 1930, interpretation by the JCPC generally restricted the powers of the federal Parliament. See **Emergency power; Judicial Committee of the Privy Council (JCPC); "Living tree" Doctrine (constitution); Persons Case (1930); Treaty power**.

Westminster. A reference to the British Parliament, built on the site of Westminster Palace in London. Thus, references to "Westminster" or "the Westminster model" are references to the British Parliament and its practices.

Whig (interpretation of Canadian history). A reference to a political movement and party in Britain which had some relevance to the reform politics of nineteenth-century Canada (although the term "Clear Grits" was more common in Canada). The so-called "Whig interpretation of Canadian history" is a pejorative reference to the view of Canadian history as a steady evolutionary process leading to national independence notably under the auspices of the federal Liberal party and its leaders during most of the twentieth century. As the Liberal party is identified as the chief architect and defender of Canadian nationality according to this "interpretation," the Conservatives are portrayed as reactionaries, clinging to outmoded notions of British imperialism and opposed to Canada's constitutional development as an independent nation.

Whip (party). The member of a party's caucus who is responsible for ensuring the presence of party members in the legislature or at committee meetings to maintain adequate representation should a vote be held.

The division bells of a legislature sound for a vote until the party whips are satisfied that as many members of their own party as possible are present. Whips arrange "pairing" among legislators on both sides of the House which allows members to be absent without affecting the relative voting strength of the government and the opposition. The party whips are also responsible for arranging the order of members speaking in legislative debate; this facilitates the Speaker's job of recognizing members during debate.

Party discipline enforced by the whip is an integral feature of Canada's parliamentary system of responsible government. Members of parliament are elected, and governments are formed and remain in office, on the basis of the generally accepted convention of strict party discipline. This discipline is maintained in practice by the threat of withdrawal of various perquisites, denial of caucus or even potential ministerial responsibilities, and the ultimate sanction of expulsion from caucus and denial of official designation as the party's candidate in the next election.

White paper. A government document tabled in the legislature that outlines government policy in a particular area and the direction of future action possibly including legislation. Other coloured papers are official documents which discuss policy and alternative proposals and might suggest government preferences. Should a government encounter serious opposition to a white paper, it might "withdraw" it. Withdrawing a white paper after a period of "study" is less an embarrassment to a government than withdrawing legislation.

White paper on employment and income (1945). A federal government document issued in April 1945, as the Second World War was ending, which outlined the Liberal government's policy for postwar social and economic reconstruction. In the white paper, the federal government committed itself to: the maintenance of a high and stable level of income and employment; the acquisition of exclusive powers to levy personal and corporate income tax; the achievement of federal-provincial co-operation to develop a welfare state; and the development of an international economic order based on principles of free trade (*Employment and Income with Special Reference to the Initial Period of Reconstruction* [Ottawa: King's Printer, 1945]). The white paper, preceded by the report in 1940 of the Rowell-Sirois Royal Commission on Federal-Provincial Relations, along with the proposals in the Green Book of 1945 and the Dominion-Provincial Conference on Reconstruction in the same year, set the agenda for Canadian national economic development policy and for subsequent federal-provincial relations.

World Trade Organization (WTO). Successor to the General Agreement on Tariffs and Trade (the GATT) under which since 1947 signatory nations have periodically negotiated the removal of barriers to international trade.

Nations seek membership in the WTO in order to enhance their export trade, but must comply with WTO regulations that prohibit policies and practices, such as tariffs, import quotas, marketing boards and government subsidies that effectively protect domestic industries from foreign imports or enhance the competitiveness of domestic products in international trade. If a country loses a case before the WTO, it must either comply with the removal of the relevant trade barrier, or the complainant nation can impose penalties on the offending country's exports.

Canada's experience with WTO adjudication has been mixed. It has, for example, won a case against Brazil's subsidies to its aerospace industry, in competition with a Canadian firm for the supply of airplanes. But it has lost cases, for example, regarding the export of asbestos and beef to the European Union, and subsidies and an excise tax to protect the Canadian periodical industry.

The WTO is one of several organizations, such as the International Monetary Fund and the World Bank, designed to foster the international flow of goods and services, but which critics complain effectively enhance the larger and more globally competitive firms at the expense of the economies of smaller, less developed nations and hence of their societies. Thus, the trend to globalization has both its supporters and critics. See **Globalization (globalism)**; **Social movement organizations**.

Writs (election; referendum). The formal announcements of legislative elections or a referendum, issued by the governor general (lieutenant-governors in the provinces), in the name of the Queen. Within the constitutional five-year term of the legislatures ("from the Day of the Return of the Writs for choosing the House...", *Constitution Act*, s.50; also, Canadian Charter of Rights and Freedoms, s.4), the governor general (lieutenant-governor) virtually always accepts the prime minister's (premier's) advice on the dissolution of Parliament and the date for an election. In federal elections, the chief electoral officer transmits the writs to the returning officers of each constituency who then administer the election. Following the vote and any judicial recount that may be required, each returning officer returns the writ to the chief electoral office, certifying the results.